TEACHING **Reading &**
Language Arts

Second Edition

an effective and high-powered approach

Dr. Joyce Bowling

Kendall Hunt
publishing company

Cover images © Shutterstock.com

www.kendallhunt.com
 Send all inquiries to:
4050 Westmark Drive
Dubuque, IA 52004-1840

Copyright © 2018, 2019 by Kendall Hunt Publishing Company

Text ISBN: 978-1-7924-6897-1

PAK ISBN: 978-1-6843-8

All rights reserved. No part of this publication may be reproduced, stored
in a retrieval system, or transmitted, in any form or by any means,
electronic, mechanical, photocopying, recording, or otherwise,
without the prior written permission of the copyright owner.

Published in the United States of America

Table of Contents

Preface

Teacher preparation is crucial when readying the teachers to teach reading and language arts. Research tells us that the teacher has the ability to make a difference in reading instruction, students' reading ability, and also make a difference in the lives of their students. High-powered teachers are effective teachers who make a difference. They are also lifelong learners who reflect, make decisions, plan purposeful assessments, design authentic instruction, and engage their students in strategically planned collaborative activities that are designed to meet the needs of all of their students. High-powered teachers know their students, their interests, learning styles, academic needs, and their learning levels. In this edition of *Reading and Language Arts* you will learn how to teach phonics, phonemic awareness, spelling, writing, language arts, reading strategies, engaging activities, comprehension strategies, vocabulary, fluency, differentiation, and learn diverse methods of assessment. You will also learn the importance of reflecting, planning, building classroom rapport, and the importance of becoming a high-powered elementary and middle-school reading teacher.

The first half of *Teaching Reading and Language Arts* is a step-by-step guide designed to teach young educators effective and proven strategies to teach reading, writing, and language arts with passion and creativity. *Reading and Language Arts* emphasizes the importance of, and also how to design, differentiated instruction, assignments, and assessments. You will learn how to teach phonics at the very basic level of reading, how to implement daily reading strategies that engage young readers with the text, and also how to design collaborative reading activities that motivate all students while allowing them to experience learning through hands-on activities.

The second half of *Teaching Reading and Language Arts* emphasizes the importance of becoming a high-powered middle school reading teacher. You will learn to design age-appropriate, purposeful, and authentic learning opportunities for all learners, as well as engaging strategies to motivate students, while also building classroom rapport. Each chapter in both sections contains research-based information about designing effective reading instruction, importance of planning, examples of engaging activities, insightful strategies, tiered vocabulary, parent and home connections, pages for student reflections and note-taking, and also suggested readings for both the teacher and students.

Acknowledgments

There are many people to whom a great debt of gratitude is owed for continually encouraging and supporting me, and for helping me achieve my dreams. First and foremost, I want to thank my Lord and Savior Jesus Christ, for life, salvation, and His daily guidance. I would also like to thank all the people who provided me with meaningful and personal quotes, my pastor, Gary Harris and his wife Fonda, for their guidance and encouragement, and Mr. Bill Lyttle, for supporting and encouraging me, and for always believing in me.

I would like to dedicate the second edition of, *Teaching Reading and Language Arts an Effective and High-powered Approach*, to the following people whom each hold a large piece of heart; my mother, Mossie Smith, who inspires me to dream. My sister, Jackie Hibbard, who reminds me that nothing is impossible, and my brother, Wayne Smith, for always standing up for me. I also dedicate this edition to; my husband, Dennis Bowling, who believes in me and supports me, our son, Jonathan Bowling, who forever changed my life and who motivates me daily, and our daughter, Bethany Brock, who is also my best friend, my go-to person, and my secret-keeper. I also want to dedicate, *Teaching Reading and Language Arts*, to our daughter in-law, Keisha Bowling, and our son in-law, Corey Brock, for making our family complete. Finally, I would like to dedicate my book to our five grandchildren, who give our lives purpose and who are living reminders of why I strive to find ways to improve our communities, our schools, and our future; Jozie RoxAnna Brock, Tinnley Dean Bowling, Noah Aiden Brock, Alexa Grace Bowling, and John Maddox Brock. I thank each of you for always supporting me, believing in my dreams, being my biggest fans, and for just being the wonderful people that you are. I love you all.

About the Author

Dr. Joyce Bowling is an associate professor of education at the University of the Cumberlands in Williamsburg, Kentucky, an author, and a retired elementary teacher.

Part One

Chapter 1
A High-Powered Literacy Teacher Makes the Difference

Teacher Quote

"High-powered teachers teach from the heart!"

~ Dr. Joyce Bowling

Modern classrooms are different than the past days when students quietly sat in their seats listening while the teacher gave instruction. Classrooms have evolved into communities of learners where students assume more responsibility for learning. When you walk into a modern classroom, don't be surprised by the hum of students' voices as they collaborate in small group and discuss a topic, a book, or a project they are working on. Students are also more culturally and linguistically diverse, which includes more English Language learners than in the previous years. Literature teachers not only instruct, but also guide and nurture their students' learning through research-based instructional strategies, engaging activities, and curriculum-aligned reading programs to help them reach their highest potential and ultimate goal of being successful readers.

High-powered literacy teachers instruct their students through balancing explicit instruction and authentic application while also addressing state standards. These teachers also integrate reading and writing using standards-based textbooks and relevant trade books, while also implementing digital technologies into their literacy instructions. They differentiate instruction to meet the needs of every student, while also correlating assessment and instruction.

An effective high-powered literacy teacher makes a difference in the lives of his or her students. They are the key to ensuring that the students successfully learn to read and write. Researchers agree that a teacher's quality is the most important factor in determining how well the students learn (Vandervoort et al.). It is vital for a teacher to know how students learn to read and write, how to teach literature, and how to respond to the needs of all students, including leveled readers, struggling readers, gifted and talented readers, and English Language learners.

For example, some struggling readers make less than one year's growth each academic year which indicates that by fourth grade the same struggling reader may only be reading at the second grade reading level. If they have a high-powered literacy teacher during their fourth grade and are able to make a whole year's growth, they will have a high-probability of learning to read at least at a third-grade reading level; however, they are still one level below their grades. Research shows that when a student falls below their desired reading grade-level by one year, it typically takes three years of rigorous and engaging instruction for them to make up for that lost year, thus leaving them even farther behind.

Think of it this way: A fourth-grade student still reading at third grade reading level often spends their day in a fourth-grade classroom(s), where almost every lesson is focused on fourth-grade-level curriculum, content, and fourth-grade-level students. All too often, the reading lesson is based on a fourth-grade core reading program or fourth-grade curriculum, a text nevertheless, that is difficult for the struggling reader. Thus, rarely, if ever, will the struggling reader benefit much from the fourth-grade reading lessons. In other words, the lessons go over the struggling readers' head. This is where a high-powered literacy teacher must know their students academically. They must also be prepared and knowledgeable in their content area, know how to modify, adapt, and or replace reading lesson materials so that the struggling readers will benefit, thus preventing them from being stagnant in their learning and ensuring that the struggling reader gains necessary skills to move forward and be a successful reader and writer, while also making a difference in the lives of all of their students.

Chapter Questions

- ✦ *What is reading?*
- ✦ *Why is learning to read successfully at an early age important to students' academic success?*
- ✦ *What are the characteristics of a high-powered literacy teacher?*
- ✦ *How do high-powered teachers promote reading success for all students?*

Author Reflection

I recall the thrill of planning my very own first-grade classroom for the first time! What an exciting time it was. What color would I paint my classroom? How would I arrange my student's desks? What colorful display would I put on my bulletin board? Questions consumed me and an unexpected fear engulfed me. Reality was staring me in the face. I was going to be responsible for 18 6-year olds. I was going to be responsible for teaching them how to write, solve math equations . . . and how to read! Quickly, I tried to recall what I had learned in my undergraduate reading courses. I had taken two classes that were supposed to prepare me for teaching reading in grades K-5. My mind was blank! The most vivid memory that I could recall was creating an annotated bibliography made up of a particular number of children's books. I knew there must be more information, strategies, plans, activities, or ideas taught in those classes. I was only able to recall a few specific instructional strategies that I felt would help me teach my students how to read. I felt a surge of panic.

I'll never forget the first day inside my very first classroom with my very own students. The fear that I had been feeling dissipated with the first glimpse of my students smiling faces. It was going to be a successful year. My students were going to be successful. It was going to be a hard work, but they were going to become well-rounded students who were also successful readers.

That first year was a true testament of teachers being lifelong learners. My students grew with great strides, so did I. I gained insights from veteran teachers who helped answer many of my questions and who gave me wonderful suggestions. I willingly observed veteran teachers, reading classes. I scoured the Internet for research-based strategies and called upon the district literacy coach often. I attended reading and writing conferences and professional development trainings. I also took time getting to know my students, every day both academically and personally, while gaining as much knowledge about teaching reading as I could possibly consume. My first year in the classroom helped mold me into an effective high-powered literacy teacher.

Upon retiring from the P-12 classroom and beginning a new journey as a professor of higher education, I was elated that I was given the opportunity to teach reading and writing for both elementary and middle school teachers. I was going to have the opportunity to share my years of experience teaching reading with new upcoming teachers. I knew right away that I didn't want my students to experience the fear of not recalling what they had learned in their college reading and language arts courses. I knew that pedagogy, research-based strategies, and collaboration were going to help guide my students to become high-powered literacy teachers. My students were going to gain and experience a wide variety of reading strategies that would increase content knowledge and critical thinking skills, and promote comprehension, while experiencing meaningful grand discussions. My students were going to learn how to encourage fluency, assess their students, analyze data, increase their student's vocabulary and writing skills, while also learning to interact and collaborate with them. I would involve my students in hands-on activities that they would not forget. They would not experience the panic and fear that I, as a first-year teacher, felt those first days, even weeks, before entering my classroom. My students would be prepared!.

As semesters quickly passed, I found that I was still scouring the web, searching books, and pulling resources from various places to ensure that my students were receiving the best-quality instruction, research-based strategies, and the content necessary for their success. After several years of picking and choosing resources from various places, I decided to design and write a book that my students could learn from, grow with, and also take into their first classroom as a reference book to help alleviate the fear and panic of searching for helpful resources to ensure their student's success.

What Is Reading?

Reading is a skill, a vital skill in student's learning and their success. Teaching students to unlock the full meaning of the texts they read is the single most powerful outcome a teacher can promote. Reading is a complex cognitive process of decoding symbols in an effort to construct or interpret meaning from print. Reading can also be defined as a multifaceted process that involves word recognition, analytical thinking, comprehension, and fluency. Reading involves visual and thinking skills that are necessary to understand the text, along with many other developmental accomplishments such as attention, memory, language, and motivation. Reading is more than a cognitive psycholinguistic activity, it is also a social activity. Readers don't just look at the words on a page and automatically understand the meaning; reading is a complex process, which involves an essential set of components and skills.

Reading components include phonemic awareness, phonics, word identification, vocabulary, fluency, and comprehension.

In addition, modern students are exposed to a wide variety of print beyond the typical textbook including digital print, computers, hand-held devices, social media, and videos. As a result of students' exposure to culturally diverse and technological learning environments, teachers are now faced with the challenge of providing effective reading instruction that will empower their students to not only learn to read, but also grow and become active participants in a rigorous and ever-changing information-based world.

Learning to read is not a simple task. Reading can be challenging for many children. While learning to read, children need to attain a set of skills that, with the guidance of a high-powered and effective literacy teacher, will help them arrive at their destination of becoming successful readers. It is essential that children acquire the skills necessary that will enable them to reach their desired reading goal, allow them to be able to read and comprehend, while also applying what they have read in all content areas. Children must acquire skills that include, but are not limited to, the following:

+ Phonemic awareness, which is hearing individual sounds in spoken words
+ Recognizing and identifying letters
+ Phonics
+ Word identification; understanding the concepts of printed language
+ Increasing vocabulary (oral language)
+ Connecting reading and writing
+ Decoding words accurately and fluently
+ Comprehension

Children's ability to learn to read often grows from their desire to learn more about letters, and how to manipulate letters to create written words. Writing is often the starting place where a young child's journey of learning to read and write begins. Young children become aware of letters and words in the world around them at a relatively young age. For example, young children may recognize their favorite restaurant by the sign, or their favorite food from the packaging label. Media and television also enhance children's curiosity about letters, and how letters form words. Through diverse exposure young children often become curious about the spelling of their own names or their pet's name.

Through strategic and rigorous research-based instruction, effective modeling, and active engagement in planned activities, collaboration, and independent work, children become aware of sounds, letters, and manipulating letters to form words. As children gain experience, knowledge, skills, and confidence, they increase their vocabulary, while also making necessary connections to reading and writing. As children learn to write, they must learn a similar set of enabling skills which will guide them along their journey to reach the ultimate goal of writing. The five stages of the writing process include the following:

+ Handwriting both upper and lower case letters
+ Understanding writing conventions
+ Being able to encode thoughts into print
+ Spelling
+ Prewriting
+ Drafting
+ Revising
+ Editing
+ Publishing

Reading and writing are reciprocal. The components of both reading and writing are complementary, and also reflect a strong and supportive relationship while students learn to be effective readers, and writers. Students need to receive explicit instruction, guidance, and be mentored to become successful readers and writers.

Why Is Learning to Read Successfully at an Early Age Important to Students' Academic Success?

The ability to read is a key factor in living a healthy, happy, and productive life. Reading is the skill that makes all other learning possible. Literacy is a tool for achieving economic, social, and personal goals. Students arrive in the public classroom with diverse backgrounds as well as vast differences in their literacy development. For example, some students would have read hundreds of books, while other students may have only been read a handful, and even others who have never been exposed to reading in any form. Some students will arrive in the kindergarten class from preschool programs, while others will arrive from home. Some students will have extensive vocabularies, and other students will have small or limited vocabularies. These factors often result in some children being more ready to read than others. Research shows that teachers can create kindergarten classrooms that reduce, or expand, these initial differences that students bring to the class.

High-powered literacy teachers can make a difference in their student's reading skills through creating and maintaining a safe community of learners. Getting to know their students through meaningful conversations, both formative and summative assessments, and observations are key at any grade-level, but very important in kindergarten to determine possible reading deficits and also to determine how each student learns.

High-powered literacy teachers analyze assessment data and formulate individualized plans of action that include instruction designed on their students' learning styles through modeling, and incorporating research-based instructional practices, which helps to ensure their students' reading success at an early age.

When students learn to read successfully at grade-level in the primary grades, they are not only reading, they are engaging with the text regardless of the genre. Successful primary readers also read fluently, which allows them to gain the skills they need to interact with as well as comprehend the text, and apply the knowledge that they gain in all content areas. Finally, students who learn to read successfully at a young age are less likely to struggle in future grades, make greater academic strides, and be successful in other content areas. Students who learn to read successfully at a young age are also less likely to require intervention, are better writers, and typically enjoy reading for pleasure more than the students who are struggling readers.

What Are the Characteristics of a High-Powered Literacy Teacher?

The characteristics of high-powered literacy teachers define the type of educator they are, ensuring their student's success, while also contributing to their school as a whole, and to their community. It is difficult to list all characteristics of a high-powered literacy teacher as each teacher brings their own unique talent and personality to their classroom. However, their vigilance in maintaining the expectation is one consistency among high-powered literacy teachers that it's not okay to not even try. Every student learns with a high-powered literacy teacher in a classroom. Expectations are high, even for the students who don't yet have high-expectations for themselves. High-powered literacy teachers also praise their students for their efforts but do not confuse effort with mastery. We will explore, define, and revisit each of the characteristics below throughout the text as we delve deeper into the process of teaching reading and language arts to both elementary and middle-grade students.

Read the characteristics below and think about how each characteristic applies to you as an educator. Ask yourself a question about each characteristic. For example, how will you create and maintain a safe community of learners? How will you get to know how your students learn? Record your answers on the note-taking page located at the end of the chapter before reading the remainder of the chapter.

1. High-powered literacy teachers create and maintain a safe community of learners.
2. High-powered literacy teachers know how students learn.
3. High-powered literacy teachers know their students as readers through the use of assessments.
4. High-powered literacy teachers analyze assessment data and formulate an individualized plan of action to ensure students' success.
5. High-powered teachers teach the essential components of reading through research based instructional practices.
6. High-powered literacy teachers model reading and writing daily.
7. High-powered literacy teachers differentiate instruction to ensure success for all students.
8. High-powered literacy teachers scaffold students' reading and writing.
9. High-powered literacy teachers involve family and community through effective collaboration.
10. High-powered literacy teachers are life-long learners.

High-Powered Literacy Teachers Create and Maintain a Safe Community of Learners

We all wish that the world were a safer place for our children. However, in reality, bullying, peer pressure, domestic violence, physical and mental abuse, as well as discrimination are all things that school children can face daily. A high-powered teacher can be a hero for their students through listening and providing a sympathetic ear, while also helping them solve their problems, all the while providing a safe place for learning.

High-powered literacy teachers create and maintain a safe community of learners through implementing InTASC Standard 3. They work with others to create environments that support individual and collaborative learning, and encourage positive social interaction, active engagement in learning and also self-motivation. High-powered literacy teachers continually strive to maintain a positive and safe environment where students also feel academically safe, safe to ask and answer questions, to express themselves, and feel comfortable collaborating and interacting with their peers as well as their teacher, and also a place where they feel physically safe to learn. High-powered teachers create this environment through meaningful classroom conversations, timely feedback, both written and oral, as well as student recognition, while also making learning fun and stimulating, through implementation of rigorous instruction and engaging activities. High-powered literacy teachers make learning fun and their classrooms welcoming with a comfortable atmosphere that students feel they are an important part of.

High-Powered Literacy Teachers Know How Students Learn

High-powered literacy teachers know their students. They get to know them through collaborative meaningful conversations, observations, daily work, and a variety of assessments. They also know how to analyze their collected data to determine how each of their students learns best. This cannot be achieved through one assessment, but through a variety of both formative and summative assessments. When teachers know how their students learn, they can then design instruction, activities, and assignments that will help meet individualized needs and the needs of all of their students.

High-powered literacy teachers understand how students/learners grow and develop. They recognize patterns of learning and how student's development varies with each individual within and across the cognitive, linguistic, social, emotional, and physical areas. High-powered teachers also design and implement developmentally appropriate and challenging learning experiences based on InTASC Standard 1: Learner Development (Council of Chief State School Officers [CCSSO]).

High-powered literacy teachers also implement InTASC Standard 2: Learning Differences. They use understanding of individual differences and diverse cultures and communities to ensure inclusive learning environments that enable each learner to meet high standards (CCSSO). At the heart of the educational process is the classroom. This is also the forefront of equity for all students.

High-Powered Literacy Teachers Know Their Students as Readers Through the Use of Assessments

High-powered literacy teachers implement InTASC Standard 6, which involves assessment. The teacher understands and uses multiple methods of assessment to engage learners in their own growth, to monitor student's progress, and to guide the teacher's and learner's decision-making (CCSSO).

Teachers in a public school system regularly work with an assessment system that allows them to measure their student's progress in a manner similar to state assessments but with greater frequency. This type of assessment is often carried out several times a year. High-powered literacy teachers strive to get to know their students through a variety of assessments, both formative and summative. Getting to know students academically can be fun, challenging, but also very beneficial. High-powered teachers begin this process on day one through a variety of fun and engaging activities. They can get to know their students as readers by conducting a grade-level reader's interest survey. This allows the teacher to learn what topics, books, and genres their students are interested in, while also learning about their student's reading habits and aspirations for their own reading goals. High-powered literacy teachers assess continually not only through summative assessments, but also through observing and listening to their students read in a variety of settings such as, oral reading, guided reading, small group reading, collaborative reading, and independent reading. High-powered literacy teachers use checklists or running records to document important information to help guide their future instruction.

High-Powered Literacy Teachers Analyze Assessment Data and Formulate an Individualized Plan of Action to Ensure Student's Success

Again, high-powered literacy teachers assess their students through a variety of both formative and summative assessments. They collect data obtained through assessments, analyze it to gain insight into who their students are as readers, and also formulate an individualized plan of action to ensure students' reading and writing success.

High-powered literacy teachers proficiently examine the data not only to find who got what right and what wrong, but also to gain insight and clues to help them determine how students are thinking, processing text, and why they answered the question correctly or incorrectly. When teachers analyze and engage in assessment of data, it can result in a systematic plan of action that gives insight into their own instruction, while also allowing them to formulate a plan of action that will enable students to succeed. High-powered teachers have a process for turning results into reteaching moments, which are useful for both the students and teachers. They also use data to better understand how to spend their time in the classroom, and also how to teach better in the time they allocate to each topic.

How Do High-Powered Literacy Teachers Promote Success for All Students?

CCSSO, through its Interstate Teacher Assessment and Support Consortium (InTASC), developed a set of model core teaching standards that outline what teachers should know and be able to do to ensure every K-12 student reaches the goal of being ready to enter college or the workforce. These standards outline the common principles and foundations of teaching practices that cut across all subject areas and grade levels, which are necessary to improve student achievement (CCSSO).

These Model Core Teaching Standards articulate what effective teaching and learning look like in a modern public classroom. They are also designed to empower every learner to take ownership of their learning that emphasizes the learning of content and application knowledge as well as skills that connect to real-world problems. InTASC standards are designed to value the diversity that each learner brings to the classroom and the learning experience that also leverages rapidly changing learning environments through recognizing the possibilities they bring to maximize learning while also engaging the learners. Thus, these standards describe and outline what effective teaching consists of, and what high-powered teachers do daily both inside and outside their classrooms that leads to improved student achievement.

High-powered literacy teachers know that teaching begins with the learner. They ensure that all students learn new knowledge and skills with an understanding that learning and developmental patterns differ with each student. High-powered teachers also know that each individual student brings their own individual and unique personalities as well as their own unique differences to the learning process, and also that the students need a supportive and safe learning environment to flourish.

High-powered Literacy teachers have high expectations for every student. They also create challenging learning experiences in diverse learning environments that encourage and help students meet objectives and achieve their goals. High-powered literacy teachers ensure student progress and success through a combination of factors such as professional knowledge, understanding of how cognitive, linguistic, social, emotional, and physical development occur, while also recognizing that students are individuals who arrive in their classroom with diverse individualized skills, family backgrounds, personalities, interests, and talents.

High-powered literacy teachers collaborate with colleagues, students, administration, families, and with their community. Communication, collaboration, and assessment allows teachers to better understand their students and their student's needs. When high-powered teachers know and understand their students, it enables them to maximize their instruction, thus, maximizing student's learning and student success.

High-Powered Literacy Teachers Implement Research-Based Instructional Practices

High-powered literacy teachers make connections and follow, InTASC Standard 7: Planning for Instruction. The teacher understands and uses a variety of instructional strategies to encourage learners to develop deep understanding of content areas and their connections, and build skills to apply knowledge in meaningful ways (CCSSO). High-powered literacy teachers also implement, InTASC Standard 8: Instructional Strategies to ensure that they are teaching the essential components of reading.

High-powered literacy teachers deal with standards every day. Most teachers will make intentional references to a standard in daily lessons, whereas a high-powered literacy teacher distinguishes all the standards that she or he will cover for the next month, breaks them up into objectives, and then decides what activity will best accomplish each day's objective. Many teachers ask themselves, "What will I do today?" A high-powered literacy teacher asks, "How will I accomplish what I need to master today?" The first question allows the possibility of the teacher becoming distracted by the qualities of the activity: Will it be fun? Will it allow room for technology? Will it be exciting? Will the students enjoy it? However, the second question focuses the teacher on the goal: Precisely what do I want my students to be able to do when the lesson is over? Both of the scenarios/approaches are teaching standards and both might be implementing rigorous instructional strategies. However, the discipline of the second approach is more likely to yield results. High-powered literacy teachers first plan objectives, then instruction, then assessments, and then the activities.

A high-powered literacy teacher understands and uses a variety of instructional strategies to encourage learners to develop deep understanding of content areas and their connections, and to build skills to apply knowledge in meaningful ways. High-powered literacy teachers ask rigorous and challenging questions to challenge students to think deeply, more critically, and also to assess their student's knowledge of a texts, full meaning and relevance. High-powered literacy teachers integrate reading instruction into their classrooms in a way that will be productive and will keep the students accountable. High-powered literacy teachers teach with research-based instructional strategies to ensure their student's success, not only inside but also outside the classroom.

High-Powered Literacy Teachers Model Reading and Writing Daily

High-powered literacy teachers make connections to InTASC Standard 4: Content Knowledge, and they also understand the central concepts, tools of inquiry, and structures of the discipline(s) he or she teaches, and creates learning experiences that make these aspects of the discipline accessible and meaningful for learners to ensure mastery of the content (CCSSO). A high-powered literacy teacher also models reading and writing on a daily basis for their students. Modeling allows students to know what the teachers' expectations are, feel comfortable and confident, while also setting an example for students. Modeling both reading and writing also allows teachers to implement fun and engaging activities that help ensure students, reading and writing success in all content areas.

High-powered literacy teachers understand how to connect concepts and use diverse perspectives to engage learners in critical thinking, creativity, and collaborative problem-solving related to authentic local and global issues (InTASC Standard 5: Application of Content (CCSSO)).

High-Powered Literacy Teachers Differentiate Instruction to Ensure Success for All Students

The roots of differentiated instruction go all the way back to the days of one-room school house, where one teacher had all students of all ages in one classroom. Gradually, as the educational system transitioned to grading schools, it was assumed that children of the same age learned similarly. However, in 1912, achievement tests were introduced and the scores revealed the gaps in student's abilities within grade levels. In 1975, congress passed the Individuals with Disabilities Education Act (IDEA), ensuring that children with disabilities had equal access to public education. To reach this student population, many educators used differentiated instructional strategies. Then came the passage of No Child Left Behind in 2000, which further encouraged differentiated and skill-based instruction. (Weselby).

High-powered teachers realize that just as each person has a unique fingerprint, each student has an individual learning style. They know that not all of their students understand a subject in the same way, or even share the same level of ability. In an effort to better deliver their lessons and instruction to reach *everyone* in class, they get to know their students, academically and as individuals. High-powered literacy teachers understand that students have individual learning differences, come from diverse cultures and communities, and they establish inclusive learning environments that enable each learner to meet high standards (InTASC Standard 2: Learning Differences [CCSSO]).

High-powered literacy teachers get to know their students through a variety of assessments, conversations, and observations, which allow them design differentiated instruction and scaffolding to ensure success for all students. They design lessons based on students' learning styles, group students by shared interests, topics or ability for activities, and assignments, assess student's learning using both formative and summative assessments, manage their classroom to maintain a safe supportive environment, all the while continually assessing and reflecting on their own teaching, and adjusting content to meet the needs of all students.

High-Powered Literacy Teachers Scaffold Student's Reading and Writing

The term scaffolding was introduced by Wood, Bruner, and Ross in an attempt to operationalize the concept of teaching in the zone of proximal development. Scaffolding refers to a variety of instructional techniques used to move students progressively toward stronger understanding and, ultimately, greater independence in the learning process. High-powered literacy teachers provide successive levels of temporary support that enable students to achieve without assistance. Much like physical scaffolding, the supportive strategies are incrementally removed when they are no longer needed, and the teacher gradually shifts more responsibility over the learning process to the student.

Scaffolding is considered to be an essential element of effective teaching. High-powered literacy teachers use scaffolding to bridge the learning gaps. For example, if students are not reading at the required level to understand a text being taught, the teacher might use instructional scaffolding strategically and gradually to progressively improve a student's reading ability until they can read the required text independently.

High-powered literacy teachers reduce negative emotions and self-perceptions that students may have when they experience frustration, intimidation, or when they feel discouraged when attempting a difficult task without the assistance, direction, or understanding they need to complete the assigned task. High-powered literacy teachers strategically scaffold student's reading and writing by knowing their students as readers and writers as well as analyzing student assessment data. Through successful scaffolding students read and write based on their own individualized level and gain much needed confidence, which ultimately leads to success.

High-Powered Literacy Teachers Involve Family and Community Through Effective Collaboration

Successful and high-powered literacy teachers enjoy collaborating with families and their community. When parents feel connected to their child's classroom through collaboration with the teacher, they become familiar with the content that is being taught (Richardson). Through consistent communication, parents are better informed and prepared to help their child with given tasks and homework assignments. These better-informed parents also know and understand the classroom rules and expectations that apply to both students and parents. When parents maintain open communication with their child's teacher, they in turn feel more comfortable with the teacher, the teaching methods employed, and the content being taught, which maximizes student's overall success.

When teachers and schools build partnerships with families that respond to their concerns and honor their contributions, they are successful in sustaining valuable connections that are aimed at improving student achievement. Research suggests that parental involvement is not only positively correlated to academic achievement, but also takes precedence over household income as a determiner of student success. Parental involvement is a major contributing factor to student's academic success.

High-powered literacy teachers strive to establish and maintain partnerships and collaboration with parents to support student learning through a variety of methods. Effective communication, via the context of ongoing exchanges, is essential to create strong school–home partnerships and increase parental involvement. Teachers require skill and knowledge to effectively communicate with their parent community. Strong communication is fundamental to this partnership, as well as in building a stable community between home and school. High-powered teachers continually develop and expand their skills in an effort to maximize effective communication with their students' parents. When teachers implement parental involvement and make it a natural part of their teaching practice, it results in increased parent comfort of content, parental involvement with the teacher and the classroom, and even more importantly leads to meaningful interactions with their children at home.

Parent-teacher and community collaboration can be effectively implemented in a variety of methods. These methods include, but are not limited to, guest speakers, field trips, parent teacher nights, open house, parent conferences, newsletters, interactive writing, blogs, and also through class websites or dojos. High-Powered teachers have the ability and power to influence the partnership that can bridge the gap between parents, communities, and schools.

High-Powered Literacy Teachers Are Life-Long Learners

High-powered teaching is an art. Great art relies on the mastery and application of foundational skills, learned individually through diligent studies. Teaching is a complex work that people have to be taught to do. High-powered literacy teachers are life-long learners. With advanced training, high-powered teachers learn to combat social and economic factors that affect student's ability to meet the challenges of academic life.

High-powered literacy teachers learn through reflection. They reflect on their instruction and assessment data daily to better understand how to create new and challenging instruction, but also to discover new ways to improve their instruction to be more meaningful, rigorous, and also meet the needs of all of their students. Reflection is also a key to design engaging activities that allow students to think critically, collaboratively, and interact with their peers to gain a deeper understanding of the concepts and content they are presented with.

High-powered teachers are life-long learners who further their education, attend content-rich conferences and trainings, and collaborate with colleagues. They also stay up to date by reading current content-based research articles, and meaningful how-to books. High-powered teachers make connections to InTASC Standard 9: Professional Learning and Ethical Practice, by engaging in ongoing professional learning and using evidence to continually evaluate their practice, particularly the effects of his or her choices and actions, on students, families, colleagues, and community, and also adapting practice to meet the needs of each student.

They also seek appropriate leadership roles and opportunities to take responsibility for student learning, to collaborate with learners, families, colleagues, other school professionals, and members of the community to ensure learner growth, and to advance the profession, InTASC Standard 10: Leadership and Collaboration (CCSSO). High-powered literacy teachers ask themselves daily, "What have I learned today that will improve my instruction and ensure that my students will reach academic success?"

High-Powered Teachers Have Knowledge

"I have not only gained knowledge from reading, I have also gained confidence, which is beneficial to my career and life."

~ Tom Hurt

Teachers' knowledge cannot be defined with a simple definition. Effective high-powered literacy teachers must have knowledge of their content, know their students, understand the importance of assessment, and also understand how students learn.

Knowing your students and understanding how they learn impact how you will teach. Let me say that again. Knowing your students and understanding how they learn *will* impact how you teach. How so? When you, the teacher, observe your students reading in a variety of settings, know their reading preferences, and determine through assessment and observations how each student learns best, you gain the knowledge and capability to strategically design, plan, and scaffold your instructions to meet the needs of each of all of your students.

High-powered literacy teachers know how to lead a whole-class discussion, design a sequence of lessons based on a specific learning objective(s), elicit and interpret individual student thinking, reflect, and also analyze their instruction for the purpose of improving it. High-powered literacy teachers are also avid readers and continually strive to gain new knowledge in their content to improve themselves as teachers, improve their instruction, and ensure their student's overall success.

Summary: High-Powered Literacy Teachers Make a Difference!

"High-powered teachers continually strive to improve themselves, their instruction, their methods, and the lives of their students."

~ Dr. Joyce Bowling

High-powered literacy teachers make a positive difference in the lives of their students. They inspire their students by encouraging them to fulfill their potential. Students who are inspired by their teachers can accomplish amazing things. Moreover, that motivation almost always stays with them. High-powered literacy teacher's students make daily progress in both reading and writing as a result of the benefits of being part of a safe community of learners, receiving meaningful standards-based instructions, being exposed to rigorous research-based strategies, collaborating with their peers through engaging activities, collaborating with their teachers, and also through receiving timely feedback on daily work and assessments.

It is not an exaggeration to say that a high-powered teacher can change a student's life. There are endless stories attesting to the benefits of a strong positive relationship between a teacher and a student. It isn't easy to change a student's life, which is why it takes a great teacher to do so. Some students just need an extra push. For example, a student whose reading grade is a few points below their desired goal, while other students may be facing struggles in their personal lives, which impedes their learning. And yet another student may need a gentle nudge to go above and beyond their current level, resulting in leading him or her to an above-level status. Regardless the student's needs a life-changing high-powered teacher will be there for each of their students.

High-Powered Teachers Implement Grammar in Reading Instruction

Grammar and writing are often separated from reading instruction. High-powered teachers strategically embed threads of both writing and grammar in their daily instruction. They implement grammar through engaging activities that are standard-based, and aligned to their grade-level curriculum. For example, kindergarten students should begin learning about nouns through verbal identification, labeling, and fun engaging games. When young students can identify nouns as being a person, place, thing, or idea, they can begin learning about proper nouns. As students advance through primary grades, grammar can be strategically scaffold to allow students to reflect on prior knowledge, which in turn allows them to build new knowledge. For example, first grade students arrive in the classroom with a base-knowledge of nouns, which is necessary for teachers to begin teaching their students about adjectives and verbs.

High-powered teachers reinforce students' knowledge through carefully planned daily writing, and oral language activities, which provide needed opportunities for students to practice writing, while also being required to use punctuation to end sentences, reinforcing their understanding of the basic parts of speech as they learn them. High-powered teachers do not withhold vital instruction from their students, instead they plan, design, and implement fun and engaging activities that help their students establish knowledge about grammar and correct uses, while also challenging their students through carefully planned daily assignments. High-powered teachers also continually search for engaging technologies that will reinforce reading, writing, and learning grammar.

Establishing a Face-to-Face and Virtual Classroom Community

High-powered teachers are more than teachers. High-powered teachers are leaders, and they are **community builders**. As a community builder, high-powered teachers begin building a community within their classroom before the academic year begins. They begin building a community by setting the tone for the class culture by creating, establishing, and facilitating the classroom norms and procedures, but also through getting to know their students as a whole and also individually. High-powered teachers know that when students feel that they belong to a classroom and feel confident and comfortable in their surroundings, rapport begins to build, as does the layers of learning.

Districts rely on various methods for teachers to get to know their students. Districts might schedule meet and greet sessions prior to the first day of the academic year to allow teachers to get to know their students and their student's parents. However, with the challenges that educators all over the world have recently been faced with, this option was not always available due to social distancing, and the demand for virtual learning. Nevertheless, the importance and the need for teachers to get to know their students remains the same. So, how will you, the high-powered teacher, meet and greet your students, both in-seat and virtually?

From day one, getting to know your students on a relational level is vital. High-powered teachers have protocols they follow to get know their students. While some teachers administer surveys, others play meet and greet games, and still others set up one-on-one conference sessions with their students. High-powered teachers have established methods to build their community in a face-to-face setting. But, what does it mean to build a community and get to know your students in hybrid and virtual environments? High-powered teachers have an answer to that questions. High-powered teachers get to know all of their students both in person and online. They build and establish a thriving community both inside their physical classroom and inside their virtual classroom where students feel safe, can be engaged, work collaboratively, be excited about learning, and most of all a place where students feel confident and included.

Virtual learning is an educational experience that is delivered through an online platform and can be accessed outside the classroom allowing students to use computer software, the Internet, or both to deliver instruction to students. Teachers have the ability to interact with their students via Internet through videos, online forums, emails, and chat sessions. Virtual learning can be for an individual student, or for the entire class.

High-powered teachers begin by building their virtual classroom based on their district's preference of technology, platforms, forums, and guidelines. They create colorful, fun, and vibrant classrooms that students are excited to explore. High-powered teachers build a virtual classroom that is as inviting as their physical classroom. They know their virtual classroom must look appealing, be easy to maneuver, and also be engaging to attain and maintain student's attention and compete with social media and other popular technology.

High-powered teachers also establish and maintain **virtual office hours**. Office hours can be a specified time where students or parents can go to ask questions, have a brief conference, or sometimes just to say hello and share an idea or talk about what's going on in their lives. Establishing a scheduled time for communication helps alleviate much of the chaos and confusion that can come from online questions. Both parents and students will appreciate your time of availability.

Once the virtual classroom is built, high-powered teachers create resources for students and their student's parents. They create tools that will enable them to be successful. Tools may include virtual tours through prerecorded videos, outlined instructions, power points with details and reference for possible troubleshooting, and contact information. High-powered teachers also provide students and their parents with instructions for logging into class, location of audio tools, microphone, and where the camera is located as well as how to turn them on and off and instructions how to utilize the available resources that their virtual classroom offers.

Now, it's time to set up **virtual meet and greet appointments**. This valuable resource can be utilized by both in-seat students and virtual students prior to the first day of school. Automatically, you've begun building your community. High-powered teachers introduce themselves with enthusiasm and with a smile that says, "I'm glad to have you in my classroom."

During the virtual meet and greet, you may **review the procedures** for logging into class and all of the basic instructions for audio, video, submitting work, typing answers, raising hands, and other available options. High-powered teachers also take this time to listen to their students as they talk about themselves, as well as their parents. Keep the virtual meet and greet simple, personable, relevant, and professional. Allow the students and their parents to view you as a genuine person, not just an online figure that will assign and grade work, but rather someone who is approachable, available and ready to teach, help, ask and answer questions, participate, and above all, someone who cares about them.

Remember, teaching is inherently relational and high-powered teachers at every level care deeply about their students, their student's parents, their school, and their community.

Now, It Is Your Turn

For this assignment you will be required to interview a veteran teacher. What constitutes a veteran teacher? A teacher who has completed five or more years inside the classroom. You will be required to design and ask the teacher at least twenty questions pertaining to reading and writing. You will also be required to write a reflection about the interview. See syllabus for details.

What Can Parents Do to Help?

Parents play a vital role in the success of their children's education. Students' whose parents read every night to them, asking them open-ended questions, and interacting with them are proven to make greater strides in both reading and writing. Whereas the student who does not have a parent that reads nightly with them progresses at a much slower rate.

Parents can help increase their child's reading and writing through maintaining close communication with their child's teacher. This can be accomplished through phone conversations, electronic apps, emails, newsletters, interactive websites, or dojos. Parents can also attend open house or parent–teacher nights to have one-on-one conversations with their child's teacher. This is an opportunity for parents to ask questions about their child's progress, content, and also a time to review their child's daily work as well as their scores.

High-powered literacy teachers establish a relationship with the parents of their students, involve them with the activities in their classrooms and their students, while also working closely with them to maintain communication in effort to increase parent–student interaction.

Becoming a High-Powered Literacy Teacher

High-powered effective literacy teachers are the key to ensure that students learn to read and write successfully. Rigorous, innovative, and effective instructions are critical for student's success. Research tells us that it is the teacher who makes a difference in both reading and writing instructions. As a literacy teacher, you will need to take time to think deeply about your teaching styles and your instructional decisions in effort to meet the needs of all of your students. This can be an overwhelming thought. However, this book will become a personal tool, an insightful and informative resource, and a personal guide that will help you succeed in becoming an effective and high-powered literacy teacher.

Authors Tip

Every teacher should be a life-long learner, an avid reader and researcher who strives to continually improve themselves by gaining new knowledge, and who implements new innovative and engaging reading and writing activities in their classroom. Every teacher should be a strategic planner. Teachers should make and take time to get to know their students both personally and academically. It is vital for teachers to know their students to ensure effective planning, effective instruction, and effective strategies and activities, thus leading to effective learning.

High-powered teachers get to know their students through one-on-one meaningful conversations, surveys, grand classroom conversations, readers' interest surveys, grading daily work and assessments, analyzing assessment data, reflecting on their instructions, are not afraid of change, and are willing to step outside of the box and their comfort zone to reach their students. Most importantly, effective high-powered teachers establish and maintain a good rapport with their students, colleagues, and their student's parents.

Applications

To help guide you through the chapter and upcoming chapters, you will need to be familiar with the following key terms:

- ✦ InTASC Standards
- ✦ Phonemic awareness
- ✦ Phonics
- ✦ Vocabulary
- ✦ Fluency
- ✦ Comprehension

+ Reading strategies
+ Reading skills
+ Rigor
+ Formative assessment
+ Summative assessment
+ Collaborative learning
+ Differentiate
+ Scaffold

In-Seat Activity

We learn by reflecting on instruction, what we've read, discussed and by the questions that we ask. Take a few minutes to review your notes, and reflect on the chapter, the discussion, and the activities that we've completed. Work with your randomly selected partner and create three questions that you would like to have answered, or would like to know more about. Be prepared to share your questions orally with the class in fifteen minutes.

Reflect and Answer the Following Questions

+ *What is reading?*
+ *Why is learning to read successfully at an early age important to students' academic success?*
+ *What are the characteristics of a high-powered literacy teacher?*
+ *How do high-powered teachers promote reading success for all students?*

Student Reflection Page

Reflection is key to a teachers' instructions. It allows the teacher to reminisce, review, and critique their instruction and instructional practices. Timely reflections are beneficial for teachers to plan and modify their instruction through analyzing and recording their thoughts about what worked during a lesson they've taught, what did not work, and why. Daily reflections also have the power to guide good teachers to be an effective high-powered reflective teacher.

This page is reserved for you to reflect about information that you found insightful and what you have learned from Chapter One.

Student Note Page

Annotating is an effective learning strategy. Annotations are typically recorded along the outside edges within the text. However, sufficient room is not always available. Therefore, this page is reserved for you to annotate (*take notes*) record potential questions, and also to refer back to when studying, completing assignments, and also to help you gain a better understanding of Chapter One.

Suggested Readings

Brown, Peter C. *Make It Stick: An Imprint of Harvard University Press*, 1st ed. Belkin Press, 2014.

Marzano, Robert J. *The Art and Science of Teaching*, ASCD, 2007.

Chapter References

Council of Chief State School Officers (CCSSO). *Interstate Teacher Assessment and Support Consortium (InTASC) Model Core Teaching Standards*, Apr. 2011, https://www.ccsso.org/sites/default/files/2017-11/InTASC_Model_Core_Teaching_Standards_2011.pdf. Accessed 7 July 2018.

Richardson, W. *Blogs, Wikis, Podcasts, and Other Powerful Tools for Classrooms*. Corwin Press, 2010.

Vandervoort, L. G., A. Amrein-Beardsley, and D. C. Berliner. *National Board Certified Teachers and Their Students' Achievement*, 2004, http://epaa.asu.edu/ojs/article/view/201. Accessed 8 Nov. 2017.

Weselby, C. *What Is Differentiated Instruction? Examples of How to Differentiate Instruction in the Classroom*, 2014. https://education.cu-portland.edu/blog/classroom-resources/examples-of-differentiated-instruction/. Accessed 13 Nov. 2017.

Chapter 2
Differentiating Instruction

Teacher Quote

"Children believe in themselves... when their teacher's belief in them is evident."

~ *Dr. Joyce Bowling*

Chapter Questions

✦ *What is differentiated instruction?*
✦ *How can I differentiate literacy instruction?*
✦ *How should I group students for instruction?*
✦ *How can I challenge the above-level students?*
✦ *What are tiered literacy activities?*
✦ *How can I address the struggling readers' problems?*
✦ *How can I address the struggling writers' problems?*

Differentiation has been a part of the classroom since the days of the one-room school house. Differentiation remains a common *"buzz"* word today inside all education classes. It is also a common term in ARC meetings, the teachers' lounge, PLC meetings, professional development trainings, and inside public classrooms. So, what does the term, differentiate mean? It simply means to distinguish, perceive, and determine the difference(s) from other things; to change or make difference by modification. In the public classroom, differentiation involves assessing, monitoring, analyzing, recognizing, distinguishing, and modifying instructions and assignments to meet the academic or social needs of all students. Differentiation can be based on academic needs, cultural needs, and social needs.

Differentiating instruction consists of designing lessons based on students' learning styles, grouping students by shared interest, topic, or ability, assessing students' learning using multiple formative assessments, and also managing the classroom to create a safe and supportive environment where all students can learn (InTASC Standard 2, 3, Council of Chief State School Officers [CCSSO]). High-powered teachers establish and maintain a warm and accepting classroom where differentiation is a normal part of daily work. High-powered teachers teach their classroom community to honor differences and embrace diversity. This is achieved through establishing an environment where students can demonstrate his or her potential or aptitude to learn and also to perform. High-powered teachers create and establish an environment that is noncompetitive, individualized, and open which allows students to advance at their own pace of learning.

In this chapter, you will learn more about differentiating instructions to meet the needs of all of your students. You will learn the importance of reflection, analyzing data, and how to modify content, topics, instructional strategies, student projects and assignments to meet the needs of all learning styles and levels. You will learn effective strategies to help the struggling reader and writer, the advanced reader and writer, and learn ideas to motivate all of your students. Keep in mind, if you, the teacher, displays an evident and observable faith in your students, they will gain confidence and have faith in themselves.

Author Reflection

- -

"A classroom of students is comparable to a box of assorted chocolates.
You don't know what the center of a chocolate is until you take it apart...
just as we don't know the capability or learning style of our students
until we get to know them, assess them, and analyze the data.
~ Dr. Joyce Bowling

Imagine a first-grade classroom filled with twenty-nine to thirty six-year olds, each with their own unique personality, dreams, beliefs, learning styles, learning impediments, schemas, socioeconomic status, and their own culture. I have always and continue to compare a classroom of students to an unlabeled box of assorted chocolates. Just as we may not know what the center of the candy contains until we take the chocolate apart, teachers do not truly know what type of students enter their classrooms each year, until they get to know them personally and academically, assess them formatively and summatively, reflect on the assessment data, analyze data to determine their learning style, reading level, their interests, or their strengths and weaknesses.

Regardless the grade-level, or content that I taught, I began every year in the same manner. I found fun and creative ways to get to know my students both personally and academically in an effort to be better prepared to teach my students. I found that student-friendly surveys were a success with students of all ages. Students found them easy to complete, fun, and engaging. I created surveys to learn more about them personally, as a reader, a writer, and about their interests. I also read through their permanent folder each year to gain academic insight into their previous school years to better understand any diagnostic assessment data that was recorded, previous grades, and also to determine if they had an existing **IEP** (*individualized education program*), a **504**, and also to learn about attendance issues. I also administered a grade-level readers' interest survey to gain insight into their reading habits, desires, and fears. Once I had collected documentation on each of my students, I created a folder for each student where I could add documentation, artifacts, and also data for future use.

After the folders were filled with the desired documentation, I made time to interview each student. I conducted student interviews at random and opportune times until I had interviewed every child in the class. In the interviews, I ask each student the following questions: *what are your aspirations, your hopes for this year? What do you want to accomplish? What are the three academic goals you hope to achieve? What is one personal goal that you want to achieve? Why do you want to achieve these goals? Do you have any reservations or fears about first grade? Why do you think you have this fear? What would you like for me to do to help you achieve these goals? What will you do to achieve your goals? How should I reward you for achieving each goal? And finally, who do you consider to be your hero?*

I recorded and dated students' answers in their folders. Student folders were not filed away to collect dust. I revisited the folders periodically with each student to talk about their progress. Students' goals were also recorded on sentence strips or index cards and laminated. They were placed in their personal work folder where students were required to revisit their goals once a week. I also wrote goals for myself each year, and continue this practice even today, and revisit them weekly. I found that this served as a reminder, an inspirational and motivational tool when I was able to star, highlight, or check-off the accomplished goal. My students found it inspiring and motivational as well. I discovered that students enjoyed creating new goals throughout the year. Their goals consisted of MAPS scores, KPREP scores, weekly assessments, books read, AR points, spelling scores, behavior, and much more. This was a fun method of getting to know my students personally, academically, all while motivating them as well.

The bottom line: get to know your students, implement a variety of formative assessments to better know them academically, to assist you in designing personalized and differentiated instruction. Continue to monitor the progress of your students throughout the year, and also be a "**kid watcher**" in other words, observe your students in various settings, take anecdotal notes, document information that concerns you, observe students while they are working, observe them during assessments, when they are working collaboratively, and when they are socializing. The better you know your students, the easier it is to differentiate to meet their needs.

Be the teacher who sees potential in every child. Be the teacher who meets the needs of every child. Be the teacher who scaffolds instructions and assignments to allow students to understand, interpret, to realistically challenge them, to allow them to learn in the style that they learn best in. Be the teacher who creates and maintains a positive and safe learning environment for all students. Be the teacher who sets goals, monitors, and encourages students. Be the teacher who praises students for their hard work and acknowledges their success. Be the teacher who makes a difference in the lives of all of your students. Be the teacher who they remember gave them opportunities and realistic challenges and helped them set goals. Be the high-powered teacher who students recall helping them, inspiring them, teaching them, motivating them, and the teacher who taught them to be the best student and person that they could be.

Differentiating Instruction

High-powered teachers know that all students are not alike. They know that their interests will vary, cultures will vary, and their ability to read and write will vary. They also know that all students do not learn the same. High-powered teachers know and value the importance of these differences.

High-powered teachers know that **differentiated instruction** is based on their understanding of how their students differ in important ways. According to C. A. Tomlinson, differentiating instruction means shaking things up inside the classroom so that students have multiple opportunities and options for taking in information, making sense of ideas, and expressing what they learned.

High-powered teachers know the importance of differentiating instructions for struggling readers and writers who are not reading or writing at grade-level. They strive to personalize their instruction to meet the needs of all of their students, while providing additional support for struggling readers and writers, and also challenging the advanced students to ensure the academic success of all of their students. High-powered teachers ask the following questions to ensure that they are implementing differentiated instructions:

- ✦ *Am I continually maintaining a commitment to meeting grade-level standards for all students?*
- ✦ *Am I assessing to determine the needs of all of my students?*
- ✦ *Am I analyzing data and reflecting on the findings?*
- ✦ *Am I planning instruction based on assessment data?*
- ✦ *Am I incorporating flexible grouping allowing students to work collaboratively and independently?*
- ✦ *Am I rotating groups to reflect students' achievement levels, or their interests?*
- ✦ *Am I teaching with a wide variety of books and reading material at varying difficulty levels.*
- ✦ *Am I designing activities based on students' academic needs and learning styles?*
- ✦ *Am I modifying my instruction to meet the needs of my students?*
- ✦ *Am I setting goals for all of my students and do I respect their progress?*
- ✦ *Am I focusing on individual students or the classroom as a whole?*

High-powered teachers are reflective, analytical, and they are also planners. They have the mindset that all students can be successful and that all students do not learn the same and will not reach their goal at the same time. They know their students. They know who is working at grade-level, who is working above grade-level, and also who is working below grade-level. With this knowledge, they reflect and analyze assessment data, running records, anecdotal notes, and plan their instructions based on their findings. High-powered teachers are also willing to modify their instruction when necessary to ensure that all students are receiving what they need to be successful (InTASC Standard, 1, 2, 3, CCSSO).

Teacher Quote

"Utilizing multiple assessments and analyzing the data is the only true way a teacher has to determine if students are learning what has been taught."

~ *Dwight Harris, Elem. Principal*

High-powered teachers provide specific ways for students to learn as deeply as possible in an efficient manner. High-powered teachers are patient and strategic as they know that every student doesn't learn the same way or at the same time. They know that students travel different routes while all working toward the same goal of grade-level reading and writing, but they know that every student will not arrive at their ultimate destination of success at the same time. High-powered teachers ensure their students success through rigorous instruction, flexible instructions, and also through complex and strategic instructions designed with a purpose in mind. They know that just walking into the classroom and delivering instructions on the spur of the moment, or what is commonly referred to as, *"winging it"* will not ensure that their instructions are purposeful and designed to meet the needs of their students. High-powered teachers also avoid *"busy work"* that is often created last minute and in a panic due to lack of proper planning. High-powered teachers ensure that they

+ Plan and provide **rigorous instructions** which are challenging and also encourage students and promote engagement and collaborative learning experiences.
+ Plan and provide **relevant instructions** that address the literacy standards to ensure that students learn essential knowledge, learn multiple strategies, and gain necessary skills.
+ Are **flexible** and implement a variety of instructional procedures and multiple techniques as well as collaborative opportunities.
+ Provide **complex and explicit instructions** that promote and engage students in deep-thinking and problem-solving in all content areas.

High-powered teachers recognize the diversity of learners. They know that all students do not need to participate in the same learning activities, or in whole-class reading and writing for the entire day. High-powered teachers modify their instructions in a variety of ways to ensure that they are meeting the individual needs of their students. For example, they modify the ***content*** that students are required to learn, their ***instructional process*** they use to teach students, and also the ***products*** that students create to demonstrate what they have learned.

High-powered teachers differentiate the content, however, they assess students' knowledge of the content before teaching to gain a better understanding of their literacy knowledge, knowledge of strategies, and level of skills they are expected to learn at each grade-level. Their content is reflective of state standards, content standards, and grade-level standards. High-powered teachers know the content well before teaching. They design and plan their instruction based on the assessment data to meet the needs of all students. They maintain a clear and precise focus on teaching the essential content, while also striving to meet the needs of all learners by providing additional instructions and practice for some students, and less for others, and also by planning for early finishers as well. High-powered teachers also increase the complexity of the content to present a realistic challenge for students who are already familiar with the content, while also increasing the complexity of instructional activities and strategies (InTASC Standard, 4, 7, 8, CCSSO).

High-powered teachers know the **differentiating process**. In other words, they know the *"how"* of teaching, the instruction that teachers provide, the materials required, the activities that engage their students, and what strategies to implement to ensure that their activities are differentiated for all learners. High-powered teachers also know how to group students for instruction and select appropriate and grade-level reading materials that will allow students to learn and make steady academic progress. They know how to make decisions about involving students that allow and encourage them to apply what they're learning through multiple opportunities such as oral retelling, collaborative learning, written expression, hands-on experiences, and also visual and auditory learning (InTASC Standard 4, 5, CCSSO).

High-powered teachers also **differentiate the product**. The product is the result of what's been learned. High-powered teachers know the product demonstrates what the students have learned, how well they have learned it, and how well they can apply what they have learned. High-powered teachers require students to create diverse projects to demonstrate their knowledge of the content. For example, they may require some students to create storymaps, storyboards, or posters. They may require other students to complete written reports, or even require them to perform through readers' theater to demonstrate their level of knowledge and understanding. High-powered teachers may also require students to create projects that incorporate technology such as power points, trailers, and multimodal reports.

High-powered teachers may require students who are performing at various reading levels to be involved in diverse activities, or create different projects in effort to ensure that all students arrive at the same destination of understanding the initial purpose for the lesson through activities and assignments that are designed to align to their learning style and academic needs. High-powered teachers plan for and design projects and project requirements that align to students' academic needs and reading level. In other words, high-powered teachers differentiate and scaffold the complexity of the projects that they ask their students to create and complete by modifying the level of thinking required to complete the project.

High-powered teachers create and maintain a **classroom culture** that allows their students to feel safe to take academic risks, feel confident and accepted, regardless of individual learning differences. A high-powered teachers' classroom is also conductive in matching instruction to individual students. They know that establishing a community within their classroom where respect is given, where students have mutual respect for each other, and where students work well collaboratively, learning will take place. In this type of community, students can focus on their work rather than on what their peers are doing or what they are not doing. High-powered teachers also know that a safe learning environment promotes independence and encourages students to be responsible for their own learning (InTASC Standard 3, CCSSO).

High-Powered Teachers Group Students for Differentiated Instruction

High-powered teachers group their students for differentiated instruction. They group their students into three grouping patterns. They encourage and promote learning through **whole-group instruction and collaboration, small-group instruction and collaboration**, and also through **independent learning**. High-powered teachers plan for instruction as well as the method of grouping based on the purpose of the lesson, complexity of the activity, and students' specific needs. High-powered teachers use a combination of collaborative grouping, instructional strategies, instructional materials, and also diverse activities.

During whole-group instruction and collaboration, high-powered teachers incorporate basal readers and literature-focused units. During **whole-group** they introduce the book or topic, vocabulary, incorporate word-walls, model strategies, and also read orally to their students, and collaboratively with their students. High-powered teachers incorporate read-alouds during whole-group instructions, which often lead to grand conversations. They know that read-alouds have the ability to pique students' interest in the topic, promote student collaboration, and also increase students' comprehension.

Small-group instruction is used for rereading the text, practicing vocabulary and skills through engaging activities, and also working in centers. High-powered teachers incorporate workbook assignments and related texts during independent learning. They also teach mini lessons during small-group instruction creating opportunities for students to read and discuss collaboratively, solve problems in their groups, and also create projects together. High-powered teachers incorporate **small-group instruction and collaboration** flexibly to provide a better instructional match between the students and their academic needs. However, these teachers do not group repetitiously, instead they regroup their students often. They do not always group students based on their academic-achievement-levels or with the same peers (InTASC Standard 8, CCSSO).

Differentiated Questioning

However, high-powered teachers know from experience that differentiating through grouping cannot occur at all times in the classroom. They know that asking **frequent, targeted**, and **rigorous questions** to all students is a powerful differentiating strategy. High-powered teachers tailor questions to individual students. They rephrase questions for clarity if necessary, while also asking further questions that challenge students who answer the initial question correct. This method of questioning promotes a deeper level of understanding, and also increases critical thinking at all learning levels.

High-powered teachers take time to strategically plan leveled and targeted questions prior to instruction. Every student has questions that are designed to meet their academic needs, reading levels, and learning styles. This method allows all students to be engaged during questioning, and also ensures that all students can be successful. High-powered teachers teach, encourage, and require all of their students to be active listeners during discussion and questioning. High-powered teachers use discussion and question time to incorporate, **Pass the Question**, which encourages listening, comprehension, and participation. Pass the Question is a simple questioning technique that requires a student to reiterate a previous student's answer and elaborate on their answer. This questioning technique requires students to listen to the teacher, peers, and be prepared to repeat an answer and also extend an answer when they are called to do so. In summary, high-powered teachers know their students and their academic reading level and learning style. They plan for meaningful instructions, differentiated and purposeful questions, and tailor-made questions for every student in their class. High-powered teachers involve every student in the class in purposeful, fun, and collaborative meaningful conversations to promote enhanced learning.

Guided Reading

High-powered teachers incorporate guided reading with beginning readers in primary grades. However, guided reading can also be incorporated in any grade-level. Guided reading is especially beneficial for English learners and struggling readers to ensure that students are receiving the required additional support. Guided reading is an instructional approach that allows teachers to work with a small group of students who have similar reading behaviors and similar reading levels. During guided reading teacher's support is more prevalent which allows students to gain confidence while working to decode and also to comprehend text. Guided reading also reinforces comprehension of learning strategies, which promotes readers' independence. High-powered teachers know that reading and writing are reciprocal. Thus, they incorporate guided writing during guided reading as well.

High-powered teachers divide their instruction into three segments during guided reading. The segments include **before reading, during reading, and after reading**. Before-reading instruction typically consist of briefly introducing the text and allowing their students to begin reading the text. During reading, teachers allow their students to read independently. Teachers may ask their students to whisper-read or read silently during reading. They do not incorporate a round robin style reading where students take turns reading, instead, they make their way around a small group of students, monitoring them as they read, and also providing one-on-one support for brief periods of time as needed. High-powered teachers know that all students learn differently and know that different students may require different strategies. For example, a student might need support using first-letter cues, while others may need help monitoring comprehension. High-powered teachers know their students as readers and know how to scaffold instruction and assistance during reading to meet their students' need and help every reader be successful.

High-powered teachers check students' comprehension after they have read. They check for understanding through a basic discussion question such as, "How did the character change from the beginning of the story to the end of the story?" High-powered teachers also ask their students to write about the text. They know that this provides them with a writing sample, as well as encourages students to go back to the text to locate textual evidence for their answers.

High-powered teachers know that guided reading is a valuable time to monitor students reading, while also prompting them to dig deeper into the text. During guided reading, high-powered teachers prompt readers by asking questions such as, does that make sense? Does that sound right? High-powered teachers also ask students to use their finger to check their answers. and They also promote decoding skills by asking students to say the first part of the word and check the picture. They encourage students to break words apart and chunk them. They also encourage readers to look at patterns and prompt them to think of words that look similar to the word they are struggling with. For example, the teacher might prompt students who are struggling with the word, *bright*, to think about a different *ight* word that they previously learned, such as *light*.

Guided reading is also an opportunity for teachers to work with students to increase fluency. High-powered teachers encourage students to read the text without pointing, speak like the character might speak, and read smoother through prompting them to put words together to flow better. They also promote vocabulary with support through prompting the reader to identify words that they do not understand, to look for context clues to help them determine the meaning, remind them to use illustrations and pictures for clues, and again, to look for chunks of the word to help them determine the meaning.

In summary, high-powered teachers incorporate small-group guided reading to enhance students reading comprehension through teacher support and guided instruction with prompting and cueing. High-powered teachers ask periodical questions before, during, and after reading. They ask questions such as what's happening on this page? Is there a confusing part? What you don't understand? They also ask students to make predictions. For example, they may ask students to explain why they think a character acted in a certain way, or what they think the character will do next. During guided reading, high-powered teachers teach, guide, monitor, informally assess through the use of running records and checklists, and later reflect on their findings and regroup accordingly. They know that guided-reading groups are not etched in stone and that students progress at different rates, therefore they must provide differentiated instruction and scaffold projects at diverse times.

Scaffold Activities

"Each cell in the human body contains about 25,000 to 35,000 genes, which carry information that determines your traits. Each Gene can determine exceptionalities in any one of us. So why would we, as Educators, present material in one way knowing that we are all so vastly different. Differentiation is the avenue in which knowledge is transferred to EVERY student."

~ Dr. Virginia West, University of the Cumberlands

High-powered teachers are flexible, creative-thinkers, who carefully plan, and scaffold instructional strategies that focus on the same essential knowledge, but vary in complexity. They know that by strategically designing scaffold activities they are enabling students to reach the same goal, to read at grade-level. High-powered teachers know that all students learn differently and "one-size-fits-all" activities are not beneficial for on-grade-level students, support struggling readers, or challenge advanced students. High-powered teachers know that scaffold activities increase the likelihood that all students will be successful. They ensure that all activities are interesting, engaging, and that each activity, regardless the academic level, requires the same amount of effort from all students.

High-powered teachers scaffold activities in a variety of ways. For example, they scaffold them by complexity of thinking. They create recall-leveled activities that require some students to identify, retell the story, or summarize, while other students might evaluate, make inferences, or draw conclusions, and yet another level of students might be creating. High-powered teachers also scaffold activities based on the level of the text. They incorporate books and other types of print, such as multimodal text that is leveled to match students' reading level.

High-powered teachers often require their students to complete a project at the end of the activity to apply what they have learned. High-powered teachers strategically design activities and how they should be completed by scaffolding how students will present their completed projects. For example, one group of students may be required to complete a graphic organizer, while a different group may be asked to complete a written essay, and still another group of students might create a hands-on project. High-powered teachers also scaffold completed activities by the form of expression. For example, students may be involved in oral, visual, and written expressions as they complete an activity based on their learning style. Examples of completed projects include charts, posters, dioramas, dramatizations, oral retelling, stories, songs lyrics, poetry, or even role play. Nevertheless, high-powered teachers know that by creating scaffold activities, they are engaging, challenging, and promoting learning for all students, regardless the learning style or reading level.

Struggling Readers and Writers

As stated previously, high-powered teachers know that all students do not learn the same nor do all children progress at the same rate. They know that many underlying factors can contribute to children's reading progress and learning rate. For example, they know that children with strong oral language skills and those who are engaged in early literacy experiences are more likely to be successful in reading. Whereas students who are not fluent English speakers, children whose parents had difficulty learning, and writing, and those from low socioeconomic area are more likely to have difficulty reaching grade-level proficiency in reading or writing (Strickland).

High-powered teachers know that students who struggle in reading or writing, often have significant struggles in other content areas, which affects their learning in all content areas. They know the importance of identifying students early who are at risk for reading. High-powered teachers also know that it is ideal to identify areas of concern when students are in kindergarten or first grade. However, they also know that not all students are identified as being a struggling reader in primary grades. They know that some students do not exhibit reading difficulties until fourth and sometimes fifth grade. Nevertheless, high-powered teachers, regardless the grade-level, know that it is vital to get to know their students as readers through multiple observations, formative and summative assessments, listening to students read in various settings, documenting evidence, reflecting on the data, and finally analyzing the data (InTASC Standard 6, CCSSO).

High-powered teachers know that struggling readers exhibit a variety of difficulties and are observant and prepared to quickly recognize students who exhibit areas of concern. For example, some students may have difficulty decoding, other students may exhibit difficulty developing concepts about written language, letter names, phonemic awareness, and phoneme/grapheme correspondences. They also recognize students who have a slower than typical response rate when identifying words, decreased vocabulary knowledge, and remembering or recalling what they've read. High-powered teachers quickly recognize areas of concern when observing and assessing students' writing. Areas of concern may include having difficulty developing and organizing ideas, struggling with appropriate word choice, writing complete sentences, and using correct grammar. Other students might display basic writing skills, but struggle with the writing process and incorporating writing strategies.

High-powered teachers recognize when students complain that their hands hurt when asked to complete writing assignments, display little to no interest in writing, and those who become frustrated when asked to write. Regardless the area of concern, when high-powered teachers suspect that a student is struggling, they quickly take action by administering further assessments to help diagnose possible problems. If an area of concern is identified, they quickly intervene accordingly with appropriate measure to ensure that the student is receiving reading or writing intervention.

High-powered teachers know the value of providing high-quality classroom instructions and including intervention. They also know that there isn't a prescribed quick fix for low-achieving students. High-powered teachers know that helping struggling students requires both high-quality, rigorous, differentiated classroom instruction and also providing meaningful intervention that is personalized to meet the needs of the reader. High-powered teachers know that a balanced approach combined with explicit instruction in decoding, fluency, vocabulary, comprehension, and writing combined with multiple daily opportunities for students to work collaboratively with peers and create meaningful projects is effective for all learners. They know that the quality of classroom instruction has a profound impact on how well students learn to read and write. Research shows through studies of exemplary teachers that teaching expertise is the critical factor (Block et al.).

Interventions

High-powered teachers are well educated about interventions and availability of intervention programs that are available in their schools to help accelerate literacy learning. They know that intervention is designed to help children at risk. They know that intervention is not meant to replace high-quality classroom instruction, but to build on what is being taught in the classroom. They know that classroom interventions promote reading growth. High-powered teachers monitor, assess, reflect, analyze, collaborate, and plan high-quality interventions. They know that high-quality intervention should include the following:

✦ **Daily planned scheduling** where interventions take 20–45 minutes, depending on the students' age or instructional needs.

✦ Working daily with students in **multiple settings** such as individual and small-group instructions.

✦ **Incorporating text** that **match students' instructional level** as well as their independence level. Including material that is interesting and engaging that provides somewhat of a challenge.

✦ **Planning daily explicit instructions** that include rereading familiar books to build confidence, reading new books, phonics, word-identification, and vocabulary, and also writing opportunities.

✦ Providing **additional opportunities daily** for students to spend time reading and writing to practice and also to apply what they have learned.

✦ **Monitoring and assessing** students on an ongoing basis, collecting work samples, data, and also diagnostic test data to determine students' academic growth, and also to analyze their growth compared to grade-level standards.

✦ Continue **professional development** to improve teaching expertise to ensure that they are providing the best possible instructions and also to help assist and ensure that instructional assistance and volunteers who may work inside the classroom are well trained.

✦ Creating and maintaining **home–school partnership** by keeping parents informed about students' progress and strive to involve them in supporting independent reading and writing at home.

Reading Recovery

High-powered teachers know their students and also know when to refer them for additional intervention. Interventions may include programs such as **Reading Recovery**, which is the most widely known intervention program for the lowest achieving first graders (Clay, *Reading Recover*; *Literacy Lessons: Designed for Individuals, Part One*; *Literacy Lessons: Designed for Individuals, Part Two*). Reading Recovery was developed by clinical child psychologist Marie Clay. It is an early intervention program that is designed to reduce reading failure in the first grade for the lowest performing 20% of students. The goal of the program is to help low-achieving students catch up to the desired and established first-grade reading-level. Reading Recovery involves a 30 minute rigorous daily one-on-one tutoring session. It is taught by a highly qualified and trained teacher. Reading Recovery lasts for 12–30 weeks and includes the following components:

✦ rereading familiar books
✦ independently reading the book introduced in the previous lesson
✦ learning decoding and comprehension strategies
✦ writing sentences
✦ reading a new book with teacher support

Once students who are participating in Reading Recovery reach grade-level standards and demonstrate that they can work independently in their classrooms, they leave the program. The results of **Reading Recovery** program are very impressive. Research has proven that up to 75% of students who complete the Reading Recovery program meet grade-level literacy standards and continue to be successful thereafter.

Author's Experience

As a veteran first-grade teacher, I have personally witnessed a high success rate with first-grade students who were struggling in reading and writing. I have, and will continue to be an active advocate for this early intervention program. Each student who completed the Reading Recovery program is a success story, and has their own unique story. However, one particular student will forever remain etched in my memory. The story goes as follows: a six-year-old male student who was not previously enrolled in our school enrolled in my first-grade classroom days after the year had begun. After researching his background, I discovered that he hadn't attended kindergarten or a head-start program. He had attended a military school in the North Western part of the United States.

I began the year as usual with summative as well as standardized assessments to determine the students, reading level. The data showed a less than desirable reading level and also some disturbing evidence. I continued to informally assess the student through daily observations, one-on-one summative assessments, all while recording documentation on a detailed running record and incorporating a checklist. I soon discovered that the student did not know the difference between letters and numbers. He could not make any connections to phonemic awareness or phonics. However, I did determine that he retained everything that I taught in explicit instruction. He could recall site words, he could make connections with the letters that I had recently taught. With data in place, I asked the Reading Recovery specialist to assess him for the program. She determined that he could be accepted into the program and intervention began soon thereafter. The student completed the Reading Recovery Program in a timely manner, showed growth inside the classroom, received help at home, and exited first grade reading slightly above grade-level. This student is now a successful young man who excelled throughout his years in public school, and graduated during his planned year. This is a successful reading intervention that is available for struggling readers in the first grade who do not have an established IEP and receive intervention otherwise.

Author Quote

"Reading Recovery provides an academic nudge that promotes learning and confidence for many struggling readers and writers."

~ Dr. Joyce Bowling

Reading Mastery

Reading Mastery is a supplemental reading program used with students who have a moderate to severe reading disability, and for students who may have not been successful in traditional reading programs. Reading Mastery is also used as a supplemental reading program for students that have been identified as high risk of failure. It is also recommended for English Language Learners.

Reading Mastery was developed by Siegfried Engelmann under the title, *Distar Reading*, which was used in Project Follow Through as part of the direct instruction teaching model, and was published by SRA/McGraw-Hill. Reading Mastery is a direct instruction program designed to provide explicit, systematic instructions in English language reading. It is available in two versions. Reading Mastery Classic level I and level II, which is used in kindergarten through third grade. It is available in what is known as Reading Mastery Plus, which is an integrated reading-language program for kindergarten through sixth grade.

Reading Mastery program is systematic and strategically designed. Lessons typically begin by teaching phonemic awareness, sound-letter correspondence, and transitions to word and passage reading, vocabulary development, developing and building oral reading fluency, and also comprehension. As students' progress, the teacher teaches and emphasizes accurate and fluent decoding, while also teaching students necessary skills to read and comprehend a variety of genres. The lessons in Reading Mastery are designed to be rigorous and fast-paced as well as interactive, and are typically taught in 30–45-minute. The teaching materials are carefully scripted and reading material is appropriate for skill-level. Students are typically grouped based on similar reading levels, which are determined by the program placement tests. High-powered teachers incorporate Reading Mastery to help students read at their level, they know that the program includes placement assessments, and also a continuous monitoring system, which helps them to accurately assess and track their students' progress.

Response to Intervention

High-powered teachers also know when students require intervention. They know, understand, and follow the process of **RTI** (response to intervention). They know that RTI is a schoolwide initiative to identify struggling students in an efficient manner, promote high-quality classroom instruction, while also providing effective interventions and increasing student success. High-powered teachers know that the RTI process involves three tiers as follows:

+ **Tier 1 consists of screening and prevention**. High-powered teachers provide high-quality instruction supported by scientific research, students are screened to help identify those at risk for academic failure, and then monitor students' progress. If students are not making adequate progress toward meeting grade-level standards, they move to the next tier, that is tier 2.

+ **Tier 2 consists of early intervention**. High-powered, trained, and qualified reading teachers provide enhanced, individualized instructions that target students' specific areas of difficulty. If the intervention is successful and students' reading problems are resolved, the student returns to Tier 1; however, if students make some progress, but still require additional instruction, they remain in Tier 2. If students do not display improvement or progress, they move to Tier 3, where the intensity of intervention increases.

+ **Tier 3 consists of intensive intervention**. High-powered special education teachers provide more intense intervention for individual students and small groups. They also monitor progress more frequently. Special Education teachers focus on resolving students' problem(s) area(s) and teaching compensatory strategies.

RTI is a schoolwide instructional and assessment program that incorporates data-driven decision-making. Special education teachers are qualified and proficient at using data to examine, and also to go beyond reading data to determine who got an answer correct and who did not. They analyze wrong answers for clues to better understand students' thinking and then engage in systematic action and planning as a result. They are also optimistic that RTI will be a better way to diagnose learning-disabled students, while also providing them with quality education.

Challenging the Above-Level Students

"My career requires me to travel from coast to coast. Reading has been a beneficial part of my travels. Reading has taken me to places that I have never been before, prepared me for upcoming travels, and given me a working knowledge of cultural traits that I would experience during my next journey and upon arriving at my next destination."

~ Tom Hurt

High-powered teachers know how to design reading and writing activities for struggling as well as above-level or gifted students. They get to know their students through observations, assessment, reflections, collaborating with them as well as listening to them in grand conversations. High-powered teachers look beyond the surface of the child, but rather work to unveil the joy and uniqueness of each child. They discover their interests and design meaningful activities that promote critical, deep, and analytical thinking based on their interests. They do not overwhelm above-level students or early finishers with extra work. High-powered teachers know that this is unfair and also can become frustrating to their students. They do not place unrealistic expectations or pressures on their students.

In other words, high-powered teachers know how to differentiate the curriculum to address differences in the rate, depth of knowledge, and pace of learning. High-powered teachers know that this enables all students in the class to learn about a specific area by creating projects at their own ability level. High-powered teachers are flexible with the curriculum and take advantage of real-life experiences that can be translated into problem-solving academics for students. They also make the curriculum student-centered and engaging. High-powered teachers allow and encourage above-level students to pursue independent projects based on their own individual interests. They assign independent projects based on ability level to involve the entire classroom. They encourage creativity and original thinking, while also allowing students to explore ways of connecting unrelated issues in creative ways.

High-powered teachers encourage peer collaboration, but do not rely on above-level students to always be peer tutors. Peer tutoring can be a fun occasional challenge for gifted and talented or above-level students, but can quickly become a nuisance and also be boring to students. High-powered teachers know that the emphasis should always be on working together in the classroom in a meaningful and engaging manner that promotes deep learning. High-powered teachers cluster or group above-level students together at a table within the regular classroom and utilize advanced materials, resources, and modifications that are designed to meet the exceptional needs of advanced students.

High-powered teachers integrate creative and meaningful opportunities for advanced students, while also not placing unrealistic expectations on their students. Some of the creative practices to challenge above-level students are as follow:

✦ Asking deeper questions to encourage students to move from factual to conceptual. Encouraging them to make connections, instead of just stating facts.

✦ Assign research to particularly strong learners requiring them to use a variety of sources such as websites, books, and blogs.

✦ Encourage divergent thinking by requiring students to contribute more than just an essay, instead requiring them to complete a poster, diagram, collage, or even a power point.

✦ Incorporate Project-Based Learning assignments where students work independently to complete projects as a group outside of scheduled class time. Project-Based Learning encourages students to explore, envision, support, create, and present.

✦ Encourage students to create and publish. For example, a class newsletter, which encourages higher order thinking, motivates and helps students to take ownership of their ideas, and complete the work. High-powered teachers set guidelines, goals, and also provide rubrics for students to self-assess.

High-powered teachers strategically group their students, organize, and provide leveled-resources for each group that present a realistic challenge, address desired standards, engage students, and promote learning. They assess their students, teach their students, encourage and motivate them, collaborate with them, and also challenge them. They provide them with timely and meaningful feedback that addresses their strengths and outlines designated areas for improvement. High-powered teachers also believe that all students can be challenged, can learn and grow socially and academically through well-planned and designed leveled instruction.

In summary, high-powered teachers get to know their students through multiple and ongoing assessments, which consist of diagnostic tests, formative assessments, summative assessments, observations, collaboration, grading daily work, and listening to their students. They also reflect on data, analyze the data, and begin planning instructions that fit the needs of all of their students whether they are below reading level, at reading level, or above reading level.

> *"When teachers give an assessment, they are not only assessing how well the students' performed, they are assessing how well they, as a teacher, did preparing their students."*
>
> ~ *Dwight Harris, Elem. Principal*

Language Link

A differentiated classroom includes all students, and the belief that all students can be successful. High-powered teachers differentiate writing instruction and writing assignments based on students' reading levels, their interests, and also their learning profiles. High-powered teachers design writing prompts, questions, and extended response questions that are designed to meet the needs of each student. They differentiate the required writing assignment by scaffolding the text and writing prompt using the following website; http://newsela.com.

High-powered teachers select a text from the newsela library. When desired lexile level is entered, the text is automatically modified to match the desired reading level. Students are given leveled texts to read that are all based on the same concept, but modified to match individual reading levels. Thus, reducing students' frustration, promoting comprehension, fluency, and also allowing all students to learn about the same topic at their reading level. After students have read the text, they may be required to answer text-based questions, or respond with an extended answer that may contain a sentence, two sentences, or a paragraph based on students' reading level.

High-powered teachers use the newsela website or app to create leveled articles for grammar as well. For example, if students in a primary class are working on identifying parts of speech in a sentence, they may be required to read the leveled text, and then asked to highlight verbs, nouns, adjectives, pronouns, or the part of speech that they are currently learning. High-powered teachers incorporate leveled texts from newsela to enhance students' reading skills, writing skills, and also content knowledge. They know that the learning possibilities are endless with this easy to use website.

What Can Parents Do to Help?

High-powered teacher communicate, inform, and involve their students' parents in their children's education. They realize the struggle that parents face when helping a struggling reader. They encourage parents to motivate and encourage their children to read through offering packets of diverse reading material and options that appeal to students. Materials can include leveled readers from different genres, age-appropriate magazine articles, comic books, and age-appropriate and teacher-approved websites, links, and apps.

High-powered teachers do not assign homework that is consistently too hard, but rather designed and leveled to fit the developmental needs of each student. High-powered teachers cleverly disguise and tuck upcoming spelling words in various assignments such as preprinted stories, sentences, and fun engaging word sorts. This allows students to read, write, and experience hands-on learning while also increasing their spelling awareness and skills. High-powered teachers design folder games that require students to make choices, answer questions, roll dice, or spin spinners, all of which require them to engage with words. In other words, they make learning meaningful, fun, and also interactive without undue stress on the parents.

Finally, high-powered teachers include praise stickers that can be given to young readers and writers when they complete the assigned work. Praise stickers encourage and motivate students and the parents. For older students, they give praise tickets for completing assignments successfully. Praise tickets can include, but are not limited to, the following: add two points to your lowest grade, 10 minute free time in the class library, be the line-leader for a day, pass out papers, etc. Both stickers and praise tickets are meant to praise students for their hard work, and also recognize them for their accomplishments.

Above all, high-powered teachers maintain constant, open communication with their students' parents. They provide them with timely graded work with clear and precise feedback of what their child completed successfully and also with areas of concern and growth. In turn, parents are informed, motivated, and focused on what their child can do, and encouraged to support and help build on his or her strengths and excited to help their child grow emotionally, socially, and academically.

Differentiating in the Virtual Classroom

High-powered teachers know that teaching virtually does not mean giving up high-powered best practices. Virtual learning can be defined, implemented, and described as diverse as the culture within the district. Virtual learning may occur for students who have a preference of in person instruction or online instruction creating a mix of in person and online students as the teacher's responsibility. And, still at other times, all students might be restricted to virtual learning. Whatever, the case may be high-powered teachers know the challenges that come with each scenario as well as the challenge of differentiation both in person and inside the virtual classroom. Differentiation can be about offering two and maybe three versions of an assignment for virtual students. Instead of selecting one assignment for the entire class, high-powered teachers select specific students for specific tasks. Differentiation can be one-on-one instruction, providing leveled readers, allowing options for the final product, and also simply engaging with your students much like you engage with them face to face. High-powered teachers are creative, confident, and willing to take risks. They know that if one method of in-seat and or virtual instruction isn't successful, they can pull from their tool box of strategies to implement a different strategy. High-powered teachers don't give up after the first try. They strive to ensure success of all of their students, both in-seat and online students.

Virtual Guided Reading

High-powered teachers implement guided reading in the classroom to scaffold and differentiate to meet the needs of all learners much like they utilize guided reading in the virtual classroom to meet the needs of all students. Yes, high-powered teachers still conduct guided reading when teaching virtually. They make this happen through simply creating and or inviting small groups in their virtual classroom.

High-powered teachers utilize several online reading resources that allow them to provide their students links to specific reading material. With the link, students can swipe through the assigned reading independently. Teachers may also share their screen and have students follow along for oral reading, group reading, and even echo reading. High-powered teachers include think aloud, read aloud, and also model strategies such as decoding and breaking apart difficult words or digging deeper in the comprehensive aspect of reading. Guided reading can be utilized for phonics, fluency, pacing, expression, and comprehension. Guided reading can become a setting where specific needs are targeted for diverse groups of students. Guided reading can become a scheduled time to ensure student's needs are met in a small group setting.

Audio Books

High-powered teachers know that audio books can be a great resource for differentiating, especially for students with dyslexia. Audio books is a method of differentiation that allows the student to access texts that they may not be able to read independently, but may comprehend when read aloud to them, thus acting as a read aloud. High-powered teachers know that audio books can be effective for emerging bilingual students to experience listening to native English speakers. High-powered teachers know that audio books that include text allows students to follow the

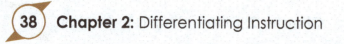

reader in a virtual one-on-one session that in turn helps strengthen student's ability to read from left to right and also to be engaged in the story, characters, plot, and much more. Audio books can also be a great resource for students who have been diagnosed with left/right confusion. High-powered teachers also know that audio books are a great resource for strengthening student's pacing, expression, and fluency. Audio books can be used as a diverse method of differentiating to meet the needs of individual students.

Early Finishers and Gifted and Talented Students

High-powered teachers know that one of the most effective methods of differentiating is to go straight to the source: their students! High-powered teachers give their students opportunities to share what support(s) they need, what feels too hard, what seems too easy, and where they would like to be challenged. High-powered teachers know that both in-seat and virtual students have little to no problem sharing their thoughts aloud in a group, while others struggle to share their thoughts, ask questions, or answer questions. High-powered teachers solve this problem both in the face-to-face setting and the virtual setting through the use of exit slips, virtual forms of check-ins, and also through collaboration.

Once high-powered teachers have had the opportunity to get to know their students through collaborative conversations, formative and summative assessments, and listening to their students, they begin planning accordingly. Differentiation for the early finisher can be as simple as offering two or three different reading responses based on different books that are leveled to meet the student's academic needs. High-powered teachers create the same template and then quickly modify them and select specific students to ensure that they're meeting the needs of every student.

High-powered teachers may also allow the early finisher to respond in diverse methods. Differentiating the product can be as simple as: asking students to respond through written responses, or oral presentations for those who do not mind speaking in the virtual setting, submitting recorded answers, or illustrations. The possibilities for differentiating the product are vast. Finally, high-powered teachers know the key to successful differentiation for the gifted students and the early finishers, both in-seat and virtual, is knowing their students, and creatively designing and offering opportunities that present a slight, but realistic challenge, that engages the students and helps extend the already established knowledge. High-powered teachers also know that busy work is NOT the best method of challenging and engaging the early finisher.

Now It's Your Turn

For this assignment, the candidate will work **one-on-one** with four students in their clinical placement in the content area of reading and writing. You will need to collaborate with your cooperating teacher to determine the students you will work with. This is meant to be a diverse learning experience to help you gain a better understanding of how to differentiate instruction based on students' needs at various levels. The students' reading level should already be determined by the teacher as, **above-level, at-level, below-level**, and **struggling**. The struggling student can be an **IEP** or **ELL** student, but doesn't have to be. You will be required to write a five paragraph reflection about your experience. Reflect on how this experience helped you prepare for teaching, gave you a better understanding of what is meant by the term, differentiation, scaffolding assignments, and working one-on-one with diverse students. Describe what you thought was successful, your strengths, and areas for improvement. You will be required to submit the reflection as well as copies of students' graded work at all levels. Be sure to include meaningful feedback on graded work. Specific details for the assignment are located on the content page of blackboard.

Application

To guide you through Chapter Two and upcoming chapters, become familiar with the following key terms for a deeper understanding of Chapter Two:

- ✦ Differentiate
- ✦ Diverse instruction
- ✦ Individualized educational program (IEP)
- ✦ 504
- ✦ Rigor
- ✦ Rigorous instruction
- ✦ Relevant instruction
- ✦ Explicit instruction
- ✦ Whole group instruction and collaboration
- ✦ Small-group instruction and collaboration
- ✦ Independent learning
- ✦ Guided reading
- ✦ Scaffold activities
- ✦ Intervention
- ✦ RTI (Response to Intervention)
- ✦ Reading recovery
- ✦ Reading mastery
- ✦ Differentiated questioning
- ✦ Pass the question

In-Seat Activity

Reflect on what you have learned about differentiating in the classroom. You will be randomly partnered with a peer. Working collaboratively with your partner, and based on the partner number that you randomly select from the box of numbers, match your number to the scenario in the stack of scenarios that's on your table that has the same number as your partner number. Scenarios will differ, with some describing shared reading, others may describe a vocabulary activity, or a reading activity. Scenarios may contain ELL students, struggling readers, multiple reading levels, visually impaired students, dyslexic students, or gifted and talented students. Read the scenario closely, identify the needs, and work collaboratively to determine how the teacher in the scenario should plan, scaffold, and differentiate to meet the needs of the students. Be prepared to review your scenario and your solution to the teachers' problem with the class. You will be given 15 minute to plan and prepare and 5–6 minute to present. Both partners must participate in the informal presentation.

Reflect and Answer the Following Questions

✦ *What is differentiated instruction?*
✦ *How can I differentiate literacy instruction?*
✦ *How should I group students for instructions?*
✦ *How can I challenge the above-level students?*
✦ *What are tiered literacy activities?*
✦ *How can I address the struggling readers' problems?*
✦ *How can I address the struggling writers' problems?*

Student Notes

Annotating is an effective learning strategy. This page is reserved for you to annotate *(take notes)* record potential questions, and also to refer back to when studying, completing assignments, and to help you gain a better understanding of Chapter Two.

Student Reflection

High-powered teachers reflect. This page is reserved for you to reflect about information that you found insightful and what you have learned from Chapter Two.

Suggested Readings

Fountas, I. C., and G. S. Pinnel. *Matching Books to Readers: Using Leveled Books in Guided Reading, K-3.* Heinermann, 1999.

Szymusiak, K., and F. Sibberson. *Beyond Leveled Books: Supporting Transitional Readers in Grades 2-5.* Stenhouse, 2001.

Chapter References

Block, C., et al. "The Expertise of Literacy Teachers: A Continuum from Preschool-Grade 5." *Reading Research Quarterly,* vol. 37, 2002, pp. 178–206.

Clay, M. M. *Reading Recover: A Guidebook for Teachers in Training.* Heinemann, 1993.

Clay, M. M. *Literacy Lessons: Designed for Individuals, Part One: Why? When? and How?* Heinemann, 2005a.

Clay, M. M. *Literacy Lessons: Designed for Individuals, Part Two: Teaching Procedures.* Heinemann, 2005b.

Council of Chief State School Officers (CCSSO). *Interstate Teacher Assessment and Support Consortium (InTASC) Model Core Teaching Standards*, Apr, 2011, https://www.ccsso.org/sites/default/files/2017-11/InTASC_Model_Core_Teaching_Standards_2011.pdf. Accessed 7 July 2018.

Newsela | Instructional Content Platform, 2018. www.http://newsela.com. Accessed 18 Mar. 2018.

Strickland, D. S. "The Importance of Effective Early Intervention." *What Research Has to Say About Reading Instruction*, 3rd ed. edited by A. E. Farstrop, and S. J. Samuels. International Reading Association, 2002, pp. 69–86.

Tomlinson, C. A. *The Differentiated Classroom: Responding to the Needs of All Learners*, 2nd ed. Association for Supervision and Curriculum Development, 2014.

Chapter 3
Phonics and Word Identification

Teacher Quote

"Teaching phonics is a vital part of teaching young children how to read, write, and spell. When teachers provide students with explicit and strategic phonics instruction, they're not only teaching them phonics, they are giving their students an advantage and a key to unlocking the mysteries of print that they will use the rest of their lives."

~ Dr. Joyce Bowling

Chapter Questions

- ✦ What is the alphabetic code?
- ✦ What is the alphabetic principal?
- ✦ What is phonemic awareness?
- ✦ What is phonological awareness?
- ✦ What is phonics?
- ✦ How do children decode words?
- ✦ Why is it important to teach spelling and reading together?

Many young children learn a great deal about reading in their preschool years. They begin to think about written language as a system and become curious about how it works. Children as young as two often respond to oral directions and can draw a picture about a given topic when asked to do so. Two-year-old children often make squiggly lines to represent text when asked to write about their picture. So, how does this connect to reading? Even at the young age of two, children begin to make important connections with pictures and print, which is the beginning stage of cracking the alphabetic code.

English is an alphabetic language. Children crack the alphabetic code as they learn about phonemes, graphemes, and graphophonemic (*recognition of letters and understanding of sound-symbol relationships and spelling patterns, often referred to as phonics*) relationships. Children learn about phonemes as they notice rhyming words, when they segment words into individual sounds, and also through creating silly words by playing with and manipulating sounds. Children also learn about letters at a young age through songs such as *Alphabet Songs*. They learn the names of the letters in the alphabet while also learning to spell their names. Learning to read is a strategic journey that opens doors to ensure students' success in all content areas. For the teachers to understand how to teach their students to read, it is important for them to understand the structure of language and equally important is to know the learning styles of each of their students.

The Alphabetic Code

The terminology used for reading can be confusing and a bit overwhelming to young teachers. One of the reccurring statements, or questions, that I encounter semester after semester is: *the reading terms are confusing, what do they all mean?* Students also ask how the terms are correlated. Each semester there's an underlying confusion with phonics and phonological awareness. I want to alleviate this confusion through detailed definitions, descriptions, and examples of the terminology that you will need to be better prepared with to teach students to read.

Some of the terms that might be confusing or difficult to distinguish and understand might include *phonics, phonemic awareness, graphemes, phonemes, the alphabet*, and the *alphabetic code*. To alleviate the confusion, let's begin by breaking down some of the terms that you, the teacher, will need to know in order to make necessary connections throughout this text as a student and also as a teacher. Let's begin with the **alphabetic code**. This is a term that you will see time and time again as a student and as a teacher.

The English language has an interesting history, which has resulted in a complex **alphabetic code** for the writing system. The 26 letters of the alphabet represent 44 or so smallest sounds identifiable in English speech in three complicated ways as follows:

✦ One sound **(phoneme)** can be represented by one, two, three, or four letters: e.g., /a/ a, /f/ ph, /igh/ igh, /oa/ ough.
✦ One sound can be represented by *multiple spelling alternatives* (**graphemes**): e.g., /oa/o, ow, oe, o-e, eau, ough.
✦ One **grapheme** (letter or letter group) can represent *multiple sounds*: e.g., 'ough' /oa/ though, /or/ thought, long /oo/ through, /ou/ plough, /u/ thorough.

You may have noticed or remember seeing one or more large colorful Alphabetic Code charts hanging on the walls in a primary classroom. Alphabetic Code charts serve multiple purposes for the teachers and the students. Teachers often use these charts in phonics instructions. These colorful charts can also serve as reminders and guidance for young readers and writers who are learning to crack the alphabetic code. Students can also refer to these charts to help decoding words as well as assistance in spelling.

The Alphabetic Principle

The **alphabetic principle** is another term that you will learn about. It is the knowledge of letter/sound relationships. In other words, the understanding that letters represent sounds/phonemes, and that sounds are represented by letters arranged to form words. Research teaches us that, children begin learning oral language at the time of birth, and is an ongoing process. They learn, either on their own or with assistance, that spoken words have individual speech sounds/phonemes. Letter-sound knowledge is a prerequisite for successful word identification. Similarly, children's reading development depends on their understanding of the alphabetic principle. As children learn that there are predictable relationships between sounds and letters, they begin to better understand how to apply these relationships to both familiar and unfamiliar words, and also begin reading more fluently. However, students need to recognize speech at its most basic level, that is, the individual sounds of phonemes.

The Alphabetic principal includes recognizing, naming, and producing letters of the alphabet, using letter-sound knowledge and syllables to decode written language. The alphabetic principle is composed of three primary components, which include **Letter-sound correspondence/Phonemic awareness:** Understanding that letters represent sounds and that sound can be represented by letters, which is phonics. **Blending:** Understanding that sounds are blended from left to right. **Phonological recoding:** Blending sounds together to represent a word that has meaning. Phonological recoding can also be defined as a systematic relationship between letters and phonemes to retrieve the pronunciation of an unknown word or to spell words, such as regular word reading, irregular word reading, and advanced word analysis.

High-powered teachers teach their students a variety of syllable strategies using a variety of texts, while also teaching them to use letter-sound knowledge for conventional spelling. The ability to use letter-sound correspondences to decode words is an indicator of a successful reader. Letter-sound knowledge can be taught through strategic and explicit instruction and collaborative and engaging activities. It is important to know that teaching alphabetic principle also leads to gains in reading acquisition/achievement (InTASC Standards 1, 4, 5, CCSSO).

What Is Phonemic Awareness?

Phonemic awareness is the ability to hear and manipulate the sounds in spoken words. It also involves an understanding that spoken words and syllables are made up of sequences of speech sounds. Phonemic awareness can also be defined as the basic understanding that speech is composed of a series of individual sounds, and provides the foundation for phonics and spelling (Armbruster et al.).

For example, when children can choose a truck as a toy whose name begins with /t/ from a collection of toys, identify the words, *duck* and *luck* as rhyming words in a song, and blend the sounds t/r/u/k/ to pronounce the word *truck*, or blend the sounds of /l/u/k/ to pronounce the word *luck*, which demonstrate phonemic awareness.

Another definition or description of phonemic awareness can be defined as an awareness of children's ability to take words apart and put them back together again with the emphasis on the sounds of spoken words, not on reading letters or pronouncing letter names. It is vital for young readers to develop phonemic awareness skills to be equipped to successfully read, spell, and write words. When young readers learn to identify and manipulate the sounds of oral language, they are

phonemically aware and understand that spoken words are made up of sounds. They also learn to distinguish and blend sounds in spoken words.

Teaching Phonemic Awareness

Teaching phonemic awareness is a daily, strategic, and consistent process. There are many interactive strategies to incorporate in daily instructions that allow teachers to model, guide, and teach students to better understand phonemic awareness (InTASC Standards 1, 4, 5, CCSSO).

For example, imagine a first-grade classroom of 20–24 students. It's 8:15 on Tuesday morning. Mrs. Bowling's students have just completed their morning message and are now gathered around her on the carpet ready to begin their morning phonics lesson. The weekly sound is the sound /k/, and the spelling *c*. Mrs. Bowling points to the Sound/Spelling card, which displays an uppercase and lowercase *c*, a colorful illustration of camera, and the letters *ck* and *k* below the picture of the camera. Mrs. Bowling asks students what they know about the Sound/Spelling card. After listening to her students, she then explains the name of the card, *Camera*, and reminds the students that there are multiple spellings associated with this card, but that they will only work on one at a time. She explains that they will begin working on the *hard c* sound today.

Mrs. Bowling explains to her students that she will read them a fun jingle to help them remember the /k/ sound. She demonstrates the sound by making the sound of the *hard c* throughout the following jingle.

> Camille has a new camera. When she takes pictures,
> her camera makes a clicking sound like this: /k/k/k/k/k/
> In the vegetable-garden Camille takes pictures of caterpillars
> crawling on the corn: /k/k/k/k/k/.
> At the park, Camille takes pictures of a duck and a colorful kite: /k/k/k/k/k/.
> At her house, Camille takes pictures of her new kitten,
> cozy in her bed: /k/k/k/k/.
> Can you help Camille take pictures with her camera?
> (Ask students to orally join in and chant) /k/k/k/k/k/.

She then reviews the name on the card, *Camera*, the sound /k/, and the spelling *c*. She then writes the letter *c* on the board and reviews the letter formation stroke, while also asking students to use their index fingers to practice writing the spelling several times in the air, on their leg, on their palms, or on their desktops as they repeat the sound. She also asks several students to come to the board and write the spelling of the letter, while other students continue to write the spelling on their hands or personal whiteboards. Mrs. Bowling also finds it beneficial to have students use actions/motions as an aid in remembering the sounds for some spellings. For example, for /k/ spelled *c*, she also asks students to pretend to take pictures with an imaginary camera while they recite, /k/k/k/k/k/.

A daily review of the letter of the week with a variety of manipulatives, engaging activities, and a variety of texts will enhance students' comprehension and use of the letter. In Mrs. Bowling's first-grade class, she writes the following words on the board; *cattle, case, cape, cake, clean, common, creeping, color, snake, rake, back, black, snack, kitten, kettle,* and *key.* She then points to each word, recites each word aloud, and urges the students to recite the words after her, placing special emphasis on the *hard c* sound. This is a simple yet effective strategy referred to as, "*I say...you say.*"

Mrs. Bowling may also ask students to brainstorm other words they know that begin with the (*hard c*) sound of /k/. She writes words that students suggest on the white board and reviews them orally when this activity is complete. Another engaging and beneficial strategy is asking students to explore the names of the students in their class to determine whose name contains the *hard c* sound. This can be completed independently or collaboratively, which is engaging and fun for young students as they are learning to read, while also reinforcing social skills and collaborative learning.

The object of the above phonemic awareness lesson and activities is to determine if the students can recognize the /k/ sound in words. Please note that the above example is basic phonemic awareness instruction and the importance of recognizing the sound is the primary focus, whether the sound is with the letter *c, k,* or *ck* doesn't matter (InTASC Standard 4, CCSSO).

Picture flashcards are excellent tools to help children who do not have strong phonemic awareness skills. For example, create a series of flashcards with pictures that the student(s) are familiar with. The teacher will then ask the students to name the picture on the card. After the students says the name of the picture, the teacher will ask them to identify the beginning sound, and or the ending sound of the name of the word. This activity helps students realize and reinforce their understanding that words are made up of a series of sounds/phonemes. Whereas, the students who need to be challenged can be given picture and letter cards to match the name of the picture with either a beginning sound, ending sound, or medial sound. For advanced students, teachers may provide a choice of letter cards such as, *the hard c card*, the *ck card,* and or the *soft c card* and ask students to sort picture cards to match the sound/letter card.

Nevertheless, high-powered teachers do not limit student's progress. They know that each year their classrooms are filled with students with diverse learning styles, academic levels, and diverse needs. Thus, requiring scaffold instructions and assignments. Teaching phonemic awareness involves more than the examples provided in this section. Teaching phonemic awareness involves strategic and scaffold assignments that should provide a learning experience that is explicit, strategic, and engaging regardless the level (InTASC Standards, 2, 5, 7, 8, CCSSO).

Phonemic awareness is a necessary prerequisite to reading. It is also a very important component of reading or prereading instruction. Phonemic awareness allows students to be better able to identify and hear the syllables while also identifying the separate phonemes in the syllable. Having phonemic awareness allows students to be successful in developing phonics skills as they learn to identify the individual sounds in words. If students are unable to hear these sounds, phonics will provide little help for them when learning to decode words. Children who lack phonemic awareness skills have difficulty in grouping words with similar and dissimilar sounds such as, *mat, mug, and sun*. They also face difficulty in blending and splitting syllables such as, (*f-oot*). Students who lack phonemic awareness also struggle blending sounds into words as simple as the word (*m-a-n*). Phonemic awareness allows students to detect and manipulate sounds with words. For example, replacing the letter *r* in the word *run* with an *s* to create the word *sun*. When students lack the ability to manipulate sounds into words, they are often identified as a struggling reader. Research tells us that the ability to hear and manipulate phonemes plays a critical role in the acquisition of beginning reading skills (Smith et al.).

In summary, when phonemic awareness is combined with letter-name knowledge, students attain a new conceptual understanding, the alphabetic principle (Byrne et al.). This understanding is vital for students to progress in their reading development, particularly in learning about phonics. As students become more aware of the alphabetic principal, teachers can then provide effective phonics instruction (InTASC Standards, 7, 8, CCSSO).

What Strategies Help Promote Phonemic Awareness?

High-powered teachers ensure that their students learn about phonemic awareness through explicit and strategic instruction as well as engaging activities (InTASC Standards 1, 2, 7, 8, CCSSO). Children learn to manipulate spoken language through identifying sounds in words, categorizing sounds in words, substituting sounds to create new words, blending sounds to form new words, and also segmenting a word into sounds.

✦ **Identifying Sounds in Words:** Children identify a word that begins or ends with a particular sound. For example, when shown a *basket, a doll, or a car*, they can identify car as the word that ends with /r/.

✦ **Categorizing Sounds in Words:** Children recognize the *"odd"* word in a set of three words. For example, when the teachers say the words *son, sock, and ring*, they recognize that *ring* doesn't belong.

✦ **Substituting Sounds to Make New Words:** Children remove the sound from a word and substitute a different sound. Sometimes they substitute the beginning sound, changing *sun* to *run*. Or, they change the middle sound, changing the word *hat* into *hot*, or substituting the ending sound, changing *cape* to *came*.

✦ **Blending Sounds to Form Words:** Children blend two, three, or four individual sounds to form a word. For example, the teacher says /b/a/t/, and the children repeat the sounds, blending them to form the word *bat*.

✦ **Segmenting a Word into Sounds:** Children break a word into its beginning, middle, and ending sounds. For example, they segment the word *feet* into /f/e/t/ and *go* into /g/o/.

Children use each of these strategies for blending and segmenting, decoding, and spelling the words. Children use phonics to sound out a word, for example, they say the sounds represented by each letter and blend them to read the word. Similarly, to spell a word, children say the word slowly to themselves, segmenting the sounds, thus resulting in their progress and success in reading, spelling, and in written expressions.

What Is Phonological Awareness?

Phonological awareness is a critical accomplishment for emergent readers. Phonological awareness is often confused with phonemic awareness. However, there are significant differences. Simply put, the difference between phonemic awareness and phonological awareness is when one possesses phonological awareness, they are aware of individual words and syllables as objects. Phonological awareness develops when young children become aware that language is an object that can be analyzed and manipulated by them in a variety of ways, such as rhyming, playing word games, and talking about words as objects. Emergent readers gradually become aware of language as an object.

Speech therapists and speech pathologists work with students who require speech therapy to help them strengthen the ability to physically formulate spoken sounds (InTASC Standard 2,

CCSSO). Teachers can also witness this inside their classrooms when students begin to manipulate sounds and substitute one word for another at the end of a repeated sentence, play rhyming games in oral language, and later segment a spoken word, such as the two syllables that make up the word *into*. An important initial step on the way to phonemic awareness is becoming aware of language as an object (*phonological awareness*) that can be manipulated and analyzed. Research has shown that a student's level of phonological awareness at the end of kindergarten is one of the strongest predictors of future reading success, in grade one and beyond.

High-powered teachers constantly observe their students through a variety of formative and summative assessments. Formative assessments can be as simple as observing students through both oral and written work. High-powered teachers also analyze the data and findings from assessments to better design the instruction to meet the needs of all students (InTASC Standard 6, CCSSO). They also recognize when a student has difficulty with phonological awareness skills and modify their instructions to better assist the student and enhance their understanding and skills. High-powered teachers also begin communicating and seek help from their school's speech pathologist to help determine if a struggling student requires speech therapy to help him or her achieve the level of required phonological awareness necessary to be successful in reading, oral language, writing, and spelling (InTASC Standard 2, 7, 8, CCSSO).

Phonics

What do you think of when you hear the word ***phonics***? When I ask students this question, I am often given the same answer. Most students think of phonics as a strategy of sounding words out and refer back to their teacher(s) or parent telling them to sound a word out. However, there is a significant amount of knowledge for students to learn about unlocking the code of written language. Knowledge and understanding of the development of phonics and other decoding skills are vital for effective assessment as well as effective teaching. Research has shown that systematic phonics instructions have been proven to be effective and should be implemented as a part of literacy programs to teach beginning readers as well as to prevent and remediate reading difficulties (Ehri et al.).

In this section of the chapter we will take a close, evidence-based look at what children need to know and be able to do effectively to *"decode"* words using word identification skills as well as phonics. We will also take a close look at the teacher's role in guiding the learning process.

What Is Phonics?

Phonics refers to how alphabet spellings relate to speech sounds in systematic and predictable ways (letter-sound relations or **graphophonemic knowledge**), and how this knowledge can be used to identify words in print. To better understand phonics, one must understand and know the difference between **word identification** and **word recognition**.

Word identification involves the skills students learn that help them determine the pronunciation of a word in print. This is what the old teaching prompt, *sound it out*, means. When a reader sees a new word in a text, such as the word, yesterday, he or she must be able to blend the speech sounds together that are represented by the letters *yes/ter/day* to pronounce the word correctly. The act of correctly pronouncing the word in print is what is meant by the term, **word identification**.

During the process of word identification students are breaking the code of written words and translating the letters, affixes, and syllables back to a spoken word.

Word recognition, on the other hand, has to do with connecting the pronunciation of a printed word with its meaning. It is possible for students to use word identification skills to pronounce a word in print. However, when students are unable to connect the pronunciation of the word to its meaning, this often results in students' failing at word recognition. Students may be able to use word identification skills to pronounce a word, yet have no idea what the word means. When we think of phonics, structural analysis, application of onset, and rime, and so on, we are referring to word identification.

Teaching Phonics

Phonics instruction is a way of teaching reading that stresses the acquisition of letter-sound correspondences and their use in reading and spelling. To meet the diverse learning needs of all students, high-powered teachers establish what students already know about phonics. They provide ample opportunities for students to demonstrate their phonics knowledge in different ways. High-powered teachers plan for and differentiate phonics instruction to meet all student's needs. They also group students responsively to better accommodate the needs of all students. They are also flexible and change as students' needs change. They help draw upon students' prior knowledge, while helping to establish prior knowledge for those students who do not have past experience with phonics. These teachers help students to make vital connections to their prior knowledge to enhance their learning experience. Finally, high-powered teachers provide a challenge for all students to ensure they are making academic growth (InTASC Standards 1, 4, 5, 7, 8, CCSSO).

Teaching phonics is a strategic process proven to help students become successful readers. However, phonics instruction is made up of a variety of terms, rules, patterns, and exceptions. It is vital that teachers understand the vocabulary terms and rules that are involved with phonics instruction. As a young teacher you will need to familiarize yourself with the terms that are located at the end of this chapter in the applications section.

Most state and local school districts have either developed or purchased a standard-based reading program that provides a plan and sequence of reading skills to assist teachers, thus helping them know what reading skills should be taught at each grade-level. The primary value of a well-designed, standard-based reading program is to assist and also ensure that teachers approach decoding instruction in an explicit, systematic, and strategic manner to ensure that their students are successful. An additional value of teaching with a standard-based reading program is that it promotes consistency in classroom instruction across the district. Thus ensuring that students who change schools within a district receive similar instructions, working with similar content, and engaged in similar curriculum, which results in consistent learning while also decreasing any possible gaps.

The single, most efficient phonics generalization to teach is identifying beginning consonant sounds in words. Teaching beginning consonant sounds is the best place to begin phonics instruction as consonants represent consistent phonemes more regularly than vowels do. In other words, consonant sounds tend to be more constant or reliable compared to vowel sounds. However, it is important to realize and understand that not all consonants are created equal. Some consonants are more concrete than others. Refer to **Table 3.1** for examples of concrete consonants. **Table 3.2** explains and gives examples of consonants that are not consistent. It is vital for reading success that students are aware of and also understand that consonant sounds can change.

The C Rule

Letter *c* is an irregular consonant because it represents more than one phoneme. In other words, it can be used to represent two other phonemes that are already represented by the letter *k* and sometimes by the letter *s*. Typically, when the letter *c* is followed by the letters *a*, *o*, or *u*, it will represent the sound that is most often associated with the letter *k*, also known as **the hard c sound**. Examples of words beginning with the hard c sound include *cut*, *cute*, *cake*, and *craft*. However, the letter *c* can also represent the sound associated with the letter *s*. This is referred to as **the soft c sound** and is usually produced when the letter *c* is followed by *e*, *i*, or *y*. Some of the soft c words include *circus*, *cent*, and *cycle*. When students understand the concepts of the hard and soft c, they are better prepared and decode words with more success, read with more fluency, while also increasing their spelling skills.

Table 3.1: Example of Concrete Consonants

Sound	Spelling and Percentage of Use in English	Example
/b/	b (97%)	bat
/d/	d (98%)	dog
/h/	h (98%)	hat
/l/	l (91%)	last
/m/	m (94%)	man
/n/	n (97%)	no
/p/	p (96%)	pen
/r/	r (97%)	rat
/t/	t (97%)	top
/v/	v (99.5%)	view

Table 3.2: Examples of Consonants That Are Not Consistent

Sound	Spellings and Percentage of Use in English	Example(s)
/f/	f (78%), ff, ph, lf	fat, stuff, phone, wolf
/g/	g (88%) gg, gh	gift, egg, ghost
/j/	g (66%) , j (72%) dg	giraffe, juice, smudge
/k/	c (73%), cc, k (13%), ck, lk, q	cat, stucco, rack, clock, chalk, bisque
/s/	s (73%), c (17%), ss	same, cent, dress
/y/	i (55%), y (445)	onion, yell
/z/	z(23%), zz, s (64%)	zag, jazz, easy

The G Rule

G is a key symbol for the phoneme we hear in the word *girl*. The consonant g is also irregular. *G* has a soft and a hard sound. The rules are the same as the letter *c*. When g is followed by the letters *e*, *i*, or *y*, it represents a soft g or /j/ sound. For example, this sound is associated with words such as *giant*, *germ*, and *gym*. If *g* is followed by the letters, *a*, *o*, or *u*, then it typically represent the hard *g* sound. Some words associated with the hard *g* include *gift*, *go*, *gain*, and *goggles*.

The CVC Pattern

Reviewing vowels every day shouldn't become a dreaded chore to the teacher or students. High-powered teachers are creative in their instructions and repeat and implement reviewing vowels in multiple ways. For example, reciting vowels as students line up to leave the classroom, in the morning before reading instruction begins, with fun matching games, using technology, song, and with the, *I say you say*, approach. Nevertheless, repetition is powerful when teaching young students about consonants, vowels, and also vital to their success in reading (InTASC Standards 1, 3, 7, 8, CCSSO).

The **CVC** pattern is defined as when a vowel comes between two consonants. It typically represents what is referred to as a *short* vowel sound. Examples of words following the **CVC** pattern include *pat, sat, rat, man, dad, get, pen, let, sit, win, bin, hot, mop, mom, sun, fun*, and *cup*.

When high-powered teachers teach young readers about the CVC pattern, their instruction and activities are strategic, yet engaging and fun (InTASC Standards 1, 7, 8, CCSSO). The focus should primarily be on one short vowel at a time. For example, the vowel of the day can be *short a*. Using a visual, such as an alphabet card, introduce or review the sound of *short a* with students. Ask students to repeat the sound of the *short a* aloud. Incorporate the fun game of **Quick Erase** on the whiteboard. Quick erase is simply writing a word such as *cat* on the board. Ask students to read the word. Once they reply, change the letter *c* to an *h* then ask them to read the word. This can be repeated with the beginning consonant or the final consonant for several rounds of fun. This is an engaging and fun way to involve students as well and enhance their knowledge of *short a* sound and also practice segmenting sounds within words, which will help students better understand beginning, medial, and ending sounds. This will create a buzz in the classroom and engage students with the letter, which leads to them taking risks and also taking ownership of their learning.

Next, ask students to write the letter *a* with their finger on their desks, lap, or in the air. Ask them to practice both an uppercase *a* and a lowercase *a*. Once students have practiced writing the letter a with their finger, ask them to write the letter a on either paper or whiteboards. This will allow them to practice penmanship while also allowing you to formatively assess the students as you walk around the class observing. I also suggest that each time the students write the letter *a*, they whisper the short sound of *a*. End this fun and interactive lesson with students self-assessing their own writing with a familiar and easy to understand rubric.

Vowel Digraphs (CVVC)

Vowel Digraphs are often difficult for young readers to understand. **Vowel digraphs, CVVC** pattern, form when two vowels come together in a word. The first vowel usually demonstrates what is known as the long vowel sound and the second vowel is the silent vowel. This occurs especially often with the *ee*, *oa*, and *ay* combinations. Such as, *road*, *feet*, and *say*. However, there are clever and fun ways to teach students to better understand, recognize, and use the **CVVC** pattern correctly. A common jingle that I found to be very beneficial when teaching vowel digraphs to help students better remember the pattern and rule was, *"When two vowels go walking, the second one is quiet and the first one does all the talking."* After repeating this jingle during instruction, I witnessed students whispering this jingle as they decoded words.

The VCE (Final Silent E) Pattern

When two vowels appear in a word and one is the letter *e* located at the end of the word, the first vowel is typically long and the final *e* is silent. Some examples of this pattern include *make*, *rope*, *bake*, *bike*, and *ripe*. I found that using the following jingle helped students to better understand the VCE or the final silent e sound. *"The ending e is silent and the boss, it makes the first vowel say its name."* Eventually, students recognize and understand the silent *e* and no longer require the jingle to understand the rules of the **VCE** pattern. Repetition and exposure to a variety of words that contain the VCE pattern in a variety of texts is beneficial for students' awareness and understanding of the VCE pattern.

The CV Pattern

The **CV pattern** happens in a word when a consonant is followed by a vowel, the vowel usually produces a long sound. This is especially easy in two-letter words such as, *me*, *be*, *go*, and *so*. Repetition and jingles are again an important factor for students grasping the concept of the CV pattern. One beneficial strategy for young readers is to mimic a side-line cheer. For example, *"G-O-go, G-O-go, pause G-O-go...go, go, go!"* This was a great strategy for increasing spelling, written expression, and also word recognition.

R-Controlled Vowels

The **R-Controlled Vowel** patterns occur when a vowel appears before the letter *r* and is usually neither long nor short. However, the vowel tends to be overpowered or consumed by the /r/ sound. Some examples of words with the **R-Controlled Vowel** include *are*, *barn*, *fern*, *player*, *her*, *person*, and *star*. This can be a fun vowel pattern to teach to young readers. I often referred to the R-controlled vowel as, *"the bossy pirate r."* Students enjoyed making the pirate sound and motion when learning this vowel pattern.

It is important for students to identify words in text that contain the particular vowel or the consonant that they are currently working on. Providing students with text through age-appropriate magazines, worksheets, sentence strips, then asking them to highlight or circle the words that contain the vowel or consonant that they are learning is highly recommended. This is a fun activity to complete collaboratively in teams or independently. Students also enjoy racing to beat the clock for activities such as this. Thus, it teaches them to work quickly and efficiently, while learning to manage their time. This type of activity can be differentiated to fit the need of all students, which can challenge the above-level students, while also not frustrating the struggling readers.

Finally, ask students to use paper and pencil to complete independent work to further enhance their understanding of the vowel or consonant they are learning about. Activities for primary

students can be as simple as matching pictures to words, or coloring pictures that contain the vowel or consonant in question. For example, pictures might include illustrations of a hat, mop, cat, pen, and a dog. The objective could be for students to only color the pictures that contain the short a sound. An extension could be challenging the students to write the word beneath the picture.

In summary, phonics instruction should be engaging, fun, stress-free, and differentiated to meet the needs of all learners. Phonics instruction should involve explicit phonics instruction, phonics games, phonics worksheets, as well as the use of technology through online phonics games or interactive apps. Providing students with multiple opportunities to learn, involving them in whole-group activities, small collaborative groups, and also requiring them to work independently encourages students to take risks, learn from peers, gain confidence, and also become successful independent readers (InTASC Standards 1, 2, 3, 4, 5, 7, 8, CCSSO).

Important Phonics Terms and Skills

The abovementioned phonics patterns and rules are the most common. However, there are many other terms that high-powered teachers are familiar with that enable them teach their students to be successful readers. There are several terms, definitions, and examples of other phonics skills related to consonants and vowels, which are identified and defined in the following sections.

Consonant Digraphs

Consonant digraphs include two consonants that produce only one speech sound including, *ch*, *sh*, and *ng*. Examples of words containing consonant digraphs include *children*, *change*, *merchandize*, *which*, *chunk*, *search*, *which*, and *church*. Other examples include *thank*, *think*, *author*, *that*, *father*, and *smooth*. *Ng* words include *sing*, *ring*, *sling*, *long*, *rang*, and *wrong*.

Consonant Blends or Clusters

Two or more consonants coming together in which the speech sounds of all the consonants can be heard *(bl, fr, sk, spl)* are referred to as **consonant blends** or sometimes as **clusters**. Examples of words containing **consonant blends** include *black*, *blink*, *block*, *froze*, *frost*, *friend*, *fruit*, and *fresh*. Other examples include *sky*, *skunk*, *skirt*, *desk*, and *mask*. Examples of *spl* words include *split*, *splash*, and *splash*.

Schwa

The schwa sound is sometimes audible when two vowel letters produce the /uh/ sound, which sounds much like the *a* sound in the word, *affect*. **Schwa** is represented by the backward upside-down *e* (ə) symbol on phonics charts. Some examples of words containing the schwa sound are; *a-about*, *china*, *America*, and *comma*. Examples of words for the schwa sound with vowel *e* include *happen*, *label*, and *effect*. For the *o* vowel, some examples include *mother*, *second*, and *other*.

High-powered teachers find creative ways to teach the schwa sound to ensure that students are pronouncing words correctly, and also spelling words correctly (InTASC 7, 8, CCSSO). A beneficial way to teach young children about the schwa sound can include asking students to say their name and listen for the *schwa* sound. Ask them to circulate the room checking other names for the schwa sound. Students can then graph names with markers to find out how many students' names in their class contain the schwa sound. This also integrates a math skill as well in the lesson. Students that understand the schwa sound are more strategic and accurate spellers.

Diphthongs

When two vowels together in a word produce a single, glided sound such as, *oi in soil, oy* in the word *toy*, and *ou* in the word *out*, this is known as **diphthongs**. Some examples include words *down, flower, towel, bowl, oil, toil, voice, void, out, spout, double, our, count,* and *about.*

Onset and Rime

An **onset** is the part of the syllable that comes before the vowel, the rime is the remaining part of the word. Even though all syllables must have a **rime** not all syllables require an onset. The following are a few examples of onsets and rimes in words.

Word	Onset	Rime
a		*a*
in		*In*
sat	*s-*	*-at*
spin	*sp-*	*-in*
bring	*br-*	*-ing*

New teachers may wonder about using onset and rime in their classrooms. High-powered teachers know through experience that when teaching young children to read, spell, and identify parts of a word, they are also better able to identify the spelling of whole rimes than individual vowel sounds. Also, young children, even those in kindergarten, can transfer what they already know about one word to another word, for example, *at, hat, cat,* and *that*. Finally, though many traditional phonics generalizations with vowels are very unstable, even irregular phonics patterns seem to remain stable within rimes. For example, the *ea* vowel is typically consistent with the exceptions of the letters e-a-r in the word *bear*. Nearly 500 primary-level words can be derived through incorporating the following combination of **rimes**.

-ack, -at, -ide, -ock, -am, -ate, -ight, -oke, -ake, -aw, -ill, -op, -ale, -ay, -in, -or, -all, -eat, -ine, -ore, -ame,

-ell, -ing, -uck, -an, -est, -ink, -ug, -ank, -ice, -ip, -ump, -ap, -ick, -ir, -unk.

Many students find it much easier to identify new words in print by locating familiar rimes, or parts of words also known as chunking. It has been proven that students' spelling increases as rimes are matched with onsets to create new words. High-powered teachers find it beneficial to teach rimes with rhymes. For example, using the following jingle with young readers can help them hear, recognize, and manipulate the *uck* rime.

> *While walking in the rain,*
>
> *My friend and I saw a d**uck**…*
>
> *In a puddle of mud beside a red tr**uck**.*
>
> *The d**uck** was really st**uck**!*
>
> *We carefully helped the d**uck** from the m**uck**.*
>
> *The d**uck** was happy about his good l**uck**!*

Chunking

Structural analysis is very beneficial for decoding unfamiliar words. Structural analysis allows readers to use their own knowledge of meaning, *"chunk"* within words. It is easier for some students to recognize chunks, rather than trying to decode a word through letter-phoneme or onset and rime. It is a simple strategy that enhances students' decoding skills. An example of this strategy is as follows: a reader encounters a word, typically a multisyllable word that is unknown to the reader in print. The student may know word when he or she hears it, but not be familiar with it in print. For example, a very young reader might encounter the word captain within the following sentence, *He was the captain of the ship,* and doesn't recognize the word, captain. The student can immediately look for a chunk of the word that he or she knows. For example, they might pick out the small word, *"cap"* within the word. Incorporating other strategies such as context clues and rereading the sentence the student is better prepared to decode the word as being, *captain*.

High-powered teachers know that structural analysis is more than just chunking familiar smaller words within a word. Structural analysis also involves identifying prefixes that are familiar to the reader. For example, the prefix *un* in the words *untie, unreal,* and *unhook* might help a student to decode the word *unbelievable,* while also helping them to determine the meaning of the word. Structural analysis of words takes decoding to a new and even higher level. This is a very important strategy for students in second and third grades, as this is typically the time when students are working with multisyllable words.

High-powered teachers teach their students about the process of structural analysis through a variety of diverse activities and much practice. They also teach their students that words are made up of basic meaning units known as **morphemes**. Morphemes may be divided into two categories: bound and free. **Bound morphemes** must be attached to a root word, otherwise known as a base word, to have a meaning. Prefixes and suffixes are bound morphemes, for example, *pre-, un-, dis-, en-, inter-, extra-, -ed, -ies, -ir, and –ing*. **Free morphemes** (base or root words) on the other hand are units that can stand alone independently and still have meaning. Sometimes two free morphemes come together to create **compound words**. Meaning that each morpheme can stand alone independently and still have meaning. Examples of compound words include *outside, playground,* and *tonight* (InTASC Standards, 1, 4, 5, CCSSO).

High-powered teachers also help students practice structural analysis of words in the same way they teach onset and rime. The idea is to emphasize to students that when a good reader comes to an unfamiliar word and is unable to identify it through context and phonics alone, the reader can sometimes look within the word for a recognizable base or root word and its accompanying prefix, suffix, or ending to decode and determine what the word is. High-powered teachers teach their students to strategically look for something that they know within the unfamiliar word (InTASC Standards, 4, 5, 8, CCSSO).

Putting It All Together

Evidence-based reading research suggests a general sequence of early literacy skills that directly relate to word identification. When readers become proficient in following word identification skills by the end of third grade, or before, and who also practice them routinely in reading, no matter if it's in the classroom, or at home for pleasure, will attain a high degree of fluency. Benchmarks vary from district to district. Many of the expected benchmarks you set for your students are identified within the school or districts-adopted reading program, or within their individualized required curriculum.

With the implementation of the **Common-Core Standards**, teachers of all grades and content areas are given a guide for what skills they are expected to teach and what their students are expected to master in each grade-level. High-powered teachers assess their students to determine prior knowledge and then carefully design their instructions around the data acquired from the assessment and with the grade-level standards or benchmarks to help ensure that all students are successful readers.

High-powered teachers deliver high-quality phonics instructions using auditory, visual, and kinesthetic activities that acknowledge student's different learning styles and encourage them to activate as many of their senses as possible. Activities can involve using magnetic letters, writing with sticks or their fingers in sand, imaginary writing, whiteboards, smart boards, and a variety of uses of technology, with paper and pencil, and also collaboratively (InTASC Standards 1, 3, 4, 5, 7, 8, CCSSO).

High-powered teachers create and design phonics instructions to allow students opportunities to practice and apply their developing knowledge. This can be achieved using decodable texts, which are often designed and scaffold to enhance and reinforce phonics learning at all reading levels.

In 2000, The National Reading Panel confirmed through research that systematic and explicit phonics instructions are more effective than nonsystematic instructions or programs that ignore phonics. When taught as part of a comprehensive reading program, one that also includes expansive and vast vocabulary instruction, reading practice through the use of diverse genres and a variety of texts, and also implementing writing development and strategically incorporating phonics instructions, children can become successful, enthusiastic life-long readers.

There are several approaches to design phonics instruction proven to be successful when combined with standard-based reading programs. They include **synthetic phonics instruction** where students learn how to manipulate letters or letter combinations into speech sounds, then blend them together to form words. This is referred to as *sound it out*. **Analogy-based phonics instructions** consist of a variety of onset and rime instructions that encourage students to use their knowledge of word families to identify new words that have that same chunk/part of word.

A combination of diverse phonics-based instruction that is carefully planned, taught with explicit and inspiring instruction allows students to become engaged in the text. When students are engaged with the text, their learning is elevated to a higher level (InTASC Standards, 1, 2, 3, 7, 8, CCSSO). According to Cynthia Hynd et al., "Engaged readers negotiate textual understanding by linking information both within and outside of the text(s) that they are reading".

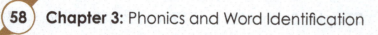

Phonics Through Spelling Instruction

Phonics through spelling instruction require students to segment words into phonemes and also write letters that represent those sounds to create the word in print. For example, students can sound out a word to spell it correctly. Words such as *mat* can be sounded out and written phonetically. However, creating word families helps students as they begin to write and spell words containing more than two or three letters. For example, a word family can include the words, *oat, boat, moat, coat*, and *goat*. Challenging words can be included for students who need to be challenged. Challenge words may include *boating, coats,* or *oatmeal*.

As students learn to spell words using word families their reading becomes more fluent as they quickly recognize words throughout the text. Note that many words in word families are also site words. Site words are words that typically cannot be *"sounded out"* as they often break the rules of phonics. These are the words that students should recognize quickly without involving sounding or decoding. Site words can be included in spelling or learned as a group of words through the use of games, flash cards, technology, written expression, and also through repetition in printed text.

In summary, high-powered teachers use a variety of teaching methods and instructional strategies to ensure that all students are successful (InTASC Standard 8, CCSSO). They appeal to the senses and the needs of each of their students through incorporating visual aids, manipulatives, audio, oral, motions, written expression, as well as technology to ensure that all students are learning and that all students are reading and writing. Not only do high-powered teachers use a wide variety of diverse methods of instruction and include an array of strategies and activities, they also administer ongoing diverse methods of formative and summative assessments (InTASC Standard 6, CCSSO).

Assessments and Running Records

High-powered teachers are continually assessing their student's progress through a variety of assessments, both formative and summative. It is vital that the teachers follow student's development, knowledge, and use of phonics skills throughout the year. When teachers assess their students and analyze the data gathered, they are not only focusing on what students know or don't know, they are analyzing the data to design, redesign, and enhance their own instruction. High-powered teachers are continually searching for new innovative ideas to better their instruction, thus enhancing their student's knowledge, learning experience, and overall success (InTASC Standards, 6, 7, 8, CCSSO).

A running record is a method of assessment that I, as well as other teachers, have found to be successful. Running records have been incorporated in the classroom since the early 1900s and are still being used. Some well-designed reading programs include running records for teachers' use. With the availability of the Internet, a wide variety of running records can be retrieved in a matter of minutes.

High-powered teachers also design their own running records based on what concept and knowledge they wish to assess. **Table 3.3** provides a simplistic example of a running record. This record is being used to assess a students' letter recognition, if they can identify in print, know the sound(s), and if they can give a word including the letter. Note that the student receives a *tally mark* for correct answers and an *x* for incorrect answers. The teacher also annotates misconceptions to gain insight, knowledge, and to better know their students' knowledge of the letter(s), while also referring back to the running record to better prepare individualized instructions for each of their students. What can you learn about this the student through the information recorded in **Table 3.3**?

Table 3.3: Running Record Example

Letter	Identifies in Print	Sound(s)	Example(s)
A, a	//	//	Apple if student gives a word that does not begin with the letter a, record with an x and the word they stated
B,b	/ x b = d	/	Boy
C,c	//	/ x soft c	cat
D,d	/ x d = b	/	X = student wrote a b for a d

Running records can be as simplistic as the record in **Table 3.3** or as detailed as you need them to be. Running records can also be implemented in all content areas and administered randomly or strategically. It can also be used for teacher data, peer-assessment, and also as a method of self-assessment. Running records are one of the many formative assessments that high-powered teachers incorporate and administer daily inside their classrooms to ensure their students are performing, reading, solving, spelling, etc, where they need to be in order to be successful.

Virtual Ideas for Teaching Phonics and Word Identification

High-powered teachers are creative, tech savvy, and flexible. High-powered teachers are also willing to step outside of their comfort zone and explore the endless possibilities and benefits of virtual teaching regardless if only a small portion of their students are attending through virtual connection, or all of their students are working from home. Regardless the method of learning, high-powered teachers strive to locate, create, and perfect strategies and activities that enables them to teach phonics and word identification both inside the classroom, and in their virtual classroom. Whether their instruction is in person, or online, high-powered teachers are advocates for building classroom community and also teaching all students the skills they need to be successful. They know that success begins with routines, expert modeling, and also varied practice to help build mastery and memory.

High-powered teachers also know that strategies and activities will heavily depend on their district's preferred platform. For example, if a teacher is implementing instruction through Google Classroom, they can exercise the *"ask a question"* feature that allows students to respond to the question. High-powered teachers also implement virtual turn and talk strategies that work similar to the in-seat, think-pair-share strategy. Depending on the platform used, the virtual turn and talk feature can create fun and engaging conditions for students to message their partner with an answer to the question. High-powered teachers may also ask students to **respond with emojis**.

For example, teachers may ask, or post a question on the screen, and designate each answer with an emoji, or a character. Students will answer and reply by posting with the emoji or character in the chat. Nevertheless, high-powered teachers will strive to design their instruction to meet the needs of all students.

Phonics and word building can be fun, exciting, diverse, and also a challenge. High-powered teachers do not allow the challenges of virtual teaching to define their instruction. They dip into their creative resources and create opportunities to guide students through prerecorded sessions that students can access to listen to teacher's instruction, rewind and listen again if necessary, and also opportunities to engage with them in one-on-one virtual sessions. However, high-powered teachers are also actively engaged and visible in their virtual classrooms. Students can interact with the teacher while they use strategic methods of the gradual release of responsibility through the, **I do, we do, now you do**, strategy. They know that repetition and exposure is key to student's success when building words by stringing together individual sounds. High-powered teacher's use repetition and encouragement to mimic their motions and movements, encourage and build muscle memory and also to make connections.

High-powered teachers teach double-letter consonant sounds, spelling patterns, and vowel sounds through deliberate and precise articulation. They also provide multiple examples to ensure students have multiple methods of recalling the information. High-powered teachers use the same resources for both in person instruction and online instruction. They allow the camera to view them **physically modeling their instruction** on the smartboard, whiteboard, and also using manipulatives so that students can virtually be a part of the instruction. They know when students are included at this level of instruction and modeling, given time to ask and answer questions prior to working collaboratively, they are better prepared to work independently.

High-powered teachers require student responses in various forms, which include oral responses and written responses. They may require both in person and virtual students to create a phonics journal. Teachers dictate words daily for students to write in their journals to strengthen their spelling skills. For example, high-powered teachers teach CVC words through listening for sounds much like they would in person. Games can be incorporated both in person and virtually to help students make connections. Games may include "**I Spy**" where students visually find objects whose name is a CVC word, or a CVVC word, or any other phonetic pattern. Teachers may also require both in person and virtual students to play the **matching game** where students are required to match a CVVC word with the correct picture. Word charts can also be implemented in person and virtually. In other words, high-powered teachers find creative ways to incorporate and blend the instruction that in person students are participating in with virtual students.

High-powered teachers know the importance of student engagement and also alleviating the feeling of isolation, which might happen with virtual students. High-powered teachers involve all students and create opportunities to partner with an in person student or with a virtual student. If the entire class is working live with the teacher in the virtual classroom, they may implement think-pair-share, turn and talk, listen and respond, ask and answer questions, or practice word identification to help encourage collaboration. In summary, high-powered teachers know their content, they know their students, and they also know that how to deliver high-quality instruction within the four walls of their classroom, through prerecorded instruction, virtually online, and in one-on-one settings both in person and online, while also actively engaging with their students to ensure their students are academically and socially successful.

Now It's Your Turn

Design a running reading or phonics record that you could implement in your classroom to assess your students. Design the running record for the grade that you would like to teach. Once you have designed the running record, you will be required to write a five paragraph reflection about your experience designing the running record, how you plan to implement it in your future class, and what you hope to achieve from it.

What Can Parents Do to Help Their Child?

Parents play a vital role in their child's success (InTASC Standard 10, CCSSO). Research shows that students' reading skills improve when parents/guardians read with their child for at least 20 minutes each night. Parents/guardians should sit down with their child and interact with them during this time to enhance the student's phonological awareness skills. Parents can also use activities such as words from pictures, which allow the child to glue pictures from magazines onto paper. Pictures can be organized and categorized by beginning sounds, medial sounds, ending sounds, vowels, or consonants. Parents can challenge young children by also allowing them to paste pictures onto a piece of paper in chronological order to tell a story. Rhyming picture cards with words beneath the picture are a great way to help students with rhyming words and word families. Matching picture cards to letter cards is also beneficial for basic knowledge. These are simple ideas for beginning readers. The strategies are simple, but also fun engaging, and can be very beneficial and enhance their classroom experience as well as their reading ability.

For children who are reading, regardless of their reading level, their parents can spend an allotted 20 minutes an evening with their child, listening to them read while also following along with their child as they read to ensure that they are not just calling random words, or words they think fit the story. Parents should not automatically correct their child when they make a mistake, they should encourage them to self-correct through encouraging them to reread or read on to ensure what they are reading makes sense. After listening to their child, parents should ask questions about what their child has read to promote comprehension. Questions should consist of beginning with multiple words such as why, when, how, does, can, etc. Parents should encourage their child to interact with the text by making inferences, predictions, and also summarizing what they have read. This should be a fun time of learning for both the parents and children, not a stressful time.

Keep in mind that this designated time should also be consistent. For example, this can be 20 minutes that is set aside especially for reading just before bed time. However, it doesn't have to be the only time that parents and their children read together. Parents can listen to students reread while they are riding in a car, doing household chores, lying around the pool, sitting on the front porch, and any other time when both participants have a few minutes of free time.

Parents should also maintain regular communication with their child's teacher to stay up to date on their child's progress as well as with the content that is being taught. Reading at home is also a great opportunity for parents and their children to complete a reading log, which you will learn more about in upcoming chapters, to help hold parents and students accountable. A signed reading log helps hold parents accountable for their time spent reading with their child and helps students become accountable for their time reading outside the classroom. Reading for 20 minutes together can be a win-win situation for both parties involved!

*"Let us tenderly and kindly cherish, therefore, the means of knowledge.
Let us dare to read, think, speak and write."*

~ *John Adams, 2nd President*

Author's Tip

As a first-grade teacher, I found that a strategic and consistent approach to phonetic instruction helped young students become successful readers. I began the year with my first-grade students with a weeklong review of the kindergarten reading curriculum. This allowed me to find out student's base knowledge through various formative assessments, such as checklists and running records, before planning instructions. I also conferenced when possible with my student's previous kindergarten teachers about students that I had concerns about. Reviewing curriculum, conferencing with previous teachers, and reviewing past data allowed me to better know my students as readers, become familiar with any difficulties they had previously encountered, determine who was previously considered to be a struggling reader in kindergarten, or who may have been a gifted and talented student. This allowed me the data and knowledge that I needed to design instruction to fit the needs of all of my students.

I also found that working with one letter per week with beginning readers was beneficial and did not overwhelm the students. Note that all students do not learn the same way, once students have mastered a letter, remember that it's okay to provide them with a challenge. Young students enjoy peer-tutoring. Early finishers or higher performing students can be partnered with struggling readers. Students learn well from other students. Peer-tutoring can be a win-win situation for both the early finisher and the struggling student.

Students should also experience learning each letter through multiple strategies. Strategies such as the use of visual aids, alphabet cards, word/picture associations, songs, rhymes, motions, and opportunities to engage in written expression. Instruction should be purposeful, carefully planned, consistent, and fun. Remember learning should be fun in a safe environment where all students feel comfortable in taking risks, and stepping outside of their comfort zone. Formative assessment is a vital component of teaching and can be implemented without students being aware they are being assessed. Track data through running records, reflect on accumulated data, and plan your instruction and activities around the data. Above all, be patient, creative, and motivating. Remember, learning to read should be a pleasurable and memorable experience for all students.

Applications

To help guide you through the chapter and upcoming chapters you will need to be familiar with the following key terms.

- ✦ Alphabetic principal
- ✦ The C rule
- ✦ The G rule
- ✦ Phonemic awareness

- ✦ Phonological awareness
- ✦ Vowel digraphs (CVVC)
- ✦ The CVC pattern
- ✦ The VCE (final silent E) pattern
- ✦ The CV pattern
- ✦ R-controlled vowels
- ✦ Consonant digraphs
- ✦ Consonant blends or clusters
- ✦ Vowel digraphs
- ✦ Schwa sound
- ✦ Diphthongs
- ✦ Onset and rime
- ✦ Structural analysis
- ✦ Phonemes, morphemes, and graphemes
- ✦ Prefixes and suffixes
- ✦ Running record
- ✦ MSV analysis: semantic, structure, and visual
- ✦ Cueing strategies

In-Seat Activity

Turn to your partner and review the card that is on your table. Each card contains a different term, such as, Schwa sound, onset and rime, phonemes, morphemes, graphemes, etc. Each team will have approximately 5 minutes to discuss their terms and be prepared to present it to the class. Each member of the team will be required to participate in the collaborative conversation as well as the presentation. Explain the term to your peers and give three to five examples of words that demonstrate the term.

Reflect and Answer the Following Questions

- ✦ *What is the alphabetic code?*
- ✦ *What is the alphabetic principal?*
- ✦ *What is phonemic awareness?*
- ✦ *What is phonological awareness?*
- ✦ *What is phonics?*
- ✦ *How do children decode words?*
- ✦ *Why is spelling important to early readers?*

Student Notes

Annotating is an effective learning strategy. This page is reserved for you to annotate *(take notes)* record potential questions, and also to refer back to when studying, completing assignments, and to help you gain a better understanding of Chapter Three.

Student Reflection

High-powered teachers reflect. This page is reserved for you to reflect about information that you found insightful and what you have learned from Chapter Three.

Suggested Resources

To learn more about word recognition and the important role it plays during the reading process, explore these online resources.

Cunningham, P. M., and J. W. Cunningham. "What We Know About How to Teach Phonics." *What Research Has to Say About Reading Instruction*, edited by S. E. Farstrup, and S. J. Samuels, International Association, 2000, pp. 87–109, http://www.learner.org/workshops/readingk2/support/HowToTeachPhonics_1.pdf. http://www.learner.org/workshops/readingk2/support/HowToTeachPhonics_2.pdf. http://www.learner.org/workshops/readingk2/support/HowToTeachPhonics_3.pdf. Accessed 15 May 2018.

Staudt, D. "Intensive Word Study and Repeated Reading Improves Reading Skills for Two Students with Learning Disabilities." *The Reading Teacher*, vol. 63, no. 2, 2009, pp. 142–51, https://eric.ed.gov/?id=EJ860806. Accessed 16 May 2018.

(This article describes how a teacher improved reading for two struggling readers by focusing on word analysis instruction and poetry.)

Chapter References

Armbruster, Bonnie B., et al. *Put Reading First: The Research Building Blocks for Teaching Children to Read*. US Department of Education, 2001.

Council of Chief State School Officers (CCSSO). *Interstate Teacher Assessment and Support Consortium (InTASC) Model Core Teaching Standards*, Apr. 2011, https://www.ccsso.org/sites/default/files/2017-11/InTASC_Model_Core_Teaching_Standards_2011.pdf. Accessed 7 July 2018.

Ehri, Linnea C, et al. *Evidence from the National Reading Panel's Meta-Analysis*, 2001, http://journals.sagepub.com/doi/abs/10.3102/00346543071003393. Accessed 1 Dec. 2017.

Hynd, Cynthia, et al. *Thinking Like a Historian: College Students' Reading of Multiple Historical Documents*, 2004, http://journals.sagepub.com/doi/abs/10.1207/s15548430jlr3602_2. Accessed 10 Dec. 2017.

National Reading Panel (NRP). *Report of the National Reading Panel: Teaching Children to Read.* National Institute of Child Health and Human Development, 2000.

Presidents' Day: Educational Quotes by U.S. Presidents. https://www.alphabest.org/presidents-day-educational-quotes-by-u-s-presidents/. Accessed 19 May 2018.

Smith, S. B., et al. *What Reading Research Tells Us About Children with Diverse Learning Needs: Bases and Basics.* Lawrence Erlbaum Associates, 1998.

Chapter 4
Readers
Writers

Teacher Quote

"Academic instruction is language-based. In order for a child to successfully access the curriculum, language skills must be intact. The American Speech and Hearing Association defines spoken language and written language and their associated components (i.e., receptive and expressive) are each a synergistic system comprised of individual language domains (i.e., phonology, morphology, syntax, semantics, pragmatics) that form a dynamic integrative whole (reason). Our educational system should work to support language development to ensure the success of students in the classroom."
~ Lona Cormier, M.A., CCC/SLP, speech and language pathologist

Chapter Questions

- ✦ *What is the structure of language?*
- ✦ *How does children's oral language dev...*
- ✦ *What link does oral language have to lite...*
- ✦ *How is oral language assessed?*
- ✦ *What are the developmental stages of reading...*

Children arrive in classrooms each year with a variety of diverse language skills and backgrounds. The modern classroom is more diverse than ever before. Many students have limited social skills, often resulting in a decreased vocabulary and decreased oral language skills. Whereas other students often referred to as social butterflies by their teachers, are quite the opposite. The latter group of students often have siblings, interact with relatives on a regular basis, attend social gatherings, and also interact with other children their age. Many of these social students have a background of attending Sunday school or formal daycares. Students with a rich social background typically have a larger vocabulary and better oral language skills, both expressive and receptive, which gives them an academic advantage.

Every year teachers are faced with gaining a better understanding of each individual students' language skills in effort to address each child's academic and social needs. High-powered teachers understand the structure of language, how student's oral language skills develop, and also the importance of how oral language affects literacy. These teachers understand how learners grow and develop, recognizing that patterns of learning and development vary individually within and across the cognitive, linguistic, social, emotional, and physical areas. High-powered teachers know how to assess students' oral language skills and plan instructions accordingly. They design and implement developmentally appropriate and challenging learning experiences through standard-based lessons that include rigorous and engaging activities to help create and enhance student's oral language skills (InTASC Standard 1, Council of Chief State School Officers [CCSSO] 11).

The Structure of Language

High-powered teachers know and understand the value of early language development. They also know that the development of oral language is directly linked to success in reading and writing abilities. Children come to school with literally thousands of words knowledge (words in their head) that they can hear and recall, understand, and use in their daily lives. When students have been exposed to a large vocabulary, they are already on the path of learning to be a successful reader. However, children who come from language-deprived backgrounds need immediate attention to have a better chance to be successful readers (National Research Council).

Language is made-up of verbal (speech sounds) and visual symbol (printed letters and words) system used in human society that is capable of representing the full range of our knowledge, experiences, and emotions. All humans use language as a tool for meeting their needs. Language is used to communicate, solve problems, and for thinking and planning. Language is both expressive and receptive. Expressive language requires the sender of a message to encode or put his or her own thoughts into symbolic systems (verbal and visual) of the language. Whereas, receptive language requires the receiver of a message to decode or unlock the code of the language symbol systems used by the sender in order to construct meaning. Both expressive and receptive languages take the forms of spoken sounds or written symbols, but can also be represented visually through gestures, art, pictures, video, or dramatization.

Language can be divided into seven interrelated components. (1) *phonology*, (2) *orthography*, (3) *morphology*, (4) *syntax*, (5) *semantics*, (6) *etymology*, and (7) *pragmatics*.

1. **Phonology** refers to the study of the sound structure of oral language and included both understanding speech and producing speech.
2. **Orthography** refers to patterns linking letters or graphemes to sounds or phonemes in spoken language to produce conventional word spellings.
3. **Morphology** refers to the study of word structure.

4. **Syntax** refers to the rule system of how words are combined into larger language structures, especially sentences.
5. The **Semantic** component of language involves connecting the reader's own background experiences, their knowledge, interests, attitudes, beliefs, and perspectives with spoken or written language to comprehend the meaning of that language.
6. **Etymology** is the study of how word meanings and language meanings change over time in popular culture.
7. **Pragmatics** is the study of how language is used by people in societies to satisfy their need to communicate.

Research tells us that reading teachers who are aware of the structure of oral language, oral language developmental stages, and average rates of oral language development are more likely to be effective in raising children's oral language development to new and higher levels (Braunger and Lewis). High-powered teachers understand that rates of oral language development will vary among their students as well as how children learn oral language and how they learn to read. They know how to scaffold instructions, pacing assignments and expectations of their students accordingly to meet the diverse needs of their students.

How Does Children's Oral Language Develop?

Young children's exposure to everyday words, conversations, and interactions are vital for their oral language to develop. Interactions with parents, siblings, and peers help young children learn new words, thus enhancing their vocabulary. Children's oral language becomes more diverse as they are exposed to different words in different settings. For example, children who commonly play with other children on the playground will gain words from their peers. Children who attend Sunday school or take swimming lessons gain new words from their instructors as well as others in the class. Many students will come to the classroom with words and language skills they have learned from television, whereas other students may not have been exposed to television.

Children continue to develop oral language skills, competence, and confidence at school through a variety of both receptive and expressive opportunities. For example, engaging literacy activities such as interactive read-alouds enhance student's oral language skills as they interact with the teachers and peers. High-powered teachers read orally to their students, pausing to ask and answer student's questions. They also design engaging activities that allow students to collaborate, discuss, problem solve, make predictions, and even present. They involve their students in activities such as, Think Pair Share, which allow students to work with a partner to think about the text, discuss their findings, and then present their findings/answers as a team to the class. When children listen and interact with their teacher and peers, they are learning new vocabulary while also gaining more in-depth diverse sentence structure. This interaction enhances both their receptive and expressive language skills.

High-powered teachers explore a wide variety of books in all genres to help develop and enhance student's oral language development. They select popular and colorful picture books that specifically introduce new vocabulary, pique student's curiosity, and encourage listening and speaking, while also promoting higher order thinking. They select books that appeal to all of their students. They read with enthusiasm and expressions, and often implement storyboards for a visual learning experience to increase student's interest and level of engagement. High-powered teachers also engage students in the story through random questioning and predictions to pique curiosity, interest and help them recall facts, and make inferences based on what they know about the story. Student engagement of this level, often results in grand conversations, which increases student(s) vocabulary. When students are engaged in this type of grand conversations they are encouraged to repeat words and phrases from the book or from their peers. High-powered teachers also encourage students to summarize or retell stories. Retelling (summarizing) encourages oral language development, articulation, and also enhances comprehension.

When children's oral language is developing through engagement and instruction it is comparable to how children learn a second language. Most children learn a second language best in an active and engaging classroom with their peers with strategic and planned instruction. When young children are encouraged to participate and have the opportunities to use their newfound skills, and newfound language, they become fluent in oral language skills as well as in a second language in a culturally diverse classroom.

Students gain word knowledge in the English language as they hear the English language spoken. When this language is put into motion with the use of textbooks, photographs, and physical actions students acquire conversational English, also known as **Basic Interpersonal Communicative Skills**. However, basic interpersonal communicative skills can take up to two years to develop, whereas academic English, known as **Cognitive Academic Language Proficiency**, can take six to eight years to acquire. High-powered teachers continually strive to enhance students' academic English fluency through introducing and incorporating new academic vocabulary in their daily instructions. Academic vocabulary and more in-depth strategies will be addressed in Chapter Seven.

Societal and cultural factors influence language acquisition; children's personalities, their attitudes toward their cultural group, and their teacher(s) expectations all play a role (Otto; Samway and McKeon). Thus, it is vital that educators ensure that rich engaging activities are implemented into their daily instruction to help develop student's oral language skills. High-powered teachers exercise understanding of individual differences, diverse cultures, and diverse communities to ensure inclusive learning environments that enable each learner to meet high standards (InTASC Standard 2, CCSSO). They also strive to establish and maintain a learning environment that supports individual and collaborative learning, and that encourages positive social interaction, active engagement in learning, as well as self-motivation (InTASC Standard 3, CCSSO).

Activities for developing oral language should include expressiveness, wordplay, and word knowledge. Wordplay activities are a beneficial addition to strategic and standard-based instructions. Wordplay activities will vary across grade-levels, but all students regardless the grade or age benefit from rigorous and engaging wordplay activities. Wordplay activities can include shared reading and read-alouds for very young students. Kindergarten student's expressiveness activities can include collaborative conversations, grand conversations, interactive read-alouds, structured show and tell, interactive writing, story boards, and story retelling. However, these activities are not limited to kindergarten, each activity can be beneficial in increasing oral language for all grade-levels.

Proven activities that help develop oral language for older students can include choral reading, KWL charts, interactive word-walls, word sorts, quick writes, graphic organizers, and semantic feature analysis also help in the development of oral language. Other activities can include book talks, speeches, and presentations. High-powered teachers know how to adapt expressive activities to fit the needs of their students. They know that consistent exposure to a wide variety of words as well as opportunities to use those words in various contexts, leads to enhanced development of students, oral language skills.

What Link Does Oral Language Have to Literacy?

High-powered teachers plan and design their instructions with standard-based content that provides a strong foundation for literacy learning. Children who do not show strong oral language development before first grade have difficulty keeping pace with their classmates (Hart and Risey; Snow et al.). Having vocabulary knowledge is also an important predictor of young children's reading success. Students who can internally and orally define words are better able to decode words, thus increasing their comprehension and also increasing receptive and expressive language skills. Although there are other factors such as letter knowledge and phonemic awareness that enable students to decode words, these factors do not promote comprehension or fluency.

How Is Oral Language Assessed?

High-powered teachers monitor young children's oral language development because they understand that it is a vital component for their students' academic progress and their overall academic success. These teachers use a variety of formative assessments to gain insight about their students' oral language skills, as well as monitor their oral language skills. They understand and use multiple methods of assessment to engage learners for their own growth, to monitor learner progress, and to guide their students' as well as their own decision-making (InTASC Standard 6, CCSSO). Listed below are examples of formative assessments that high-powered teachers use to assess, analyze and plan instructions for their students:

+ Running records to document data
+ Enforcing the Rule of Five

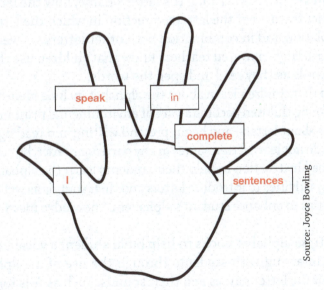

Source: Joyce Bowling

+ Random selection for questioning to ensure all students are actively engaged
+ Participating in discussions
+ Asking diverse questions to recall, predict, and make inferences
+ Collaborative partner work
+ Reader's theater
+ Show and tell

High-powered teachers use the above observations and formative assessments combined with running records, anecdotal notation, and checklists to monitor their students and record their findings. They review the recorded data, analyze their findings, reflect, and use the information to better understand their students' growth and needs, while also helping them to plan and design activities for future instruction that addresses the needs of all students. High-powered teachers observe their students to determine if they are manipulating or playing with words appropriately as they speak in general conversation and also when they are writing. High-powered teachers strive to foster a love of words, oral language, reading, and writing through careful planning, collaborative interaction, and engaging activities.

Readers and Writers Develop in Stages

High-powered teachers know that reading and writing develop in stages. When young children come to school, their knowledge about reading and writing expands quickly. High-powered teachers know that as young children interact and participate in meaningful experiences with reading and writing their oral language develops as does their knowledge about the use of words with reading and writing.

With the implementation of the Common Core Standards for English Language Arts also came a more strategic emphasis on the importance of fostering children's interest in reading and writing as well as their development and understanding of concepts about both reading and the written language.

How Do Children Learn the Alphabet?

Where does it all begin? Research shows us that young children learn about alphabets in stages. The components of these stages include learning the letter's name, how the letter is formed, upper and lower-case print, distinct features of the letters, direction in which the letter is turned, sounds the letter represents in isolation and in combination with other letters, as well as the sound the letter represents within a word. High-powered teachers know that children use their knowledge of letters to decode unfamiliar words as they read and spell the words.

The very basic skills that children learn about the alphabet include identifying and forming letters as they begin writing. Young children become aware of environmental print in their surroundings, they learn songs and rhymes about letters, and begin pretend writing and reading. High-powered teachers also know that children do not learn letter names in any particular order, but rather follow strategic and consistent standard-based instruction to help their students learn the alphabet. High-powered teachers implement engaging activities to introduce letters and their sounds as well as enhance students oral vocabulary. Some activities to enhance student's alphabetic knowledge may include:

+ Reading aloud from alphabet books to help build student's vocabulary.
+ Consistently interacting with students through the use of an alphabet chart. Reminding students daily of the letter names and their sounds. Such as A-is for apple, B-is for ball, and etc.
+ Using and allowing students to use whiteboards to demonstrate and practice the formation and writing letters.
+ Implementing letter sorts, which allow children to sort objects and pictures representing letters.
+ Using inexpensive cookie sheets and magnetic letters to practice letter identification and forming words.

High-powered teachers plan instruction carefully. They plan instruction that support every student in meeting rigorous learning goals by drawing upon knowledge of content areas, curriculum, cross-disciplinary skills, and pedagogy, as well as knowledge of learners and community context. They implement a variety of instructional strategies to encourage learners to develop deep understanding of content areas and their connections, while also building skills to apply knowledge in meaningful ways (InTASC Standards 7 & 8, CCSSO).

High-powered teachers provide their students with multiple opportunities, such as the activities listed above to ensure their students can identify the letters, know the sounds each letter in the alphabet represents, and how the letters are used to formulate words. They encourage student interaction with letters through visual, verbal, and written activities, and through physical manipulation of letters. They capitalize students' interest through collaborative experiences. Students are not only interested, they are engaged, and feel safe while learning. High-powered teachers also assess their students' knowledge of the alphabet using a checklist.

Three Stages of Reading and Writing

High-powered teachers know that all children do not learn to read and write exactly the same. They know that most young children develop both reading and writing skills in stages. The three stages include emergent readers and writers, beginning readers and writers, and fluent readers and writers.

Stage One: Emergent Readers and Writers

During the emergent stage of reading and writing, children become aware of the purpose of print and begin to develop an interest in reading and writing. They gain insight into how both reading and writing are communicative. As they notice environmental print through their surroundings, they begin to develop ideas and concepts about print from their teachers and their classmates. High-powered teachers help enhance students, understanding of the connection between oral language and writing. They demonstrate the art of story writing through pictures and word manipulation. High-powered teachers also encourage students to dictate their own stories to them as they scribe/write and record the story for them. Active engagement, consistency, and opportunity are vital in students' success as they emerge as readers.

Young readers should accomplish the following during the emergent stage:

+ *Emergent readers acquire concepts about print, become aware of environmental print, and distinguish between writing and drawing.*
+ *Emergent readers and writers gain interest in reading and writing, pretending to read and write letters, and begin scribbling to represent print.*
+ *Emergent readers gain knowledge of books, book parts, their purpose, and how to handle books.*
+ *Emergent readers identify letters and the sound(s) that each represent and gain directionality.*
+ *Emergent writers develop handwriting skills and write their first and last names and some words.*
+ *Emergent readers and writers learn to recognize and write 20 or more high-frequency/site words.*
+ *Emergent writers use sentence frames to write sentences.*

Most children are identified as emergent readers and writers while in kindergarten. However, students who have been read to by their parents or siblings on a daily basis typically learn to read and write before students who did not gain this valuable experience.

High-powered teachers interact with young readers through a variety of experiences including; modeling, oral reading, interactive reading, and shared reading. For example, students may listen to their teacher read aloud during shared reading and interact with them periodically through predictions and questions. High-powered teachers realize the importance of modeling both reading and writing. Modeling allows them to demonstrate what readers and writers do, while also teaching concepts about print. They also provide their students with multiple opportunities to interact with peers and texts.

Stage Two: Beginning Readers and Writers

During stage two, beginning readers and writers grow immensely as their awareness, comfort, and their understanding of the alphabetic principal increases. During this stage young children learn more about phoneme–grapheme relationships, phonetic rules within words, and also become familiar with word families. They engage in wordplay through applying their newfound phonics knowledge to begin spelling words. Students may omit the final *e* sound as they are not proficient with all of the rules that apply to spelling, and only write the sounds that they can hear. For example, they may spell the word *light* as *lit*, or *fine* as *fin*.

High-powered teachers realize the importance of introducing and reinforcing new high-frequency/site words during this stage. During stage two, beginning readers and writers are learning to recognize and read more high-frequency words, many of which cannot be sounded out. These may include words such as *are, what, does, there, where*, and a vast amount of other words.

Young readers should accomplish the following during the beginning stage of reading and writing:

+ *Beginning readers learn phonics skills and correct names of letters and their associated sound(s).*
+ *Beginning readers and writers use beginning, middle, and endings sounds to decode words.*
+ *Beginning writers print from left to right and incorporate both upper and lowercase letters.*
+ *Beginning readers and writers recognize up to 100 high-frequency words.*
+ *Beginning readers apply reading strategies, including, but not limited to, cross-checking, predicting, and self-correcting.*
+ *Beginning readers point to words while reading, read word by word, and read at a slow pace.*
+ *Beginning writers write five or more sentences, which are sometimes organized into a paragraph.*
+ *Beginning writers spell phonetically sound by sound and can spell up to, but not limited to, 50 high-frequency words.*
+ *Beginning writers are aware of and apply capital letters to begin sentences.*
+ *Beginning writers use punctuation to indicate the ends of sentences.*
+ *Beginning readers and writers make reasonable predictions and can reread their own writing.*

Most beginning readers and writers are second graders. However, some students develop into beginning readers and writers during first grade. High-powered teachers carefully plan and design their instruction to allow students daily opportunities to read and write. With daily practice students move through the beginning stage at a rigorous pace in effort to reach the fluent stage of reading and writing.

As young readers begin reading, they often read aloud slowly and point to each individual word, while also stopping to sound out and decode unfamiliar words. With diverse practice their reading becomes smoother, less choppy, and more fluent. However, the emphasis in this stage is primarily on recognizing and decoding words, to learn that reading involves thought, which leads to comprehension. High-powered teachers model predicting and skill of interacting with the text. Through strategic and consistent modeling, students learn to pause and think about what they are reading. They begin to make connections between their own lives and what is going on around them and with the text they're reading, which leads to a meaningful and personal experience, thus enhancing their comprehension.

High-powered teachers also model how to analyze reading. They use think-alouds to model their own thoughts about text they are reading to demonstrate how to determine their understanding of the text. They teach students to monitor their own reading to recognize when it doesn't make sense, to cross-check using phonological, semantic, and pragmatic information in the text to determine the problem, while also repairing the problem. During the beginning stage of reading and writing, students also learn about story structure. They learn that stories have a beginning, middle, and ending. High-powered teachers encourage students to use this knowledge to help guide their reading, writing, summarizing, and retelling.

As students near the end of this stage they begin to develop longer sentences and also write more complex sentences. Their sentences may contain five or more words and sometimes formulate a paragraph. Beginning readers and writers also apply what they have learned about phonics and spelling to correctly spell many words, including high-frequency words. During this stage they also learn to capitalize letters that begin a sentence and also use correct punctuation to end sentences. High-powered teachers teach students to not only monitor their reading, but also what they have written, and encourage them to rewrite when necessary for clarification.

High-powered teachers also plan and create activities and opportunities for children to read and write independently. The activities that they plan emphasize the importance of engagement through thinking about what they are reading and what they are writing. They model brainstorming ideas and use simple graphic organizers to plan their writing. High-powered teachers model first, interact, and then gradually release the responsibility to the students. However, they also assist students who require a scribe and also monitor all students during the planning and writing stage.

As students near the end of the beginning stage of readers and writers they gain an interest in a variety of genres, become more fluent as they read, require less decoding, read less choppy, recognize more high-frequency words, self-correct, and also become more involved with both their reading and writing. Their handwriting is more accurate, phonics and spelling skills are more accurate, and they become more fluent writers as well.

High-powered teachers know the importance of knowing their students. They know that all students do not learn alike. They implement InTASC Standard 2 and 6 by strategically planning, instructing, modeling, assisting, and assessing for all academic levels, as well as each individual student to ensure that all students are successful.

Stage Three: Fluent Readers and Writers

The third stage of reading and writing consists of students' advancement to both fluent reading and writing. Fluent readers differ from readers in the emergent and beginning stages of reading. Fluent readers recognizes hundreds of words automatically and also knows how to use multiple strategies to identify and quickly decode unfamiliar words while reading. Fluent readers read words accurately, rapidly, and also expressively. Their reading rate has increased to 100 words or more per minute. Fluent readers typically read silently, and often at a faster pace compared to when they read orally. Fluent readers also interact on a higher level with text than emergent and beginning readers. They are able to make more connections, predictions, visualize the characters, and the plot as it unfolds while they are reading.

Students who are reading and writing fluently use the writing process to draft. They also understand how to revise and apply that knowledge in their writing to prepare it for publishing, and know how to organize their writing in a structured or sequential manner. They apply punctuation, capitalization, and spell more accurately. Fluent writers can write both independently and collaboratively, and have the capability to peer-assess in both independent settings and collaborative settings. High-powered teachers also involve fluent readers and writers in a variety of genres.

Most second-grade students reach this stage during the course of the academic year. Note that not all students learn alike or at the same pace. It isn't uncommon for an occasional first-grade student to exit first-grade reading and writing in the fluent stage, while all second-grade students may not reach or master the fluent stage of reading and writing. High-powered teachers scaffold their instruction and assignments to meet the needs of all of their students. High-powered teachers know the importance of students reaching the milestone of being a fluent reader and writer. They also know that students should be fluent readers and writers by the end of their third-grade year.

High-powered teachers know that when students are both reading and writing in the fluent stage by the end of their third-grade year, they are in turn ready for the increased literacy demands of fourth grade, which include students being expected to read longer and more difficult texts, including chapter books and literature from a wide variety of genres. High-powered teachers also strive to prepare their students to respond to the literature that they are reading through various types of writings, such as topical essays, book reports, on-demand style writing that can include both persuasion and personal narratives, while also using graphic organizers and rubrics to plan and assess their writing.

Virtual Strategies for Oral Language Development

High-powered teachers know that young children's exposure to words, conversations, and interactions are **vital for their oral language development**. They know that student's academic needs and oral language development remains the same for both in person students and virtual students. High-powered teachers strive to provide both in person and virtual students with the instruction, guidance, exposure, conversations, and interactions that will stimulate and encourage oral language development.

High-powered teachers know that children continue to develop language skills, competence, and confidence both in person and virtually through a variety of both receptive and expressive opportunities. High-powered teachers create and implement interactive **read alouds** both in person and virtual with students by reading orally to them, and also involving them in the text. Virtual students can respond through both oral answers when they are actively engaged with the entire class in whole-group setting, or when they are working independently online during an in-class session. They can also submit answers through written responses when watching prerecorded videos. Nevertheless, high-powered teachers involve all students, including virtual students, in the story through incorporating think-pair-share or turn and talk strategies.

For live virtual instruction, high-powered teachers place their camera in a position that allows virtual students to visibly see the teacher and interact with them via the preferred online platform. Students may also be asked to engage with students who are attending class in-seat at the time. This method of collaboration makes the classroom more **cohesive, collaborative**, and also **builds community** both online and in person. High-powered teachers know that when teaching primarily virtually, they can focus the camera solely on themselves and engage with the students just as if they were sitting in the classroom. Virtual learning can also include instruction that is not live instruction. High-powered teachers may choose this type of instruction as an introduction, assignment, review, or follow up to live instruction. Students may be required to watch **pre-recorded videos**, respond in **online journals**, and other times may be required to submit short video clips of themselves reading aloud to their parent, or reading aloud independently to themselves and the camera to allow the teacher to assess their oral language, reading, and or fluency.

High-powered teachers may choose to implement **guided reading groups** for virtual students that allows them to divide students into categories **of emerging readers, beginning readers, and fluent readers**. By grouping students based on their reading level, teachers can design instruction that meets that particular group of student's needs. Guided reading involves **careful scheduling**, management, and also **intense planning**. It also requires that teachers know their student's reading ability, strengths, and their areas of growth. High-powered teachers know that precise planning and structure are vital for all classrooms. They know that while they are working with a group of students in a guided reading group, the remaining students should be working independently, which takes careful planning and implementation. High-powered teachers know that **guided reading typically lasts 20 to 25 minutes**, depending on the age/grade-level, and plan their instruction for the small group and independent assignments for remaining students accordingly.

Once students who are not participating in the guided reading group are on task, high-powered teachers move to their small group of students, which may consist of either virtual or in person students, or a mix of both. During guided reading, high-powered teachers allow students to complete a book walk and read a **familiar book** to help build, activate, or establish background knowledge. They may also use this time to assess students through the use of a running record. High-powered teachers know that when students read a familiar read, they are also gaining confidence. After completing the familiar read, teachers distribute books that are based on students reading level or books that provide a small challenge to both in person and or online students. They require students to read orally through whole-group guided reading incorporating **echo reading** when necessary, while also requiring students to read independently or with their partners. Based on the concept being taught, the high-powered teachers will then require students to participate in close reading to answer questions either with their elbow partner or independently. During guided reading, high-powered teachers offer **support** through echo reading, orally reading with students, guidance and prompting, and also asking and answering questions. Guided reading is a grand opportunity to scaffold instruction and meet the needs of all students, regardless their reading level or their location of learning.

High-powered teachers also know that guided reading can be a fun and challenging opportunity to work with **early finishers** to provide a fun and **exciting challenge** that helps **prevent** and alleviate **boredom**, promote collaboration, and engagement, while also extending student's knowledge, and ensure success at an even higher level. With careful planning, above level learners can be grouped to work collaboratively or independently both in person and online to work on projects and or assignments, while the teacher is working collaboratively in smaller guided reading groups.

High-powered teachers know that half the battle of the struggles of virtual teaching can be won through structure, planning, consistency, and through creating a cohesive, engaging, and comfortable situations for all students.

Now It's Your Turn

For this assignment, you will design a reading log that is appropriate for the grade-level that you desire to teach. For example, the reading log can be a type of spreadsheet that the parents of primary students complete each night after reading with their child. You may include the date, title of what they read, amount of time spent reading, and even a place for a brief reflection by the student. You should also include a place for both the parent and the child to sign. For upper intermediate elementary and above, the reading log can be a reflective journal that the student is required to turn in weekly. The journal should contain dates of reading, titles or page numbers of a novel, and maybe questions that they have thought about while reading their book or chapters. This can even be an online journal. Nevertheless, tracking students reading is very beneficial at all grade-levels and also for all levels of reading. You will also be required to write a reflection of how you will incorporate this reading log in your future classroom, what your aspirations of the reading log are, and also include the reading log itself. Details will be discussed about this assignment in class and on blackboard.

What Can Parents Do to Help Their Child?

High-powered teachers know that parents play a vital role in their child's advancement in reading skills. They encourage their students' parents to stay involved in their child's learning and help hold them accountable for young readers through encouraging them to sign a nightly reading log. They encourage both reading and discussing what has been read with young children to help develop children's receptive and expressive oral language, develop and enhance fluency, and also increase and promote comprehension.

High-powered teachers also provide their students' parents with lists of high-frequency words to review with their child. Reviewing these words through flashcards, flipbooks, whiteboard, and a variety of fun apps provides children an advantage to increase oral language skills, reading, and writing. Words can be divided into sections and distributed based on students' individual progress. Parents should expect their child to recognize the words quickly, and also use them in oral sentences or, depending on the age, they can require them to use two to three words in written sentences. This allows students to know the words by sight, which not only enhances fluency but also allows them to know how to use them in oral language, be receptive when they hear the words being used in daily conversations, increase their writing skills, and enhance spelling skills.

High-powered teachers also realize that parents are busy and that available time is not always a convenience. They help design a plan to prevent overwhelming parents or overworking the child. This plan can be distributed to parents through weekly individualized folders. The folder should contain the precise amount of work, a five-day schedule, a reading log, reading material, designated number of high-frequency words for the week, spelling words, and include a brief greeting with an explanation of the folder. Students will return their folders each week, teachers will remove the components to be graded, and add student's work for the next week.

Once the graded work and feedback is complete the folders will then begin to be given back with graded work on the left and unfinished work on the right. High-powered teachers do not leave folders idle and they do not procrastinate. They follow through with a carefully designed cycle of folders always being graded and continually being filled with new and challenging fun assignments that is not *"busy work."* They ensure that folders contain work that is designed to fit the needs of their students. They do not use the graded work for formal grades, but rather as informal data that will help them design instructions and monitor the progress of their students, while also keeping their students' parents involved in their child's education. High-powered teachers provide timely feedback that includes a brief explanation of what students need to work on for improvement, as well as words of praise! Words such as great job, good job, way to improve, awesome, and so forth help motivate students. The use of rubber stamps with smiley faces or stickers also increase young students desire to learn, while giving them the confidence that they need to be successful.

Author's Tip

When I was eleven, I was an active energetic sixth-grade student. I was involved in sports, read every Nancy Drew book I could get my hands on, a very good speller, and what I considered to be an above average student. However, one day my teacher's 6-year-old son came into the class just in time to hear the teacher reprimanding a group of students who didn't seem to be interested in learning, and who were not performing to the best of their ability in reading and writing. She quickly whipped out the anthology of short stories that we were currently reading and handed the book to her son and simply stated, "do you mind reading this to the class?"

I recall smiling inwardly and also feeling a bit sorry for her 6-year-old son. I wondered why she would set her son up to fail. I tried to imagine how he would feel trying to read from the thick book that appeared to be weighing heavy in his small hands. However, I recall the initial shock that I felt as this 6-year-old boy read from the book without missing one word. I knew these stories! I had read and reread these stories! He wasn't faking! This 6-year-old boy was reading, and reading fluently! He was fluently reading our sixth-grade reading book! He was reading a book that had a lexile level much higher than what 6 year-olds typically read. I also recall wondering how this was possible.

The teacher quickly addressed what her son had come to see her about, and excused him to go back to his classroom. She then turned to address our class that was still sitting there with wide eyes of amazement. Some thought it was a trick to make them want to read, while others thought that he had rehearsed the story, and still others accused him of memorizing the story. I recall thinking they were wrong. Somehow I knew that he was quickly decoding every word and actually reading the book page by page.

Our teacher explained after many questions were posed and many theories were given about what we had just witnessed. She explained that she had begun labeling everything in her house when her son began to walk. Chairs were labeled simply as chairs, tables as a table, doors as a door, and etc. She explained that she exposed him to words and repeated the words to him. When he played with a ball, she showed him the word ball so that he would associate that word with that object. She further explained how as he grew the words in her house also grew. She described how at a very young age she began reading aloud to him and also playing word games with him. The word games that I recall her mentioning were simple word sorts, storyboards, and story retelling. She taught him the alphabet at the age of three and basic phonics at the young age of four. As a result of the visible exposure to words, read-alouds, word activities, and having those grand conversations with her son, he was a fluent reader at the young age of 5. His love for learning had been set in motion as was his love of reading. I recently found out through research that her son is now a college professor, earned a doctoral degree, and has been honored with several academic accomplishments. To think, his successful career began with engaging wordplay at home as a toddler.

As a young public school teacher, I decided to follow in my sixth-grade teachers' footsteps. I posted words all over my classroom. I had word walls for all subjects, everything in the room contained labels, I created what became known as, **The Word of the Day Board**, and implemented interactive read-alouds, collaborative conversations, word walls, classroom rules posted, daily writing, reading and writing centers, pen pals, academic words, show and tell, reader of the day, choral reading, presentations, book talks, and many more opportunities through daily activities. I also incorporated the eight parts of speech throughout these fun and simple activities. I reinforced students' knowledge of nouns daily during both reading and writing instructions. I also introduced adjectives and verbs verbally and gradually required them to complete simple activities of identifying nouns, proper nouns, adjectives, and action verbs. These activities would include circling pictures of the parts of speech, picking out nouns, verbs, and adjectives within sentences and circling them in different colors, engaging students in fun interactive games, using flashcards, word sorts, and incorporated daily read-alouds. I decided that my students' oral language and grammar skills would develop academically and socially.

The abovementioned activities, as well as structured and standard-based instruction, led to many success stories with student's oral language development, grammar skills, and reading and writing skills. However, the key to promoting and developing children's oral language, reading, and writing skills requires imagination, confidence, not being afraid to step outside of the box, getting out of your comfort zone, while also being consistent. In other words, words on the word wall or labels on objects are of little value or benefit to students if both the teacher and the students do not interact with those words, with their peers, and with you. I must admit that a smile crossed my face and a feeling of accomplishment and satisfaction enveloped me when one of my first grade orally read grade-levels and lexile-levels above what was expected. I felt an enormous sense of accomplishment as a teacher when a parent of a previous student whom I had in class many years ago stopped by my table while dining out one evening to thank me for instilling the love of reading in her son. My desire is for you to experience this sense of satisfaction with your students and as a teacher.

Applications

To help guide you through Chapter Four and upcoming chapters, become familiar with the following key terms for a deeper understanding of Chapter Four:

- ✦ Phonology
- ✦ Orthography
- ✦ Morphology
- ✦ Syntax
- ✦ Semantic
- ✦ Etymology
- ✦ Pragmatics
- ✦ Emergent readers and writers
- ✦ Beginning readers and writers

+ Fluent readers and writers
+ High-frequency words
+ Word families

In-Seat Activity

High-powered teachers can think on their feet, modify their instructions, and design quick activities that address the needs of all levels of learners with ease. For this activity, you will work with your collaboration group to create a five to seven minute, hands-on word activity using the supplies/materials in the box on your table. Each person must be involved. Design the activity to enhance reading in either the emergent reading stage, beginning reading stage, or the fluent reading stage. Be prepared to explain your activity, the purpose of the activity, the level of reader it targets, and also how you anticipate it to enhance student's fluency, and also how it could enhance their writing. You will present your activity to the class in the second half of the class. Don't overthink this, but try to think outside the box.

Reflect and Answer the Following Questions

+ *What is the structure of language?*
+ *How does children's oral language develop?*
+ *What link does oral language have to literacy?*
+ *How is oral language assessed?*
+ *What are the developmental stages of reading and writing?*

Student Notes

Annotating is an effective learning strategy. This page is reserved for you to annotate *(take notes,)* record potential questions, and also to refer back to when studying, completing assignments, and to help you gain a better understanding of Chapter Four.

Student Reflection

High-powered teachers reflect. This page is reserved for you to reflect about information that you found insightful and what you have learned from Chapter Four.

Suggested Readings

There is a wide variety of books available that can be incorporated within the classroom to help enhance students' oral language. Some of the books are listed below. Keep in mind that you, the teacher, should implement a diverse variety of books in your classroom that are interesting, challenging, engaging, and rich in vocabulary. I suggest that you read and explore a wide variety of children's books in all genres. Read old titles, new titles, and books published by a variety of authors. Fill your classroom library shelves with an array of both old and new titles so that you will have instant access to multicultural books and books from all genres. Your students will thank you for a well-stocked classroom library.

Suggested Kindergarten Books Include

Carle, E. *The Very Hungry Caterpillar*. Puffin Books, 2002.
Martin, B., Jr., and J. Archambault. *Chicka Chicka Boom Boom*. Beach Lane Books, 2009.
Wood, A. *The Napping House*. Harcourt, 2005.

Suggested Primary Books Grades 1–3 Include

Bunting, E. *Smoky Night*. Voyager, 1999.
Hoban, T. *Over, Under, and Through*. Aladdin Books, 2008.
Levin, E. *Henry's Freedom Box: A True Story from the Underground Railroad*. Scholastic Press, 2007.
Scieszka, J. *Math Curse*. Viking, 1995.
Scieszka, J. *The True Story of the 3 Little Pigs!* Viking, 1999.
Van Allsburg, C. *The Stranger*. Houghton Mifflin, 1996.

Suggested Reading for the Educator

Silverman, Rebecca D., and A. Hartranft. *Developing Vocabulary and Oral Language in Young Children.* The Guilford Press, 2014.

Chapter References

Braunger, J., and J. P. Lewis. *Building a Knowledge Base in Reading*, 2nd ed. International Reading Association, 2006.

Council of Chief State School Officers (CCSSO). *Interstate Teacher Assessment and Support Consortium (InTASC) Model Core Teaching Standards*, Apr. 2011, https://www.ccsso.org/sites/default/files/2017-11/InTASC_Model_Core_Teaching_Standards_2011.pdf. Accessed 7 July 2018.

Gleason, B. J. *The Development of Language*, 6th ed. Pearson, 2005.

Hart, B., and T. Risley. "The Early Catastrophes: The 30 Million Word Gap." *American Educator*, vol. 27, no. 1, 2003, pp. 4–9.

National Research Council. *Preventing Reading Difficulties in Young Children*. National Academy Press, 1998.

Otto, B. *Language Development in Early Childhood Education*, 4th ed. Pearson, 2014.

Samway, K. D., and D. McKeon. *Myths and Realities: Best Practices for English Language Learners*, 2nd ed. Heinemann, 2007.

Snow, C. E., et al., editors. *Preventing Reading Difficulties in Young Children*. National Academy Press, 1998.

Chapter 5
The Process of Reading and Writing

Teacher Quote

"Reading aloud to a child opens the magic of imagination."

~ Dr. Joyce Bowling

Chapter Questions

+ What are the stages of the reading process?
+ What are the stages of the writing process?
+ What do students need to know to become successful writers?
+ How is reading related to writing relationship?

The Reading Process

The reading process is a group of stages that involve the reader interacting with the text they're reading in order to comprehend what they've read. Note that the term text refers to all reading material. This material is not limited to textbooks. This material can include short stories, novels, magazines, articles, books, social media posts, media, labels, and even cereal boxes. Students should learn all genres and all forms of text to be real-world ready to read.

Reading is a constructive process. Reading involves reading words within the text and creating meaning. Comprehension is the ultimate goal of reading. When asked the definition of comprehension, most students will immediately reply that comprehension is understanding what you read. However, comprehension is more than just recalling the text. High-powered teachers teach reading with the goal for students to understand and recall what they've read, and also be able to apply their newfound knowledge. Students then are able to apply their newfound knowledge to answer both text-based and interpretive questions, solve problems, make inferences, and apply their knowledge to real-world situations.

High-powered teachers know that reading involves phonemic awareness and phonics. They also know that students use their knowledge about phonological system, including how to manipulate sounds in spoken words, apply phoneme and grapheme correspondences, as well as phonics rules while they are reading. High-powered teachers ensure that their students develop the ability to use this knowledge through phonemic awareness as well as phonics instruction while in the primary grades. They understand how learners grow and develop, recognizing that patterns of learning and development vary individually within and across the cognitive, linguistic, social, emotional, and physical areas, thus designing and implementing developmentally appropriate and challenging learning experiences for their students (InTASC Standard 1, Council of Chief State School Officers [CCSSO]).

Pre reading

High-powered teachers know that the reading process begins before readers actually open their books. Pre\reading is the first stage of reading and is a vital part of learning to read. It occurs as students are preparing to read. High-powered teachers know that students have both general and specific background knowledge. **General knowledge** consists of knowledge that students have acquired through various experiences such as life experiences, knowledge that they have gained at their homes, in communities, from their families, from television, and also from school. **Literary knowledge** includes what they know about reading such as text structures or genres.

High-powered teachers know that during pre reading it is vital to plan instruction, which includes **activating student's prior knowledge**. They strategically plan instruction that activates both general and literary knowledge. They encourage students to interact with the text by reading the title of their text, thinking about it, and making a prediction or inference based on the title or the illustration on the cover. High-powered teachers ask their students to open their text and examine the illustrations, read captions, and also read the first paragraph. Reflection is encouraged at this stage of the activity before asking students to make an inference based on what they know.

High-powered teachers know their students. They realize that not all students come to their class lacking **background knowledge** in a particular subject, content, or concept. High-powered teachers plan instructions and collaborative activities that help establish and build background knowledge about reading, as well as extend the background knowledge. They teach reading strategies and skills, knowledge about genres by examining the structure of the genre, and explain how reading will vary based on a particular genre. They also enhance student's knowledge of a topic by providing a carefully selected text to read based on that topic. For example, if the topic in their students' fictional story is based on the moon, high-powered teachers will incorporate informational texts about the moon.

High-powered teachers understand the importance of conversation in the classroom and will plan activities based on the topic that students are learning about to promote collaboration, vocabulary, critical and creative thinking, while also establishing content knowledge. High-powered teachers also incorporate technology to enhance students' interest and their knowledge, such as virtual field trips. They also provide and incorporate artifacts, guest speakers, and allow students to complete hands-on activities. High-powered teachers expose, teach, and incorporate content vocabulary to enhance students' understanding. Activating students' prior knowledge encourages students to make connections to the text. However, it's not enough to simply build students' knowledge about a topic; literary knowledge is also an essential component of pre reading (InTASC Standard 5, CCSSO).

Through my years of teaching reading, regardless the age, students often asked, why are we reading this? High-powered teachers know the importance of setting a purpose for reading. This purpose establishes a guide for students' reading, as well as a way for students to monitor their reading to determine if they are fulfilling their purpose. According to research, setting and sustaining a single purpose while students read the text is more effective than presenting students with a series of purposes (Blanton et al.).

High-powered teachers **set purposes for reading**, but also realize the value of students setting their own purpose(s). In most structured reading programs, literature focus units, and reading textbooks, the teachers typically explain how students are expected to read and what they will be doing after they finish reading, thus giving the students a purpose. However, high-powered teachers also encourage and require their students to set their own purposes for reading while they are collaborating in activities such as, **literature circles**, **jig saw**, and **readers' workshop**. Groups of books to be used in collaborative activities can be preselected for students by the teacher. Students are then given a choice. They can choose a text or topic that they find interesting, informative, or explain a topic that they want to learn more about from the group of books the teacher selected. High-powered teachers also allow their students to make book suggestions, if a particular book of interest to them was not included in the group of books. High-powered teachers know that as their students develop as readers, they become more effective at selecting books and also at setting their own purposes.

> *"Establishing background knowledge within a child, allows them to meet people they've never met before, and travel to places they've never gone before."*
>
> ~ *Dr. Joyce Bowling*

High-powered teachers encourage their students to plan for reading. Once the students activate or establish their **background knowledge**, and identify their **purpose for reading**, they take their first look at the text and plan for reading. Students' plans will sometimes vary among themselves, as all students do not learn the same, and also based on the type of text they're preparing to read. For example, for stories, students might make predictions about characters and events in the story, often basing their inferences on book's cover illustration, or title. Students may also make predictions based on previous stories that they've read by the same author or genre. High-powered teachers know that students use this information to make predictions, while also using it to share their predictions orally, and at other times, they also encourage them to write predictions in their **reading logs/journals**.

Book-walks are very beneficial for students of all ages. When students are preparing to read nonfiction books or content area textbook chapters, high-powered teachers encourage them to complete a **book-walk** prior to reading. A book-walk simply allows students to browse the pages, paying close attention to the titles, section headings, illustrations, graphs, captions, and diagrams prior to reading the text. High-powered teachers also encourage their students to examine the table of contents to see how the book is organized, or ask them to search the index to locate specific words, or information that they want to learn more about, and also the text that they want to read.

These teachers also encourage students to pay particularly close attention to unfamiliar words or terminology within the first pages of the text. They ask their students to make **annotations** about words that they do not know, words that they find confusing, or even words that they want to know more about. High-powered teachers use this information to guide and plan their instruction to ensure that they meet the needs of all of their students. The words that students notate are often used to create **anticipation guides** or **grand conversations** in the classroom, which encourage text involvement and also establish and help promote a deeper understanding of the content prior to reading (InTASC Standards, 4, 5 & 8, CCSSO).

Reading

High-powered teachers know the power and impact of incorporating **read-alouds** with their students. However, they also know that for their students to be successful readers they must also be involved in a variety of readings. For example, high-powered teachers plan and integrate **shared reading experiences, guided reading**, **partner reading,** and also **independent reading**. The type of reading varies in the amount of scaffolding from full teacher support to limited teacher support.

Read-Alouds

High-powered teachers use read-alouds as an opportunity to read books aloud that are developmentally appropriate, but are written above their student's reading level, to encourage and promote reading growth. As they read, high-powered teachers engage their students in activities during the read-aloud, rather than waiting to involve them after they finish reading. This allows students to become active participants in the storyline, with the characters, and with the plot. For example, high-powered teachers involve their students by asking them to make predictions, ask and answer questions, identify big ideas, and also make connections. In addition, when teachers read aloud to their students, they are modeling what good readers do such as reading fluently, expressively, animatedly, and with smooth rhythm. Read-alouds are also an opportunity for teachers to model how good readers use various reading strategies (Cappellini). Reading aloud provides an opportunity for teachers to demonstrate thinking aloud. Think-alouds are basically modeling what you are thinking while reading, what strategies you are applying, and even what connections or questions you may have while reading.

Research shows that read-alouds are an important component of literacy instruction at all grade-levels, not just an activity or strategy for young children who can't read books on their own (Allen). High-powered teachers incorporate read-alouds during reading and writing workshops, for thematic units, and also in literature-focused units. High-powered teachers know the benefits of reading aloud to students. They know that a read-aloud is a grand opportunity to introduce diverse genres, vocabulary that is necessary for both fluency and comprehension, model reading strategies, and also an opportunity to increase students' motivation. They also know that reading aloud can help introduce new strategies, strengthen skills, create a sense of community in the classroom, and is an opportunity to help foster the love of reading in their students.

Shared Reading

High-powered teachers know the importance of shared reading. They also take time to integrate shared reading into their classrooms. **Shared reading** is often incorporated in content areas in addition to reading for primary teachers who are self-contained. Shared reading can be implemented with all grade-levels. Primary teachers often incorporate "*Big Books*" that contain colorful illustrations and large print that is visible for both large and small groups, which allows students to read along. High-powered teachers know that big books are a grand opportunity to have discussions about illustrations, story, characters, and also to ask and answer questions. High-powered teachers also use shared reading experiences to teach phonics, text patterns, and high-frequency words, at the same time modeling fluency and incorporating reading strategies. Shared reading differs from read-alouds because students often join in the reading of predictable refrains, as well as identifying and even reciting rhyming words. Once they have listened to and interacted with the text being read several times, they often remember enough of the text to read along with the teacher, which helps prepare them to reread the same text in smaller individual books.

High-powered teachers incorporate **guided reading** when working with small groups of students and sometimes with their entire class. When implementing guided reading with small groups of students, the teacher asks the students to read books that are based on or slightly above their reading level orally and at the same time, individually. High-powered teachers provide support for the students during guided reading by reading along with them when necessary, reminding them of a particular strategy that they are being asked to use, and also answering questions about the text when necessary. Guided reading is a grand opportunity to scaffold instruction and meet the needs of all students, regardless the reading level.

Guided reading usually lasts 20–25 minutes depending on the age/grade of the students. When students arrive at the small-group guided-reading area, which is often a table near the back of the room, they often reread, individually or with a partner. During guided reading students read a **familiar read**. A familiar read is a book that they've read before, either in previous guided-reading groups, or together in whole group instruction. Familiar reads helps increase student's confidence, comprehension, fluency, and expression. New and unfamiliar books can also be introduced in guided-reading groups to help prepare students for whole group reading. However, teachers are more involved when new books are introduced. High-powered teachers implement carefully planned small-group guided reading into their classroom to **scaffold** and **differentiate instruction**, assignments, and also ensure that they are meeting the needs of all of their students (InTASC Standards 2 & 8, CCSSO).

High-powered teachers observe students as they read during guided-reading lessons, and formatively assess their students during small-group guided reading by monitoring their reading ability, word knowledge, and fluency. Guided reading is also an opportunity to incorporate **whisper phones** when working with primary students. A whisper phone is a small tubular instrument that resembles a telephone. The object of the whisper phone is to allow students to hear themselves read, while reading in a whisper. Students hold the whisper phone to their ear and whisper read the text into the mouth piece of the instrument. Whisper phones decrease the noise-level, which often disturbs young students when reading, but allows the teacher to continue to monitor and assess students' expression, fluency, and reading skills. High-powered teachers monitor their students' reading, complete checklists, or running records, and make annotations about individual student's progress, accomplishments, and struggles. They reflect on the recorded data and use their findings to plan future mini lessons to help their students become successful readers and writers.

High-powered teachers integrate shared reading with older students using novels when the text is too difficult to read independently. Shared reading is meant to be a comfortable learning experience for all students. It is also meant to enhance fluency, comprehension, classroom rapport, inspire reading, and is a great opportunity to introduce and incorporate new genres. Shared reading also promotes classroom discussions, higher-order thinking, and problem-solving. High-powered teachers know that shared reading is an opportunity for all of their students to participate, scaffold instruction, and to grow as readers.

The process of shared reading with older students differs from that in the primary grades. Older students are given an Individual copy of the novel, and discussion of the book takes place prior to reading, which can be predictions or comments about the author. Students are then asked to follow along with the teacher as they read the blurb on the back of the book. These simple activities promote an interest in the book, while also clarifying misconceptions. High-powered teachers then ask students to follow along as the teacher reads aloud. They allow students to take turns reading aloud. However, the goal is not for everyone to have a turn reading. High-powered teachers use the process of **monitored random selection**. In other words, they know their students' reading ability and the difficulty of the text. Thus, they call students randomly to read a passage based on their ability to read aloud. Monitored random selection allows the teacher to scaffold the oral reading experience and also not overwhelm struggling reader(s) by asking them to read a passage that is far above their reading level, while also allowing a higher leveled reader to read a more challenging passage from the text. Monitored random selection paired with knowledge of students reading ability and knowledge of text brings equals success for everyone, and an equal opportunity to read and grow academically with confidence.

Partner Reading

High-powered teachers also incorporate **partner reading** in their class. Partner reading isn't limited to just reading. It can be incorporated in all content areas to help strengthen students' reading ability and also encourage student collaboration. During partner reading students read or reread a selection with a randomly selected or assigned partner. Partner reading increases student's social skills, problem solving skills, comprehension, promotes class rapport, and also allows students to peer assess.

High-powered teachers model partner reading prior to assigning partners to read a text. They demonstrate how to partner read with a partner. They also demonstrate the appropriate way partners support each other for word identification, how they take turns reading, and also how students are expected to listen to their partners. They also model how partners read in unison and how partners discuss what they've read in a collaborative manner. Partner reading provides the practice that beginning readers need to become fluent readers. It is also an effective and beneficial way to scaffold and differentiate when working with students with special learning needs and English learners. Partner reading is not just for younger or struggling readers. Partner reading is a beneficial strategy for all levels of reading and can be modified to fit the needs of all students.

Partner reading can also include the **Think-Pair-Share** technique. Think-pair-share technically works just like partner reading. However, after partners have read their text, the teacher requires them to answer a question(s), make an inference, solve a problem, or complete a passage collaboratively. Once the assigned task has been completed, students signal the teacher to let them know that they have completed their task and they are ready to proceed and share their answers, or their work. High-powered teachers incorporate think-pair-share in all content areas. They are also engaged with their students during the process of think-pair-share by monitoring and form-atively assessing their students. Think-pair-share encourages classroom rapport, collaboration, and the opportunity to differentiate instruction, content, and partners to ensure all students are successful.

Independent Reading

Independent reading is the most authentic form of reading and is a very important part of a balanced-reading program. High-powered teachers know that independent reading is a way students develop a love of reading as well as gain independence and self-confidence. As a result of gaining confidence, students begin to think of themselves as readers when they read independently. High-powered teachers incorporate independent reading in their classrooms at various times of the day. Some teachers schedule independent reading in the final 15 minutes of the academic day, while others may have fifteen minutes of scheduled independent reading time at the beginning of the day. The schedule for independent reading can vary from class-room to classroom to fit the needs of the teachers' schedule.

High-powered teachers know when students read independently they are capable of reading silent for their own purposes, and at their own pace. They also know that it is vital that the books students select are at appropriate reading level. High-powered teachers often make prime selec-tion books available in their classroom library for students to select from to ensure that students are reading books that are equivalent to their reading level, and are content or theme-based, while also allowing them a choice. Independent reading is typically more prevalent inside the classroom near the end of first grade, Whereas, second grades and beyond students read more fluently. Third-grade students and above often read chapter books during independent reading time for literature focus units as well as literature circles. Independent reading allows students the opportunity to read in a particular genre that they are interested in, curious about, or that they've read before. Independent reading can be a time to allow students to explore unknown genres. It also enhances and promotes the love of reading in students, while also allowing them to grow as readers.

Responding

Responding is a very important part of reading. When students respond to what they have read, while also continuing to explore the meaning after they read, they are thinking about what they've read and how they might want to respond to oral or written questions, or what they might want to add to a discussion. High-powered teachers encourage students to make tentative and exploratory comments immediately after reading. They often ask them to record their answers in reading logs, with a partner, or during a **grand conversation**.

High-powered teachers incorporate reading and writing logs to encourage students to record their thoughts, perceptions, inferences, and feelings about what they have read. While they are reflecting and writing their responses, they are also unraveling their thinking and elaborating or clarifying their responses. Reading and writing logs can be incorporated in all genres.

Reading logs do not have to be an expensive purchase. Many teachers simply staple a desig-nated number of sheets of line paper together, while others require an inexpensive folder to which paper can be added or taken out. Inexpensive wire notebooks also work well. The focus is not on the appearance of the writing log/journal, but on the content. High-powered teachers also model how to write in a reading/writing log. They model annotations, determining key words, and also how to write concisely, yet meaningful. High-powered teachers may also provide their students with text-based structured questions to prompt and guide their thinking. Reading/writing journals are meant to be learning tools. They are not meant for assessment or formal grades. The focus of this type of journal/log is the responses of the students, their ideas, and to promote reflection, thinking, and interaction between the student and the text. High-powered teachers expect their students to practice correct spelling and punctuation while writing in their journals. At the end of the story, unit, or text selection, teachers review students' logs/journals and often grade the students based on whether the he or she completed all of the assigned entries and on the quality of their ideas or expressions. High-powered teachers also provide students with explicit feedback to encourage as well as make them aware of areas for possible improvement.

High-powered teachers know that **Grand Discussions** are also an important part of responding. During discussions students talk about the text with classmates. They discuss stories, characters, plots, and theme in various genres. Students also make inferences and discuss text evidence during grand discussions. High-powered teachers also encourage their students to share their personal responses and tell what they liked or disliked in the text. Once students have shared their ideas and personal reactions, they change the focus to dig deeper into what the author may have been implying, to make connections between the text and their own lives or other texts that they have read. Grand discussion is also an opportunity for students to make predictions about upcoming chapters or the ending of a book. Grand discussions promote rapport in the classroom, encourage students to participate, ensure that everyone has a voice, share ideas, grow from collaboration, promotes differentiation, and also encourage and inspire students to continue reading or reread for a closer understanding. Grand discussions support and align with InTASC Standards 3, 6, & 7. High-powered teachers works with others to create environments that support individual and collaborative learning and encourage positive social interaction, active engagement in learning, and self-motivation (InTASC Standards 3, 6, & 7, CCSSO). Grand discussion is an opportunity for teachers to formatively assess students, plan future instruction, and assess their teaching methods.

Exploring

The initial stage of exploring is teacher-directed and the teacher is more prevalent than in previous reading stages. Students are asked to go back to the text to examine it more analytically. They reread the text or selection, examine the writer's craft, and focus on key words, sentences, and think about their meaning. High-powered teachers incorporate mini lessons to emphasize a particular strategy during the exploring stage.

Exploring can also be student-centered. High-powered teachers encourage their students to **reread** the text, to use think-alouds, participate in collaborative group discussions, and also make annotations. High-powered teachers also know that each time their students reread a selection, they benefit in specific ways. When students reread for a deeper meaning, they gain a better understanding and can better comprehend the text. Their initial focus shifts from the events of a story or the big idea in a nonfiction book to understanding the theme of a book or story. They also better understand the relationship among the big ideas in a nonfiction text.

Close Reading

High-powered teachers incorporate and value **close reading.** They know that through close reading they are better able to guide students through the process of rereading passages from text to uncover deeper layers of meaning. When students reread a difficult or complex text with a purpose, they better understand the meaning of the text, they are more likely to determine the author's purpose, and gain a much deeper understanding of the big ideas. The teacher's role in close reading is to scaffold their student's way of thinking while interacting with the text.

High-powered teachers ask text-based questions to help direct their students back into the text to reread a particular passage and encourage analytical thinking after they've reread the passage. Text-based questions can consist of one or more of the following: the author's purpose, ideas, structural elements, word choice, sentence structure, and viewpoints.

When teachers implement text-based questions they require their students to pay close attention as they reread the passage and locate evidence from the text to support their answers. For example, if a fourth-grade teacher is reading *The Miraculous Journey of Edward Tulane* with their students, they've read the first chapter, the teachers' close-reading questions should focus on word choice. The following are examples of statements the teacher might make to prompt students, and also questions that may be asked to extend students' thoughts, engage them with the text, while also encouraging them to make connections to the text.

- ✦ *Go back to the text in chapter seventeen to determine words that the author uses to help you formulate an opinion about Sarah Ruth and Bryce's home life.*
- ✦ *Are there words that suggest neglect?*
- ✦ *What tone does the author evoke in this chapter?*
- ✦ *What is the author not saying?*

As the fourth graders reread the designated chapter to determine, locate, and annotate the words that imply neglect, their comprehension and relationship with the author, the characters and the plot grow. The last question is the most thought-provoking question. High-powered teachers ask questions about what is not being said in order to promote critical thinking, interpretive reading, deep thinking, as well as encouraging their students to search for textual evidence that supports their answers and their inferences.

High-powered teachers select grade-appropriate texts that are also challenging enough to support and warrant multiple rereads. They also take time to model rereading and the process of locating key words, close reading and also analytical thinking. They realize that students will require practice analyzing a variety of genres and texts. High-powered teachers also expose their students to different formats when close reading. For example, they may incorporate newspaper and magazines articles, biographies, fiction, or even expository texts. High-powered teachers model close reading through read-alouds for primary students. High-powered teachers always pre read before assigning texts for their students to read, regardless the age or grade-level. High-powered teachers also pre teach difficult or confusing vocabulary and design questions prior to assigning students the activity of rereading a particular text. They also teach their students a variety of methods of annotation to enhance the close-reading experience (InTASC Standards, 7 & 8, CCSSO). For example, when students are unable to write directly in a text, they teach them to use sticky notes that can be attached to the page.

High-powered teachers use a variety of tools when teaching students to explore the text and examine the author's purpose. For example, high-powered teachers may incorporate the use of a storyboard, graphic organizers, highlighters, written reflections, collaborative discussions, book reports, and book talks. Word walls are a prominent décor in most classrooms. However, if the students do not interact with the word wall as a group, orally, and also independently in daily work, they become dormant and useless decoration on the walls. High-powered teachers interact with their word walls in daily instruction, collaborative work, and also as a guide and resource tool for their students. They also work with their students with a specific purpose in mind to add words to the word walls. High-powered teachers encourage their students to refer to the word wall when they write and to use the words for word-study activities such as concept definition maps, graphic organizers, open and closed word sorts, to enhance their use of vocabulary words in written or verbal expressions.

High-powered teachers also categorize words and complete semantic feature analysis charts to help their students examine relationships between words, while encouraging their students to think deeply and analytically (InTASC Standard 8, CCSSO). Words that have been added to the word wall can also guide students in locating important sentences in their texts, such as sentences containing figurative language, character traits, expressing or determining a theme. Nevertheless, a word wall is a valuable tool for the students and the teacher. Research has also proven that word walls enhance students' vocabulary, both verbal and written.

Applying

In the applying stage, students enhance their comprehension through reflection, while also valuing the reading experience in the final stage. High-powered teachers assign, encourage, and support their students through assigned projects. Teachers understand how to connect concepts and use differing perspectives to engage learners in critical thinking, creativity, and collaborative problem-solving related to authentic local and global issues (InTASC Standard 5, CCSSO). They assign projects that are strategically planned and are designed to require students to apply what they have learned. Projects are designed based on grade-level and can take many shapes and forms. For example, they may include writing stories, creating slide shows, creating a book trailer, making a diorama, creating a poster, or writing a play to perform in a reader's theater. Projects should be assigned for both independent and collaborative works. Students may work with one partner or a small group of peers, depending on the type of project.

Teachers are involved with their students in the applying stage. They offer support when necessary through answering questions, guidance, and assisting students with individualized education programs (IEP's) by acting as a scribe or a reader. High-powered teachers also monitor, encourage, and formatively assess students as they work on their assigned projects.

The Writing Process

The writing process is similar to the reading process. Similar to the reading process, writing also involves five stages. While students learn to work through the stages of writing, they gather their thoughts and ideas and organize them, write rough drafts, revise, edit, and finally publish their writing. Students learn to use the writing process to create and revise various types of writing including, stories, essays, book reports, narratives, poems, and also expository writings. The five stages of writing include **prewriting, drafting, revising, editing,** and **publishing**.

Prewriting

High-powered teachers know that during the prewriting stage students are preparing to write. They realize that students need time to gather their thoughts, that they do not always have an idea, or topic completely thought out, and are not always prepared to write. High-powered teachers encourage prewriting. They know that ideas are often developed through reflection, annotations, brainstorming, and through discussions. Prewriting should not be omitted. It is common for some teachers to omit prewriting due to time constraints, or lack of understanding of its purpose. However, high-powered teachers know that when their students are prewriting they are thinking, planning, choosing a topic, thinking about the type of writing they want to write, or sometimes creating characters while organizing their ideas. High-powered teachers encourage prewriting to allow students to not only choose a topic, but also gain interest and keep them engaged in their writing. High-powered teachers change things up inside their classrooms by presenting a range of topics for students to think about, preview, and then allow them to select a topic from preselected topics that they would like to write about. This strategy allows the students to have a voice as well as a choice in their writing.

As students prepare to write, they think about their purpose for writing. Teachers may choose an acronym to guide students. For example, high-powered teachers might use the acronym **PAT**; **P = purpose, A = audience, and T = task**. This allows the students to think about their purpose for writing. Students determine if they are writing to entertain, persuade, or inform. It also prompts them to remember their audience while they are writing. For example, if students are given an assignment to write a persuasive letter to the principal, their focus should be on the purpose of their writing, which is to persuade. They should also focus on who's going to read the letter; in other words, who their audience is. Using PAT also reminds them that their task is to write a letter. High-powered teachers encourage their students to refer to PAT throughout their prewriting to maintain a focus and purpose for their writing.

During the prewriting stage, high-powered teachers encourage their students to use a graphic organizer to organize and record their thoughts, ideas, and plans to help guide their writing. Graphic organizers help students recall previously learned content, make connections to previous experiences, and also help eliminate writer's block, while planning their writing.

High-powered teachers plan activities to engage their students while also allowing them opportunities to gather and organize ideas for writing. Activities can include research, watching short video clips, reading articles or related books, interviewing, collaborative conversations, creating collaborative or independent graphic organizers, and collaborative as well as independent brainstorming. High-powered teachers also encourage students to use a thesaurus to create a word bank of words they want to incorporate in their writing. Word banks can be as simple as a notebook, index cards, or even post it notes. Word banks are a great source and reminder of words that might go unnoticed without prewriting and the planning stage in place. Prewriting allows students to think about the beginning, middle, and ending of their writing.

Ideas

High-powered teachers know that ideas drive the message of a piece of writing. They refer to the ideas as the backbone or the heart of a piece of writing. They assign or ask students to pick an area of concern or interest, they then prompt and guide students to narrow that area of interest into a

more precise or specific idea, which results in developing their ideas into a main idea, and finally adding details. The idea is typically selected during the planning and prewriting stage, and then developed as they revise and edit.

Organization

High-powered teachers emphasize the importance of organization when teaching writing. They model how to hook the reader in the beginning of their writing with a bold statement, fact, or a rhetorical question. They teach their students to identify their purpose early in their work and also to present their ideas in a logical manner while also including transition words and phrases between ideas to help their writing to flow smoothly. High-powered teachers also stress the importance of a strong ending/conclusion of their writing. The organizational stage includes using the completed graphic organizer to create a strong opening paragraph with a hook, establish the structure of their writing, plan for transition words or transitional phrases, and establishing a strong ending or conclusion. The purpose of the organization stage is to help students know how to organize their writing and also learn how to make the structure of their writing logical to the reader. Organization typically occurs during the prewriting stage while they are developing ideas for their writing.

Drafting

Drafting is the second stage of writing when students get their ideas down on paper. During the drafting stage students write a first draft of their composition. Student's first drafts are often messy and not organized well. Their first draft may often contain eraser marks, cross-outs, lines drawn through words, and annotated notes in the margins. High-powered teachers encourage their students to write quickly and not focus on neatness or punctuation during this stage, but rather on developing their ideas. They also encourage students to refer back to their completed graphic organizer and PAT to help them stay on task.

High-powered teachers model, guide, and encourage their students to skip every other line during the drafting process to allow room for revisions. They model and encourage their students to use arrows to indicate where an area of text or a sentence will be moved. They teach their students to label their draft as *rough draft* in colored ink at or near the top of the page. Labeling their draft will indicate to the writer, as well as other students, parents, and even administrators that the composition is a draft and the emphasis is on the content, not mechanics. Labeling the paper as a draft also explains why the teacher hasn't graded the paper.

High-powered teachers often integrate technology with writing by encouraging their students to use computers to compose rough drafts, revise their writing, publish, post, or print their final product. High-powered teachers realize the benefits of using computers for word processing. For example, students are often inspired and motivated to write when given the opportunity to use a computer. Many students will write in greater length and produce neater work than hand written assignments. Students are encouraged to incorporate spell-check programs to identify and correct misspelled words. Finally, when students use computers to write they feel a sense of satisfaction, confidence, inspiration and motivation when they see their final writing complete.

Revising

During the revising stage writers refine their ideas in their work. Beginning or inexperienced writers often find this stage difficult as they think that once their draft is complete their work is finished. However, high-powered teachers model the stage of revision prior to asking students to revise their work. They provide their students with examples of rough drafts for practice and also show them a draft that has been revised. They also work collaboratively with their students to revise a composition via a smart board and then also with copies in small groups. High-powered teachers realize the importance of practicing revision, which allows their students to recognize errors, know how to notate errors, how to rewrite their paper based on their findings, and finally include these changes in their work during the drafting stage.

High-powered teachers stress to their students that the revision stage isn't a polishing stage. They teach their students that the revising stage allows them to think like a reader, which in turn allows them to meet the needs of the reader by adding, substituting, rearranging, and deleting. They instill within their students the term *"look again"* during this stage, which simply signals the writer to take a second look at their composition. High-powered teachers encourage students to work collaboratively to peer-revise and also work independently to revisit and revise their work during the revision stage. As students reread their writing, they begin to make changes and make annotations where they feel it needs additional work. This can be annotated with a question mark or using a high-lighter. Students can conference with the teacher or their peer-partner to collaboratively make the necessary changes.

High-powered teachers also encourage their students to reread their revised drafts and then distance themselves from their work for at least a day. This allows students to come back to their work with a fresh eye and perspective, which allows students to recognize errors, implement rich vocabulary, and add transition words with more ease. High-powered teacher also plan collaborative revising group time for their students, which allows them to meet in groups and share their composition with their peers. Group members respond to the writer's draft and suggest possible revisions. Collaborative groups also encourage scaffolding and differentiation across the classroom.

High-powered teachers often set up revising centers to give their students revision options. They introduce and familiarize their students with the revision centers, the tools that are incorporated in the centers, how to use the tools, and also what is the objective of the revision center. Students are often provided with a rubric or a checklist to self-assess their writings. This type of center encourages students to interact with their writing, helps develop a repertoire of revision strategies, and also allows them to personalize their writing process.

Word Choice

High-powered teachers model how students should carefully select words that enhance the meaning of their writing, while also making their composition more meaningful and interesting. Word walls and word banks are often implemented based on the genre of writing. For example, narrative writing should include dialect, characters, lively verbs, descriptive adjectives, and rich expressive vocabulary. Argumentative or persuasive writing should include a variety of transition words, vocabulary that consists of support or opposition, to solidify the purpose of their writing. High-powered teachers establish the clear goal of word choice as a way for students to express their message through word choice, while also being concise. Incorporating carefully selected words allows the writer to paint a visual image for the reader, energize their writing, and bring their writing to life with strong verbs and rich descriptive adjectives. High-powered teachers encourage their students to jot down words they might want to incorporate in their writing during the brainstorming/planning stage, and focus on word choice during the drafting and revision stage of writing.

Writer's Voice

Through careful selection of words writers establish a distinctive style often referred to as voice. When students develop a writer's voice, their personality begins to emerge and become prevalent in their writing. Voice is often established through word choice as well as word placement. High-powered teachers know that students grow as writers through modeling, collaboration, and practice. Writer's voice and tone is often developed in the drafting and revising stage.

Editing

During the editing process students are asked to put their writing in its final form. Prior to this stage the focus has been primarily on the content of their writing. However, in the editing stage the focus shifts from content to mechanics. Mechanics are the commonly accepted conventions of written standard English, which consists of capitalization, punctuation, spelling, sentence structure, usage, and formatting. During the editing stage students polish their writing by correcting spelling mistakes and other mechanical errors to allow the reader to read their words with ease. In other words, their composition flows and allows the reader to read without being distracted by mechanical errors.

Just as in the revision stage, high-powered teachers encourage their students to step away from their composition for at least one day prior to editing. After working closely with their own writing during the first two stages, students are often too familiar with their work to recognize their own errors. This allows the student to revisit their work with a fresh eye and perspective, which allows the students to identify errors that they may not have recognized prior. Once errors have been corrected students become inspired and can better visualize their final product. They also become anxious to move to the final stages of the writing process and see their work published.

Sentence Fluency

High-powered teachers help their students develop sentence fluency in stages. They teach, model, create, plan, and implement activities and create opportunities for their students to practice creating sentences that vary in length and are grammatically correct. Sentence fluency helps writing flow through rhythm that is achieved with varying the sentence length, which allows the writing to flow in a natural smooth manner and is easily read aloud. Sentence fluency consists of achieving a rhythmic flow, creating effective sentences, incorporating a variety of sentences, and also including transition words or transitional phrases when necessary.

Spelling and Mechanics

High-powered teachers teach, model, and require their students to use correct spelling in all assignments. Correct spellings are expected in the final published composition. High-powered teachers expect their students to use resources that are available to them to ensure that their writing contains words that are spelled correctly with correct word choice. They make dictionaries available for their students to check to ensure spelling accuracy, while also ensuring that students are implementing the correct word. For example, the correct use of words such as to, too, or two, dear or deer, and also words such as their, they're, or there. Common words are often spelled correctly, but often misused.

High-powered teachers know that the mechanics of writing include more than correct spelling. They know that mechanics/conventions include capitalization, punctuation, and grammar. During the editing stage, students proofread their writing, correct the spelling, and grammatical errors to enhance their writing, while also making it easier for the reader to read. Students typically correct mechanical errors during the editing stage of writing.

Proofreading

Once students have edited their paper, they proofread their work to locate possible errors that might have been overlooked in the editing process. High-powered teachers know the importance of proofreading. They know that proofreading is a unique type of reading where students very carefully and precisely read each word with a purpose to locate errors, rather than reading for meaning. During this stage students' focus on mechanics, which can be very difficult as students are accustomed to reading for meaning. High-powered teachers explain, model, and allow students to practice proofreading prior to expecting them to proofread independently.

High-powered teachers model proofreading through a variety of activities that often include sharing a piece of writing on the white board via their document camera, making copies to distribute into groups or for individuals, then demonstrate how to recognize and look for a particular type of error. They teach their students to read slowly to pronounce each word while carefully tracking with the tip of their pencil to help them maintain their focus. High-powered teachers also demonstrate how to mark when an error is located. They also incorporate editing checklists to help their students focus on particular errors. Checklists can be created and personalized based on grade-level to allow students to focus on two, five, six, or more details. For example, a first-grade checklist might consist of punctuation at the end of sentences and capital letters. Whereas, fifth-grade students might be focusing on ending punctuation, capital letters, comma usage, and run-on or incomplete sentences. High-powered teachers design and modify the checklists they provide their students with based on skills taught in the classroom. This is also a key time for teachers to scaffold and differentiate to meet the needs of their students through developing scaffold checklists.

High-powered teachers also create, model, and implement writing resources they require their students to use during the proofreading stage. Resources may include rubrics, dictionaries, and thesauri. After students have proofread their rough drafts and located as many errors as they can find, they correct the errors either independently or with their peer partners. Once students have corrected as many mechanical errors as possible, or have met their teacher for a final editing conference, the proofreading and editing stages are considered complete.

Publishing

Publishing is the final stage of writing and also one of the most exciting and satisfying stages for students. Students bring their writing to life as they write their final copy and share them with their teachers, parents, and peers. The publication process can be a powerful and motivational stage of writing as students are motivated to continue writing, and encouraged to improve the quality of their writing through the five stages of writing.

High-powered teachers require their students to publish their writing in a variety of formats. For example, they publish their writing in the form of simple booklets where students can also design and create a cover as well as write a blurb on the back cover. These booklets can simply be pages stapled together between the folds of copy paper or incorporating construction paper for the cover. Nevertheless, the results are satisfying and rewarding for the student to see their final composition complete, neat, with illustrations, and a cover that they designed and created.

High-powered teachers model how students should present their work to their peers before requiring them to present their writing to the class. They model by reading a sample of their own writing, allowing students to watch short video clips of other students presenting to the class, and through discussion of what they are expected to do during a presentation. The student reading is asked to sit in a designated chair and read their writing aloud to classmates. Classmates are given time to ask questions once the author/student has finished reading their work. High-powered teachers take this opportunity to formatively assess their students, listening and speaking skills. When students share their work in class, it promotes classroom rapport, enhances social skills, and also enhances speaking skills.

High-powered teachers implement a variety of presentation methods in their classrooms. For example, they might include formal presentations at parent–teacher night, displaying their work in a designated area in the school such as a display in the library, contributing their work to a classroom anthology, posting their work on the schools' webpage, or the classroom website, or even submitting their work to a children's literary magazine. Moreover, high-powered teachers know the benefits of students sharing their writing with others. They know that sharing work they are proud of promotes self-confidence, engagement, collaboration, academic growth, and also motivates their students to challenge themselves to grow as a writer.

Presenting the Final Product

High-powered teachers teach their students how to make final products presentable. Presentation of the final writing focuses on the appearance and making the final copy look good. Based on the format of the text that students are writing, enhancing the final product can include adding subtitles, headings, illustrations, adding a cover, charts, graphs, captions, or titles and even page numbers. Students typically work on the presentation of their final product to enhance and maintain the reader's interest and the purpose of their writing.

High-powered teachers strategically plan instructions, create activities, and opportunities for their students to practice each of the stages of writing to ensure that they are internalizing what it takes to be a good writer. They learn to recognize good writing, develop vocabulary for both verbal and written expression, and also enhance spelling, mechanics, and grammar skills. They also incorporate mini lessons with guided practice to help perfect and energize their writing, while also helping them to become confident writers in multiple genres.

Teaching Writing for English Learners

One of the most asked questions among new teachers is: how do I teach my students to write? Writing can be a very challenging task, especially for English learners. High-powered teachers set high expectations for all students including English learners in an effort to make them more fluent with English vocabulary, spelling, mechanics, and sentence structure, thus helping them to become good writers. High-powered teachers model for all of their students. They also create and plan activities so that they can be involved with the writing process daily. However, they are mindful of the increased linguistic challenges and demands often placed on English learners. They use their understanding of individual differences and diverse cultures as well as communities to ensure inclusive learning environments that enable each learner to meet high standards (InTASC Standard 2, CCSSO). High-powered teachers plan instruction and activities taking into consideration these challenges, and they teach writing accordingly.

High-powered teachers encourage students to write about topics they are familiar and comfortable with such as their family, friends, vacations, pets, or sports. They also work collaboratively with ELL students to nudge their writing along as they make advancements. This can be done through shared writing where the teacher contributes a page of writing to a story and then the ELL student writes a page. This type of collaborative activity increases the students' confidence as they are learning more about writing and the English Language rules and expectations. They also implement peer-tutoring to enhance students writing skills.

High-powered teachers collaborate with ELL students to model, and assist them in planning their writing through one-on-one conversations and also in small group conversations. During conversations they talk about what they want to write about. Collaborative conversation is also an opportunity to enhance creativity and also an opportunity for ELL students to annotate ideas or words into a word bank to use in their writing. High-powered teachers may also give ELL students a word bank of commonly used words to guide them during the writing process. Both word walls and word banks can be modified to fit the needs of all students (InTASC Standards 2, 7, 8, CCSSO). High-powered teachers create, incorporate, and allow their students use them during writing.

Reading and Writing Are Reciprocal

High-powered teachers know that reading and writing are reciprocal. They know that both reading and writing are constructive and meaning-making processes. Much research has been conducted which suggests that better readers make better writers. According to Tierney (1983) and Shanahan, integration of reading and writing improves both areas. It is also suggested through research that reading and writing involve same type of thinking and also have comparable and interchangeable activities.

Reading and writing both involve concurrent, complex transactions between the writer as a reader and the reader as a writer. High-powered teachers encourage students to purposely focus on the structure of writing when they are reading, while also annotating for new ideas. They also encourage their students to purposely focus on vocabulary words that authors use in a variety of genres to help expand their student's vocabulary, while also learning how to incorporate their newfound words in their own writing. They know that this type of reading experience enhances students writing and often leads to writing success. When teachers think of their readers as writers and their writers as readers, they are better able to create and plan purposeful activities that encourage their students to use background knowledge, set a purpose, determine importance, and also monitor and revise their own writing.

High-powered teachers integrate reading and writing activities such as asking their students to read a text and then write about it. They require students to write in their reading logs, write reports, reflect in journals, and write a story or a poem based on the newfound information. High-powered teachers know that integrating reading and writing also helps students to better understand authors' purpose as well as viewpoints. Reading and writing integration should be introduced as low as kindergarten and continued through each grade thereafter.

What Can Parents Do to Help?

Parents play a vital role in students' success in both reading and writing. They serve as a role model, a resource, and a support mechanism. Parents can encourage their child to be better readers through interactive reading, reading aloud to them, asking questions during or after reading, and also encouraging them to write and share reflective responses about their reading. Parents can help enhance their child's vocabulary by helping them with newfound words to incorporate in both verbal and written expressions. Parents can also help their child by being aware of assignments, homework, by being available to answer questions that may arise while their child is completing their homework, and finally ensuring that their child has completed their assignments in a timely manner. Positive feedback is also very important for children. Parents can serve as a mentor by giving support when needed through positive feedback and praise. For struggling readers and writers, parents can request additional support material or ideas from their child's teacher to use to help enhance their child's reading and writing (InTASC Standard 10, CCSSO).

Author's Tip

As a public school teacher of various grades, I found that, regardless the grade that I taught, the students progressed as a reader through writing experiences and grew as a writer through reading experiences. I cannot stress the impact and opportunity that teachers have to influence their student's reading and writing through read-alouds. Read-alouds provide opportunities for teachers to model fluency, expression, voice, rhythm, and also to teach word choice, pique student's curiosity, and much more.

Read-alouds are effective in all grades. Teachers can modify their approach to a read-aloud based on the age or grade of their students. With primary students implementing big books, so that students can see with ease and also to allow the teacher to point to text features and draw attention to the illustrations. However, with students who are reading independently, teachers should seek out vocabulary-rich novels or texts that students will find interesting and yet challenging. They should require their students to read along in their personal copy of the novel or text that the teacher is reading. They should also require their students to annotate with sticky notes throughout the book paying close attention to interesting quotes, rich vocabulary, character traits, and also those aha moments, which allow the reader to make personal connections to the book.

Finally, a read-aloud becomes a story that is read aloud if the teacher does not take the time to involve their students in the story. I encourage you to allow your students to become an active part of the read-alouds by allowing them to make predictions, inferences, change the ending, portray the characters, and also have grand conversations about the plot, dialogue, characters, and connections. Read-alouds enhance students' understanding of the concepts of text, allows them to get to know the characters, interact with the text, enhance their writing, and also increase their comprehension. Read-alouds provide a golden opportunity to embrace diversity, introduce new genres, bring an element of excitement into the classroom, while also instilling the love of reading in your students through a rich literature.

"Reading aloud with my students was a designated time that my students as well as myself, looked forward to every day, regardless the grade. The look of anticipation, curiosity, and their level of enthusiasm inspired me to take reading to the next level, to involve them in the story, and an elevated desire to watch them grow as readers and writers."

~ Dr. Joyce Bowling

Engaging Virtual Students in the Reading and Writing Process with Read Alouds

I truly believe the following quote, "*Reading aloud to a child opens the magic of imagination.*" I found that my time spent reading aloud to my students, regardless the grade-level or age, was a magical time for both the students and myself. Reading aloud to students motivated and inspired me as much as it did the students. It was a time that helped instill the love of reading within the students and also engage them with rich genres, new authors, exciting characters, and it was also an engaging and fun opportunity to increase their reading, and their writing skills.

Reading is a constructive process that involves the stages of **prereading, reading**, and **after reading**. High-powered teachers know that each stage of the reading process involves the reader interacting with the text they are reading or with the text that is being read orally to them. Active engagement with the text, and or with the reader, provides opportunities to establish, build, extend, and enhance student's comprehension, enhance vocabulary, and also improve fluency. High-powered teachers know the importance of interacting with the students during a read aloud at each stage of reading and strive to ensure the engagement is relevant and aligned to the standards and or objectives. They also incorporate writing in the various stages of the reading process. High-powered teachers find it effective to implement the same strategies for both in-person and virtual students. However, they know and plan according as the strategies are implemented differently, yet work as effectively.

High-powered teachers set the stage for reading during the prereading by asking students to make **predictions** about the text based on the cover, the blurb, illustrations, or previously read chapters. They work to build **anticipation** through the use of **anticipation guides**. Both strategies can be implemented in person or virtually. When working live with virtual students, the strategies are implemented the same as in person instruction. High-powered teachers may choose to record their read alouds on the district approved platform, and still others might prerecord their read alouds on their personal YouTube channel. The prerecorded recording might consist of questioning during the prereading, introduction of the anticipation guide and directions for use. High-powered teachers also model with think-alouds during the reading as well as stopping and asking questions. They also include questions after the read-aloud and ask students what their

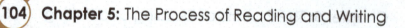

anticipation guide looks like. For example, they might ask if their anticipation guide is complete, or do they have additional questions they've written down. The teacher then asks students to record their written responses and or questions in their online journal, reading logs, and or anticipation guides and submit them electronically. High-powered teachers know that requiring student responses from various stages of the read-aloud helps them to remain accountable for their learning. Once the student's work is submitted, the teacher reads and responds with applicable feedback, and often an, **I Wonder Question**, for students to think about before the next read-aloud.

High-powered teachers know that nothing replaces live face-to-face interaction with students. However, they also know the importance of read alouds. Read alouds are grand opportunities to introduce new genres, new vocabulary, model fluency and comprehension, and also an opportunity to introduce and model diverse reading strategies through the use of think-alouds. Most importantly, high-powered teachers know that engagement is vital for meaningful read alouds, whether the read-aloud is conducted in person or virtual. High-powered teachers read to students with high expectations of interaction and engagement. They plan accordingly and expect and require all students to respond through verbal communication as well as written responses. Once the students have responded or replied, high-powered teachers ensure that students are given quality applicable feedback through verbal replies, or through written expression. High-powered teachers work tirelessly to provide a rewarding and collaborative experience through reading aloud to and with their students to ensure students have a rewarding experience that allows them to grow as readers and writers.

Now It's Your Turn

- -

You will be required to select a book, poem, article or excerpt from a novel for a read-aloud that you will present and read to the class. Online students will be required to record their read-aloud. Your book/text should align with your major and your emphasis area. The text should also be appropriate for the grade-level that you desire to teach. You will also be required to write a reflection after you've presented your read-aloud to the class, or uploaded your video. (Refer to the syllabus for specific directions, which may vary from semester to semester, detailed guidelines, and rubric that will be scored by during your read-aloud and also for specific directions for the reflection.)

Applications

- -

To help guide you through Chapter Five and upcoming chapters, become familiar with the following key terms for a deeper understanding of Chapter Five:

- ✦ Pre reading
- ✦ General knowledge
- ✦ Literary knowledge
- ✦ Prior knowledge
- ✦ Setting a purpose
- ✦ Literature circles
- ✦ Jig saw
- ✦ Reading workshop
- ✦ Book-walks

- ✦ Annotations
- ✦ Anticipation guide
- ✦ Grand conversation
- ✦ Read-aloud
- ✦ Shared reading
- ✦ Guided reading
- ✦ Partner reading
- ✦ Independent reading
- ✦ Monitored random selection
- ✦ Whisper phones
- ✦ Think-pair-share
- ✦ Exploring
- ✦ Responding
- ✦ Grand conversations
- ✦ Applying
- ✦ The writing process
- ✦ Prewriting
- ✦ Drafting
- ✦ Revising
- ✦ Editing
- ✦ Publishing

In-Seat Activity

Using the books that are provided, turn to your partner and partner read, and be able to share answers to questions about the text you read.

Reflect and Answer the Following Questions

- ✦ *What are the stages of the reading process?*
- ✦ *What are the stages of the writing process?*
- ✦ *What do students need to know to be successful writers?*
- ✦ *How is reading and writing reciprocal?*

Student Notes

Annotating is an effective learning strategy. This page is reserved for you to annotate (*take notes*) record potential questions, and also to refer back to when studying, completing assignments, and to help you gain a better understanding of Chapter Five.

Student Reflection

High-powered teachers reflect. This page is reserved for you to reflect about information that you found insightful and what you have learned from Chapter Five.

Suggested Readings

There is a wide variety of books in all genres that are great for guided reading, independent reading, and also for read-alouds that are available today. Some of the books are listed below. However, this is just a sample of the books available. As you begin to build your classroom library you will discover new books, old books, used books, and classic books that you will implement in your classroom in more ways than one. Nevertheless, never underestimate the power of a good book. Rich literature can promote and foster the love of reading within your students and help them to excel in both reading and writing. As stated earlier, your students will thank you for a well-stocked classroom library. Happy reading!

Suggested Kindergarten Books Include

Campbell, R. *Dear Zoo*. Little Simon, 2007.

Diesen, D. *The Pout-Pout Fish*. Farrar, Straus & Giroux, 2013.

Suggested Books for Primary Grades 1–3 Include

Daywait, D. *The Day the Crayons Quit*. Philomel Books, 2013.

Dicamillo, K. *The Tale of Despereaux*. Candlewick Press, 2003.

Dicamillo, K. *The Miraculous Journey of Edward Tulane*. Candlewick Press, 2009.

Suggested Books for Intermediate Grades 4 and 5 Include

L'Engle, M. *A Wrinkle in Time*. Farrar, Straus & Giroux, 2012.

Lewis, C. S. *The Lion, the Witch, and the Wardrobe*. Harper Collins, 2008.

Lowery, L. *The Giver*. Houghton Mifflin, 2011.

Sachar, L. *Holes*. Random House, 1998.

Suggested Books for Middle Grades 6–9 Include

Collins, S. *The Hunger Games*. Scholastic Press, 2008.

House, S. *A Parchment of Leaves*. Random House, 2003.

Picoult, J. *The Storyteller*. Simon & Schuster, 2013.

Zusak, M. *The Book Thief*. Random House, 2005.

Suggested Reading for the Educator

Anderson, J. *Mechanically Inclined*. Stenhouse, 2005.

Buehl, D. *Developing Readers in the Academic Disciplines*. Stenhouse, 2017.

Chapter References

Allen, J. *Yellow Brick Road: Shared and Guided Paths to Independent Reading*. Stenhouse, 2000, pp. 4–12.

Blanton, W. E., et al. "The Role of Purpose in Reading Instruction." *The Reading Teacher*, vol. 43, 1990, pp. 486–93.

Cappellini, M. *Balancing Reading and Language Learning: A Resource for Teaching English Language Learners, k-5*. Stenhouse, 2005.

Council of Chief State School Officers (CCSSO). *Interstate Teacher Assessment and Support Consortium (InTASC) Model Core Teaching Standards*, Apr. 2011, https://www.ccsso.org/sites/default/files/2017-11/InTASC_Model_Core_Teaching_Standards_2011.pdf. Accessed 7 July 2018.

Tierney, R. J. "Writer-Reader Transactions: Defining the Dimensions of Negotiation." *Essays on Theory and Practice in the Teaching of Writing*, edited by P. L. Stock, Boynton/Cook, 1983, pp. 147–51.

Chapter 6
Developing Fluency in Reading and Writing

Quote

"Children who are read to learn two things: First, that reading is worthwhile, and second, that they are worthwhile."

~ First lady, Laura Lane Welch Bush,
(Cerritos Library, First Ladies Collection)

Chapter Questions

✦ *What is fluent reading and fluent writing?*
✦ *What is the relationship between fluency and comprehension?*
✦ *How do young readers develop reading and writing fluency?*
✦ *How is reading and writing fluency assessed?*
✦ *What strategies can help develop and enhance reading and writing fluency?*

Author Reflection

As a student, I was grateful for the opportunity to observe experienced teachers as they taught reading. I enjoyed gaining valuable insight and learning strategies that would better prepare me to teach reading to my future students. I recall the confidence that I felt with my newfound knowledge of phonics and phonological awareness, I even felt confident and excited about teaching comprehension, but I was very nervous about teaching fluency. I remember watching young students struggle to read as they worked hard to decode and make sense of the text. I didn't want my students to struggle, but if they did, I wanted to be ready to help them overcome their reading struggles. I wanted all of my future students to become fluent readers and writers. I was anxious for the opportunity to observe a veteran second-grade teacher teaching reading.

I recall watching Mrs. Landon as she moved around the room with a level of excitement and enthusiasm that seemed to radiate and spill over to her second-grade students. They were attentive and seemed to hang on every word she said. All eyes were on her! I sat quietly in the back of the classroom and absorbed the positive atmosphere that consumed me and quietly took notes as I literally inhaled the excitement that hung thick in the air of the second-grade classroom. I wanted to know her secrets. How did she gain and maintain their attention in such a mesmerizing manner?

I was mesmerized as I listened to Mrs. Landon read a book about ant's homes while her students followed along in their own individual copies of the book. She explained that she had read the book the day before orally to the class as a read-aloud and that today they would track her, the reader, and then take randomly selected turns to read from their text. I loved hearing those sweet little voices read the words with confidence and with such a beautiful flow, and even the students who struggled didn't seem to feel intimidated, but rather encouraged by Mrs. Landon's prompting and cueing as a reminder to use the strategies that they had been working on. She explained that a familiar read helped build student's confidence and also helped enhance their fluency. She also stopped reading periodically to question students about the story, which seemed to pique their interests even more.

Once the students finished reading the book, they worked in small collaborative groups to examine ant farms. They turned the ant farms over and examined them closely through the glass using magnifying glasses. They worked collaboratively to think of and write down interesting and important words pertaining to the ants and their homes on a large sheet of white paper. Mrs. Landon moved quietly around the room with a checklist in hand, making periodical checks beside each student's name. She explained that the checklist was her method of informally assessing the number of words per minute her students read, how they answered questions, and also their use of vocabulary and written expressions. She also encouraged me to maintain checklists or running records of data to track my students' progress. Once the students completed their word lists, Mrs. Landon asked them to work with their peer-partner to write a specific number of sentences using words from their lists in their writing journals. She reminded them that their sentences must include an exclamatory, interrogative, declarative, and also an imperative sentence with correct punctuation.

While the students were writing, she eagerly showed me word walls displayed on the classroom walls. She explained the number of high-frequency words required for the second-grade students to learn by the year-end. She also pointed out science vocabulary words, a word wall of verbs, adjectives, and prepositions, and also a word wall of current spelling words. She stressed the importance of her students expanding their word knowledge to enhance their vocabulary, reading fluency, and also their writing fluency and how they used the word walls daily as a resource to help them achieve writing as well as reading fluencies.

She enjoyed describing the reading and writing strategies that she and her students had previously been working on. She also described the strategies they would be working on in upcoming days. She elaborated how the current strategies would prepare them for upcoming strategies and help them build the prior knowledge that they would need in upcoming weeks. She stressed the fact that the book they had worked from today was a familiar read and also stressed the importance of a familiar read. She further described how the students had completed a book-walk of the same book the day before and how they had partner read the book after she read it as a read-aloud. She explained the purpose for the repeated exposure of a familiar text and how this enhanced student's fluency and also helped build comprehension, but she explained that it was more than just exposure to the text, she described the experience as working the text.

Mrs. Landon's students were learning science content, while also enhancing fluency, gaining new vocabulary, and incorporating writing, all while having fun with ant farms. I was in awe and also inspired by the multiple methods of learning that I had witnessed all in one short hour in Mrs. Landon's reading class. I couldn't wait to return to her class and soak up even more knowledge and insight into teaching reading from such an inspiring teacher.

I returned the following day to observe students scattered about the room working in small collaborative groups. One group of students was taking turns reading independently and fluently to their peers. They were reading the same book about ants. A second group of students that Mrs. Landon was working with were also reading. However, the students that had struggled the day before with a few of the words were not struggling as much today, but were able to quickly recognize and decode the text, and continue reading. I loved the immediate feedback that Mrs. Landon provided when each child finished reading their text.

I was also intrigued as I observed the students who had read fluently the day before. They were given a collaborative challenge to complete a Venn diagram comparing and contrasting two books. They were comparing the familiar nonfiction book with a second fiction book about ants. I also enjoyed watching Mrs. Landon review the vocabulary words with all of the students. She was excited about the words and seemed to bring the content alive with motions, animation, and a thirst for learning. The students didn't just recall the words, they were required to use the words in a sentence and occasionally give a synonym for the word. They recognized the words, knew the definition of each word, and also knew how to use it in a sentence. The students were reading, writing, recalling, problem-solving, defining, exploring, learning about animals homes, incorporating English language arts, and becoming fluent readers as well.

I loved how well the students worked together in groups and how they seemed to know exactly what to do and what was expected of them with little guidance. I soaked up all of the knowledge I could while I observed both Mrs. Landon and her students. I was impressed how well the students worked together in collaborative groups and with Mrs. Landon's classroom management. A desire to teach intensified and a fire ignited within me as I imagined myself interacting with my future students much like Mrs. Landon did with her students. I would definitely remember this observation above all of the others! Great teaching is an art and Mrs. Landon was truly a great teacher! I wanted to be a teacher that set high expectations for my students, to help them gain confidence, and to inspire them to want to be successful fluent readers!

According to Lemov, one consistent finding of academic research is that high expectations are the most reliable driver of high-student achievement, even in students who do not have a history of successful achievement. It was evident in Mrs. Landon's teaching that she had high expectations for her students, and they had high expectations for themselves.

What Is Reading Fluency?

Reading fluency is the ability to read quickly, accurately, and with expression. It is made up of three components: **automaticity, speed, and prosody**. Research suggests that fluency is one of the critical building blocks of reading and is also directly linked to students' ability to comprehend what they have read. All students learn differently and at different rates. However, most students reach the stage of fluency during their second-grade year, while others will reach the stage of fluency near the end of the first grade, and still others may not read fluently until the third grade. High-powered teachers know that reading fluency is vital for students' overall academic success.

High-powered teachers strategically plan instruction to help young readers achieve reading fluency through a combination of explicit instruction and large amounts of authentic daily reading and writing opportunities. They follow InTASC Standard 7 to plan instruction that supports every student in meeting rigorous learning goals by drawing upon knowledge of content areas, curriculum, cross-disciplinary skills, and pedagogy, as well as knowledge of learners' and the community context (InTASC Standard 7, Council of Chief State School Officers [CCSSO]). They also set high expectations for their students and strive to ensure their students can read and write effortlessly and also efficiently with accuracy and can decode words automatically, while reading grade-level appropriate texts with speed, appropriate volume, and expression. High-powered teachers know that fluent readers read as they speak. They also model this level of fluency and encourage their students to read accordingly. They know that it is vital for students to achieve reading fluency as both readers and writers and be able to focus attention on meaning, rather than on decoding. They know that fluent readers are better able to comprehend what they are reading than readers whose focus and attention is primarily on decoding the text. They know that reading fluency contributes to reading comprehension and comprehension leads to reading academic success.

Assessing Student's Word Fluency

Assessing fluency is vital in understanding and planning effective fluency instruction. High-powered teachers know the importance of fluency assessment and also recognize that their classrooms will be filled with diverse reading levels. They also know that one single method of fluency instruction will not meet the diverse needs of all students. High-powered teachers informally assess their students' reading fluency prior to planning instruction. They begin assessment by assessing student's word fluency with multiple types of word automaticity assessments. High-powered teachers also understand and implement diverse methods of assessment to engage in their own growth, to monitor their students' progress, and also to guide their instructional decisions (InTASC Standard 6, CCSSO).

Assessments are made up of high-frequency words, also referred to as Fry words sight words, or Dolch words. Using the list of words and a checklist the teacher points to words on the list and waits a couple of seconds for the student to read. If the student spells the word correct the teacher checks the word on the checklist. If the student doesn't know the word or calls the word by a different name, they place an X beside the word on both the checklist and the record what the student thought the word was.

This type of informal assessment is given throughout the school year, typically biweekly. High-powered teachers manage their time wisely and assess up to five students per day until all students have been assessed and then the process begins again. Once students are assessed the data is reviewed and reflected upon and the instruction is planned, designed, and taught based on their findings. In other words, high-powered teachers use the data to drive their instruction.

Automatic Reading Also Known as Automaticity

Automaticity is a common word used in classrooms currently. It helps translate letters to sounds, and sounds to words effortlessly and accurately. While children read fluently with automaticity, they are recognizing familiar words automatically without conscious thought. However, they also recognize unfamiliar words without conscious thought with swiftness and ease. High-powered teachers know that it is vital for students to know and recognize most of the words in a text as they're reading to prevent them from reading at a slower pace due to trying to decode words.

When students achieve automaticity, they are able to recognize a large number of high-frequency words, apply phonics knowledge to decode unfamiliar words, decode new words by connecting them to familiar words, and also break larger words into syllables or chunks to decode them effectively. Students who have reached the stage of automaticity also read swiftly with **speed**. They are able to read at least 100 words per minute. However, high-powered teachers know that students speed may vary based on their purpose and or text complexity. Students who are reading with automaticity are better able to chunk words into phrases, read smoothly with few pauses, read with expression, and read at an appropriate pace that is comparable to speech.

High-powered teachers require their students to have a large inventory of words that they recognize automatically and read correctly to prevent them from analyzing every word that they encounter while reading. The conventional wisdom is that students can read a text successfully when they know at least 95% of the words; that averages 19 out to of every 20 words or 95 of every 100 words (Tompkins). However, R. L. Allington challenges this notion, suggesting that students need to know 98% or 99% of the words to be considered a fluent reader; otherwise, they're stopping too often to figure out unfamiliar words. Research has proven that repeated exposure to words through strategically planned reading and writing instruction and activities as well as experiences allows students to develop **automaticity** (Samuels).

High-powered elementary teachers are familiar with the Dolch or the **Fry high-frequency** word lists. They put more effort in teaching high-frequency words to beginning and struggling readers. High-frequency words comprise the most common words that readers use time and time again. **High-frequency words** are comprised from words which account for more than half of the words that people use to read and write. J. L. Eldredge has identified the 300 high-frequency words that make up nearly three quarters of the words people use in reading and writing. These words also account for 72% of the words that beginning readers read, with students being required to know the most common 100 words by year end of first grade, thus helping them to become automatic readers. See **Table 6.1** for a suggested list of site words for primary grades.

Table 6.1: Suggested Site Words for Primary

A	Am	An	And	Away	About
At	Ate	Fat	Fate	Hat	Hate
As	Ask	Asked	Asks	Asking	Ax
About	After	Again	All	Along	Always
Animal	Another	Above	Again	Ant	Aunt
Be	Bee	Been	Before	Behind	Because

(Continued)

Ball	Baby	Bear	Began	Beside	Bead
Bed	Bull	Bottom	Bet	Better	Bird
Blue	Blew	Boy	But	By	Brown
Beautiful	Bring	Brought	Borrow	Burrow	Beauty
Call	Called	Calling	Came	Come	Can't
Can	Coin	Circus	Cent	City	Child
Children	Could	Couldn't	Cry	Cried	Crying
Dark	Day	Do	Door	Did	Didn't
Doing	Down	Done	Dew	Doubt	Debt
Eat	End	Each	Ever	Every	Even
Everyone	Eye	Everything	Easy	Egg	Except
Fat	Fast	Father	Feather	Friend	Find
Found	Fine	Fly	For	First	From
Garden	Girl	Get	Gave	Go	Going
Got	Good	Give	Great	Green	Grow
Has	Had	His	He	Head	Hear
Her	Him	Have	Happy	How	Hello
House	Hope	Hill	Help	Heat	Hang
I	I'll	In	Inside	Into	Is
Isn't	I'm	If	It	It's	Its
Ice	Icing	Include	Ill	I've	Instill
Jump	Jumping	Jumped	Jumps	Joke	Juice
Joy	Join	Jingle	Juggle	Jog	Jogging
Keep	Key	Kept	King	Know	Knew
Knot	Keys	Kind	Kiss	Knowing	Keeper
Last	Left	Let	Let's	Letting	Like
Likely	Little	Live	Long	Look	Looking
looked	Loud	Loudest	Lone	Lure	Ladder
Love	Loop	Liked	Lasting	Lonely	Late
Mad	Made	Man	Many	May	Maybe

Me	Meet	Meat	Mean	Mom	More
Morning	Mother	Much	My	Must	Might
Name	Number	Need	Never	New	Next
Nice	Night	No	Not	Note	Nothing
Now	Nod	Nickle	Nap	Napping	Neat
Of	Off	Often	On	One	Once
Oh	Old	Only	Or	Other	Our
Out	Over	Oil	Owl	Outside	Odd
Pig	Put	Pull	Pulled	Picture	Place
People	Picture	Pitcher	Play	Playing	Pout
Pain	Person	Purse	Palace	Pretty	Pound
Ran	Rain	Rat	Rabbit	Run	Red
Read	Ride	Right	Road	Room	Rear
Rule	Row	Rise	Raise	Rich	Riddle
Sat	Saw	Say	She	Show	Said
Show	Sister	Sky	Sleep	Small	So
Some	Something	Soon	Start	Started	Stay
Still	Stop	Story	Stories	Sun	Soak
Take	Tell	Took	Than	That	That's
The	Their	Them	Then	There	These
They	Thing	Things	Thin	Think	This
Thought	Three	Through	Threw	Time	To
Too	Two	Together	Toad	Told	Took
Top	Tree	Three	Truck	Trunk	Try
Up	Us	Under	Until	Unless	Upward
Very	Vast	Victory	Vote	Vow	Vice
We	Was	Wait	Walk	Walked	Want
Wanted	Water	Way	Well	We'll	Went
When	Where	While	Who	Why	Will
Wind	Witch	With	Wizard	Woman	Write
Word	Work	Would	Wouldn't	Write	Wrong
Yes	You	Your	Yours	You're	Yesterday

However, the full list of Fry words extends to over 1,000 words, first published in 1957 and revised in 1980. Fry compiled his list from the American Heritage list, which ranks the frequency of words taken from materials used in grades 3–9. Fry's words also include all parts of speech and are listed by frequency (Readsters, LLC). Edward Fry was born in 1925 and died in 2010. He wrote extensively about how to teach reading. His books focused on what became known as the Fry words. He covered topics such as reading, vocabulary, and assessment. Dr. Fry was a professor at Rutgers University in New Jersey for more than 20 years (Rutgers' Faculty and Staff Bulletin). He believed that children could learn to read by having them learn the Fry 1,000 instant words in their frequency, in other words, the words that were most commonly used in each grade-level. He also encouraged teaching phonics, incorporating a wide variety of rich children's literature all while incorporating words from the Fry list (Readsters, LLC).

High-powered teachers know their students, their reading levels, as well as their learning styles. Based on this knowledge, they create their own vocabulary and site word lists, as well as modify suggested site word lists to scaffold and also ensure that that they are meeting the needs of all of their students. High-powered teachers are also planners (InTASC Standard 7, CCSSO). They pre-read material and resources that they will implement into their instruction, lesson, activities, and assignments that students will be required to read and complete. They create word lists to accommodate their instructional material modifying suggested word lists and adding any necessary word(s) to their lists to match chapters, books, or units of reading material. These words are pre-taught, used as vocabulary words, and also used to enhance students' reading fluency, comprehension, and provide them with a greater understanding of the material. **Table 6.2**, contains grade-level suggested oral reading rates that high-powered teachers use to determine whether students are reading at the suggested oral reading rate.

Table 6.2: Suggested Oral Reading Rates

Grade Level (by year-end)	Oral Reading Rate (words per minute)
1st	80–120
2nd	135–145
3rd	150–165
4th	170–175
5th	180–195
6th	200–220
7th–8th	225–230

High-powered teachers know that high-frequency words can be difficult for their students to learn because the words cannot always be decoded easily, and are often learned by sight and repetition. High-frequency words are also considered function words or connecting words, simply meaning that the words do not have much meaning. For example, primary students do not have as much difficulty recognizing the word, *elf*, than they do recognizing the word, *of*. Why? Because students can make visual connections and meaning of the word *elf* and can also decode the word with ease, whereas the word *of* cannot be decoded phonetically and students can't make a visual or meaningful connection with the word; they simply have to know the word. Students will also be required to use the word *of* more frequently; therefore, they must learn to read it, spell it, and include it in their writing.

High-powered teachers teach high-frequency words through explicit and standard-based instruction. Just as Mrs. Landon did in the author's reflection, they introduce five to six words each week. High-powered teachers also involve their students in a variety of daily activities, just as Mrs. Landon did. They carefully select words from the district approved list of high-frequency words that match or coincide and make connections to the content that they are teaching. High-powered teachers also create, incorporate, and interact with word walls that contain high-frequency words, content-specific words, and spelling and vocabulary words. High-powered teachers are also strategic planners. They plan and create the word walls that they plan to incorporate in their instruction prior to the school year beginning. However, they don't leave those prepared word walls idle or dormant. They continually add new words to the word walls throughout the year as their students master the words.

High-powered teachers also use the chant and clap procedure to practice reading and spelling words that are being placed on the word walls.

1. ***See the word and hear the word***: *Teachers point to a new word on the high-frequency word wall and slowly pronounce the word while their students observe.*
2. ***I say you say***: *Teacher repeats the word and points to the students to pronounce word as the teacher points at the word.*
3. ***Say Spell say the word***: *Both teachers and students say the word, spell the word aloud while clapping as the say each letter, and then say the word again. This can be repeated in stages while looking at the words and gradually looking away to spell the word. Teacher and students repeat the word as necessary.*
4. ***Write the word and check the word***: *Students write the word on a whiteboard or in their journals, making sure to check their spelling against the word wall for accuracy.*
5. ***Say the word again***: *Students repeat the words as the teacher points to the word.*

Identifying Words Strategically

High-powered teachers teach their students to use word-identification strategies to decode unfamiliar words. These strategies include the following; ***phonic analysis, decoding by analogy***, ***syllabic analysis***, and ***morphemic analysis***. They know that beginning readers depend on phonics to sound out unfamiliar words. High-powered teachers also know that students gradually learn to decode words by analogy and to use syllabic and morphemic analysis effectively.

When using phonic analysis, students apply their knowledge of phoneme–grapheme connections, phonics, phonics rules, and also using spelling patterns to read and write. Students using decoding by analogy use their knowledge of phonograms to deduce the pronunciation or spelling of unfamiliar words.

While syllabic analysis allows students to break a multi-syllable word into smaller parts, such as syllables, and then apply their knowledge of phonics to decode the word, syllable by syllable. Syllabic analysis allows students to chunk words, which is a strategy that high-powered teachers find beneficial with beginning readers. High-powered teachers teach their students syllabication rules which are as follows:

✦ When two consonants come between two vowels in a word, divide the syllables between the consonants. Examples include **day-light**, **win-dow**, and **soc-cer**.

✦ When more than two consonants come together in a word, divide the syllables keeping the blends together. Examples include **ex-tend**, **ex-plore**, and **pre-tend**.

✦ When one consonant comes between two vowels in a word, divide the syllables after the first vowel. Examples include **do-nut, fo-cus**, and **bo-nus**.

✦ If the previous rule doesn't apply, make a recognizable word, divide the syllables after the consonant that comes between the vowels. Examples include **ech-o, tap-er**, and **do-zen**.

✦ When two vowels together don't represent a long vowel sound or a dipthong, divide the syllables between the vowels. Examples include **po-em**, **qui-et**, and **po-et**.

Finally, morphemic analysis allows students to use their knowledge of root words and affixes to read or write an unfamiliar word.

High-powered teachers ensure that their students are practicing these strategies through participating in guided-reading activities, during reading workshops, in other content areas, and also while independently reading. They choose a strategy to focus on depending on their student's knowledge about the words as well as the complexity of the unfamiliar words. If their students struggle with using the strategy, high-powered teachers reteach the strategies through modeling the strategies demonstrating the use of the strategy, and also using the strategy of a think-aloud pertaining to the strategy that students are struggling with. High-powered teachers understands the central concepts, tools of inquiry, and structures of the reading fluency, thus creating learning experiences that make the aspects of reading fluency accessible and also meaningful for learners to assure mastery of the content (InTASC Standard 4, CCSSO).

How Can The Teacher Help Students Learn Unfamiliar Words?

The lists of sight-words required for the students to learn each year can be overwhelming to a new teacher. The overwhelming list may appear to be a daunting task for the unprepared teacher. However, high-powered teachers ensure students' success through formative assessment that helps them to know their students and to determine the words that they already know. They also make a strategic plan for explicit instruction and creative engaging activities that appeal to all learners and learning style.

High-powered teachers also assess themselves to ensure that they are doing everything possible to give their students' academic advantages, academic challenges, and also engaging them with multiple opportunities to learn. They may assess themselves through a visible checklist. In other words, they ask themselves questions about their own instruction to ensure they are meeting the needs of all of their students. High-powered teachers use the following questions to self-assess:

✦ *Have I informatively assessed all students?*
✦ *Do I have word walls posted that are visible to all students?*
✦ *Am I interacting with my students via the word walls?*
✦ *Am I incorporating high-frequency words in spelling, reading, and writing?*

✦ *Do I require students to practice incorporating high-frequency words in their writing?*
✦ *Do I pre-teach key words or vocabulary words prior to the reading or writing assignments?*
✦ *Do I teach word-identification strategies and model how to use the strategies?*
✦ *Do I implement mini-lessons to help my students gain a deeper understanding?*
✦ *Do I set mini-goals for my students?*
✦ *Am I reassessing students periodically?*

Reading Speed

High-powered teachers know that it is vital for students to develop and achieve an adequate reading speed or rate to be able to focus on meaning. In other words, to be able to understand what they are reading, they need to read without constant interruptions due to decoding words. Oral reading rate, when it assesses fluent reading, is a measure of word recognition automaticity. High-powered teachers know that fluency is also an indicator of potential reading volume and a predictor of comprehension. Appropriate oral reading rates may vary slightly with different reading programs.

Researchers have identified suggested reading speeds for each grade-level. **Table 6.2** provides suggested oral reading rates. However, high-powered teachers know that there are many underlying factors that can affect students' reading speed. There are a number of factors that could affect students reading speed in a positive aspect, but that can also affect their reading speed in a negative manner. Some factors that may include

✦ *Background knowledge. Some students will have background knowledge that will allow them to read at a swifter rate, while other students may lack background knowledge.*
✦ *English-speaking students have an advantage over ELL students.*
✦ *Students who receive parental assistance will read at a faster rate than students who do not receive any assistance outside the classroom.*
✦ *Students who have received direct and explicit reading instruction and guidance will read at a faster rate than students who have not received explicit reading instruction and guidance.*

High-powered teachers know that with strategic practice, their students learn to use speed through gained confidence and also through knowledge of reading strategies. Through daily modeling, guided reading, and strategic practice students have multiple opportunities to develop reading speed and also develop stamina. To help increase volume, stamina, and speed high-powered teachers plan strategic and engaging activities and opportunities that include a combination of teacher-guided as well as independent reading practices. Some of the reading strategies include

✦ **Guided reading**: High-powered teachers work with students in both small and whole groups to allow students to practice strategies independently, set a purpose for reading, introduce vocabulary, make predictions, and also to read orally independently, and with small groups.
✦ **Choral reading** allows students to read together orally. Choral reading also provides less skilled readers opportunities to practice and receive support prior to being required to read independently. It also provides a model for fluent reading and has also been proven to improve the recognition of sight words.
✦ **Partner reading**: High-powered teachers also partner fluent readers with a student who is less fluent to allow them to read and also reread together. Rereading a familiar

text allows students to gain confidence while also giving them an opportunity to gain reading speed.

✦ **Reader's Theater**: High-powered teachers incorporate Reader's Theater to enhance students' interest, motivation, and also to increase reading fluency. Reader's Theater allows students to read a familiar read as the script for the activity/strategy is typically implemented after the initial reading. Students have multiple opportunities to read the text during each practice session. (*Directions for Reader's Theater is provided at the end of this chapter.*)

To develop students' fluency high-powered teachers know that students' books must be appropriate in reading level. Books should be based on student's interest with 98%–99% reading accuracy. Once a student becomes a fluent reader, high-powered teachers plan more opportunities that allow the student to practice reading independently daily. They know that daily practice will increase stamina. Daily opportunities for independent reading should be carefully planned to allow an increase in reading time each day. For example, depending on the age of the student they may be required to read 10 minutes every day for a week, and read 15 minutes independently every day for the next week, and 20 minutes every day for the next week, with an increase weekly to achieve the goal of 30 minutes of independent reading. High-powered teachers know the importance of stamina and how students gradually increase stamina through daily practice. Reading stamina is much like physical stamina. Both take repeated daily practice with gradual increase of endurance.

Prosody

High-powered teachers model prosody to their students by reading expressively, and use their voice to add meaning to the words as they read to their students. They model prosody for their students to allow them to hear the correct components of prosody. The components of prosody are *expression, phrasing, volume, smoothness, and pacing*.

When a high-powered teachers model **expression** they are adding an element of enthusiasm, while also varying their expression to match their interpretation of the text. **Phrasing** is also referred to as *chunking* words, which is chunking words into phrases while reading and also applying stress and intonation correctly. High-powered teachers also model **volume** when reading aloud to their students. Volume is modeled by varying the loudness of their voice to add meaning to the text. They also read with a **smooth** flow. They model smoothness through reading with rhythm and also self-correcting when necessary. **Pacing** is also very important to fluency. High-powered teachers also model pacing by reading at the speed of conversation.

High-powered teachers model the components of prosody through **think-alouds** in effort to increase their students use of prosody while reading orally and also reading independently. During the think-aloud they are stopping to talk about and discuss the importance of prosody for fluency and also for comprehension with their students. They emphasize how meaning can be affected when reading in a monotone voice and also how it slows down their speed. High-powered teachers demonstrate this through reading orally in a monotone voice and then reading orally in an expressive voice. They ask their students which read-aloud they enjoyed the most and why. Prosody components also play a vital role during silent reading as well. Every reader has an internal voice as they read. If a student's internal voice doesn't demonstrate the components of prosody their comprehension can be negatively impacted.

Assessing Student's Oral Reading Fluency

Assessing student's oral reading fluency has often been focused on how quickly students could read a given text. This is referred to as **reading rate** or **reading speed.** The term words correct per minute has become more prevalent in schools today. High-powered teachers observe and assess reading rate, reading speed, and also give much attention to the number of words they read correct per minute (*wcpm*) to indicate the reading rate. To adequately assess fluency, high-powered teachers incorporate the following four components of assessment *accurate decoding of text*, *reading rate or speed*, *use of volume*, and *phrasing*.

Time management is one of the biggest fears and the largest growth areas that new teachers experience. It can appear to be a daunting task to formatively assess thirty or more students. However, high-powered teachers manage their assessment time well. They informally monitor student's reading by listening and assessing three to five students' reading fluency daily. High-powered teachers incorporate a checklist or a running record into their daily toolbox. As their students gain practice reading orally every day they assess them by listening for volume, accurate decoding, speed, and also phrasing.

High-powered teachers informally assess with the use of the running record during whole-group, guided reading, reading workshops, or in small group instruction, while the other students are tracking the reader silently. This type of formative assessment doesn't interfere with instructional time or learning time. The running record and the checklist help teachers to collect data used as evidences of their students' reading growth over time. High-powered teachers also use this assessment to make instructional decisions and allow it to drive their instruction. Refer **Table 6.2** for suggested oral reading rate.

Teaching Reading Fluency

High-powered teachers know that accuracy is a fundamental component of fluency. When working with beginning readers they focus significantly on the amount of instruction time on basic word recognition and also on word analysis skills. High-powered teachers are effective teachers that also plan strategic instruction that systematically presents daily opportunities for their students to learn new words, while also establishing opportunities to practice and use words in diverse content. Learning words, their meaning, and their use is a first step in becoming a skillfully motivated reader.

High-powered teachers also know that pushing students to read faster too soon can cause some students to begin guessing words, which decreases their focus on reading for meaning. High-powered teachers model fluent reading, demonstrating reading at a reasonable rate with good phrasing, intonation, and expression. High-powered teachers also plan opportunities for their students to reread familiar texts and encourage them to make their reading sound the way they talk in normal conversation. They plan reading instruction and activities that include read-alouds, choral reading, close reading, partner reading, guided reading, and also independent reading. High-powered teachers listen and also assess their students' oral reading every day. They set high expectations, plan systematic instruction, daily opportunities to read orally, informally assess their students often, analyze data, involve parents, and also provide their students with timely and meaningful feedback.

Teacher Quote

I found the use of a simple running record to be very beneficial. I used a running record to informally assess primary student's word fluency and reading fluency. I also used a running record to informally assess intermediate student's word knowledge, grammar, and reading fluency. The data that I collected proved to be beneficial for my instructional decisions, planning, intervention decisions, as well as ARC meetings.

~ Dr. Joyce Bowling

What Is Writing Fluency?

Fluent writing flows smoothly from word to word, phrase to phrase, and from sentence to sentence. Fluent writers spell words automatically and are able to write quickly while focusing and developing ideas. Their writing is focused and flows with little effort. High-powered teachers know that fluent writing is vital for writers just as fluency is vital for reading. Fluent writing is based on three components *automaticity*, *speed*, and *voice*.

+ **Writing automaticity** is defined as writers that automatically write most words accurately, without stopping and thinking about how to spell them.
+ **Writing speed** is defined as writers that are able to write swift enough to maintain pace with their thoughts.
+ **Writer's voice** is defined as writers develop distinctive voices that reflect their individuality (Spandel). Voice is also similar to prosody. Voice creates tone and emotional feelings of a piece of writing. Writers develop their voice through words they select and how they organize and structure them within their sentences.

Automatic Writing

High-powered teachers help students become fluent writers through strategically implementing writing in stages. They know that students must first accomplish automaticity writing. To become fluent writers, students need to be able to spell most high-frequency words automatically while also applying spelling strategies and including other words. High-powered teachers teach their students to write high-frequency words much like they teach their students to read them.

High-powered teachers gradually introduce five to seven new words each week and provide multiple opportunities to revisit the words, while also requiring them to practice reading and writing them in diverse activities. These activities can include requiring students to write the words in sentences, using manipulatives to spell the words correctly, asking students to share a sentence orally using one or more words, and also engaging students in interactive writing activities.

Interactive writing can be completed through implementing a morning message for them to complete, journal writing, and also peer-partner writing. High-powered teachers increase the length of writing assignments gradually in carefully planned stages based on their progress in effort to help increase student's writing stamina. Writing stamina can be increased similar to the methods used to increase reading stamina. For example, teachers may require primary students to write one sentence every day incorporating high-frequency words, the next week asking students to write two sentences, and the third week three, and so on, with the goal being a paragraph. Time allotted will depend on the grade-level and also students' individual needs.

Writing Speed

When students become fluent writers they are able to get their ideas on paper quickly, incorporating correct spelling automatically for most words while also using legible handwriting without much forethought about how to form letters. High-powered teachers help young writers and guide them by correcting their work, making them feel comfortable, and gaining confidence in their writing ability in effort to help them write smoothly, neatly, precisely, and accurately. They also know the challenges that left-handed students face when writing. They model how left-handed students should tilt their paper to the right to help them write more comfortably. They also encourage their left-handed students to slant their letters in the direction that provides them the most comfort. High-powered teachers know for both left-handed and right-handed students to write quickly and fluently they need to be comfortable and not distracted.

High-powered teachers also know students develop writing speed through required daily writing practice. They also require their students to write periodically throughout the day. Their students are required to write in all content areas as well as specifically designed writing assignments that vary with grade-levels. High-powered teachers in the primary often incorporate a morning message, which requires students to copy from the board and complete unfinished sentences, or complete a story starter. They also incorporate writing through requiring them to write sentences with spelling words and incorporating high-frequency words in sentences. They also engage students in interactive writing by asking them to write on the whiteboard, smart board, class charts, and shared writing journals. They encourage their students to visit writing centers periodically in their class to complete writing assignments and self-assess their writing using a posted rubric or checklist. High-powered teachers also require their students to write in reflective journals daily.

High-powered teachers understand that students learn differently at different levels. Students who struggle with forming letters are given more strategic practice that allows them to practice forming letters with white boards, wide ruled paper, or tracing broken letters to become more proficient with legibility. All students are encouraged to use the resources around them when in doubt of the spelling of a word, or choosing an appropriate word. High-powered teachers encourage their students to use the displayed word walls, dictionaries, and thesauri for older students. High-powered teachers also require their students to write in all content areas, at different times during the course of a school day, and also in diverse settings to ensure that they are receiving adequate writing practice and also to help enhance students writing stamina, thus increasing their writing speed.

High-powered teachers work with students to attain sentence fluency. Once they've achieved sentence fluency they begin extending their writing requirements to paragraphs and eventually their paragraphs become a complete composition. They also encourage their students to read their work orally for smoothness to ensure that their writing flows smoothly.

Writer's Voice

Writer's voice reflects the person who is doing the writing. When a writer achieves their writer's voice their writing sounds natural and not forced. As students gain experience as readers and writers, their voice becomes more prevalent. High-powered teachers carefully plan and create assignments that allow students to write about a topic they are interested in. Through creative writing experiences high-powered teachers implement a variety of diverse writing strategies to encourage their students to develop a deep understanding of the topic or subject of their writing, to make connections, build skills, and also apply knowledge in meaningful ways within their composition (InTASC, Standard 8, CCSSO). They know that when students write about something that inspires them, or a topic that they are passionate about, their writing flows without being forced, thus allowing their voice to emerge.

High-powered teachers know that as their students begin to develop their writer's voice, they learn to vary their tone based on the writing assignment. For example, students who have developed their writer's voice write with the appropriate tone which is reflected in their writing, whether they are writing to entertain, persuade, argue, or inform the reader. They understand that some types of writing requires a more formal tone than others. High-powered teachers help students to better understand diverse styles of writing through reading orally from a wide-variety of genres, the use of think-alouds, class discussions, modeling various types of writing, and also through requiring their students to practice writing in different formats, genres, and about different topics.

High-powered teachers also preteach the vocabulary that they would like their students to incorporate in their writing. For example, if the writing assignment requires their students to write a persuasive letter, they preteach them words that enhances their writing purpose to persuade, words that allows their writing to flow smoothly, while also making the purpose of the composition evident to the reader.

Assessing Writing Fluency

High-powered teachers know the importance of assessment. They observe their students writing fluency as their students are writing and then examine their finished composition. They consider the following questions:

- Is the student spelling most words automatically?
- Does the student write quickly enough to complete the assignment?
- Is the student's writing legible?
- Did the student write easily, or did they write laboriously complaining that their hands hurt?

High-powered teachers use these questions to help them determine if students are fluent writers. If their observation suggests that a student is struggling, they assist the student and provide them with ideas, writing strategies, and one-on-one instruction in effort to help them become fluent writers. If the student continues to struggle with writing they may conduct additional testing to diagnose written expression and fluency problems.

High-powered teachers assess their students for automaticity, which is their ability to spell high-frequency words and use strategies to spell other words on spelling tests and also by frequently examining their writing. They assess their students writing fluency by timing their students as they are writing an assigned task about a familiar topic. The time is determined based on the age and grade-level of the student. For example, students may be asked to write for 5 minutes about a familiar topic. After 5 minutes, the teacher will count the number of words they've written and divide that by the number of minutes they were given to determine the number of words written per minute. High-powered teachers assess student's ability to write with a writer's voice by reading and rereading several of the student's compositions to evaluate the student's tone and style.

At this time commercial tests aren't available to formally assess students' writing fluency. However, high-powered teachers know that consistent informal assessments are beneficial in determining writers with fluency problems. They know that good instruction requires that they continually assess the needs and skills of their students, plan and modify their instruction based on their students' needs in effort to meet the diverse needs of all of their students. High-powered teachers also know that reading and writing fluencies go hand-in-hand. They know that the more their students read, the sooner they'll reach writing fluency, the more students write, the sooner they become fluent readers.

Spelling and Fluency

High-powered teachers may also incorporate high-frequency words in their weekly spelling words. This can be completed through word families. High-powered primary teachers know that spelling is best learned when students are required to spell words that formulate a pattern. When students can visibly see a familiar word within a word, or extend a word by adding a prefix, suffix, or affix they are able to spell more accurately and formulate new words. For example, if a student can spell the word *out*, they can quickly learn to spell the words *shout, shouting, about, spout*, or *spouting* as well as many other words that contain the small word, *out*. High-powered teachers also integrate spelling, reading, and writing through carefully planned instructions to help students become fluent spellers.

Teaching Writing Fluency

High-powered teachers know that writing is a fundamental part of life. They also know that it is vital for their students to develop an early foundation in writing in order to effectively and efficiently communicate their ideas. High-powered teachers know that students who develop strong writing skills at an early age are equipped with a valuable tool for learning, for communication, and self-expression. These skills can be developed through carefully planned strategic writing instruction, activities, and also when students are given sufficient opportunities and time for daily writing. They also know that students learn by doing, therefore they provide them with multiple daily opportunities to learn and practice writing skills, strategies, and techniques. High-powered teachers integrate writing into their instructions in other content areas such as science, social studies, and math to provide students additional time and opportunities to write.

High-powered teachers provide adequate time for their students to write to allow them time to practice and gain confidence in their ability to write while also applying the writing process for a variety of purposes. Regardless the age, students need time to think about their purpose for writing. They need time to plan what they want to say and how they want to say it. High-powered teachers help students to think critically about their writing. They focus their writing instruction on teaching students the writing process and how to use it effectively. They model how to brainstorm quickly, complete a graphic organizer to organize their thoughts, and recall prior knowledge before they begin drafting their composition. High-powered teachers who teach very young primary students teach their students how to hold their pencil correctly and how to form letters fluently and efficiently. They teach them to spell words correctly and construct sentences for fluency, meaning, and style. Teachers who teach older students focus on writing strategies for the various components of the writing process and gradually release writing responsibilities from themselves to their students. High-powered teachers teach their students to understand and use different purposes for writing and help them to understand the concept of their audience. They teach students different techniques for writing effectively for different purposes through modeling, allowing them time to practice, and also encouraging them to share their writing.

Regardless the age, high-powered teachers know that timing students writing will help increase their writing stamina and fluency. Primary teachers may set a timer to help students stay on task and focused during their daily writing of the morning message, while older students may be timed daily after being given on-demand writing scenarios and an assigned task to complete. High-powered teachers know that students gain writing fluency through daily opportunities to practice writing.

Language Link

High-powered teachers use (DOL's daily oral language) to help students better understand the correct use of grammar in their writing. They implement daily oral language as bell ringers, in lessons, and also as exit slips. They also incorporate the parts of speech and encourage proper use of mechanics in daily instructions, daily reading, and daily writing. High-powered teachers use read-alouds and think-alouds to help their students gain insight and understanding of a particular part of speech or punctuation that they are currently working on. They also revisit previously learned content periodically by integrating, embedding, and building on previous learned content with new instruction to help students retain what they have previously learned and also gain a deeper understanding of the use of punctuation and grammar.

High-powered teachers may ask students to raise a hand or a cue card when they hear a noun, adjective, or verb. They may also ask their students to highlight prepositions in their text, and also ask students to complete word sorts to categorize various parts of speech that they are studying or have studied. High-powered teachers also require their students to include diverse parts of speech in their daily writing. Instruction and assignments will vary depending on the grade-level, age, and required standards. They also know that knowledge of the eight parts of speech and mechanics directly affects reading and writing fluency. Moreover, high-powered teachers incorporate grammar and mechanics daily in both reading and writing to ensure that their students are making steady growth and progress. They know that students who are avid readers also better understand grammar and use of correct punctuation.

What Can Parents Do to Help?

High-powered teachers know the importance of connecting fluency practice at school to the home. They have found that asking parents to incorporate closed-caption television has been an effective tool for improving students' reading fluency. This technique can also be fun, yet challenging for students and can also accommodate parent's busy schedules. **Closed-caption television** uses written subtitles and provides students with meaningful and motivating reading material. Parents can monitor and carefully select what television programs to incorporate closed-caption for their children.

Parents can also record television programs with closed-captions for their children to read, which also allows them to rewind for multiple viewings if necessary. Parents can also become involved by stopping the recorded program and asking their child to make a prediction as well. Closed-caption can also be used with and without audio. This allows very young students to read with the audio and can be muted as children become fluent readers. This type of fluency practice also stimulates multiple senses as children view the drama, hear the sound, and see the captions.

As always, high-powered teachers encourage parents to read with their children for at least 20 minutes each day modeling fluent and expressive reading. They also encourage parents to listen to their children read orally in some manner whether from teacher suggested texts, library books, or a favorite book they have at home. Writing with students is also encouraged and can vary in length depending on the age of the child. For young children writing can be made fun with magnets, soap crayons, white boards, and paper and pencil. Nevertheless, students whose parents take 20 minutes each night to read and write with them will gain much needed fluency practice that spills over into their daily work at school.

Virtual Strategies for Developing Fluency in Reading and Writing

High-powered teachers know the importance of reading fluency. They know that reading fluency is the ability to read quickly, accurately, and with expression. It is made up of three components: **automaticity, speed, and prosody.** They also know that research shows that fluency is a critical building block of reading and also has a direct link to reading comprehension. High-powered teachers strategically plan instruction to help young readers achieve reading fluency through a combination of explicit instruction and daily opportunities to practice reading. They know that virtual learning can look different than in-person learning, but also that it can be a rewarding experience for both the students and for the teacher. High-powered teachers plan their instruction accordingly.

High-powered teachers strive to provide both in-person and virtual students with the tools that can ensure reading fluency success. They introduce new applications of software that can be used at home as a study tool, inside the classroom, and also used by the virtual student to respond. Many elementary teachers across the nation are implementing resources such as **Flipgrid, Quizlet**, and also the use of **Zoom,** which has become popular across the world due to the growing demand of virtual meetings. With each of the abovementioned applications, teachers and students are able to **communicate, respond, reply**, and also to **assess**, all of which are vital for student's academic growth.

High-powered teachers know that good instruction comes from precise and planned assessment. They know that assessing fluency is vital to plan effective fluency instruction. They realize that both their in-person and virtual classes will be filled with diverse learners that require precise instruction that targets each student. High-powered teachers assess their virtual students the same as they would in-person students. They administer informal assessments through the use of running records, anecdotal notes, and through observations. High-powered teachers know the importance and also the connection of knowledge of high-frequency words and fluency.

They strive to provide time to work with in-seat and virtual students in a one-on-one setting to assess the student's knowledge of high-frequency words. For virtual students, this might consist of 20 minutes where the student quickly says the high-frequency word as the teacher points to them. Most districts have approved software that provides the opportunity to work face to face in one-on-one online settings with students. If the entire class is virtual, this will take careful and precision scheduling from the teacher. If only a few students are working virtually, while the remainder of the students are in-person, high-powered teachers may choose to work while the other students work independently or when the class is in the library, or the computer lab. Nevertheless, high-powered teachers create and maintain a schedule to provide the same quality instruction and assessment for all students.

High-powered teachers know the importance of interacting with their students, as well as the importance of consistency. Many district approved platforms have the capability of allowing face-to-face interaction as does the software application of Zoom. High-powered teachers do not rely on occasional meetings and interaction with their students, but rather they work to maintain a consistent schedule of times that they meet with each virtual student to ensure the students are receiving effective instruction, having the opportunity to communicate verbally, time for assessment, and also time to respond. High-powered teachers provide guided reading through virtual learning, as well as choral reading, and also partner read with students, or have students partner read with each other to mimic in-person reading strategies.

High-powered teachers also teach writing fluency virtually by implementing the same instruction, and also the same strategies. They know the key to virtual learning is to keep students engaged, and also strategically plan assignments that will help students be accountable for their work. They strive to ensure students become fluent writers through strategically implemented writing at various stages of the reading and writing process. High-powered teachers know that reading and writing are reciprocal, and therefore teach reading and writing together. They know that reading increases writing skills, and writing increases reading skills.

High-powered teachers require virtual students to complete the interactive morning message, work with the word of the day, and respond via written response just as they do in-person students. They know that through consistent and precise instruction, modeling, and required responses that students have the multiple opportunities to grow as fluent readers and fluent writers. High-powered teachers also respond accordingly with applicable feedback for all written responses, and also verbal responses. They conduct spelling tests orally to ensure virtual students are studying, and may ask parents to recite the word, and require their child to spell the word, and finally high-powered teachers may use software that allows the student to practice spelling words and also take virtual spelling tests online. **Spellingcity.com** is a favorite among many elementary teachers. This website allows students to manipulate words, study words, play games, and also take spelling tests. This is a great website to help prepare both in-person and virtual students for site word assessments, automaticity, help increase phonics skills, and also spelling skills. High-powered teachers strategically and diligently work to create, locate, and incorporate strategically planned instruction, intense modeling, rigor, and applicable software that engages their students and helps them to be successful and fluent readers and writers.

Now It's Your Turn

For this assignment you will be randomly placed with a peer who is seeking the same degree and emphasis area that you are in. You will be required to collaborate with your peer to create an engaging activity that includes both reading and writing. The activity should promote both reading and writing fluency. Your activity should include an age or grade-level-appropriate children's book. Your activity should describe how you, the teacher, plan to informally monitor students' reading and writing fluency. The activity should be planned for small group instructions of no more than six students. You may decide if the group of students are at-level, below-level, or above-level. You may also decide if the students are individualized education program (IEP) students or if the group includes an IEP student. Keep in mind that this assignment is a collaborative effort and will require some planning from both students. I encourage you to work outside of class time.

You will also be required to present your activity to the class. (See the syllabus for dates.) Your presentation must be no less than 5 minutes and no more than 7 minutes in length and both students should participate in the presentation. You will be required to bring the book and all documentation that your activity includes the day your team presents. For example, if you plan to informally assess your students with a running record, you would need to bring copies of the running record. Copies should include one for each of your peers. You will also need to bring a bulleted outline of the activity for each peer as well. Your peers will assess your activity and presentation. They will then give me their assessments and I will forward them to you after I review them. Each member of the team will be required to submit documentation used in the presentation and the bulleted outline in the appropriate drop box as well as a five paragraph reflection about your collaboration experience, the activity, and your aspirations for the activity. You will be required to identify your areas of strength as well as areas of growth. This should be submitted prior to the presentation date. Online students will work collaboratively and present their work in the form of a power point that will be presented in class. See syllabus for details.

Author's Tip

As previously mentioned, reading and writing are reciprocal. Reading, writing, and grammar should be taught together instead of separate. Planning instruction for reading and writing is a strategic and systematic process. I encourage all teachers to get to know their students as both readers and writers prior to planning instruction. Reader's interest surveys provide great insight to students' reading preferences, identify if they are a reader, have hopes of becoming a reader, as well as their reading and writing goals. Reader's interest surveys can also provide valuable information about student's fears of reading, or writing, apprehensions they may have as well as areas of weakness and also areas of strength. Reader's interest surveys do not have to be just about reading. I encourage you to design a reader's/writer's interest survey to include questions about both reading and writing.

I also encourage new teachers to informally assess their students to better determine their level of both reading and writing fluency, analyze the data, reflect on their findings, and then plan instruction based on the findings. Instructions should be explicit and taught with passion allowing students to engage and collaborate with you, the teacher, and with their peers. Instruction should include daily read-alouds and think-alouds. I cannot emphasize enough the

importance of modeling. Model, model, model, and then model some more! Model what you want your students to do. I encourage you to incorporate the, *I do, we do, and now you do*, strategy in your classroom for a slow release of responsibility. The theory of this strategy is that once you have modeled what you want your students to do, and have worked collaboratively with them to help them achieve what you want or expect them to do, then they are better prepared for you to release responsibility to them to work independently with confidence of being successful.

I also encourage you to teach students what the four types of sentences are and how they are punctuated through interactive instruction and through read-alouds before asking them to write correctly punctuated sentences from each category. If your students can identify them first, they will be better prepared to write them. Incorporate the parts of speech in reading and writing as well as daily activities, such as interactive games, and collaborative activities as well as daily bell ringers, exit slips, and assignments before requiring students to use them proficiently. Learning the parts of speech is a strategic process that begins with the basics, such as learning what nouns are and then learning to identify them. As students learn the parts of speech begin incorporating them into daily writing and requiring them to identify them as well as use them to write various types of sentences. Teach punctuation daily and always require students to punctuate their writing. Provide timely feedback that is applicable and allows students to know what areas they are excelling as well as areas they need to grow in. When reading and writing are taught together year after year students gain knowledge, grow academically, and advance as both readers and writers.

Finally, set high expectations and teach with passion and fire! Provide a safe environment for your students to learn and grow socially and academically. Grow and learn daily with your students. I've taught under the leadership of several different principals over the course of my career and learned a great deal from each of them. However, one principal made a positive impact on my way of teaching as well as my way of thinking. He often lingered at school after the buses had pulled out from the parking lot loaded with children eager to return home. He made routine visits to the classrooms and had conversations with the teachers who remained at school to work on lesson plans, activities, or just to catch their breath before going home. I had many memorable conversations with him about teaching. He loved to learn and loved watching the students and the teachers learn. He periodically stopped by our classrooms and would ask us what we had learned today. He also randomly stopped children in the hall, or during lunch, and occasionally in the classroom and ask them what they had learned today. It was his belief that we should never let a day go by that we don't reflect and determine what we have learned, whether it be an academic growth, social growth, or a personal insight.

I adopted his daily questions and asked my students the same questions over the years. I enjoyed hearing their responses and using their feedback to assess my teaching and also to plan instructions. I still ask my students this question and also ask myself the same question daily. My favorite principal passed away a number of years ago. However, his words of wisdom still resonate with me often. Be that teacher! Be the teacher who inspires your students to grow and learn daily. Be the teacher who learns with your students. Read when they read, write when they write, and grow as they grow. After all, we are never too old to learn. Educators are life-long learners.

Applications

To help guide you through Chapter Six and upcoming chapters, become familiar with the following key terms for a deeper understanding of Chapter Six:

+ Reading fluency
+ Reading automaticity
+ Reading speed
+ Prosody
+ Word fluency
+ High-frequency words
+ Decoding by analogy
+ Syllabic analysis
+ Morphemic analysis
+ Guided reading
+ Choral reading
+ Partner reading
+ Reader's Theater
+ Expression
+ Phrasing
+ Volume
+ Writing fluency
+ Writing automaticity
+ Writing speed
+ Writer's voice
+ Tone
+ Spelling fluency
+ Expository sentence
+ Declarative sentence
+ Interrogative sentence
+ Exclamatory sentence

In-Seat Activity

Working with your partner, practice reading the passage that you've been provided to read orally to each other. While one candidate is reading, the other will time the student reading and determine how many words per minute the student read. As you are listening to the reader you will also be required to complete a running record, which includes the following:

1. *Reader placed vocal emphasis on appropriate words.*
2. *Reader's voice tone rose and fell at appropriate times in the text.*
3. *Reader's inflection reflected the punctuation in the text.*

4. *In narrative text with dialogue, the reader used appropriate vocal tone to represent characters mental status, such as excitement, fear, confidence or sadness.*
5. *Reader used punctuation to pause in appropriate places.*
6. *Reader used prepositional phrases to pause appropriately at phrase boundaries.*
7. *Reader used subject-verb divisions to pause appropriately at phrase boundaries.*
8. *Reader used conjunctions to pause appropriately at phrase boundaries.*

Reflect and Answer the Following Questions

✦ *What is fluent reading and fluent writing?*
✦ *What is the relationship between fluency and comprehension?*
✦ *How do young readers develop reading and writing fluency?*
✦ *How is reading and writing fluency assessed?*
✦ *What strategies can help develop and enhance reading and writing fluency?*

Reader's Theater Strategy

Reader's Theater is a fun reading strategy that can inspire and engage students in a collaborative fun reading and writing experience. Reader's Theater is often recommended as a motivational way to increase students' reading fluency, but it is also an excellent practice in reading for information and to allow students to understand the thoughts and perceptions of their peers through collaboration. Reader's Theater is also an inspirational strategy to engage students in the text.

In Reader's Theater, students present a text by practicing it first and then reading aloud dramatically to the entire class. Students learn to read the text more fluently from the repeated readings of the text. However, with each practice session, they also revisit the text for a deeper understanding of the content, which is vital to content area learning. The theory behind Reader's Theater is that by the time students have read, reread, practiced, and are ready to present to the class, they are able to provide a clear, fluent, and also a thoughtful interpretation of the text, while also making it engaging and comprehensible to their peers.

Reader's Theater is typically texts that are scripted by the teacher or small groups of students. The author's original words and phrasing are generally kept intact, but divided into meaning parts much like the script of a play. Students work in small collaborative groups and are assigned specific parts of the text to rehearse. Collaborative groups can be based on students reading level or interest depending on the difficulty of the text.

Scripts can also be designed in interesting and beneficial ways. For example, students can be given various roles. Students can become multiple characters or work together to allow more than once student to read a particular part of the text that might require extra emphasis on a word or phrase to express the emotions implied. Primary students enjoy using puppets and a curtained theater to perform the play, while older students enjoy rehearsing the script and standing before the class with or without props reading and acting out the story. Reader's Theater is a very diverse strategy that can be modified year after year to fit the academic needs of the students. For at-level or above-level students, Reader's Theater can involve multiple content areas and multiple skills. For example, the teacher might require them to read a more difficult text, collaborate and reflect on the text, and then write their own version of the play to portray the meaning of the text. The theory behind this is if students can read the text, analyze it, and write a script that aligns with the text in their own words and then act it out, they truly have a deep understanding of the text that they read.

High-powered teachers implement Reader's Theater year after year to enhance students understanding, comprehension, fluency, and also to informally assess students reading fluency, writing fluency, comprehension, and their speaking and listening skills. I encourage you to implement Reader's Theater in your classroom to help enhance student's reading, writing, and speaking skills and also to provide a rich, fun, collaborative, and engaging experience that students will remember for years to come.

Student Notes

Annotating is an effective learning strategy. This page is reserved for you to annotate (*take notes*) record potential questions, and also to refer back to when studying, completing assignments, and to help you gain a better understanding of Chapter Six.

Student Reflection

High-powered teachers reflect. This page is reserved for you to reflect about information that you found insightful and what you have learned from Chapter Six.

Suggested Reading for the Teacher

High-powered teachers are life-long learners and continually strive to further and expand their knowledge to ensure that they are providing their students with meaningful learning experiences. There's a large number of resources on the market today to help teachers teach reading and writing fluency. I encourage you to continually seek out rich, inspiring books to read aloud to your students, as well as informative books to increase your knowledge of reading, and to increase your teachers' toolbox with diverse reading strategies.

Rasinski, T. V. *The Fluent Reader: Oral Reading Strategies for Building Word Recognition, Fluency, and Comprehension.* Scholastic, Inc., 2003.

Stahl, S. "What Do We Know About Fluency?" *The Voice of Evidence in Reading Research,* edited by P. MCardle, and V. Chhabra, Paul H. Brookes, 2004, pp. 187–11.

Chapter References

Allington, R. L. *What Really Matters in Fluency: Research-Based Best Practices Across the Curriculum.* Allyn & Bacon/Pearson, 2009.

Cerritos Library. *First Ladies Collection,* 1981, http://menu.ci.cerritos.ca.us/collections/first/flc_bios.html B_Bush. Accessed 28 May 2018.

Council of Chief State School Officers (CCSSO). *Interstate Teacher Assessment and Support Consortium (InTASC) Model Core Teaching Standards,* Apr. 2011, https://www.ccsso.org/sites/default/files/2017-11/InTASC_Model_Core_Teaching_Standards_2011.pdf. Accessed 7 July 2018.

Eldredge, J. L. *Teach Decoding: How and Why,* 2nd ed. Merrill/Prentice Hall, 2005.

Lemov, D. *Teach Like a Champion.* Jossey-Bass, 2010.

Readsters, LLC. *Comparing the Dolch and Fry High Frequency Word Lists,* 2013. http://www.readsters.com/wp-content/uploads/ComparingDolchAndFryLists.pdf. Accessed 7 July 2018.

Rutgers' Faculty and Staff Bulletin. *In Memoriam.* 2018, http://ucmweb.rutgers.edu/inmemoriam/?q=inmemoriam_record&id=249. Accessed 2 Feb. 2018.

Samuels, S. J. Toward a Theory of Automatic Information Processing in Reading, Revisited. *Theoretical Models and Process of Reading,* 5th ed., edited by R. B. Ruddell, and N. J. Unrau. International Reading Association, 2004, pp. 1127–48.

Spandel, V. *Creating Writers Through 6-Trait Writing Assessment and Instruction,* 5th ed. Allyn & Bacon/Pearson, 2009.

Tompkins, Gail E. *Literacy for the 21st Century: A Balanced Approach.* Pearson, 2014.

Chapter 7
Increasing Student's Vocabulary

Teacher Quote

"Every child is different. What works for one, may not work for another. Be patient, have a back-up plan (or ten), and most importantly… model, model, model! I cannot express enough how important explicit and scaffold instruction is."

~Dr. Jennifer Chambers

Chapter Questions

+ *What is vocabulary?*
+ *What is basic vocabulary?*
+ *What is academic vocabulary?*
+ *What is content-specific vocabulary?*

Author Reflection

I have always been fascinated with words. I recall growing up in the Appalachian Mountains when communication was rich with storytelling. One of my favorite evening activities consisted of listening to my grandparents, aunts, uncles, and neighbors telling stories of their childhood. I sat wide-eyed on the porch of the old country store and devoured every word they said. I paid close attention to my grandfather's vivid descriptions of farming his land, and plowing with his old mule, Pete. I can still recall how he described the plow blade digging deep into the rich dark soil creating deep furrows to drop the precious seeds in. I loved his descriptive words he used for the many stories that he told. I can vividly recall the sweat beading up on his brow like beads of glass and how he worked from sun up until sun down.

I was also mesmerized when my grandmother told stories about her colorful patchwork quilts. She described the colors as rose-red, flaming-orange, and greens that were as green as the spring-time grass. I can still close my eyes and see my grandfather standing in the freshly plowed earth behind his coal-black mule wiping his brow with his worn and faded red bandana. I can visualize the lemon-yellow, rose-red, and flaming-orange squares of scrap material that connected my grandmother's quilt. I can recall these wonderful memories and their words simply because they painted a picture that will forever be etched in my mind. They brought their stories to life! Through the years, my desire to learn more words and my hunger to use them intensified.

As a student, I loved to write. I loved to speak. I loved to use a rich combination of words to take my reading and writing to the next level. I wanted my words to come alive, much like my grandparents words did. As a teacher, I desired to instill the love of reading, writing, and the love for words in my students. I read every book I could get my hands on about teaching, reading, writing, and vocabulary. I wanted to be a wealth of knowledge for my students, while also learning and growing with them. This thirst for knowledge and desire for my students to succeed led to the idea of creating a word of the day for my first-grade students. I worked and planned how I could make the word of the day engaging, exciting, and useful. I wanted my students to love words as much as I did!

I decided to introduce what I referred to as, **The Word of The Day,** first thing each morning using a colorful photograph, I displayed the pictures with an overhead projector, posters, and eventually with a document camera, and finally as technology advanced, with a smartboard. I integrated literature with the word of the day by reading a short poem describing the picture aloud to the students. I loved what happened next! We had a meaningful conversation about the poem and the picture. I then asked them to describe the picture using their senses. I created a web on the whiteboard beside the picture and added their words in the appropriate categories of visual/sight, sound/hearing, smell, and touch. At the center of the web I drew a blank for each letter in the word. Students were encouraged to make an educated guess of the word. This game worked much like the **Hangman** game. The game was engaging, exciting, and also allowed the students to practice their phonics and phonological awareness skills while having fun, learning, and expanding their vocabulary.

After a few turns guessing the letters, or the word, I explained if the word was noun, adjective, or verb. We continued the guessing game adding letters and discussing the possibilities. Finally, the word was divulged, either by myself or by a student. The picture, word, and the web remained on the board throughout the day. I incorporated the word throughout the day in instruction, conversations, different content areas, and also in assignments.

Students interacted with the word throughout the day as well by adding synonyms or antonyms in the appropriate columns on the board. I also encouraged them to be word detectives. When they heard me using the word during the day they were asked to quietly stand up. This encouraged them to listen and helped them to better understand the word and its use in different contexts. When students orally used the word of the day, the level of excitement radiated throughout the room. When I heard them use the word I added a marble to their vocabulary party jar! The object of the party jar was to encourage students to use the word of the day in a casual yet meaningful way, and also as an incentive to have a word celebration party when the jar was finally full of marbles.

The words were added to a word wall each afternoon. The word-wall wasn't left unattended or dormant. We revisited the word-wall often! Students were encouraged to incorporate the words in daily conversation and also in their daily writings. Our first-grade wall contained a menagerie of words. At times the word wall displayed words such as evaporate, buoyancy, honey, verse, journey, mammal, bright, sturdy, glossy, coarse, foul, rapid, and many more accumulated words. We also created a classroom dictionary, which was a collaborative effort. The words were alphabetized as a group. We wrote the words in a big book, determined a useful definition, and then the students would take turns writing the definition in the book and illustrating colorful pictures to represent each word. The book was kept on display on an easel at the front of the room. Students were proud of their book year after year and were inspired to use the dictionary as needed during daily work.

The idea for the word of the day grew and spread quickly throughout the school. Over the years it became a word of the day for the entire primary hall. I posted the word of the day in the hallway each day in a visible location where all of the students could see it. Teachers loved interacting with the word and incorporating it into their morning messages and in writing assignments. The words were removed and added to a bulletin board near the lunchroom entrance that students passed throughout the day. Students were eager to watch the wordlist grow and learn new words each day. The thirst for knowledge grew year after year with the students, so did the activities that surrounded the concept of the **word of the day**.

One summer while attending a reading conference, I was approached by a colleague whose son had previously been a student in my first-grade. She thanked me for all that I had done for her son, who was then a senior in high school. She specifically mentioned his use of words. She thanked me for teaching him to love words. She stated through misty eyes, "I can still hear you when I hear him using rich vocabulary in day to day conversations. Thank you for enhancing his writing, reading, and expanding his vocabulary." I think this was one of those teacher moments that make up for all of the extra time planning, reading, researching, learning, teaching, and reteaching, that truly allow the teacher to feel that they have come full circle and know that they truly made a difference in the lives of their students.

Shortly thereafter, I wrote the quote, *If you will teach it...They will learn*, which was inspired by one of my favorite movies. This quote hung above the board in the front of my classroom year after year. I still recite this to my college students today who are aspiring to be teachers. *If you will teach it...They will learn*. Keep this quote in mind as you advance through the sections of this chapter.

In this chapter, you will learn how high-powered teachers increase their student's academic vocabulary. You will also learn engaging and interactive activities to help develop students' word knowledge. You will learn strategies that will pique your students' interest in discovering, exploring, learning, and using new words both inside the classroom and in everyday life.

Author Quote

"If you will teach it...They will learn."

~*Dr. Joyce Bowling*

Vocabulary

High-powered teachers believe that the basis of a student's desire to learn, as well as their academic success, heavily relies on a solid vocabulary. They believe that for students to succeed in school and beyond, they need to build a robust vocabulary. However, they also consider a lack of vocabulary knowledge to be a primary reason for student's poor comprehension, thus resulting in academic struggles in all content areas. High-powered teachers know that a strong vocabulary helps foster understanding, increase communication, and also enhance reading.

However, many teachers struggle with how to teach vocabulary effectively so that students will be able to make connections to help them better understand the word and also to use the words effectively in all content areas as well as written and verbal expressions. High-powered teachers teach words through various methods. They teach vocabulary synonyms for a word that students already know or are familiar with. However, they also teach new information as well as new words that are related to the topic, subject, or information they are teaching. High-powered teachers also teach their students to learn about words and their meanings. They teach students to be constructive detectives of meaning. In other words, they teach them through explicit and strategic instructions, multiple opportunities to collaborate and engage in meaningful activities, and also equip them with the knowledge they need to quickly and automatically look for clues to enable them to deconstruct the word. They teach them how to use **morphemic analysis** to determine the meaning of unfamiliar words.

High-powered teachers also build their instruction around students' prior knowledge or concepts. They know that a concept is an idea and that concepts are categorized in the brain as a memory. In other words, they know that concepts are bits and pieces of already acquired knowledge that is stored in the brain. This information is also known as **schema**. High-powered teachers assess to determine the level of students' already acquired word knowledge. Based on their data, they work to establish and build students' word knowledge prior to teaching specific vocabulary. For example, a student may understand the concepts of floating (*something that stays on top of the water*) before they learn the word *buoyancy*. Their knowledge of the concept allows them to make connections to the new vocabulary word, buoyancy. However, high-powered teachers know that not all concepts are familiar to all of their students, which leaves the student without base knowledge about a topic, faced with learning both the concept and the vocabulary word that describes the concept. In this case, high-powered teachers plan interactive and engaging activities that help establish the concept before teaching the vocabulary words to ensure their students make connections to the necessary prior knowledge needed to be able to truly understand the vocabulary word.

According to R. J. Marzano, D.J. Pickering, and J. E. Pollock, teaching word meanings, especially before reading, has been found to be effective for word learning and text comprehension. High-powered teachers agree with research and know that vocabulary instruction, associated with extensive dictionary time and creation of random sentences that contain the words, is not effective enough to warrant the time used for it (Beck et al.; Nagy). They strategically plan vocabulary instruction that piques the interest of their students. They involve their students with interactive learning strategies, while also creating multiple opportunities where students can practice using vocabulary words. They know that students, on an average, acquire approximately 3,000 words per year, which estimates to be 8–12 new words each day that averages out to about 100–150 words per week. High-powered teachers ensure that their students learn these words through explicit daily instruction, teaching vocabulary strategies, providing daily reading, and writing opportunities in various settings and content areas, while also engaging their students in grand conversations.

High-powered teachers also ensure their students learn meanings of words through instructions, exposure, opportunities to use the word, and also by maintaining a word-rich environment. They carefully plan explicit instructions that allow their students to have multiple daily opportunities to read vocabulary-rich texts in various settings such as independent reading, partner reading, choral reading, and also involving them in carefully selected read-alouds. They know that students also learn a large number of words incidentally through reading outside the classroom such as television, advertisements, books, conversations, family activities, social gatherings, Internet, social collaboration, and also interacting with their peers. With this knowledge in mind, high-powered teachers plan accordingly to help expand their students' vocabulary by teaching specific words and implementing word-learning strategies that encourage students to use newly learned words in daily life outside the classroom. They also strive to foster students' interest in words through rich literature.

High-powered teachers know that word knowledge and reading success are closely related. They know that students who have a larger vocabulary are typically better readers. High-powered teachers encourage students to read by introducing and involving them in reading through engaging reading activities, incorporating a variety of genres, and also making their own love of reading evident to their students. They also know that students who are capable readers have a larger vocabulary, primarily because they read more. They know that the more books students read, the more exposure they will have to new and challenging vocabulary, which results in the student having an expanded vocabulary. High-powered teachers also know that word knowledge is a vital part of comprehension and that students are required to learn words at more than one level. They implement the three-tier method. These three tiers consist of ***basic words, academic words***, and ***content-specific words***.

1. **Tier 1: Basic vocabulary**. Basic words are common words used socially, in informal conversations, at home, and on the playground.
2. **Tier 2: Academic vocabulary**. Academic vocabulary are words that can be applied in various content areas.
3. **Tier 3: Content-specific vocabulary**. Specialized terms are defined as words that are content-specific and often abstract.

Basic Vocabulary

High-powered teachers know that basic vocabulary is not taught through explicit instructions. They know that their students build their basic word knowledge through hearing the words used in conversation, and also repeated use of the word in their own daily oral conversations, through reading them in text, and also incorporating them in written expression. Basic vocabulary consists of words such as *baby, food, clock, happy, no,* and many other words that are learned and also used daily. However, they also realize that students' word knowledge is not equal. They know students arrive in their classrooms with diverse basic vocabulary knowledge.

High-powered teachers know that some students arrive at school with very limited vocabulary. They strive daily to ensure they are providing every opportunity and advantage possible to help establish and build all of their students' basic vocabulary, regardless of their basic level of word knowledge. High-powered teachers plan and provide students with meaningful learning opportunities that assists them in recalling and making necessary connections to words. They know that students need to learn words deeply to retain the words and be able to apply them in various settings. High-powered teachers ensure that students are gaining necessary basic vocabulary required to be successful in life (InTASC, Standard 2, Council of Chief State School Officers [CCSSO]).

High-powered teachers teach vocabulary interventions that are powerful enough to accelerate their students' vocabulary, not just advance it. They teach vocabulary that will empower their students and also help them make up academic deficits by learning to read, speak, and also write with a strong word knowledge. They know that students learn words when they actually experience the words multiple times in various forms of exposure. Research suggests that students need to be exposed to the words and also experience words at least six times to truly learn the word and be able to use it correctly. However, high-powered teachers know that all students do not learn the same and do not limit their instructions and students' experience to vocabulary words, instead they revisit words throughout the academic year to ensure that their students "*own*" the words. High-powered teachers cleverly integrate basic vocabulary in their class using words they want their students to use. Students are exposed to the basic words without direct and explicit instructions, but rather in a comfortable environment where a wide use of vocabulary is the norm.

Expanding Basic Vocabulary

High-powered teachers introduce words through in-class conversations, daily oral read-alouds, trade-books, library books, think-alouds, engaging activities, word games, technology, diverse texts, diverse genres, written assignments, and also oral instructions. High-powered teachers also model what they want their students to do, even how they want their students to speak, and what vocabulary they want their students to use. They also make their own love of reading and use of words evident for their students, while also interacting with them in a variety of strategic and planned activities and sporadic conversations (InTASC, Standard 5, CCSSO).

Conversations and Vocabulary

Instructional conversation is a research-based strategy for encouraging academic conversations with students. High-powered teachers know that discussion is also an important tool of learning. They know that it engages students as well as broadens their perspectives, promotes understanding, and a higher level of thinking. High-powered teachers incorporate academic conversations by planning a theme and deciding what they want their students to know at the end of the discussion. High-powered teachers facilitate the conversation in a way that students can participate and actually do most of the talking (InTASC Standard 3, CCSSO). They also use this conversation to cleverly weave in and embed background knowledge while also allowing students to explore and understand topic, theme, and content.

High-powered teachers also know that some of the most meaningful instructional conversations occur sporadically. They know that students' questions will often open the floodgates of opportunities to not only answer them, but also involve the entire class in rich academic conversations. During this conversation, teachers ask open-ended questions, restate student's comments, pause briefly and strategically, and also ask students to elaborate on their answers. This helps promote the students' bases for statements or opinions by asking questions that make the student dig deeper. Questions may include, asking students what else they know about a subject, can they elaborate on their answer, or allowing them to respond with a question to promote and encourage the conversation.

High-powered teachers know that engaging students in instructional conversations about vocabulary in all content areas, results in students exploring new ideas, furthering their knowledge of a topic, while also enhancing their base-knowledge and their basic vocabulary, preparing them for tier-two and tier-three vocabulary instruction. In other words, high-powered teachers realize the power of instructional conversations. They know that instructional conversations can expand student's vocabulary, and also promote their oral and receptive language, speaking and listening skills, as well as create a positive classroom rapport where students feel a sense of community and trust where they feel safe to learn and exercise their opinions (InTASC Standard 3, CCSSO). High-powered teachers know that true and meaningful discussions are not just summarizing ideas or simply searching for a correct answer. They also know that **grand conversations**, whether they are planned or sporadic, can help students develop new ideas, a deeper understanding, and inspire them to dig deeper to learn more about the topic.

Interactive Read-Alouds and Vocabulary

High-powered teachers also know that interactive read-alouds is another way to create an interest and promote conversation among their students. Teachers carefully select vocabulary-rich literature that contains thought-provoking vocabulary. High-powered teachers select texts for their read-alouds that does not simplify the text for beginning or inexperienced readers, but rather a text that will pique their students' interest and prompt them to ask questions. They also model the strategy of a **think-alouds** while they are reading to encourage conversation (InTASC Standard 4, CCSSO).

They incorporate novels such as *The Miraculous Journey of Edward Tulane* by Kate DiCammilo, categorized as a fourth-grade Lexile-reading level, to use as a vocabulary-rich read-aloud. The book is not only vocabulary-rich, it also has multiple plots that are interesting and contain diverse characters. The book is very entertaining, which promotes interesting academic conversations. For example, read and think about the following paragraph located on page two of the novel, *The Miraculous Journey of Edward Tulane:*

> *The rabbit's name was Edward Tulane, and he was tall. He measured almost three feet from the tip of his ears to the tip of his feet; his eyes were painted a penetrating and intelligent blue.*
>
> *In all, Edward felt himself to be an exceptional specimen. Only his whiskers gave him pause. They were long and elegant as they should be, but they were of uncertain origin. Edward felt quite strongly that they were not the whiskers of a rabbit. Whom the whiskers belonged to initially, what unsavory animal, was a question that Edward could not bear to consider for too long. And so he did not. He preferred, as a rule not to think unpleasant thoughts.*

High-powered teachers realize the wealth of words within this rich excerpt of the novel. They implement this type of book as a method of inspiration, entertainment to prompt higher order questioning, enhance students' comprehension, while also fostering a love of reading within them, all while creating multiple opportunities for instructional conversations that will expand students' vocabulary, and also enhance their comprehension. High-powered teachers read novels

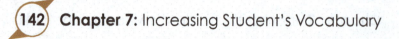
such as, *The Miraculous Journey of Edward Tulane*, with expression and focus on drawing students' attention to rich-vocabulary words that are cleverly woven into the text. They engage their students in interactive discussions emphasizing the use of rich-vocabulary words. In addition, they incorporate think-alouds, ask thought-provoking questions, and encourage peer-collaboration with think-pair-share. Thus, enhancing socialization, vocabulary, comprehension, classroom rapport, and also establishing and expanding students' vocabulary.

What Is Academic Vocabulary?

J. Burke defines academic vocabulary as words that students use frequently in all content areas as well as see them in library books, trade books, magazines, newspapers, and even in advertisements. High-powered teachers know that students' knowledge of academic vocabulary, also known as **high-frequency words**, is part of their background knowledge, and that it affects their school success (Marzano et al.). High-powered teachers implement academic vocabulary into daily instruction, assignments, **mini-lessons**, and also in discussions. They know that it is very important for students to know these words as they are exposed to them in multiple formats and expected to use them in multiple ways.

High-powered teachers know that students are exposed to and use academic vocabulary in all content areas, which intensifies their academic value. They are also aware of the vital role that it plays in both reading and writing success. High-powered teachers explicitly teach students about academic vocabulary. Their instruction is rich, deep, and can be extended. In other words, they teach their students about the words, and they provide them with multiple opportunities to encounter words through a variety of texts as well as writing opportunities to ensure that they not only know the word, but also know how to use the word correctly.

Planning to Teach Academic Vocabulary

High-powered teachers assess students to determine their level of word knowledge and use the data from their preassessments to design instruction, conversations, activities, and assignments to help build the necessary background knowledge. They also preteach or review some unfamiliar or confusing words that students may encounter within the text before they independently read a book or study a topic. As high-powered teachers plan instruction, they consider what students already know about a word, does the word have multiple meanings, or does it represent a new concept (InTASC Standard 7, CCSSO).

High-powered teachers assess their students to determine their academic progress often through multiple formative assessments. After determining their students' prior knowledge about a word(s), high-powered teachers prepare themselves with necessary information about the topic that they want to provide to their students. In other words, they know the topic well and can answer student's questions that may arise about the topic. High-powered teachers plan instruction implementing guided practice through repetition of saying the vocabulary word, using it in conversations, applying the words in small collaborative groups, or playing a game that allows them to use the word in sentences, definitions, synonyms, or even as antonyms.

High-powered teachers plan and implement **mini-lessons** about specific words. They also provide background information about words, including definitions and contextual information, and also engage students in thought-provoking activities to encourage them to think about the words, their definitions, and their uses. mini-lessons can be implemented prior to reading to pre-teach. They can also be arranged after reading. Some of the mini-lessons for teaching academic vocabulary may include introducing vocabulary prior to reading through posters, word maps, examples, anticipation guides, word chains, word sorts, interactive read-alouds, and interactive games.

When a high-powered teacher designs a mini-lesson to expand their students' academic vocabulary, they think about how they will introduce a topic. Introducing the topic should bring an element of interest, pique students' curiosity, and motivate them to want to know more. It is also a time to informally observe and make notes about what level of prior knowledge or lack of knowledge students have about the topic. After selecting how they will introduce the topic, they determine what types of examples they will share with their students. Examples can include visual objects, photographs, written examples, text, music, and so on.

High-powered teachers involve their students with words through listening, talking, reading, and writing. They also teach specific words through collaborative and engaging activities. High-powered teachers design instruction to allow students multiple opportunities to encounter and experience vocabulary words. They also teach word-learning strategies to equip students with knowledge and skills to determine the meaning of unfamiliar words. High-powered teachers strive to develop students' word consciousness, and their awareness of words, as well as their interest in words through inspiring literature, interactive read-alouds, and also through modeling the vocabulary.

High-powered teachers want their students to have fun and develop the habit of becoming word-detectives. They want their students to always be curious about words. They know that innate curiosity and inspiration to take academic risks with new words are very important to the beginning of word consciousness. High-powered teachers provide students with multiple opportunities to play with words. They know that students gain necessary confidence and motivation through fun and rewarding experiences.

High-powered primary teachers promote vocabulary through fun wordplay using word books, games, art, music, and even drama. They get their students up and moving and allow them to experience words though multisensory opportunities. High-powered primary teachers involve their students through a combination of visual, auditory, kinesthetic, and tactile activities, which also ensures that they are meeting the needs of all learners (InTASC Standard 2, CCSSO). They know that vocabulary instructions that involve multisensory activities can help students internalize new words, which continue to develop word schema, while also bringing an element of excitement to learning. Finally, high-powered teachers formally assess their students, analyze the data, reflect, and then determine their students' academic growth from the initial preassessment prior to explicit instruction.

Content-Specific Vocabulary

High-powered teachers introduce **content-specific** vocabulary in tier-two, but teach the vocabulary explicitly in tier-three in **content-specific instruction**. Content-specific vocabulary contains those technical words that are content-specific and can be abstract. Examples of content-specific words can be scientific terms such as metamorphosis, larva, or condensation. Content-specific vocabulary exists in all content areas. High-powered teachers know that content-specific vocabulary should be taught specifically and also prior to instructions to enable students to understand and comprehend what they have read, as well as have the ability to apply their knowledge in various formats.

High-powered teachers know the importance of prereading a text prior to instruction to determine words that may give students difficulty or decrease their understanding of the text. They carefully plan how they will introduce students to the newfound words, how they will incorporate them in instructions, without spending a large amount of time on the words. They introduce their students to the words, briefly explain them, provide examples, and incorporate them in academic conversations prior to requiring their students to read the text to help build background knowledge and a better understanding of the text.

High-powered teachers also teach and model how to dissect an unfamiliar word, to look at all components of the word, such as the root-word, prefix, affix, or suffix for clues that would help them determine the meaning of the word. High-powered teachers know that not knowing one word in a sentence can result in not understanding the entire sentence. To enhance students' word-knowledge, high-powered teachers plan daily activities to help students better understand how to determine the meaning of a word through examining parts of the word also known as **morphemic analysis**. Flip charts are a fun and beneficial visual activity that helps demonstrate how manipulating parts of a word can change the entire meaning. Remember, morpheme, is the smallest unit of a language that expresses meaning or serves grammatical function. For example, let's look at the word, *unfairness*.

+ *UN—is the prefix, which is a morpheme added at the start of a word.*
+ *FAIR—is the root word, which is the core of the word and carries the major component of the meaning.*
+ *NESS—is the suffix, which is a morpheme added at the end of a word.*

Now, if we take away the prefix of *UN*, the entire meaning of the word has changed. Also keep in mind that the prefix and suffix cannot stand alone. Teach students to look for the root word to determine the word and then look at all parts of the word to determine the words' meaning. Flipbooks can easily be constructed to help young readers better understand the parts of words. Seek out creative ways to help students better understand morphemic analysis through apps, websites, and manipulatives.

High-powered teachers know that when students are introduced to new vocabulary, they experience it in multisensory activities, and can also use morphemic analysis as well as context clues to determine the meaning of a word in a passage, they are truly in control of their own cognitive awareness of words. They are also aware that when students know how to systematically determine what a word is, as well as what the word means, they are ready to apply the required strategies in all content areas (InTASC Standard 8, CCSSO).

Assessing Student's Vocabulary Knowledge

Some research suggests that teachers do not assess students' use of vocabulary in a way that assesses or evaluates learning, and have concerns that teachers do not use the results from assessments to help them plan for future instruction. However, high-powered teachers know and value the importance of vocabulary assessment. They know that vocabulary instruction begins with assessment, occurs daily in an informal manner, and also that vocabulary instruction ends with summative assessments. They know that regular and ongoing assessment helps them to better know their students, plan for instruction, evaluate their teaching, while also understanding their students' vocabulary knowledge and their use of vocabulary (InTASC Standard 6, CCSSO).

High-powered teachers plan for vocabulary assessment just as they plan for vocabulary instruction. They think about the goals and the purpose of the assessment. For example, will the assessment data be used to help them plan instruction, or will be it be used to measure students' academic growth? High-powered teachers evaluate and assess students' vocabulary through observations, running records, recording anecdotal notes, and also through analyzing students' work. They understand and value the purpose of summative assessments. They also know the importance of formative assessments and incorporate them through daily observations, student work, and daily conversations.

High-powered teachers not only assess students' word recognition, such as site words, but they also assess students for depth of vocabulary knowledge. They realize that students will be required to complete a wide variety of assessments including standardized tests. They also know that the degree of difficulty and question formats will vary with different forms of assessment. High-powered teachers model and ensure that their students gain sufficient practice with diverse questioning techniques to truly understand the questions they may face in standardized tests. They also preteach **assessment vocabulary** to enhance their students' understanding of what is being asked of them. They know that when students are confident about questioning techniques, they can focus on the answer, resulting in a higher comprehension, as well as overall academic success.

Language Link

High-powered teachers know that vocabulary should not be isolated, but integrated in all content areas. Instead of thinking of vocabulary as being a confined unit of study, they ensure that students are visually seeing the words in other content areas. They know that students not only need to see the vocabulary words in other content areas, they need to learn that the words may also be relevant in other areas. High-powered teachers hold their students accountable for old vocabulary words in new units of instruction. In other words, they expect their students to be able to recall the previously learned vocabulary words and apply them when necessary. High-powered teachers revisit and cleverly weave previous vocabulary words in new instructions, assignments, and also in activities to ensure that students are being exposed to the words in multiple settings, are able to recall, understand, and apply the words in future assignments and assessments. They know when the students see that vocabulary words extend beyond one content area and beyond the walls of their classroom, they're more likely to see the words' academic and real-life relevance.

In addition to explicit instructions, interactive activities, word-walls, and word of the day, high-powered teachers implement a **Word Journal** in their classrooms. They require students to keep a writing journal to help them personalize their developing vocabulary. High-powered teachers model and teach students how to keep a word journal, while also giving them specific guidelines to follow. They ask students to include the following components in their word journal.

- ✦ A word journal begins with students writing their own paraphrase of a word's definition.
- ✦ Write a dictionary-based definition for the word.

- Write a sentences using the new vocabulary word.
- If the word has multiple meanings, they require them to write a sentence for each use of the meanings/definitions.
- Primary students may also include an illustration for each word.
- Write a synonym and an antonym for each word.
- Identify if the word is a noun, adjective, or if the word can be more than one part of speech.

High-powered teachers encourage students to include a definition in their own words because they know that research suggests writing a personalized definition is good for student's memory, enhancing their comprehension, while also allowing them to take personal ownership of the word.

High-powered teachers extend the requirements, interactions, and purpose of the word journal into more than just a method of recording definitions. They require their students to complete weekly writing assignments that must include a specific number of words from their journals. Writing assignments can be fun, yet beneficial. For example, teachers may ask students to design a perfect birthday gift. Students would be required to revisit their word journal and incorporate at least five previously learned vocabulary words in their description of a perfect birthday gift. They would be required to write a narrative about receiving a gift, buying a gift, or a gift that they may be in search of, while also incorporating five or more words from their word journal. This fun lesson can be modified to fit a particular holiday theme, grade-level, or content area.

High-powered teachers know the value and positive rewards that word journals can have on students' vocabulary, daily work, word use, written expression, oral language, grammar, as well as other content areas. Word journals also help students explore new words, revisit familiar words, interact with words, strengthen their dictionary skills, as well as help them gain confidence while also learning to be independent and responsible. High-powered teachers not only hold their students accountable for building a cumulative vocabulary, they model it through daily use of rich vocabulary. They also tie vocabulary to grammar to ensure that their students are truly embracing words for long term, in other words, for life.

Vocabulary Strategies

High-powered teachers make it a priority to focus on and increase the amount of time their students talk using academic language. In other words, they know that students need practice with academic vocabulary if they are to become proficient in using and knowing the academic vocabulary necessary to succeed. They plan for opportunities to allow their students to speak the language of science, math, social studies, literature, writing, or the topic at hand to help ensure students become thinkers in the targeted discipline.

High-powered teachers strive to find diverse methods to encourage word interaction with all of their students. They know that Internet is not a complete solution, but can be very beneficial and appeal to the interest of their students (InTASC Standard 3, CCSSO). They are continually in search of new websites, apps, and games that will allow their students to interact, have fun, and also learn at all learning levels and styles. High-powered teachers encourage students to explore and participate in vocabulary-building puzzles and play vocabulary games that mimic game shows.

They also bring these games to life in the classroom through Internet via smartboard, actual game-boards and game pieces, or by simply using the dictionary.

High-powered teachers play what they refer to as, **The Dictionary Game**.

+ They post the words via the whiteboard or smartboard.
+ They ask students to create definitions for the specified word or words that students are not familiar with.
+ The teachers knows the correct definition and has them recorded on index cards.
+ Students then write their definitions and post them or the teacher may record them.
+ Students then vote for the definition they believe is correct.
+ If the answer they selected is correct, they score points.

This fun and interactive game can be played individually or as a team. It can be played with cards or via smartboard. It can be modified to accommodate all levels of learners or any grade-level. The game brings laughter, fun, and learning to the classroom and can also be used as a behavior motivational tool. The game can be played with Plickers, interactive apps, pencil and paper, or through survey-type questions where students select a, b, c, or d. No matter how the game is incorporated, students are learning through interaction and having fun.

High-powered teachers know the importance of having fun learning with interactive games. However, they also know the most obvious instructional implication of learning also relates to a well-balanced use of instructional time. They know that students need time every day, in every class, in every content area, to practice their collaborative conversational skills. Having collaborative conversations doesn't mean that teachers should sit back and turn the entire class over to their students. Instructional and collaborative conversations include the teacher who already has established expectations for the conversations, and that students are held accountable for.

High-powered teachers know that collaborative and instructional conversations can occur before and after reading, help promote comprehension, increase vocabulary, and also increase students' oral language. High-powered teachers implement the following during instructional conversations.

1. Students need to be taught the rules of conversation, which include;
   • Avoiding too many or unnecessary details.
   • Have an established purpose that students are aware of.
   • Teach students the expected rules that apply to a collaborative conversation.
   • Ensure students know what is acceptable and what isn't.
   • Don't ask more questions before the first question has been answered.
   • Do not interrupt another person who is speaking.
   • Do not contradict, especially if it's not important.
   • Do not do all the talking.
   • Be an active listener.
   • Don't always be the hero of your story (but keep an open mind).
   • Choose a subject of mutual interest or a subject that is highly interesting.
   • Do not exaggerate.
   • Be careful and use correct quotes.
   • Cultivate tact through exercising good listening and promoting a calm and harmonious atmosphere.

2. Students need to be taught how to use argumentation while interacting with their peers. High-powered teachers establish an expectation that students will engage in argumentation, not argue. The goal is for students to use acceptable and accountable language to talk, persuade, voice opinions, make statements, provide evidence, ask questions, without being disagreeable. High-powered teachers provide students with sentence frames or templates to help them make clear, precise, and meaningful contributions to the conversations.

3. High-powered teachers also establish expectations and accountability for the conversations. This allows students to know that they are responsible for producing something as a result of the collaborative conversation, thus inspiring them to produce quality work while also helping them to remain on task during the conversation.

High-powered teachers are also life-long learners and lovers of knowledge. They strive to learn new and exciting methods of instruction, strategies, and activities to ensure their students' academic success, while also instilling within them a love of learning.

"There's no special formula for the best way to teach word recognition."
~ Dr. Jennifer Chambers
University of the Cumberlands

Engaging Vocabulary Activities for all Learners, Including Remote Learners

High-powered teachers believe that the basis of a student's desire to learn, as well as their academic success, heavily relies on a solid vocabulary. High-powered teachers have recently been faced with the challenge of establishing and also enhancing both in-person and virtual student's vocabulary more than ever before. Teachers have also been faced with the difficulty of motivating virtual students to dig deep into the vast world of words that awaits them.

High-powered teachers know that learning words is time consuming and can be difficult for many students to learn independently. They realize that students become disengaged easily when activities become routine, or what students refer to as, boring. They know that students enjoy creative and collaborative activities inside the classroom and also enjoy socialization that the Internet offers. Thus, high-powered teachers implement engaging and interesting vocabulary learning strategies that do not take a great deal of time, or take time away from reading, but instead are designed with a purpose. High-powered teachers are ramping up remote learning through creating collaborative opportunities that engage students in academic technology that is also fun, rather than losing their students to the pitfall of casual technology that is ever-present in society today.

High-powered teachers know that **Graphic Vocabulary Cards** are a well-researched strategy for learning and also have the ability, if used correctly, to build and enhance student's vocabulary. They require their students to create vocabulary cards, which in turn will help them to make connections between words, examples of the word, nonexamples of the word, and the critical attributes associated with a word. Establishing a routine with vocabulary cards also helps students with their understanding of word meanings as well as key concepts by relating what they do not yet know to other concepts they are familiar with. Graphic vocabulary cards also requires students to pay attention to words for longer periods of time, thus improving their understanding of the words. In addition, vocabulary cards can become an easily accessible reference for students to access repeatedly from their vocabulary journal, or binder.

High-powered teachers know that vocabulary cards can be created and utilized by both in-person and online students. Whether vocabulary cards are implemented in person or online, the steps that high-powered teachers require students to follow are very similar. The vocabulary card acts as a graphic organizer. There are multiple patterns that can be used, but the most common requires students to create a graphic representation of each word. They're not simply writing the word, but also describing the word. To create a card, teachers ask students to do the following:

- Each card should be divided into equal sections of four much like an addition sign. In the center of the four squares, they add an oval where they will write the word in bold colorful ink of their choice.
- Students then write a **definition** from the dictionary in the top left box and a definition in their **own words** in the top right box. For example, the word, *stroll* is defined as, *to walk in a leisurely way*. And can be written as, *a casual walk.*
- Students then **list characteristics** for the word in the bottom left box. For example, the essential characteristics for the word *stroll* might be *walking casually*, and *short distances*.
- Have the students then list several **examples** and also nonexamples of the key concept. For the word *stroll*, this might be *beach, park, or yard*. For nonexamples, students might identify places where you **wouldn't** typically take a stroll. For example, a *busy street* or a *crowed mall.*
- Depending on the type of vocabulary word card, students might choose to create an **illustration** or sketch in the box on the right.

High-powered teachers reveal to their students that the cards are not just study cards, but cards that can help them prepare for a fun, challenging, and collaborative competition that awaits them in upcoming weeks. High-powered teachers plan carefully and also prepare their students to come together virtually through the fun game of, **Vocabulary Slam.** They know that building anticipation for a fun activity, such as Vocabulary Slam, is also a great method of motivation. They know that introducing the competition of a **Vocabulary Slam**, will give students a fun purpose for not just memorizing the words on the cards they created, but also to help them gain a deeper understanding of the words. Vocabulary jam is also great way to create a sense of community, and have fun while learning. A Vocabulary Slam allows students to have a friendly competition, while also increasing student collaboration.

High-powered teachers may choose to create a new list of vocabulary words, or use the preassigned vocabulary words that the students created on **Graphic Vocabulary Cards**. They determine how many questions they want to ask as well as the level of difficulty. High-powered teachers strategically plan and structure the activity around rules that are visibly posted for students to review. They also discuss the rules for the competitive vocabulary game so that students will be prepared and equipped with what is expected of them throughout the activity. Next, they determine the amount of time that students will have to answer each question. Times might range from medium to fast paced depending on the students age, grade-level, or learning level. Students are then divided into teams for mini-competitions.

- The teacher then sets a timer for the preferred time. For example, some teachers may choose to select one minute per question on the virtual timer.

✦ The teacher recites the vocabulary clue orally, and also displays it so students can visually see the clue.

✦ The timer should start as soon as the teacher finishes reading the clue, and the teams will then have the option to buzz in, ring in, or chime in depending on the technology that is being used.

✦ The teacher then announces the team that buzzed in first, and in turn the team responds with what they think the secret vocabulary word is.

✦ If the team answers correctly, they earn a point. If they do not answer correctly, the opposing team has the option to answer and earn the point. If neither team answers correctly, the word is set aside for further review and the game proceeds with the next randomly drawn word.

✦ The game continues until all of the vocabulary words have been used.

✦ The teacher may choose to review the vocabulary words that students were not able to identify after the game.

The above strategies not only help build student's vocabulary, but also increase their understanding of how to use their newfound vocabulary correctly, while also appealing to various learning styles such as the visual learner and the kinesthetic learner. The strategies can also be successful for both in-person students and virtual students. When high-powered teachers begin with an objective, build anticipation, create a fun, challenging, and collaborative purpose for students to learn their assigned vocabulary, their students will be more engaged with the content. Remember, learning does not have to be boring, and it does not have to be routine. High-powered teachers are not afraid of change, are flexible, adaptable, and also determined that all of their students will be academically and socially successful.

Now It's Your Turn

This is a fun and exciting activity. For this assignment you will be randomly paired with a peer to work collaboratively. You will work together and plan activities to teach our class. The activity must be reading-and language arts–based. It must be an activity that introduces, enhances, or promotes vocabulary. Once you've made a collaborative decision about the activity that you will coteach, you will be required to work together to plan how you want to teach the activity, the materials that you will use, and also if you want to use technology. The activity must involve your peers who will become your students while your team is teaching. It must be standard-based with an objective. It must also be engaging and involve interaction and a hands-on-experience. The activity should be no longer than 9 minutes and no less than 7 minutes. Identify the grade-level that your activity will address. Both partners should be involved with teaching, assisting, and monitoring students.

The objective must be clearly written and visible on the board and explained to your students. This can be in the form of an "I can" statement. This is not a full lesson plan, but rather an activity that can be implemented in a lesson plan. Involve your students in the activity as much as possible and have all resources ready to go! Once you've taught the activity you will be required to write a full reflection of the experience from the planning stage until the activity has been taught. Identify your strengths, weaknesses, what was successful, and also areas of improvement. More details can be found on the content page of blackboard. This is a fun activity that will enrich your teaching experience! I will assess your activity, your teaching, creativity, and how engaging your activity was for the students. Random peers will be asked to assess your activity using the TAG rubric, which is located on the content page. I will review the peer assessments and will give those back to you the following week. The rubric for your activity is also located on the content page.

What Can Parents Do to Help?

High-powered teachers know that parents play a vital role in their child's education. These teachers attain and maintain communication with their students' parents. They communicate through blogs, apps, newsletters, telephone calls, emails, and also by having face-to-face conversations (InTASC Standard 10, CCSSO). They keep parents informed of strategies, activities, and suggestions to help their child become successful. As stated in previous chapters, parents are encouraged to read with their child for at least 20 minutes each night. Interactive reading where both the parent and the child participate is encouraged, as well as the parent reading aloud and the child reading aloud. Reading with children is an excellent opportunity to expand both reading and vocabulary skills. Stopping to ask rhetorical questions about parts of the story is an opportunity for parents to encourage their child to think about the topic, descriptions of the characters, or setting while also suggesting new words that might enhance the characters or the setting. Then using those words throughout the story and also in conversations with their child. However, there is more that parents can do to introduce, enhance, and expand their child's vocabulary.

There are many simple activities that parents can do to help their child expand their vocabulary. Ideas that are often overlooked in everyday life. High-powered teachers encourage parents to introduce words in their everyday conversations with their child. Parents are encouraged to use vocabulary words from the story in daily conversations with their child to enhance their child's understanding of how to use the word correctly in daily oral language. Children are naturally curious and constantly absorbing everything that they hear. The more they hear you speaking and incorporating rich vocabulary in daily conversations, the more likely they are to mimic what they hear. Parents have the ultimate choice to enhance their child's vocabulary through a simple, day-to-day, natural conversation that doesn't take time away from their busy schedules.

High-powered teachers also encourage parents to play word games with their children. Word games can be online games, board games, or even as simple as scrabble or Hangman. Internet has a wealth of opportunities through interactive apps for diverse age levels to pique children's interest, promote technology, alleviate parents' busy schedules, while also expanding their child's vocabulary. Word apps can be cleverly woven into alleviate boredom while children ride in the car, sitting tirelessly in the waiting room, or even waiting in checkout lines. High-powered teachers encourage parents to display a menagerie of words in their house whether it is labeling items or simply posting them on the refrigerator. They also encourage them to make the words interactive by talking to their child about the words, ask questions about the words, and also to play games with the words.

High-powered teachers encourage their students' parents to take a proactive role in their child's education. They supply the parents with words that can help their child learn in all content areas, encourage them to be patient with the process of learning vocabulary as it is natural for children to mispronounce or misuse new words. They encourage parents to not reprimand their child for a mistake, but encourage them by praising their attempt, pointing out what they got right and reviewing the proper pronunciation and use of the word. High-powered teachers recommend when parents are trying to teach their child new words to choose four to five words to work with every week.

They also encourage the parents to enjoy interactive opportunities to help their child. High-powered teachers know that a positive and fun learning experience increases students' interest in learning, thus resulting in positive parent/child relationships as well as expanded vocabulary. High-powered teachers encourage the parents to become active participants of their child's education to help expand their vocabulary, enhance their language skills, communication, reading, and overall academic success (InTASC Standard 9, CCSSO).

Author's Tip

As a teacher in both the primary, intermediate, and middle grades I had a desire for my love of words, writing, and reading to spillover to my students. I wanted to make a difference in their lives. I wanted them to love learning as much as I did. Each year I was inspired and recited my quote, *If I will teach it...they will learn,* again and again to myself. One morning while reading my quote that hung above the colorful alphabet chart I realized how important quotes were to me, to my learning, my philosophy of learning, and to me personally. I decided that I would incorporate a quote of the day in my daily instructions.

After careful thought I decided based on my own experience with quotes that if my students read a memorable or thought-provoking quote each morning they too could have an inspiring experience and also gain exposure to new words. This was how, **The Quote of the Day**, became a familiar part of daily learning inside my classroom in all grades that I taught.

The Quote of the Day was incorporated by beginning the day with a quote to provoke students' interest and some higher level thoughts. I selected clever quotes, famous quotes, funny quotes, and quotes that connected to the word of the day and also planned instructions for the day. I wanted to model figurative thinking prior to posting the quotes and incorporating the quote of the day. I selected excerpts of books, poems, and books that the students were familiar with and modeled through the use of read-aloud and think-aloud to explain and model what figurative thinking was. They found this to be exciting and thought of it as a game.

Soon thereafter, each morning began with a quote on the board. I then randomly selected a different student each day to read the quote aloud. I asked the class to then read the quote together without me reading and finally with me reading it in a thoughtful and meaningful tone. I prompted students to consider the following questions.

- ✦ Are there any vocabulary words that need clarification?
- ✦ What did this quote make you think of?
- ✦ What do you think the meaning of this quote is?
- ✦ Can you make any connections to the quote?

I would then randomly pair the students with a peer to discuss the meaning of the quote and encouraged figurative thinking, while also thinking about the questions I had asked. I allowed partners to share their answers and then we briefly discussed the quote as a whole. This was a fun way to begin the day and also encourage collaboration, high-level thinking, and to promote vocabulary (InTASC Standard 5, CCSSO). I encourage you to incorporate a quote of the day. You may modify my method to fit the needs of your students. Nevertheless, it was a positive way to begin the day, empower students with knowledge and also encourage the use of new vocabulary. I was amazed over the years how many students recalled some of the famous quotes that had been displayed on the board when they heard them again in instruction months and even years later in various content. Never underestimate the power of words!

Applications

To help guide you through Chapter Seven and upcoming chapters, become familiar with the following key terms for a deeper understanding of Chapter Seven:

- ✦ Word of the day
- ✦ Schema
- ✦ Basic vocabulary
- ✦ Academic vocabulary
- ✦ Content-specific vocabulary
- ✦ Instructional conversations
- ✦ Grand conversations
- ✦ Content-specific instruction
- ✦ Assessment vocabulary
- ✦ The dictionary game
- ✦ Quote of the day
- ✦ Word journals

In-Seat Activity

Working with a partner, select one of the trade books from the books on your table. Once you've selected a book, **think-pair-share** the book, and work collaboratively to determine five to eight vocabulary words that students might struggle with, should be pretaught and incorporated in a vocabulary activity. Write your words down and be prepared to explain why you selected the words, and give a brief overview of a vocabulary activity that your team would suggest incorporating.

Reflect and Answer the Following Questions

- ✦ *What is vocabulary?*
- ✦ *What is basic vocabulary?*
- ✦ *What is academic vocabulary?*
- ✦ *What is content-specific vocabulary?*

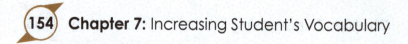

Student Notes

Annotating is an effective learning strategy. This page is reserved for you to annotate *(take notes)*, record potential questions, and also to refer back to when studying, completing assignments, and to help you gain a better understanding of Chapter Seven.

Student Reflections

High-powered teachers reflect. This page is reserved for you to reflect about information that you found insightful and what you have learned from Chapter Seven.

Suggested Readings

DiCamillo, K. *The Miraculous Journey of Edward Tulane.* Candlewick Press, 2006.

Overturf, B., et al. *Word Nerds: Teaching All Students to Learn and Love Vocabulary.* Stenhouse, 2013.

Spiegel, D. *Classroom Discussion: Strategies for Engaging All Students, Building Higher-Level Thinking Skills, and Strengthening Reading and Writing Across the Curriculum.* Scholastic, 2005.

Trelease, J. *The Read Aloud Handbook.* Penguin Random House, 2006.

Chapter References

Beck, I., et al. *Bringing Words to Life: Robust Vocabulary Instruction.* Guilford, 2002.

Burke, J. *The English Teacher's Companion. A Complete Guide to Classroom, Curriculum, and the Profession.* Heinemann, 2008.

Council of Chief State School Officers (CCSSO). *Interstate Teacher Assessment and Support Consortium (InTASC) Model Core Teaching Standards,* Apr. 2011, https://www.ccsso.org/sites/default/files/2017-11/InTASC_Model_Core_Teaching_Standards_2011.pdf. Accessed 7 July 2018.

DiCamillo, K. *The Miraculous Journey of Edward Tulane.* Candlewick Press, 2006.

Marzano, R. J., et al. *Classroom Instruction That Works: Research-Based Strategies for Increasing Student Achievement.* Association for Supervision and Curriculum Development, 2001.

Marzano, R. J., et al. *Building Academic Vocabulary: Teacher's Manual.* Association for Supervision and Curriculum Development, 2005.

Nagy, W. E. *Teaching Vocabulary to Improve Reading Comprehension.* International Reading Association, 1988.

Chapter 8
Promoting Reading Comprehension

"Reading is magical! Reading can allow the reader to escape reality, visit far off lands, travel through time, open doors of knowledge, allow them to meet unforgettable characters, and transport them to places they've never heard or dreamed of. Yes, reading is a magical experience!"

~ Dr. Joyce Bowling

Chapter Questions

- ✦ *What is literal comprehension?*
- ✦ *What is inferential comprehension?*
- ✦ *What is critical comprehension?*
- ✦ *What is evaluative comprehension?*
- ✦ *How do children develop reading comprehension?*
- ✦ *What are effective reading comprehension strategies?*
- ✦ *How should I assess children's reading comprehension?*
- ✦ *How can I motivate my students to read?*

Author Reflection

Comprehension is the heart and soul of reading. Even when my primary students were learning, how letters form words, I encouraged and promoted reading comprehension through interactive read-alouds. I wanted my students to have a desire to read rich literature, to enjoy the plot, to get to know the characters, and also be able to recall the story. To help instill the love of reading within my young students, I emphasized the importance of comprehension in all content areas, every day.

I enjoyed incorporating fun and interactive read-alouds and think-alouds daily, which allowed me to model fluency and comprehension. Incorporating engaging interactive activities also created multiple opportunities to question students about the text, which promoted thinking, which in turn promoted reading comprehension. I wanted my students to be engaged in the text, interact with the author, with the characters, and to be involved with the plot. I wanted my students to become strategic readers, to comprehend the text, and also to love reading.

Comprehension cannot be taught with one chapter or one book. Just as comprehension cannot be taught in a week or even in a month. Comprehension should be taught in all subjects every school day at all grade-levels. After all, comprehension is the ultimate purpose of reading! Students need multiple ongoing opportunities that allow them to practice and incorporate comprehension strategies daily. Participating in collaborative and engaging reading activities and having multiple opportunities to practice using the strategies daily inside the classroom helps ensure students' reading comprehension success.

In this chapter, you will learn what comprehensions is, and the various levels of thinking involved with reading comprehension. You will learn how students develop reading comprehension, and also effective strategies that help promote comprehension. You will learn inspiring techniques that high-powered teachers use to motivate their students to be readers.

In the second half of this book, we will dig deeper into effective comprehension instruction, learn new strategies that can be incorporated at all grade-levels, while also learning new innovative ways to engage students in collaborative reading activities that will help enhance students' reading comprehension. But for now, let's take a closer look at the definition of comprehension and techniques to promote young readers' reading comprehension.

What Is Comprehension?

Comprehension can be defined as a complex process, intentional thinking during reading, or as a multifaceted thought process that occurs while reading allowing the reader to creatively interact with the text. Comprehension has been defined by countless researchers, teachers, and professors with a multitude of different definitions. However, no matter the definition of comprehension, high-powered teachers know the purpose of reading remains the same, which is to construct meaning of what has been read. They also know, in order for students to understand what they're reading, they must make sense of the words in the text to be able to maintain an interest in what they're reading, become strategic readers, and enjoy what they're reading. In contrast, they know that struggling and frustrated readers do not typically understand what they're reading, which can lead to frustration, lack of self-confidence, and lack of enjoyment in reading (InTASC Standard 1, Council of Chief State School Officers [CCSSO]).

Research shows that there is a strong correlation between well-developed word-recognition skills and reading comprehension. High-powered teachers know that both the ability to decode unfamiliar words and recognize a group of words by sight are good predictors of comprehension as students progress through elementary grades. M. Pressley states that reading comprehension instruction begins with teaching decoding skills.

High-powered teachers teach their students that once they recognize a word within the text, they should use context clues to determine the definition or if the word has been properly recognized. Context clues that reinforce comprehension can include reading on to find out more information, simply meaning that students read the remainder of the sentence or paragraph to determine if they decoded the word correctly. Another context clue can be as simple as looking at the pictures or reading the captions. Research shows that extending students' vocabulary improves both reading fluency and reading comprehension.

However, high-powered teachers know that comprehension involves a series of behaviors that occur over time. According to research, students must be explicitly taught not only to understand and remember text, but also comprehension strategies (National Reading Panel; Pressley). High-powered teachers know that the comprehension process begins during prereading as students begin to activate prior knowledge and preview the text. Comprehension continues to develop as students read, respond, explore, and also apply their reading. High-powered teachers know that for their students to become strategic readers they have to be able to think about the text that they are reading at different levels. They know that comprehension involves diverse levels of thinking that include *literal comprehension, inferential comprehension, critical comprehension*, and *evaluative comprehension*.

+ **Literal comprehension**: It is the most basic level of comprehension that involves the reader picking out main ideas, sequencing details, determining similarities and differences, and also identifying explicitly stated information.
+ **Inferential comprehension**: It is a higher level of comprehension. In the inferential level students use their own knowledge along with the information that is presented in the text, as well as implied information to make inferences. The reader also makes predictions, recognizes cause and effect, and determines the author's purpose.
+ **Critical comprehension**: At this level, readers analyze the symbolic meanings, distinguish and determine fact from opinion, and also draw conclusions.
+ **Evaluative comprehension**: This is the most sophisticated level of comprehension where the reader judges the value of the text using generally accepted criteria or their own personal standards. They detect and identify bias, faulty reasoning, and determine the effectiveness of persuasive techniques and assess the quality of the text.

High-powered teachers know the importance of readers engaging in all of the above-mentioned levels of comprehension. They know the importance of involving their students in higher order thinking, asking multi level questions, and in engaging collaborative activities that require them to use inferential, critical, and evaluative comprehension. High-powered teachers know that comprehension is a creative and multifaceted process. Their goal is to engage students every day in activities that allow them multiple opportunities to interact with the text independently, with the teacher, and with their peers. However, they also include comprehension activities designed to engage the entire class, while others are designed for collaborative groups, and still other activities allow partners to work together with the ultimate goal of students being able to apply reading comprehension strategies independently.

High-powered teachers know that providing ongoing opportunities for students to experience engaging reading comprehension activities will help them get accustomed to applying different comprehension strategies without even thinking about applying them. In other words, practicing comprehension strategies with their peers will help them learn the strategies, become comfortable with them, know when to apply them, and ultimately allow them to take ownership of the strategies, to become a natural part of their reading and learning (InTASC Standard, 8 CCSSO).

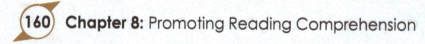
High-powered teachers know when students arrive at this level of reading, they are comfortable, confident, and have the ability to use comprehension strategies independently. In other words, the student is becoming a **strategic reader**.

How Do Children Develop Comprehension?

High-powered teachers know that teaching students strategic reading comprehension strategies in the primary grades and beyond assures that students are learning to effectively, effortlessly, and fluently recognize words, as well as process them to gain meaning of the text. They know that students need to read extensively and receive expert and explicit reading comprehension instructions which are focused on vocabulary and comprehension strategy acquisition.

High-powered teachers also know that students need explicit comprehension instructions, guided-instructions, guided assistance, and multiple opportunities to select and use multiple comprehension strategies to process a variety of texts in order to become fluent and competent readers who understand what they have read, and who can also apply what they have learned from the text. High-powered teachers also know the value of interacting with their students during rich comprehension instructions as well as the importance of peer collaboration and teacher-student collaboration, while incorporating a wide variety of diverse texts and genres.

High-powered teachers know that students' reading comprehension development focuses on higher order processing, activating, and also relating prior knowledge to text content. They also know that reading comprehension focuses on consciously learning, selecting, and also being able to control the use of a variety of cognitive strategies to ensure they are recalling, remembering, and learning from text. They also know that reading comprehension is influenced by **schema theory**, which explains how information is stored in the brain and retrieved to help gain new knowledge. Schemas are mental representations of stereotypical situations. These are described and compared to a filing cabinet of information that is stored in the brain that contains concepts, events, emotions, roles, as well as life's experiences. High-powered teachers know that all students' schemas vary in size, as all students do not have the same experiences or opportunities to develop schemas. They also know that the size and content of schema is influenced by both direct and vicarious experiences.

According to Kintsch, the **situation model** is what the text is really all about: objects, ideas, people, characters, processes, or significant events. Situation models are integrated mental representations of described state of affairs. High-powered teachers know that the situation model is also remembered days, months, and even years of experiences. They know that processing text occurs in cycles that involves multiple cognitive processes. The cognitive processes involved in eventually formulating a *situation model* are influenced by *the reader's knowledge about the topic, text, or message, the reader's motivation, the reader's goal(s), the reader's choice and use of strategies, the type of text, genre, and also the difficulty of the text, and finally the context in which the text was processed.* For example, was the text read independently, collaboratively, through guided reading, in a crowded classroom, a quiet area, etc. High-powered teachers know that the physical setting is related, and also vital, to students' reading comprehension.

High-powered teachers know that two phases of mental processing occur during reading. They know that for each phase the reader encounters a **construction phase** and an **integration phase**. In the two-phase process, the reader initially constructs meaning from the text and then integrates it with prior knowledge to formulate what Kintsch refers to as the **situational model** that is stored and retrieved from long-term memory. In the **construction phase**, a lower level of processing occurs such as activating prior knowledge and experiences, making connections, retrieving words and their meanings, examining the surface of the text, the structure, grammatical structure, text elements, formulating ideas, making inferences, and trying to construct meaning of the text. Whereas, in the **integration phase** the ideas from the text are strongly interwoven with prior knowledge and strengthened through the process of what applies to the meaning of the text and what does not. Readers in this phase are able to disregard, deactivate, and delete concepts that do not fit or apply to the text, or to the integrated knowledge. Thus, they are able to determine the main idea of the text, and gain a deeper meaning of the text.

High-powered teachers know that all readers do not develop reading comprehension at the same rate or in the same way. Again, they know that all students do not learn the same and that each of their students arrive in the classroom with their own *schemas, diverse culture, socioeconomic status*, and *unique experiences*. They know to ensure reading comprehension success, they must first get to know their students as readers to effectively design explicit and beneficial reading comprehension instruction that is designed to meet the needs of all of their students. High-powered teachers know their students as readers. They know how their students read, what their students read, and also where their students read best (InTASC Standard 7, CCSSO).

How and When Should I Assess Children's Reading Comprehension?

High-powered teachers know what reading comprehension is, how to promote it, and they also know their students as readers through interacting and engaging with them, and finally through multiple assessments. High-powered teachers get to know their students as readers through multiple forms of formative reading assessments, observations, listening to them read aloud, asking questions, and also through summative assessments. High-powered teachers collect data through incorporating running records, check lists, and through formal data collected through various diagnostic tests such as MAPS, STAR, weekly assessments, AR, KPREP, and other standardized assessments. They assess students at various times of the academic year, near the beginning of the year to determine each students' academic reading level and throughout the year to monitor their progress. In other words, high-powered teachers implement the integrated instruction–assessment cycle to ensure that students are growing in their ability to understand complex texts and to use increasingly more sophisticated strategies to deepen their understanding of grade-level texts (InTASC Standard 6, CCSSO).

High-powered teachers know reading comprehension assessment is composed of several essential components, for example, the reader, the text, the activity, and the social context. They also know that since reading comprehension is multifaceted, it cannot be adequately measured with a single approach, with one process, or with one particular text or assessment. High-powered teachers make decisions about how they will teach comprehension strategies as well as other reader factors, and they also decide how they will monitor students' progress during instruction and evaluate it afterward. High-powered teachers assess their students informally on a daily basis through monitoring them. For example, they listen to the comments that students make during grand conversations, conference with students, and also examine their entries in reading logs. High-powered teachers implement diverse reading comprehension assessments, which include listening to students read orally every day, asking diverse-leveled questions, allowing and listening to students make predictions, observing students' while they are problem-solving, encouraging and listening to students during grand conversations, literature circles, and also working independently to answer leveled questions.

High-powered teachers also reflect and analyze data to determine academic reading levels, comprehension reading levels, and also fluency levels. High-powered teachers compare various forms of collected data from diverse assessments to ensure that the data justifies their academic decision of a students' reading level, comprehension level, and also their fluency level before planning individualized explicit instructions. This allows teachers' to scaffold instruction to meet the academic needs of all of their students. In other words, high-powered teachers use the data from multiple assessments to drive their instruction (InTASC Standard 6, CCSSO).

Reader and Text Features

High-powered teachers know that comprehension involves both reader and text features. They know that when students are reading, they should be actively engaged with the text. They model and teach their students to think about the things that they comprehend in the text. High-powered teachers use a variety of diverse methods to help students understand how to think about the text. They know that students must have adequate background knowledge to comprehend the text, understand the majority of the words in the text, and be able to read fluently. High-powered teachers know that when any of these prerequisites for comprehension is missing, or lacking, students are less likely to understand what they are reading.

High-powered teachers also teach students to examine the text, make predictions, make connections to their own experiences, visualize and create mental images, draw inferences, and monitor their own understanding. High-powered teachers know that reader features include what the reader brings to the reading process. Reader features also include strategies that a reader uses while he or she is reading, as well as their engagement and motivation while reading. Text features include the author's ideas, words, and phrases that the author uses to express ideas, and also includes organization of how the ideas are presented in the text. High-powered teachers know that both reader and text features affect students' comprehension (InTASC Standard 5, CCSSO).

High-powered teachers know that one of the most effective ways to assess students' reading comprehension is through retelling the story. They know when students retell or summarize the story or information, they are reconstructing the entire text, including major or important elements of the text, including details, and important elements of the plot. During the retelling process students can also make inferences, describe the characters, and make predictions, thus allowing the teacher to assess their understanding of the text. The teachers carefully listens and record anecdotal notes on a running record while students are summarizing, noting important information and areas of concern. High-powered teachers use diverse texts for oral retelling which include expository texts, narrative texts, and informational texts. An example of a running record used for assessing reading comprehension can be found in **Table 8.1**. A comprehension checklist rubric can be found in **Table 8.2**.

This type of running record can be modified and duplicated to fit the needs of all grade-levels, and all texts. High-powered teachers incorporate comprehension checklists to assess and gain a better understanding of their students' comprehension. They know that unlike multiple choice questions, this type of formative assessment gives a deeper understanding of students' comprehension of the text. High-powered teachers include copies of checklists that they have completed over a period of time in an organized data-book. **Data-books** serve as a method of organization of various types of data, student work samples, and anecdotal notes, which can be used for progress monitoring, reflection, instructional planning, and also as a source of documentation of students' progress and areas of concern, which can be useful in ARC meetings, and parent–teacher meetings.

Table 8.1: Comprehension Running Record

Check	Concept	Notes
	Big Idea: An ant is an insect.	
	Detail: Ants have eight legs.	
	Detail: Ants don't have ears.	
	Detail: Ants don't have lungs.	
	Big Idea: All ants live in colonies.	
	Detail: Some ants live in smaller colonies.	
	Detail: Some ants live in large colonies.	
	Detail: Ants hear by feeling vibrations.	
	Big Idea: There are three major kinds of ants in a colony.	
	Detail: There is a queen ant.	
	Detail: Female worker ants	
	Detail: Male worker ants.	
	Detail: Ants have jobs.	
Scoring:	Tally the marks for the big ideas and details. Place the total number of each in the blanks below	
# Big Ideas: _____/3	# Details: _____/10	# of Prompts required _____
	Sequentially retold story: Circle: Yes No	# of inferences _____
Other ideas recalled:	# of Real-life Connection _____	Concerns:

Table 8.2: Comprehension Checklist Rubric

5	✦ Reader includes all main ideas and supporting details. ✦ Reader sequences correctly. ✦ Reader makes inferences beyond the text. ✦ Reader makes real-life connections. ✦ Reader retells story with detail. ✦ Reader doesn't require prompting. ✦ Reader understands text organization.
4	✦ Reader includes most of the main ideas and supporting detail. ✦ Reader sequences correctly. ✦ Reader makes some inferences beyond the text. ✦ Reader makes some real-life connections. ✦ Reader retells story well with minimal mistakes. ✦ Reader requires minimal prompting. ✦ Reader understands text organization.
3	✦ Reader includes most of the main ideas and details. ✦ Reader sequences most of the material correctly. ✦ Reader makes minimal inferences. ✦ Reader makes minimal real-life connections. ✦ Reader retells story with some mistakes. ✦ Reader requires occasional prompting. ✦ Reader understands text organization.
2	✦ Reader includes minimal information about the main ideas and details. ✦ Reader has some difficulty sequencing. ✦ Reader doesn't make inferences. ✦ Reader doesn't make real-life connections. ✦ Reader's information and retelling isn't all relevant to the story. ✦ Reader requires prompting. ✦ Reader doesn't fully understand text organization.

1	✦ Reader omits main idea and gives minimal details.
	✦ Reader has poor sequencing skills.
	✦ Reader doesn't make inferences.
	✦ Reader doesn't make real-life connections.
	✦ Reader gives irrelevant information to the story and doesn't retell story.
	✦ Reader requires prompting.
	✦ Readers doesn't understand text organization.

Characteristics of Effective Comprehension Instruction

High-powered teachers know that reading comprehension begins with teaching decoding skills. Research shows that there is a strong connection between well-developed word-recognition skills and reading comprehension. High-powered teachers know that the ability to decode unfamiliar words and recognize site words in the primary grades predicts and promotes good reading comprehension. They know that once a student recognizes a word, they should be taught to use context clues, the surrounding print, or even the pictures to evaluate whether the word has been properly recognized.

High-powered teachers explicitly teach vocabulary, comprehension strategies, and read a wide variety of texts. They ensure that their students are guided through multiple opportunities to practice application of comprehension strategies across a variety of text types. High-powered teachers also ensure that they involve their students in collaborative reading study groups, a variety of texts, rich-discussions, engaging activities, multiple reading comprehension strategies, and above all they provide multiple opportunities for students to read aloud, in groups and silently (InTASC Standard 8, CCSSO).

Strategies That Promote Comprehension

High-powered teachers know that in order for students to effectively comprehend what they are reading, they need to learn how to coordinate and use a set of key comprehension techniques before reading, during reading, and also after reading. High-powered teachers provide and equip their students with tools and strategies that they will need to comprehend all types of text. They design and divide their instruction into a three-part framework, with specific activities used before, during, and after reading.

What Are Effective Reading Comprehension Strategies?

How will I know which reading comprehension strategies are effective? This is a question that every teacher has asked. Reading comprehension is composed of four different components that each play a vital role in reading comprehension. The four components of reading comprehension include the *reader*, the *text*, the *activities*, *strategies*, and the *situational context*. High-powered teachers ensure that their students are equipped with reading comprehension strategies designed to help the reader prepare for and successfully comprehend what they have read (InTASC Standard 8, CCSSO).

However, high-powered teachers know that teaching comprehension strategies one at a time and explicitly to students can be effective, they also know that all students do not learn the same, thus one strategy does not fit all. They know that students need to learn how to effectively orchestrate, coordinate, and self-regulate the applications of a variety of reading comprehension strategies to effectively construct meaning when reading a variety of texts. They also know that realistically readers do not use only one reading strategy at a time, and that they do not use an individual strategy for weeks at a time, as every strategy does not apply to the same text. High-powered teachers know that students need to be equipped with a multitude of reading comprehension strategies that they can apply to different texts or genres.

High-powered teachers know that teaching their students' to self-regulate their comprehension through integrating and using multiple comprehension strategies is beneficial for students' reading comprehension. They also know the value as well as the difficulties of providing collaborative experiences, teaching multiple comprehension strategies, and also the need for explicit instruction can be difficult and complex. They also know that effective teaching begins with thorough understanding of the concept, strategy, and content. Effective teaching also requires a goal, objective, and motivation. High-powered teachers realize that every first time implementation of a reading strategy and activity may not be successful, thus perseverance and repetition are a must. They don't give up on a strategy just because it wasn't as successful as research stated it would be or didn't happen as they envisioned it to. Instead, they reflect on their instruction, the implementation, and students' knowledge to determine what worked and what didn't. High-powered teachers then make necessary modifications to the lesson, strategy, activities, and. also by thinking outside the box. High-powered teachers are innovative, creative, and flexible.

Regardless of when or where teachers help their students to self-regulate the application of multiple comprehension strategies during reading and discussion of texts, high-powered teachers know that three important conditions should be in place for the instruction to be effective. They first implement and model the **"I do, we do, you do"** in their classroom, which simply means they provide explicit instructions, then engage with their students, and finally release responsibility to their students to work independently. In other words, they gradually shift the responsibility to the students. Second, multiple comprehension strategies instruction focus on the process of constructing meaning from the text rather than on the product of that construction. In other words, the teachers provides explicit instruction, and modeling for students. They incorporate think-aloud(s) to demonstrate how to make decisions about what is worth knowing in the text, or how a text could be interpreted. High-powered teachers then ensure that students are actually beginning to adopt, adapt, and apply reading comprehension strategies in their own reading. Finally, high-powered teachers know the value of modeling in a collaborative, highly interactive, and engaging setting how to strategically orchestrate, coordinate, and also how to apply a collection of reading comprehension strategies to comprehend the text.

High-powered teachers teach their students that reading comprehension strategies are an essential tool for constructing meaning from text, for them to check their own understanding of the text, and also how to take certain actions when they are experiencing difficulty in understanding a text. In other words, teaching multiple reading comprehension strategies requires a highly interactive, collaborative social setting for discussing text. High-powered teachers promote independence through explicit modeling and showing students how to select and apply each and every reading comprehension strategy in the set of multiple strategies. They ensure their students can effectively do this by beginning with explicit instructions, and then quickly moving to combine multiple strategies while also interacting through the text over time. Finally, high-powered teachers gradually release the responsibility over to their students to allow them to work independently, while they continue to monitor and provide assistance for students whom might be struggling.

Making Predictions

High-powered teachers know that humans are wired to infer and predict. They know that students' watch people's facial expressions, body-language, and their reactions. They know that every day students make predictions about books, foods, television shows, and even their teachers. In other words, they know that making predictions is a natural process. They also know that making text predictions is a processing skill strategy. Making predictions in reading is the process of combining the current text information with the readers' own experience to create meaning of what is not directly stated in the text.

High-powered teachers know the value of this strategy. They know that making predictions allows the reader to use information from the text, which can include *titles*, *captions*, *pictures*, *diagrams*, *cover* of a book, and book *title*. They also know the value of students creating connections and making educational guesses that go beyond the author's exact words or images. They also know the value of and encourage students to use their own background knowledge and experiences to anticipate what they are about to read.

High-powered teachers know the importance of involving their students in the text, even before reading the text. They model how to make predictions to ensure that students understand the process, as well as inspiring them to become engaged with the text. High-powered teachers know that a reader who is involved in making predictions is focused on the text at hand, continually thinking ahead, refining, revising, and also verifying his or her predictions. High-powered teachers know that making predictions also encourages and enhances students' ability to make connections between prior knowledge and text, as well as text-to-text inferences/predictions. Nevertheless, predictions can be made at various times. For example, before reading, during reading, and also after reading. Each type of prediction promotes students' involvement in the story and enhances reading comprehension.   #2

+ **Before Reading:** *Look at the title and the cover. What do you think the story is about?*
+ **During Reading:** *Stop! Ask yourself what happened and record any prediction and clues.*
+ **After Reading:** *Check your predictions. Were they correct?*

High-powered teachers incorporate predictions during *read-alouds*, *think-alouds*, *collaborative team work*, and also encourage students to make predictions independently, while recording their answers in a graphic organizer or writing journal. High-powered teachers know that good readers make inferences and predictions while they read. They may draw on their background knowledge or look for clues in the text to supply information about characters, plot, or events that the author has not provided direct details about. High-powered teachers know that students may

initially be more comfortable making predictions about fiction than nonfiction or informational texts. However, they also know that the strategy of making predictions is important to all genres. High-powered teachers make sure to include time for instruction, modeling, and also practicing to help students gain confidence in how to make predictions. When teaching students' to make predictions, high-powered teachers also ensure that students have sufficient background knowledge before beginning to read the text. High-powered teachers also incorporate predictions in other content areas such as science to help promote students skills at processing information, eliminating, and also recalling information. We will delve deeper into the strategy of making predictions and inferences in the second half of this textbook, but for now take a look at an example of a simple graphic organizer in **Table 8.3**. This graphic organizer can be used to help students make predictions based on prior knowledge and also determine if their predictions were correct.

Table 8.3: Making Predictions

What I Already Know	My Prediction Is...	Was I Correct?	Supporting Evidence

KWL Charts

High-powered teachers guide their students through explicit instructions and systematic strategies that activate students' prior knowledge. They know that activating all students' prior knowledge, including ELL students, is vital in promoting reading comprehension. They activate students' prior knowledge through various activities including implementing a **KWL chart**. However, they know KWL Charts are more effective when they read the text prior to incorporating the strategy, and when the questions are designed to guide the KWL process to ensure that the appropriate knowledge is activated to act as an interpretive framework for reading the text. High-powered teachers know the value of incorporating a KWL chart with informational texts to activate prior knowledge and also establish background knowledge. They also know that KWL charts can be implemented successfully with all genres.

KWL charts are based on three questions. The three questions are as follows: What *do I already know? What do I want to know? What did I learn?* High-powered teachers ask their students to brainstorm collaboratively or independently about a particular topic. They may also ask them to categorize what they know through the use of a **graphic organizer**. Once their brainstorming list is categorized, they encourage their students to look within the list of information to determine if there are other categories within the list. Depending on the age or grade, graphic organizers can be completed in collaborative teams, independently or as a class on the whiteboard.

Once students have activated or established what they already know about the topic, character, theme, setting, or plot, they begin the second step of the KWL chart, which is based on the question: What do you want to know? While answering this question, students begin to realize that there are existing gaps, inaccuracies, discrepancies, and possibly disagreements in their prior knowledge and what they want to know more about. High-powered teachers play a vital role in pointing out these areas by helping students design questions. The questions should focus on what students want to have answered. High-powered teachers may model questioning with saying, "*I wonder.*" Once students begin to formulate questions that they want answered, they are encouraged to write the questions down to be answered later.

Finally, after reading, high-powered teachers ask students to write down what they have learned from the text. Students may refer back to the questions they recorded in the KWL chart for what they wanted to know to determine if they can answer the questions, and did they learn what they wanted to by reading the text. High-powered teachers encourage students to reflect on their findings. This can be completed as a whole-group effort with all students contributing to one large KWL chart, in small collaborative groups, or independently. Much of this will depend on the age and grade of students. Nevertheless, KWL charts have been shown to be effective in improving reading comprehension by systematically causing students to think about, activate, organize their knowledge, and also reflect on what they have learned.

Collaborative Learning Teams

High-powered teachers also know that collaboration is key to language acquisition as students collaborate, have discussions, present their findings, and also listen to their peers, all while negotiating language. They know that peer and class collaboration as well as collaborative group discussions and grand conversations are also key in helping English Language Learner (ELL) students develop comprehension. However, high-powered teachers also know that collaborative team discussions help students to attain a higher thinking level, while also allowing them to preserve discussed information for longer times than when working independently.

High-powered teachers strategically group their students to allow them collaborative time to discuss their ideas, perceptions, evaluate text, make inferences, and also to listen to their peers' thoughts and ideas. They know that more information about a text is discussed within a collaborative group, thus helping them to make connections, establish necessary background knowledge, gain valuable insight, while also helping them retain the information in their long-term memory. High-powered teachers believe that the idea of collaborative learning aligns with Vygotsky's idea of the **zone of proximal development**, which considers what a student can do if aided by peers and adults. Thus, resulting in an increase in student awareness of other concepts.

High-powered teachers incorporate collaborative learning teams in their classroom as follows.

✦ **Establishing group goals:** High-powered teachers know that effective collaborative learning involves establishing group goals, while also stressing individual accountability. Establishing goals and objectives prior to beginning the assignment saves time and also helps ensure that groups remain on task.

✦ **Controlling size of groups:** High-powered teachers know that a moderate size group of four to five students is ideal for collaborative learning. They know that small groups of three or less do not provide enough diversity and may not allow divergent thinking to take place. They also know that when groups are too large it is difficult to equally share the conversations, which results in member(s) being stagnant and inactive participants.

✦ **Establishing rules:** High-powered teachers model appropriate behavior in collaborative teams prior to making assignments. They teach their students to listen to others, be tolerant of peer's ideas, views, and perceptions. In other words, they encourage flexible norms that change with the situations.

+ **Successful interpersonal communication**: High-powered teachers emphasize the importance of trust within a team. They stress the importance of explaining concepts thoroughly to each other and uninterrupted listening.

+ **Create group roles**: High-powered teachers also incorporate assigning team members different roles. For example, one member might become the researcher, while another is the reader, or the fact checker, and yet another member might be assigned the job of being the reporter. Nevertheless, this is a great time-saver and also helps in deconstructing a difficult task.

+ **Assessment:** High-powered teachers may also establish a goal for their teams through the aspect of assessment. This type of assignment gives the team a goal and also ensures that learning is a priority. It also allows the teacher to gauge the effectiveness of the group. High-powered teachers may also incorporate a survey. Surveys can be online or hand written that individual members complete to allow more insight into the collaborative effort and success of the team, while also allowing members of the group and teachers to measure the depth of comprehension about the particular topic discussed.

Jigsaw

Collaborative learning has been proven to help promote students interest as well as enhance comprehension, all while increasing classroom rapport and diversity. High-powered teachers use a wide variety of strategies to allow students to work and learn collaboratively. They incorporate activities such as the **jigsaw** strategy. They know that the jigsaw strategy improves social interaction in learning and also supports diversity, is research-based, and also increases students' comprehension. Much like the pieces of an actual jigsaw puzzle is necessary for the puzzle to be complete...each person involved in the jigsaw strategy is essential for the completion and full understanding of the final product. High-powered teachers know that each studens' part is essential, each student is essential, and as a result that is exactly what makes the jigsaw strategy so effective.

Jigsaw strategy involves dividing an assignment into subtasks, where individuals research their assigned areas. High-powered teachers know that students with the same topic from different groups might meet together to discuss ideas between groups, which result in students gaining new insight about a topic, resulting in deeper understanding. The Jigsaw strategy is very simple to implement. There are ten basic steps that include the following:

+ **Step One:** Divide students into five or six person groups. The groups should be diverse in terms of gender, race, ethnicity, and ability.

+ **Step Two:** Appoint one student from each group to be the leader. This should be the most mature and responsible student.

+ **Step Three:** Divide the day's lesson, topic, or chapter into five or six segments. For example, if you want your students to learn more about a character from a book, you might divide a short synopsis of the character into stand alone segments such as in the beginning of a story or novel, near the middle of the book or story, at the climax of the story, or the character near or even at the end of the story.

+ **Step Four:** Assign each student to learn one segment. It's very important that students only have direct access to their segments only.

+ **Step Five:** Allow students time to read over their assignment at least twice and become familiar with it.

+ **Step Six:** Form temporary "expert groups" by allowing one student from each jigsaw group join other members of a group who have been assigned the same segment. Then give students in the expert groups time to discuss the main points of their segment and time to rehearse the presentations that they will make to their own jigsaw group.

+ **Step Seven:** Bring the students back into their jigsaw groups. Students return to their primary groups after researching their topic to explain their findings and educate others about the topic.

+ **Step Eight:** Ask each student to present his or her segment to their group. Encourage others in the group to ask questions for clarification.

+ **Step Nine:** The teacher will circulate around the room from group to group, observing the process. If any group encounters trouble, make an appropriate intervention. Depending on the grade-level, the group leader may be able to handle small situations that might arise. Leaders can be trained by the teacher whispering an instruction on how to intervene, until the leader gets the hang of it.

+ **Step Ten:** At the end of the session, give a quiz on the material. Students realize quickly that these sessions are not just fun and games, but they really count. Thus, enhancing their efforts, collaborative skills, and their overall comprehension of the task at hand.

High-powered teachers know that this type of collaboration allows students to become proficient with the assigned topic. They know that if each student's part is essential, then each student is essential; and that is what makes this particular strategy so effective. They also know that the jigsaw strategy is a research-based cooperative learning technique that has been proven successful over the years. They know that students gain confidence from the knowledge and also gain a deeper meaning, which results in enhanced comprehension.

There are countless reading comprehension strategies available in books, professional development meetings, conferences, and at teacher's fingertips on the Internet. Are they all successful? High-powered teachers know that a reading strategy that was successful with one group of students, may not be as successful with the next group. They also know that reading strategies that are successful for one teacher, may not be as successful for all teachers. #4 The success rate of a reading comprehension strategy depends on how the strategy is implemented, the level of the teachers' enthusiasm, students' enthusiasm, clear objectives, sufficient modeling, and also clear and precise instructions and expectations.

High-powered teachers integrate reading comprehension strategies and activities in their classrooms in all content areas. Reading comprehension is vital for students' understanding. They do not isolate reading strategies in reading, but bring reading alive in social studies, science, math, and other content areas to enhance their students' content knowledge, while also strengthening their reading and comprehension skills. High-powered teachers also know the value of integrating reading and writing in all content areas.

Motivation

"As a special education teacher, I have always said that no matter how severe the disability, every child can learn something."

~ *Mrs. Bonnie Butcher*
University of the Cumberlands

Motivation can be defined as intrinsic and innate curiosity that makes students want figure things out and learn more about something. Motivation involves feeling self-confident, belief in self, believing that you will succeed, and also imagining the activity or book to be enjoyable. However, for students motivation can be social. Students enjoy socializing, sharing ideas, and also participating in collaborative group activities (InTASC Standard 9, CCSSO).

High-powered teachers know that students' motivation to become a better reader or writer can be a powerful tool during the primary years. They also know that students' motivation often diminishes when they reach middle grades, however, they strive regardless the grade-level to motivate their students. They also know that struggling readers demonstrate significantly less enthusiasm for reading and writing than other students do. Thus, high-powered teachers continually strive to motivate students through various collaborative activities, words of encouragement, and whole-group discussions where everyone participates. They also scaffold work to decrease the feeling of stress and being overwhelmed and increase students' self-confidence. High-powered teachers continually provide meaningful feedback pointing out growth areas as well as students' strengths.

These teachers know that many factors contribute to students' engagement and involvement in reading and writing. High-powered teachers know that everything they do affects their students' interest and engagement with literacy, and they also know the four most important factors which include: *the teacher's attitude, the community that teachers create in their classroom, their instructional approaches, and finally their reward system.*

High-powered teachers show students that they care about them, they display excitement and enthusiasm about what they teach, and they also stimulate their students' curiosity and their desire to learn through well-planned instruction and collaborative activities. High-powered teachers build a positive environment inside their classrooms and encourage their students to treat each other with respect, while also giving their students respect. High-powered teachers know that motivation can be contagious. They work tirelessly to do the following: engage their students, focus on students' long-term and short-term learning, set realistic goals, employ words of praise, and provide timely applicable feedback. High-powered teachers also expect their students to be successful, they don't employ negative language or doubt, they minimize competition, treat everyone as equals, and insist every day that everyone can be successful.

High-powered teachers also allow students to have a voice, invite inspiring guest speakers and readers, teach their students what they need to know to be successful, they work with all students to meet their needs, and also provide words of encouragement for all students on a daily basis. High-powered teachers have meaningful conversations with their students. They also read inspiring literature with and to their students daily. They also listen to their students. They reflect on their day and continually strive to improve their instruction, and strive to create fun, innovative, and collaborative learning experiences to motivate their students (InTASC Standard 9, CCSSO).

Language Link

High-powered teachers know that students develop an awareness and appreciation for correct word usage when they encounter it on a regular basis. Students encounter words everyday inside the classroom and in various other places. High-powered teachers teach their students to become word detectives and encourage them to incorporate a variety of words in their daily writing. They also teach students to be aware of the impact that word usage has on the message or the meaning that the author is trying to convey to the reader.

High-powered teachers incorporate a variety of literature to help young readers gain a better understanding of the parts of speech. For example, for their primary students, they might incorporate the book, *The Very Hungry Caterpillar* (Carle) or *Goodnight Moon* (Brown) to teach plural nouns. They may select a different book to teach adjectives such as *Many Luscious Lollipops* (Heller) or *The Napping* House (Wood) to teach synonyms. Nevertheless, high-powered teachers carefully select rich literature that inspires young readers, while also addressing and teaching the particular part(s) of speech they are teaching.

High-powered teachers also incorporate the use of word walls to encourage students to think beyond the obvious word when writing. The word wall can be designed around the content of a particular book that is currently being read to the students, or it can simply provide examples of different parts of speech that students can refer to when they are writing to enhance their writing skills and also to enhance their understanding and use of the parts of speech. See **Table 8.4** for an example of incorporating stronger words in students' writing.

Table 8.4: Selecting Stronger Words

(Noun)	House:	Shack, cottage, condo, mobile home, apartment, dwelling, cabin
(Noun)	Automobile:	Car, truck, van, camper, sports car
(Verb)	Said:	Yelled, shouted, declared, exclaimed, whispered, screamed
(Verb)	Walk:	Skipped, rambled, hiked, strolled, ambled, meandered
(Adjective)	Bright:	Shiny, dazzling, glittering, shimmering, glistening
(Adjective)	Sad:	Depressed, upset, unhappy, blue
(Adverb)	Fast:	Swiftly, speedily, quickly, rapidly
(Adverb)	Slowly:	Gradually, reluctantly, leisurely

Incorporating Virtual Gallery Walks to Promote Reading Comprehension

High-powered teachers know that reading comprehension is the heart and the soul of reading. They encourage and promote comprehension when students are still learning letters, and also when they are decoding words. They also promote reading comprehension before reading, during reading, and after reading. High-powered teachers also strive to adapt many of the strategies they use inside the classroom for in-person learning for their virtual students. However, they know that distance learning often requires students to work more independently than they're used to, so as their teachers, they adjust the methods that they use to help them read the required text.

Reading is an act of constructing meaning. When high-powered teachers provide students materials to read, they also provide them with the necessary tools to understand the text. They provide students with the required tools in a different manner than in person, remote learning requires a greater degree of intentionality in effort to support students as they become increasingly independent.

High-powered teachers strive to create stimulating and collaborative activities that can be conducted both in person and online. **Gallery walks** rank among one of the most preferred strategies for diverse content areas, and also among a wide variety of grade levels. High-powered teachers incorporate virtual gallery walks to build and **activate prior knowledge** and also to **pique student's interest** prior to reading the text. Gallary walks also allow students to work collaboratively in groups to formulate opinions, complete graphs, formulate questions, answer questions, make predictions and or inferences, and also to enhance student engagement and motivation.

High-powered teachers implement gallery walks within their classroom, and also online for virtual learners. A gallery walk is an effective reading strategy that allows students to interact and be engaged as they either walk throughout the classroom, or browse designated folders online. When participating in a gallery walk, both in person and online, students will work in small groups of three to five students depending on the size of the class. They browse designated **charts, posters, graphs, projects,** and or **illustrations** and **collaborate** to **discuss** and **share ideas**.

Virtual gallery walks make a perfect **prereading assignment** and also allow students to interact with various prompts, questions, and also with various images in a creative way that generates curiosity, generates questions, and also helps students **make inferences** and **draw conclusions**. Gallery walks can also be used after **a postreading activity** by including illustrations or events that students place in chronological order to summarize the text. Still other teachers may choose to create a walk that allows students to complete a **character analysis** of various characters within the text. High-powered teachers know that the possibilities are endless.

High-powered teachers plan the virtual gallery walk based on the following steps:

It all begins with your **virtual set-up.** You will need to choose a platform to organize and also to facilitate your virtual Gallery Walk. You might choose to use **Zoom** *or* **Google Slides**. You might even decide to use a combination of the two. High-powered teachers know that an organized setup and a structured plan will help to ensure that there are few, if any problems when their students begin the activity, which will work much like an in-person gallery walk.

✦ Before class, create a separate poster for each in-seat team. For in-person students and online folders or Google Docs for online students. Each poster or Google Doc will contain tasks that teams will be required to complete. Tasks might include, a question(s), a prompt based on the current topic, illustration, or a chapter from a class novel.

✦ Host an initial video meeting with all students to explain the **Virtual Gallery Walk**, familiarize students with expectations and instructions. This also provides an opportunity to activate prior knowledge and get the discussion started. Provide log on instructions, links if you plan to use links, and also date and time of the walk if students will be working independently rather than in groups in real time. This initial meeting can take place the day of the walk if students are going to be completing the walk during real time, or can be prerecorded and scheduled for students to work independently. The choice is yours.

✦ Each folder or poster should be numbered to align with the assigned teams/student's number to maintain organization and guide students to their designated area of the gallery walk.

✦ If using Google Docs or Word documents for online students, then poster/documents should be set up similar to the poster or display that is used for in-person gallery walks.

✦ Before the synchronous class begins, create teams or groups, and number them to match the numbers on the online folders or posters for in-person students.

✦ Prior to beginning the Gallery Walk, create breakout rooms for small groups of students to collaborate and analyze the sources in your premade presentation (*remember to post your slides to Google Classroom or provide a link in the Zoom chat feature*). Students will break out after the initial video meeting to complete their Virtual Gallery Walk.

✦ Predetermine the amount of time that teams will spend in their breakout room. Set the timer accordingly.

✦ Teachers may choose for students to maintain a log that contains the poster numbers or folder numbers for submission, if necessary.

✦ Place students into breakout groups for the first prompt. Students will then access their teams' documents from their designated folders. During the breakout sessions, the teacher may visit various groups to ensure effective collaboration is taking place in each group. Teams will record their answers and or findings. The timer will exhaust and students will automatically be returned to the main meeting room.

✦ **(Rotation Option)** Once students have recorded their teams' answers on their log, the teacher may choose to signal for teams to move to the next group to complete the question and or prompt for that poster or folder. Once teams are in their designated location, start the second breakout rooms. Repeat this process until all the groups have cycled through all the documents.

✦ At the end of the breakout sessions, students will automatically be bumped back to the original video meeting regardless if they rotate or attend a single breakout room. Teachers may then choose to host a quick closing meeting with students to discuss answers, ask questions, present and compare findings, and also to address any misconceptions. Elect a speaker from each small group to share the group's responses, ideas, and questions.

High-powered teachers strategically modify the **research proven strategies** they utilize inside their classroom into rigorous and engaging strategies when teaching students online. They model, set goals, and explain resources while also working to create, modify, and incorporate new innovative strategies and ideas to promote reading **comprehension** and **collaborative opportunities** for all students.

Now It's Your Turn

Getting to know your students is fun, engaging, and also very beneficial. Getting to know your students as readers is vital. Reader's interest surveys are a great source of information. You gain insight to your students' reading preferences, how often they read, where they read, when they read, and genres they want to explore. You will discover students who do not like to read, but will find out what their interests are, which in turn can lead to introducing them to reading materials based on those interests. By better understanding your students as readers, you will be able to provide them with reading material they may not have access to otherwise. The collected data from this survey will help you plan for instruction, suggest books, create collaborative partners, and teams. The data collected is valuable and the possibilities are endless!

For this assignment, you will design a reader's interest survey to administer to the students in your clinical placement. The survey should be aligned to the grade-level and age of students. You may research reader's interest surveys on the Internet for inspiration to create your own tool. This will be a great tool that you can take into your own classroom later. Once you've designed the reader's interest survey, you will need to administer it, evaluate the data, reflect on the process of how you created the survey, how you administered it, and what the results were. In at least a five paragraph reflection you will be required to explain: how you created the survey, what you learned from this assignment, what struggles, if any, did you encounter, and what you would change before administering it again. You will also be required to include how you plan to use the survey in your future classroom. Be sure to describe areas of growth and strength. You will be required to submit a copy of the survey with your written reflection as well as three completed student surveys. Follow confidentiality policy please. Further details are available on blackboard.

What Can Parents Do to Help?

High-powered teachers establish and maintain good communication with their students' parents (InTASC Standard 10, CCSSO). Through good communication, parents stay informed about their child's progress and receive helpful information and ideas to help promote their child's comprehension. One idea that high-powered teachers have found to be successful is providing each student with a packet of three books to take home to read with their parents. The books are scaffold based on difficulty and genre. Each book contains a comprehension card. Comprehension cards are simply bulleted questions and prompts listed on laminated index cards and tucked in the front of each book. The comprehension cards provide parents questions and prompts to incorporate with the book that can either be read aloud by the parent or by their child. Parents are encouraged to read and listen their child read. Parents are also encouraged to create their own questions and make their own predictions to make the reading time more engaging, personalized, and interactive.

High-powered teachers found providing parents with a choice of books to be very successful as well as inspiring. They also found that parents typically incorporate all three books during the course of the week. On Friday, the students return their packet of books and rotate their books with classmates. High-powered teachers encourage their students to think deeply about the books they've read by selecting one student each week to participate in a book talk. Book talks, are simply the student telling the other students about their favorite book. The student who presents is also required to briefly summarize the book in sequential order, include main ideas, key details, and also their personal rating of the book. Book talks encourage students to recall information, promote comprehension, and also inspire other students to read the book. High-powered teachers replace the book that students present with a different book for a couple of weeks, and then adds the book back to the packets. High-powered teachers also provide simple handwritten thank you notes in their students' packet each Friday to allow the parents to know that they are appreciated for their hard work. They include the notes as a means of inspiration, motivation, and also to increase parent involvement.

Author's Tip

From the beginning of the school year until the end of the year, I felt inspired to be an advocate of reading. I had a desire to help my students apply meaning to print by providing effective comprehension instructions for listening and reading. I wanted my students to think about what they were reading, make predictions about what was going to happen in the text, make connections to prior knowledge, visualize the characters and setting, and also question the author. Regardless the age of my students or grade that I taught, I carefully planned instruction implementing reading strategies that equipped students with the tools they needed to understand what they had read that encouraged them to dig deeper into the text, and ultimately to enhance their comprehension.

Each morning as I prepared the classroom for daily instruction I wrote the word of the day as well as the quote of the day on the whiteboard. I also added a colorful poster that described the reading strategy of the day. For example, the *"Making Inferences"* poster that I made for primary students included the following information: what I know already, clues that I found in the text, what questions I have, and my inferences (**Table 8.5**). Students knew that the strategy poster was a clue to the strategy that they would be working on throughout the day. I laminated the posters to be able to write on them with dry erase markers. I worked collaboratively with the students in whole-group discussions to complete the strategy chart to allow students hands-on experience, to help them gain knowledge and confidence, and also to serve as a guide for independent worktime.

I incorporated the, *"I do, we do,* and *now you do,"* strategy with each of the strategy posters to ensure that students knew how and when to implement the strategy. I found this type of instruction and strategy to be very beneficial. It also targeted various learning styles through having a visual aid, a hands-on instrument, and experience, and also providing explicit instructions before releasing responsibility.

Table 8.5: Making Inferences Chart

What I Know Already	Clues That I Found in the Text	What Questions I Have	My Inferences

Applications

To help guide you through Chapter Eight and upcoming chapters, become familiar with the following key terms for a deeper understanding of Chapter Eight;

- ✦ Reading comprehension
- ✦ Literal comprehension
- ✦ Inferential comprehension
- ✦ Critical comprehension
- ✦ Evaluative comprehension
- ✦ Schema
- ✦ Construction phase
- ✦ Integration phase
- ✦ I do, we do, you do (gradual release of responsibility)
- ✦ Strategic readers
- ✦ Situational model
- ✦ Text features
- ✦ Reader features
- ✦ Predictions
- ✦ KWL chart
- ✦ Graphic organizers
- ✦ Zone of proximal development

In-Seat Activity

Select one of the trade-books from your table. Choose a book that you are not already familiar with. Once you've selected a book, do a **book-walk** (*browse the cover, do not read the content, browse the pages, look at the illustrations, and then read the blurb, if there is a blurb available.*) Once you've browsed the book, complete the **inference chart** that is provided for you on the table. After completing the chart, read the book, and go back and review the inferences that you made. Were your inferences correct? Were you able to answer your questions? What have you learned?

   (*The books are arranged by **lexile level**. Select a book that coincides with the grade-level you desire to teach and also matches the degree you are seeking. For example, if you are seeking a middle-school certification, select a book that is appropriate for middle-school students; elementary teachers, select a book that you would use with the grade-level that you would like to teach*).

Reflect and Answer the Following Questions

- ✦ *What is literal comprehension?*
- ✦ *What is inferential comprehension?*
- ✦ *What is critical comprehension?*
- ✦ *What is evaluative comprehension?*
- ✦ *How do children develop reading comprehension?*

✦ *What are effective reading comprehension strategies?*
✦ *How should I assess children's reading comprehension?*
✦ *How can I motivate my students to read?*

Students Notes

Annotating is an effective learning strategy. This page is reserved for you to annotate *(take notes,)* record potential questions, and also to refer back to when studying, completing assignments and to help you gain a better understanding of Chapter Eight.

Student Reflection

High-powered teachers reflect. This page is reserved for you to reflect about information that you found insightful and what you have learned from Chapter Eight.

Suggested Readings

High-powered teachers are life-long learners and continually strive to further and expand their knowledge to ensure that they are providing their students with meaningful learning experiences. There's a large number of resources on the market today to help teachers teach reading and writing fluency. I encourage you to continually seek out rich, inspiring books to read aloud to your students, as well as informative books to increase your knowledge of reading and your teachers' toolbox with diverse reading strategies.

Brown, M. *Goodnight Moon*. Harper Festival, 2007.

Carle, E. *The Very Hungry Caterpillar*. Philomel Books, 1994.

Silverstein, S. *The Giving Tree*. Harper Collins, 1997.

White, E. B. *Charlotte's Web*. Harper and Row, 1952.

Chapter References

Brown, M. *Goodnight Moon*. Harper Festival, 2007.

Carle, E. *The Very Hungry Caterpillar*. Philomel Books, 1994.

Council of Chief State School Officers (CCSSO). *Interstate Teacher Assessment and Support Consortium (InTASC) Model Core Teaching Standards*, Apr. 2011, https://www.ccsso.org/sites/default/files/2017-11/InTASC_Model_Core_Teaching_Standards_2011.pdf. Accessed 7 July 2018.

Heller, R. *Many Luscious Lollipops*. Puffin Books, 1998.

Kintsch, W. *Comprehension: A Paradigm for Cognition*. UP, 1998.

National Reading Panel (NRP). *Report of the National Reading Panel: Teaching Children to Read*. National Institute of Child Health and Human Development, 2000.

Pressley, M. "What Should Comprehension Instruction Be the Instruction of?" *Handbook of Reading Research*, vol. 3. edited by M. L. Kamil, et al. Erlbaum, 2000, pp. 545–61.

Wood, D. *The Napping House*. HMH Books for Young Readers, 2009.

Part Two

Chapter 9
Getting to Know Your Students as Readers

Teacher Quote

"Someone can tell you a story, you can visually watch a story, but nothing enhances your imagination like reading a story."

~ Mr. Bill Lyttle

Chapter Questions

✦ *How well do you know yourself as a reader?*
✦ *Why is it important to know your students as readers?*
✦ *How can I get to know my students as readers?*
✦ *What is a general-interest survey?*
✦ *What are reading-interest surveys?*
✦ *What are reading habits?*

I have often been asked what I like to read. My typical answer is that I like to read a wide variety of books, and that it would be hard to pinpoint one particular genre. I like to include several of my favorite books to the conversation as well. However, I was once faced with the question of, describing myself as a reader. I thought about this question long and hard, and asked if I could get back to them with an answer. My thoughts were consumed for a couple of days with books that I liked to read. With the images of some of my favorite books and series whirling around in my mind, I decided to create a running list of all the different things that I read each day for a week. My list consisted of: *Reading articles on some of my favorite websites and blogs, an occasional magazine article, weekly newspapers, social media posts, the bible, fiction, nonfiction, textbooks, students' work, emails, texts, messages, labels, online news articles, reports, students' transcripts, and my own written work.*

As my list grew in length, I began to think about what and who influenced me to read. I reflected on various teachers who had inspired my love of reading. I recalled fond memories of primary teachers reading fun stories aloud to our class. I visualized interactive Greek mythology read-alouds with my favorite high-school teacher. I enjoyed memories of reading Nancy Drew mysteries with my best friend at her house. Her mom was an elementary librarian and always kept a well-stocked library at home, which we willingly took advantage of. I smiled as I recalled the excitement that I felt when the book mobile pulled into our driveway during the summer months. I remembered watching my mom read while she drank her afternoon coffee and reading with my sister at night before we went to bed. I recalled my grandparents faithfully reading the bible and the weekly newspaper.

After my trip down memory lane, I came to the conclusion that I came from generations of readers. Finally, after much thought, I decided to describe myself as a reader as a person who's culture, family, and friends inspired me to read and who also helped me develop a love and appreciation for reading. I also included in my description that I am an avid and diverse reader who loves to read for relaxation, entertainment, knowledge, and pleasure. I found myself immersed in details about my reading profile. I also included that I liked to read at night before going to sleep, I liked to read on both electronic devices and books, but preferred reading books. I recorded that I loved to read outside while sitting on the front porch, and swinging in the shade beside the creek, in doctors' offices, during lunch, and early morning hours in the comforts of my favorite chair. I explained that I could read in almost any setting, if I was interested and engaged with the characters and plot. I had never really thought about or considered all the details and components that described a persons' reading identity, until now. This was definitely a positive learning experience and one that I wanted to incorporate in my classroom. I wanted to get to know my students as both people and readers. Excitement surged through me as I began the planning process of how I would incorporate this newfound knowledge in my classroom.

In this chapter, you will learn more about yourself as a reader, and the importance of knowing your students as readers. You will also learn how to get to know your students as readers, and discover tools and innovative ideas and activities that you can incorporate in your classroom to help you gain insight about your students as readers, and also how to motivate them to delve deeper into new and exciting literature.

How Well Do You Know Yourself as a Reader?

Researchers continually search for answers to explain why **emergent** readers are not learning to read well by fourth grade. Researchers, teachers, and professors also continue to search for answers to explain why intermediate students do not have a desire to read, or why they have lost interest in reading. Still further research is continually being conducted in search of answers as to why secondary students are reading less and less each academic year. Teachers' concern continues to rise each year as they analyze data from standardized tests. They are concerned with how to increase students' interest in reading as well as reading-comprehension skills. They face daily challenges to create interesting and engaging lessons in an effort to increase students' declining reading comprehension, which wreaks havoc on their daily grades, weekly assessments, standardized test scores, and their overall learning experience in all content areas.

Educators are faced with many questions. What can we do to cultivate, motivate, and instill the love of reading within our students? Why are reluctant readers becoming more prominent, and why are they reluctant to read in the first place? What happened along their educational journey that detoured them or discouraged them from reading? How do we create life-long readers? How can we help them improve reading comprehension? What can we do to ensure that students are college- and career-ready? In other words, teachers are concerned about their students reading ability, motivation to read, and also how they apply what they learn from reading in real-world situations (InTASC Standard 1).

High-powered teachers know themselves as readers. They know how to cultivate the love of reading within their students. They know that their own love of reading must be evident to their students. As high-powered teachers prepare for a new academic year, they reflect on previous instruction, activities, strategies, and their overall reading experience inside and outside the classroom. They also reflect on their personal reading inventory (InTASC Standard 9). They ask themselves the following questions: *Did I inspire my students to read? What did I read with my students? What didn't I read to my students? Did I try new strategies? Was my class engaging and fun? Did my students' reading scores increase? Did my students reach reading mastery? What can I do to improve my reading instruction? What books did I read during summer break? Did I read from a variety of genres? Where did I read? Why did I read? Did I explore new authors? What did I read out of obligation? What didn't I read? Did I read and research new innovative ideas to enhance reading? And, how will I generate excitement, love, and appreciation for reading in my students this year?*

Each summer before beginning a new academic year high-powered teachers answer questions about themselves and then analyze the data to measure their growth as readers to determine what genre(s) they may not read enough from, what genre they prefer to read, have they read enough, what their reading comfort zone is, and much more valuable information. High-powered teachers analyze their answers to the questions listed above as well as many other questions related to reading through **general-interest surveys**, **reading-interest surveys**, and **reading-habits surveys**. Each of these surveys can be created to tailor fit any grade-level or can be found on the Internet.

After reflecting and analyzing the data, high-powered teachers voluntarily make an effort to step out of their own comfort zone to read new and exciting novels in various genres in an effort to expand their interests, knowledge of literature, and have available answers for students who may ask about a particular genre. They also challenge themselves to reread classics, new authors, and even unheard-of authors. High-powered teachers also challenge themselves to read for more than just pleasure, to read resource books in their field of expertise to increase their academic knowledge, to gain insight to new and innovative strategies, and also to enhance their teaching skills (InTASC Standard 8).

In other words, high-powered teachers are life-long learners and readers who continually seek to increase their content knowledge, improve their teaching skills, increase their knowledge of reading strategies, expand their own personal reading inventory, gain valuable insight to new diverse literature, and also gain personal insight into their own reading interests. High-powered teachers know themselves as readers in order to get to know their students better as readers. According to Leigh A. Hall, the term reading identity refers to how capable individuals believe they are in comprehending texts, the value they place on reading, and their understandings of what it means to be a particular type of reader in a given context.

High-powered teachers not only know themselves as readers, they enjoy sharing their reading experiences with colleagues, friends, and most of all with their students. They enjoy telling them about new and exciting books they've read, or about revisiting a classic novel they haven't read in years. They get excited about sharing what they have learned or gained through reading specific books. High-powered teachers intentionally tell their students on a regular basis about new and exciting

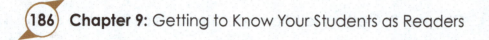

books they've read or want to read. They even share with their students where they like to read, and why they enjoy reading in a specific location. High-powered teachers inspire their students to be life-long readers through allowing them to see them, hear them, and know them as a passionate reader.

> *"To plan for meaningful instruction...we must first know our students."*
> ~ Dr. Joyce Bowling

The Importance of Knowing Your Students as Readers

Just as high-powered teachers know the importance of knowing themselves as readers, they also know the importance of knowing their students as readers. They know that students enter their classroom each year with all types of reading experiences. They know that all students do not possess positive experiences in reading. By middle school, most students have an image of themselves as either a reader or a nonreader. High-powered teachers know that students who do not see themselves as a reader often see reading as a talent that they do not have rather than an attainable skill. High-powered teachers know that reading is an attainable skill, and they strive to inspire those students who do not see themselves as a reader, and work to motivate the unmotivated student(s) (InTASC Standard 3).

High-powered teachers know that students are categorized as readers based on their standardized reading scores and their desire to read outside the classroom. For example, students who do not perform well on standardized tests are categorized as **struggling readers**. Whereas, students who don't read books outside of school or require constant encouragement to read library books are often categorized as **reluctant readers**. Some students may be categorized as both. High-powered teachers use various methods of reading assessments to gain insight into students' reading levels. Assessments may include both formative and summative types. Summative assessments may include dibbels, STAR, Accelerated Reading, MAPS, weekly unit assessments, and many other forms. The data produced from this type of assessment is valuable and allows the teacher to plan instruction that can be scaffold to fit the needs of all students, while also providing valuable insight into students' reading ability (InTASC Standard 6). However, the data limits the teacher's knowledge of a students' true reading identity.

High-powered teachers know that each of their students possesses a different reading identity. For example, a fifth-grade teacher who has 147 students, will have 147 unique and diverse reading identities. Some students enjoy the same genre and authors, gain similar scores on standardized tests, enjoy the same book(s), etc. However, high-powered teachers know that no two students have exactly the same reading identity. For example, some students may enjoy reading informational texts, while others may enjoy fiction, and still others may enjoy biographies. Some students may enjoy reading from electronic devices, while a large majority prefer books. High-powered teachers know their students, their reading preferences, and reading habits.

Just as high-powered teachers are required to read literature in their content areas on a regular basis to continually improve their teaching and expand their knowledge, they also know and consider the fact that their students are required to read obligated material. Reflect for a moment about how you feel when you are required to read a nonfiction text for class. Be honest, how did you feel? High-powered teachers know that dealing with assigned texts or obligated reading is no different for their students than it is for the teacher. They consider the diverse reading identities that students bring to their classrooms and how their identities could affect their reading, and work to create opportunities where students have a choice of materials to read including magazines, newspapers, novels, comic books, and also electronic books.

They also know that students' academic identities matter and are significant when considering their abilities and their willingness to meet the literacy demands in learning within content areas. High-powered teachers also know that their role as a teacher and mentor is critical for developing students as readers, writers, and also as thinkers in all content areas at all grade levels. Research has proven that the language teachers use when speaking in the presence of their students and also speaking to their students is powerful. High-powered teachers know that they can encourage students who may think of themselves as being an unmotivated reader, or having difficulty in math, or even refer themselves as not being a science person. Once again, reflect for a moment. Have you ever stated that you are not a math person, or that you are not a science person? Teachers have the power to encourage or discourage their students both intentionally and unintentionally by the language they use in their classrooms. High-powered teachers strive to maintain a positive attitude and never possess negativity about a discipline in the presence of their students. High-powered teachers are motivators. They motivate their students in all content areas and strive to know their academic strengths, their weaknesses, their interests, disinterests, and also their reading identities both inside and outside the school setting.

General-Interest Surveys

Surveys hold a wealth of information that can be very beneficial for teachers. High-powered teachers implement a variety of surveys at the beginning of each academic year to gain useful nuggets of information about who their students actually are. General-interest surveys are often given first to break the ice, create a comfort zone, and also to gain a better understanding of students' general interests, individual preferences, and also their personalities. General-interest surveys can be created quickly or found on the Internet. General-interest survey questions may include, but are not limited to the following:

- ✦ *What is your favorite television show?*
- ✦ *Who do you consider your hero?*
- ✦ *Who is your favorite sports figure?*
- ✦ *What is your favorite movie?*
- ✦ *What are your hobbies? List three of them.*
- ✦ *What is your favorite food?*
- ✦ *What is your least favorite food?*
- ✦ *Do you have a pet?*
- ✦ *Who is your favorite singer?*
- ✦ *What is your favorite season?*
- ✦ *What is your favorite holiday?*

High-powered teachers then analyze the surveys for information that will help them create student profiles that provide them with useful information to help them get to know their students, and also information that can be useful for encouraging their students to read. After analyzing the surveys and making notes to refer back to, a reading-interest survey is given to students. Reading-interest surveys allow the teacher to better know their students' past reading experiences, reading preferences, and also reading aspirations.

Reading-Interest Surveys

Every teacher has hopes and dreams that their students will be readers. They envision them with their nose buried within the pages of a book, begging for a few more minutes to read. But in reality, they know that all students' desire to read is not that evident or prominent. As a teacher, you will have students that read voraciously, if and only if the book is about sports figures. You may also have students who will read anything that they can get their hands on. You will also have students who really wants to read dystopian novels, but just don't understand the plot. You will also have students who want to be readers, but in reality are truly just not interested in reading. And even still, you will have students who resist reading all together. The question at hand is how will you know this valuable information about your students' reading habits, desires, struggles, and also their fears?

High-powered teachers know the value of finding out about their students as readers is crucial to their planning, instruction, assessment, and ability to motivate their students. They also know that finding out if a child is a struggling reader or an unmotivated reader is the first step in motivating them to read. They know that they must determine students' independent, instructional, and also their frustration reading level. They know they must determine their interests, where they read, why they read, or why they do not read, what family members, if any, read, and also what they are interested in and what they are not interested in (InTASC Standard 4). High-powered teachers know the power of a reading-interest survey. Just as they self-assessed their own reading interests and inventory, they administer interest surveys to their students at the beginning of each academic year in an effort to learn more about their students' reading habits and preferences, as well as to prepare activities, lessons, instruction, and also their classroom library for them (InTASC Standard 5).

Reading-interest surveys are completed in various ways depending upon the age of the students completing the survey. For example, teachers administer surveys in small groups for young primary students, and independently for older, more independent students. Reading-interest surveys can be as simplistic as necessary or as elaborate as needed. Kindergarten surveys may consist of faces of interest, such as rating with a smiley face for interested, a face with little to no expression for maybe, and a face with a sad face or frown for not interested. They may also encircle the number of fingers held up on an image of a hand to show levels of interest. Whereas, a reading-interest survey for older students will obviously have explicit questions about reading preferences, where they enjoy reading, do they prefer a book or electronic reading, etc. Questions may also include, but not be limited to, the following:

+ *What is your favorite subject in school?*
+ *What is your least favorite subject in school?*
+ *What do you like to do in your free time?*
+ *What do you enjoy collecting?*
+ *Do you enjoy traveling?*
+ *If you could have a pet of your choice, what would it be?*
+ *If you could talk to any person from history, who would it be?*
+ *What kind of books do you like to read?*
+ *Who is your favorite book character? Why?*
+ *Do you read at home?*
+ *Who do you consider your hero?*
+ *How much time do you spend reading outside of school?*

An example of an intermediate reading survey is shown in **Table 9.1.** High-powered teachers combine the information that they collect from the general-interest surveys with the data from

Table 9.1: Intermediate Reading-Interest Survey

Name: _____ Date: _____

Reading-Interest Survey

1. What type of books do you like to read? _____

2. Do you have a favorite book? What is your favorite book? Why did you like this book?
   _____
   _____

   Where is your favorite place to read? Describe your special reading place.
   _____
   _____
   _____

3. Which books do you prefer? Books that tell stories, book about real people or places, or books about animals. Circle the books you like to read.

4. What else would you like to tell me about your reading? Is there anything hard about reading for you? _____
   _____
   _____
   _____

5. What would you like learn to do as a reader? What would you like to read that you've never read before?
   _____
   _____
   _____

6. What is your reading goal for this year? _____
   _____
   _____

7. Which of the following types of books do you like? Circle your favorite. If you do not know a type of book, just skip it.

   Mystery, adventure, animal stories, comics, how to, biographies, poetry, science books, folktales, newspapers, magazines, series, picture books, fantasy, chapter books, funny books, informational books, books about people, or graphic novels

the reading-interest survey to better know their students and to be able to know them as readers to ensure that books that would appeal to them are available inside the classroom, integrated into daily instruction, activities, and assignments, and also to be able to provide them book suggestions that will pique their interest and match their personalities. High-powered teachers also administer a reading-habits survey to better understand their students' reading habits.

Reading-Habits Inventory

High-powered teachers go beyond simply administering a reading-interest survey, they create a reading-habit inventory. After administering the reading-interest survey, they administer the reading-habits survey and record the data into a running record. Accumulating and maintaining this data helps teachers to discover how their students approach reading, and also helps them to identify habits that need to be modified or even relinquished. Reading-habit surveys vary from teacher to teacher, so does the inventory. However, most surveys and inventories contain questions such as:

- *How many books is student reading? (specified times will vary with grade-levels)*
- *Does student read e-books, print books, or both?*
- *How much time does student spend reading? (specified times will vary with grade-levels)*
- *Where do they do most of their reading?*
- *Do they ever pretend to read?*
- *How well do they think they read?*
- *How well do they actually read?*
- *Is their fluency improving?*
- *How well do they comprehend what they are reading silent?*
- *How well do they comprehend what another person is reading?*
- *How do they feel about reading in free time?*
- *How do they feel about reading outside of school?*
- *What obstacles might prevent them from reading for pleasure?*

Once high-powered teachers have accumulated the data from surveys and inventories, as well as reading-interest surveys, they analyze and compile a readers' profile of each student. High-powered teachers often revisit their students' reading profiles and reassess, administer new surveys, and even ask students' periodical questions about what they are reading, offering suggestions for new books to read, and also take time to listen to their students read. In other words, high-powered teachers take time, and even make time, to conduct student interviews.

High-powered teachers also know the value of interviewing their students. However, they know that time is not always available for interviews and as a result they randomly pull completed interest surveys and interview one student per week to discover if students have read in genres that they may have not read at the time they completed the survey, or even to find out if they have learned anything more about themselves as a reader. The number of students interviewed can be based on the number of students in class. For example, a self-contained classroom teacher will obviously be able to interview more than one student per week, whereas a departmentalized teacher would have more students per day and could only interview one or two students per week.

Classroom Conditions for Meaningful Reading

High-powered teachers know when instruction is well thought out, planned, standard-based, and include engaging activities is typically successful (InTASC Standard, 7). They also know that for their instruction to be beneficial, their classrooms rapport should be motivational, and for their students to truly learn to their fullest potential, their students need to be surrounded with positive words of praise, understanding, and an environment that radiated enthusiasm. In other words, their classroom environment and conditions should be an environment that fosters learning. High-powered teachers provide sufficient time for their students to practice what they are expected to learn. Their lessons are filled with daily opportunities for students to apply old and newfound skills in their library books, classroom books, content-area reading, and also in writing assignments.

High-powered teachers surround their students with books of all genres and provide multiple and ongoing daily opportunities for them to read, and be read to. They have rich, meaningful conversations about reading with their students and discuss what is being read, what students want to read, and also what insight or insightful new information they have gained through recently read literature. High-powered teachers provide students with access to hundreds of books from all genres and diverse reading levels, while also surrounding them with encouragement to read deeply and widely. They know students need to receive encouragement for the skills and knowledge they possess, while also being encouraged when they make mistakes as they work toward their goals, benchmarks, and mastery.

High-powered teachers read daily to their students, regardless the grade-level. In high-powered teachers' classrooms, reading occurs during reading instruction to model various learning goals, and also to model skills that readers need to develop reading proficiency. They read from a wide variety of genres including, fiction, informational, articles, nonfiction, textbooks, and novels. They also set reading expectations for their students. Expectations may include reading every day, exploring a new genre or new author each week, increasing the number of pages or chapters per day to increase students' reading stamina. High-powered teachers know that when they set expectations for students' reading success through words of continued encouragement, their students will work to rise to the level of the teachers' expectations. High-powered teachers also know that students need to assume responsibility and make academic choices for themselves. For example, teachers may set the number of required books and even the genres, but still allow their students to select the books or authors they want to read in the designated genres.

High-powered teachers provide their students with immediate feedback on their progress, along with encouragement, guidance, and also validation for their reading progress. They also hold frequent mini-conferences with their students, and also require them to respond through written responses such as letters or essays about their book(s), and also discuss their reading with them on a daily basis. High-powered teachers create opportunities for students to collaborate and be involved in reading activities that are enjoyable for students, and also promote the feeling of personal value as well. High-powered teachers know that when students know the reason or objective for the activity, what is being asked of them, and why, while also feeling encouraged and capable of completing the given task, they are more likely to view themselves as readers. High-powered teachers ensure that the assigned activities and assignments do not weigh the students down and create a sense of anxiety, but promote positive connections that encourage and inspire them to dig deeper into their reading.

High-powered teachers establish and maintain a positive, encouraging, and trust worthy environment that is filled with motivation where their students feel free to take academic risks. They know that this type of learning environment allows their students to feel comfortable, confident and free to learn, free to enjoy, and more willing to take academic risks that help them excel academically in all content areas. High-powered teachers do not exclude themselves from reading, they read to their students, with their students, and listen to their students read on a daily basis. During independent reading time, high-powered teachers can be found enjoying a little quality time independently reading as well. They strive to set a positive example for their students, while also promoting a meaningful reading environment where students can grow academically and appreciate the value and joy of reading (InTASC Standard 3).

Activities

It is always fun and beneficial for students to collaborate and learn about themselves as well as their peers. One activity that increases engagement and classroom rapport is student-led interviews. To conduct **student-led interviews** you will need to do the following.

+ Prepare questions based on students' age or grade-level.
+ Pair students with a partner. I prefer to randomly select partners.
+ Provide students with a list of potential questions and determine who will interview first.
+ As students answer questions and discuss their findings, they record their information on their questionnaire.
+ After both students have completed the interview process, they should let the teacher know they have completed their interviews and recorded their answers through a signal such as flipping a red/green card to green, or placing a thumbs up-thumbs down card to thumbs up, or simply raising their hands. This will depend on the grade-level. I enjoyed the red/green cards for all grades.
+ After all students have completed their interviews, students will present a summary of their partner's findings to the class.

This activity promotes more than classroom rapport and student engagement. It allows for much-needed collaboration time, enhances oral speaking skills, summarizing skills, and also cultivates reading motivation and inspiration. Student-led interviews also encourage students to begin thinking about their own personal reading identity, inspire, and also encourage them to step outside of their reading-comfort zone. Thus, establishing and enhancing reading conditions and a classroom environment that promotes meaningful reading (InTASC Standard 3).

High-powered teachers engage their students in reading through inviting them to socialize around reading. They setup book clubs where students can meet for 30 minutes weekly to discuss books they are reading. They also create book clubs for students to meet outside of school to discuss novels and share thoughts and ideas. High-powered teachers create diverse reading groups that can be scaffold by reading levels, general interest(s), gender, etc. to encourage students to read, collaborate, and create diverse projects. They also incorporate literature circles to allow students to discuss chapters, individual books, trade books, library books, and so forth, to encourage comprehension, collaboration, and promote the love of reading.

High-powered teachers also seek opportunities to be a leader in their school and also in their community. They enjoy being a role model for students, colleagues, and parents. They take responsibility for their students' learning and collaborate with families, colleagues, and members of the community to create opportunities for all children to learn, read, and cultivate a love of reading throughout their community (InTASC Standard 10). They create parents reading night, organize reading field trips to the public library, invite authors to speak to their students, and even organize a read-a-thon that all students, parents, colleagues, and administrators can be involved in. Read-a-thons can be modified for various grade-levels. For example, primary students enjoy read-a-thons that incorporate pajama day, guest readers, book challenges, partner reading, and quiet-time reading. Middle school students enjoy book challenges that involve prizes, entertainment, motivational speakers, sports figures, new and exciting literature, and awards. Middle school students also enjoy a little healthy competition that involves team work. The possibilities of reading activities for all students, families, and communities are unlimited. It begins with the desire of a single teacher. Will you be that teacher?

Language Link

Reader's notebooks are a great way to incorporate and enhance students' writing skills. They also promote reflective thinking, comprehension, deep-thinking, problem-solving, summarization, and also allow the teacher to gain valuable insight into students' momentum. Reader's notebooks allow students to write response entries to the teacher once a week. This is an easy activity that can be modified to meet the needs of all students at all grade-levels. Responses may include writing a letter to the teacher explaining their thoughts about a book that they have read during that week, are currently reading, and also why the book appealed to them or why it did not. Other responses could be a letter to the author asking questions about a book that they've read that week. Teachers can ask students to summarize a chapter of a novel that the class is reading as whole, or individual library books, or books that they plan to read in the upcoming week. Nevertheless, student's reader's notebooks allow the teacher to monitor students reading progress, what new genres they've explored, what genre they do not enjoy, or even what problems they may have encountered. In other words, reader's notebooks provides the teacher with valuable clues about their students as readers (InTASC Standards 4, 5, 6, 7, & 8, Council of Chief State School Officers [CCSSO]).

Getting to Know Virtual Students as Readers

High-powered teachers understand the challenges of motivating students to read. With these challenges in mind, they strive to create and implement various types of surveys to learn more about their students reading preferences, styles, and habits. Surveys may consist of a combination of a **general interest survey**, **reading habits inventory**, and or a **reading interest survey**. High-powered teachers found that after creating one survey with a mix of questions from each of the surveys, students were more engaged and answered the surveys in greater depth. High-powered teachers incorporate online poling as a method of gathering data. The data can reveal a wide variety of information from learning more about student's reading preferences, their favorite characters, preferred genres, and answers to chapter questions. **Poling** students produces data, but also increases student engagement. High-powered teachers use the data to select literature that students are interested in, create engaging assignments, create probing questions, while also getting to know their students as readers. Surveys can be completed in various software applications such as, **Zoom,** or **Survey Monkey.** For those that are not comfortable or have the ability to create online surveys, the option of completing a word document survey and submitting via email remains an option. However, online surveys and poling calculates the data quickly and accurately for the teachers. Moreover, high-powered

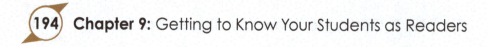
teachers know that surveys and poling can be used to get to know their students, plan instruction, and also extend instruction to enhance student's reading experience both in-person and online.

Now It's Your Turn

For this assignment, you will complete two tasks. The first task consists of completing a self-analysis of yourself. Through completing this assignment you will gain insight into your own reading habits, preferences, and also better know yourself as a reader. Please answer the following questions: *Who inspired you to read? Why? Where do you like to read? Do you like to read from electronic devices? Why or why not? Where do you prefer to read? Has your reading preferences changed over time? How? Do you have a favorite author? If so, who is your favorite author? Have you had a negative experience with reading? If so, describe the experience. Do you think the negative experience may have affected your desire to read? If so, how? Have you had to overcome reading hurdles? If so, describe the hurdle(s) that you overcome and how you did it.* Record your answers, and then write at least a five paragraph reflection describing your findings. Details for the reflection can be found in the drop box in iLearn.

For the second half of this assignment, you will be required to design general-interest survey, reading-interest survey, and a reading-habit survey that you will administer in your cooperating teachers' classroom to better know the students as readers. The surveys can be combined to create one larger survey or separate. Much of this will depend on the grade-level that the instrument is designed for. For example, intermediate, middle, and secondary students can work independently and complete the survey as a single assignment, whereas primary students might require the assignment to be divided into mini-surveys. Once you've designed the survey(s), you will be required to administer the survey(s) to the students in your clinical placement. Once you've administered the survey(s) you will be required to analyze the data and write at least a five paragraph reflection about your experience of designing your instrument, your experience administering it including what you have learned from this assignment as well as what changes you might. Explain what you feel was successful and what could be improved. Also, include at least a paragraph about how you plan to incorporate the instrument in your future classroom, as well as what you want to achieve by administering the survey(s). You will be required to submit a copy of the survey(s), as well as at least three completed surveys. Specific details for this assignment can be found in the drop box on iLearn.

What Can Parents Do to Help?

Parents/guardians are a vital component of students' academic success. Involving parents through classroom websites, parent–teacher night, conferences, and in general through good communication is key to involving parents/guardians with their child's education. Parents/guardians should be encouraged to read with their students. High-powered teachers involve parents/guardians of young students with their child's reading through nightly interactive read-alouds and reading logs. Parents of middle-school or secondary students are encouraged to read with their children as well, only not to them. High-powered teachers have discovered that some parents enjoy reading books that their child is reading. I discovered through a survey that 89% of my sixth-grade students' parents/guardians enjoyed reading, and wanted to know what their child was reading to enable them to encourage them to read. I also discovered through a student-survey that 62% of the students enjoyed the challenge of completing a book they were reading with their parent(s). This led to the parent/student reading challenge that increased students' desire to read, number of books read per year, as well as reading comprehension. Parents were equally inspired to read more for themselves and with their children.

Parents and students are both busy, both have responsibilities, and both have limited amount of time to spend on additional reading, as well as have limited quality time together. When parents read the same author, genre, or even the same book, they share a commonality, which can result in conversations about what they are reading during dinner, the drive to school, or as they walk through the local department store, or grocery store. Involving parents/guardians through constant communication, engaging them in fun interactive reading challenges that are not stressful or demanding, accepting their book suggestions, including them in community reading events, and also keeping them updated on their child's academic progress while maintaining a positive relationship will motivate parents/guardians to be an active part of their child's academic career (InTASC Standard 10, CCSSO).

Author's Tip

As a teacher, I am obsessed with cultivating a passion and a love of reading in my students. I have always loved to read. I love the opportunities that reading provides. I love that I can travel to far off places, learn about new and exciting cultures, meet rich new characters, explore the wild west, go spelunking, sail the ocean, soar through the sky, travel though time, visit new and diverse societies, and even revisit historical figures from our past. How is this possible? Through the wonderful world of reading the possibilities are unlimited. I want to open the same doors of opportunities to my students.

The first step in engaging students and cultivating a passion for reading is simple, read to them. Regardless the age or grade that I taught, I read with my students daily. We read for pleasure, for information, instructions, and to answer questions. I integrated reading in all content areas. After all, reading affects every facet of learning. I also learned through first-hand experiences that reading sometimes took the backseat to technology. Students began to discover the wonderful world of technology at the tender age of two, and sometimes even younger. By the time those students arrived in my first-grade classroom, they were often already bored with the idea of reading and were simply, unmotivated. Reading often appeared to be too much trouble for them, and it didn't come as easy for them as touching apps and playing colorful interactive games. The instant gratification they had come to enjoy with technology wasn't present with reading. I was faced with the challenge of motivating the unmotivated. I was inspired, however, each year with a small number of students whose parents didn't allow them to overuse technology, and who also encouraged reading. But, the number of students who ate, slept, and breathed gaming and technology always seemed to prevail.

After much thought, and trying various ideas to motivate the unmotivated, or inspire the uninterested readers. I decided to follow the old cliché, if you can't beat them...join them. Yes, that's right! I found that as technology became more prevalent in society and with students, I had to step up my game and be creative with technology and use it to work for the good of reading! I learned to stay on top of new and innovative uses of technology and to use my newfound technology skills to promote reading. So, instead of fighting the ongoing battle of reading verses technology, I combined the two. This allowed students to enhance technology and reading skills in new and exciting ways.

I encouraged primary students to use various apps to create alphabet books, read stories from research-based websites, interact with technology using educational websites, and also listen to exciting and colorful read-alouds from various celebrities. I also encouraged them to read on electronic readers and tablets. I discovered through incorporating fun and engaging activities on the smart board, using laptops, electronic readers, and tablets to promote reading, students were encouraged, motivated, and excited about learning in useful and creative ways. Some discovered that they actually liked to read.

While teaching intermediate and middle-grade students, I learned that they were even more absorbed in technology, their phones, and social media than primary students. I also discovered that I would have to be even more creative with technology to gain and maintain their interest in reading. I was surprised to discover that students at this age still enjoyed many of the activities and types of technology that primary students enjoyed. They enjoyed age-appropriate apps, interactive websites, and even enjoyed electronic read-alouds read by celebrities. They also enjoyed making power points, book trailers, and prezi presentations about books they were required to read, and books they chose to read. They enjoyed seeing their work on the smart board, and actually became excited about presenting their ideas to the class. They also found it less boring, as they referred to it, to create their work in exciting projects than always write about their responses. They were encouraged to write in their writers' notebooks if they could type it online rather than on paper. They also enjoyed researching various assigned topics on the Internet, reading news articles, and also researching various authors.

In other words, I found that if I included topics or settings that inspired students to read or write, students' motivation increased, reading scores steadily increased, student interest increased, collaboration increased, technology skills increased, and classroom rapport soared! I also found that I grew as a teacher, gained new insight in my own reading profile, I discovered new and innovative technology, new engaging strategies, discovered new authors via students' suggestions, enhanced my technology skills, became more motivated, and enjoyed learning with my students, while also establishing a classroom where reading was encouraged, and experienced a comfortable atmosphere where both the students and the teacher could take academic risks all the while enjoyed reading.

Applications

To help guide you through Chapter Nine and upcoming chapters, become familiar with the following key terms for a deeper understanding of Chapter Nine:

- ✦ Emergent readers
- ✦ General-interest surveys
- ✦ Reading-interest surveys
- ✦ Reading-habits surveys
- ✦ Genres
- ✦ Struggling readers
- ✦ Reluctant readers
- ✦ Student-led interviews
- ✦ Reader's notebooks

In-Seat Activity

Work with your group to research the reading strategy that you randomly select from the container of reading strategies. Be prepared to briefly inform the class about the reading strategy, why, when, and how it should be implemented. Explain how teachers can differentiate and scaffold for the strategy, and also what the objectives are for implementing the strategy. You will be given in-class time to research, collaborate, and create. This is an informal presentation of sharing knowledge and ideas with each other. Provide the website(s) where you located the information so that others can explore the website. You may post the websites on our classroom remind 101 account.

Reflect and Answer the Following Questions

+ *How well do you know yourself as a reader?*
+ *Why is it important to know your students as a readers?*
+ *How can I get to know my students as readers?*
+ *What is a general-interest survey?*
+ *What are reading-interest surveys?*
+ *What are reading habits?*

Student Notes

Annotation is an effective learning strategy. This page is reserved for you to annotate *(take notes)* record potential questions, and also to refer back to when studying, completing assignments, and to help you gain a better understanding of Chapter Nine.

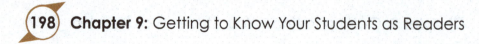

Student Reflection

High-powered teachers reflect. This page is reserved for you to reflect about information that you found insightful and what you have learned from Chapter Nine.

Suggested Readings

Miller, D. *The Book Whisperer*. Scholastic, 2009.

Miller, D., et al. *Reading in the Wild*. Jossey-Bass, 2013.

Chapter References

Council of Chief State School Officers (CCSSO). *Interstate Teacher Assessment and Support Consortium (InTASC) Model Core Teaching Standards*, Apr. 2011, https://www.ccsso.org/sites/default/files/2017-11/InTASC_Model_Core_Teaching_Standards_2011.pdf. Accessed 7 July 2018.

Hall, Leigh A. "Rewriting Identities: Creating Spaces for Students and Teachers to Challenge the Norms of What It Means to Be a Reader in School." *Journal of Adolescent and Adult Literacy, vol. 55, no. 5*, 2012, pp. 368–73. doi:10.1003/JAAL.00045.

Chapter 10
Promoting Good Study Habits

Teacher Quote

"If you will teach it… they will learn it. When they learn it… they will own it!"

~ Dr. Joyce Bowling

Chapter Questions

- *Why are good study habits important in students' learning?*
- *How can I promote good study habits?*
- *What is metacognition?*
- *What literacy strategies promote study skills?*
- *What activities can I incorporate in my classroom to promote study skills?*
- *What can parents do to help?*

The Importance of Good Study Habits

Take a little time and reflect on your personal study habits. Do you read, highlight, take notes, make annotations, create outlines, incorporate mnemonics, or recite and reread? Think about the study strategies that have been helpful to you. It is important to be aware of how you study, know what strategies have been beneficial for you, as well as know a variety of different study strategies before teaching students how to study.

High-powered teachers know that good study habits are a vital part of learning for students of all ages. They know that study habits children develop at an early age will influence how they learn throughout their school years. The international Reading Association defines study skills as, "a general term for those techniques and strategies that help a person read or listen for specific purposes with the intent to remember; commonly, following directions, locating, selecting, organizing and retaining information, interpreting typographic and graphic aids, and reading flexibility" (Harris and Hodges 245).

In other words, studying is an intentional act to remember and recall information. Study habits include study strategies that a learner applies for acquiring knowledge, skills, and ideas. Before students begin to study, they need to establish a purpose for their study session, and a goal of what they desire to achieve. High-powered teachers know that it is essential for students to establish reading goals, and it is equally as important for them to establish study goals. They know that good study habits enhance academic performance and also overall educational success.

Study habits involve a series of activities and dispositions that a learner must acquire to truly enable them to engage in academic studies. It is essential that students have an established purpose for reading. High-powered teachers know that an established purpose for reading is the basic foundation of studying. High-powered teachers also know that they cannot simply assume that their students know how to study. Students enter classrooms every year who have both independent reading and study skills, and can automatically make vital connections between prior knowledge and new information, and know how to apply what they have learned as a result of their studying. While there are also numerous students that advance from grade to grade who will require guidance, direction, and one-on-one assistance and instructions. High-powered teachers know they cannot assume that all students know how to study effectively.

High-powered teachers set yearly goals to get to know their students, their reading habits, and their study habits to better understand what study strategy(s) works best for them, as well as what strategies do not work for them. High-powered teachers know that learning styles are individualized. They also know that it isn't necessarily true that students should study only one subject at a time. They have found that some students retain more information through cross-walking or integrating two or more subjects while processing the content. They also know that some students need to concentrate specifically on one subject or one topic for an extended period of time. It is often a case of exploration, implementation of diverse activities, or what may be referred to as trial and error to discover what works best for which student (InTASC Standard 1, 2, CCSSO).

High-powered teachers know that it is vital to teach their students how to learn on their own. They also know that teaching students a variety of study strategies to enhance their study skills also means showing them through modeling, experiencing hands-on activities, and through explicit instructions for how to solve problems both inside the classroom and in real-world situations. High-powered teachers strive to prepare all students for the next grade-level, for college, for careers, and for the real world. They know *"how"* they teach is equally as important as *"what"* they teach. In other words, high-powered teachers know how each of their students learn best, and plan their instructions to meet the needs of all of their students. They differentiate through hands-on activities, one-on-one instructions, small group instructions, using manipulatives, incorporating visual aids, and also through modeling.

High-powered teachers incorporate diverse techniques and strategies to guide students to a deeper understanding, aid them in recalling information, enhance comprehension, and also to help them apply what they have learned. They provide objectives for reading that enable students to establish a purpose for their reading, which encourage them to tap into their prior knowledge, and also guide them in organizing information. In other words, they teach students how to study through diverse strategies that best suit students' individual needs or learning styles. They provide multiple ongoing opportunities for students to apply study strategies to help enhance their study skills. They also equip their students with knowledge and skills that will ensure they are college-and career-ready, along with the skills they can continue using and applying in real-world situations.

In this chapter you will learn the importance of good study habits, how to promote good study habits through innovative study strategies and activities, and revisit effective strategies and activities that will enhance your instruction and students' comprehension, all the while promoting and establishing good study habits.

Promoting Good Study Habits

One of the most useful lifetime skills that teachers can share with their students is good study habits. High-powered teachers have found that teaching one study skill each day as they begin a lesson, as a transition activity, within the lesson as a mini-lesson, or at the end of a lesson, has been effective, time-efficient, and also allows students to have exposure to a wide variety of diverse strategies that they can select from when studying independently. High-powered teachers agree that they actually save time when they teach their students how to study because it reduces the time spent reteaching material. They have also found that students are more engaged when working independently and collaboratively, and studying with more confidence (InTASC Standard 4, 5, 6, 7, & 8, CCSSO).

The Teacher's Role

High-powered teachers not only incorporate a variety of strategies to help meet the needs of their students' various learning styles. They teach them how to organize information that will enable them to store information in the brain, and also how to retrieve the stored information. They also provide their students with explicit feedback. They know that timely explicit feedback provides their students with the knowledge of their progress, what they are doing correctly, and what they need to continue working on. High-powered teachers also implement self-assessment into their classrooms. They incorporate self-assessment by requiring students to grade and correct their own work through the use of a rubric or checklist (InTASC Standard 6, CCSSO).

High-powered teachers also know the importance of student collaboration. They know that students learn best when they are actively engaged in activities and engaged in assessment. They require their students to not only self-assess, but also include time for students to work collaboratively to peer-assess. When their students peer-assess, they require the student who is scoring to provide feedback about why their peer answered a question correctly, and also why they did not answer correctly. High-powered teachers also incorporate manipulatives, a variety of study strategies, and activities that promote learning through a variety of learning modalities such as visual, auditory, tactile, and also kinesthetic processing to meet the needs of all learning styles. High-powered teachers also know that their students learn and perform best when they feel academically safe and also physically safe in their classroom. Working in a safe learning environment encourages students to take academic risks, challenges, and to think outside the box or their comfort zone. They have a sense of community that also allows them to work collaboratively to create and ask questions, and also to learn from their peers (InTASC Standard 3, CCSSO).

Finally, high-powered teachers know that for students to gain a deep understanding of content, it is vital for them to have good study skills. They know that to effectively teach diverse study skills, it is vital to make study skills a daily part of their instructions throughout the academic year. High-powered teachers teach study skills before, during, and after teaching content. For example, a social studies teacher might teach about a reading timeline, a map, or the use of a graphic organizer prior to teaching content that includes multiple timelines, maps, and graphic organizers. They know that preteaching and preparing students about particular concepts can actually save time, reduce reteaching, and also equip and prepare their students with the tools that they need to comprehend what they are reading (InTASC Standard 5, CCSSO).

High-powered teachers know that it takes exposure, time, and multiple opportunities to experience a wide variety of study skills before most students can take ownership of a personal study system. They know that students need to experience a diverse variety of study skills in different settings, situations, and also content areas before they know what study skill works best for them in different situations or content areas. They realize and teach students that a study strategy that works in one discipline may not work as well in another. For example, the study skill that a student applies in math may not be as effective for them in science. For this reason, high-powered teachers know the importance of teaching and promoting study skills in all content areas and also teaching students how to cross-walk between different content areas to promote effective and successful learning (InTASC Standard 4, CCSSO).

The Student's Role

It is vital that students recognize and understand the importance of a personal study system to establish good study habits, and what study strategy works best for them to be able to apply effective study strategies. They should know that a good study system should be flexible and allow them to apply different study skills to different learning situations. High-powered teachers encourage their students to complete a study skills checklist. The purpose of the study skills checklist is to provide students with a basic self-analysis of their study skills and their attitudes about studying. It can also help them identify areas that need improvement. An example of a **Study Skill Checklist** is provided in **Table 10.1**.

Table 10.1: Study Skill Checklist

Yes or No	I spend more time than necessary studying for what I am learning.
Yes or No	It's common for me to spend hours cramming the night before an exam.
Yes or No	The time I spend socializing often reduces my study time.
Yes or No	I usually study with the TV on or while listening to music.
Yes or No	I struggle to study for long periods of time without becoming tired or distracted.
Yes or No	I like to doodle, or daydream during class.

Yes or No	I have difficulty understanding the notes I take during class or making connections to them.
Yes or No	I usually end up writing too much information in my notes and become overwhelmed.
Yes or No	I hardly ever review my notes until the night before a test.
Yes or No	I hardly ever rewrite my notes.
Yes or No	I often struggle with what I've read or what the teacher is lecturing about.
Yes or No	I sometimes struggle with determining the main idea.
Yes or No	I struggle identifying what's important or key ideas in the text.
Yes or No	I study a little each night to prevent cramming the night before exams.
Yes or No	I have a study routine that I follow.
Yes or No	I have a designated place to study.

High-powered teachers ask their students to review their recorded answers on their study skills checklist to reflect on their study skills, the identified habits, and also to determine what they can do to improve their study skills. They require them to record their findings in a five paragraph paper to explain what they feel they have learned about themselves, their strengths, their studying habits, what improvements they can make, and also devise a plan of what they will do to improve their quality of studying. High-powered teachers ensure that their students are equipped with the knowledge of study strategies that will enable them to apply different strategies for different situations thus establishing a sound study system (InTASC Standard 4, CCSSO). In other words, high-powered teachers encourage their students to study "smarter not harder" by requiring them to do the following:

✦ *Designate a specific time to study and form a routine that helps their mental preparation to study.*
✦ *Set personal and specific goals for each study session, which helps them stay focused, which in turn helps them to evaluate their own progress.*
✦ *Follow the study plan without procrastination, as this usually results in lack of preparation for assessments and also less than desirable final projects.*
✦ *Work on the most difficult projects and assignments first when mental energies are at their highest.*
✦ *Review class notes before beginning assignments to ensure that they know what is being required of them.*
✦ *Ask for help when it is necessary.*
✦ *Take brief breaks as necessary during study time to refresh energy and refocus.*
✦ *Make plans to review what has been covered in class to identify what subject matter is most important.*
✦ *Maintain a positive attitude, even when a subject, assignment, or project seems difficult.*
✦ *Modify or shift priorities and spend a little extra time on the more difficult assignments or content.*
✦ *Be consistent with study routines.*

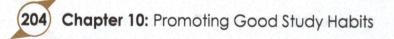

High-powered teachers know that as students develop effective study habits, their ability to assimilate and learn new information improves, and so do their grades. Moreover, and most importantly, high-powered teachers know that when students develop, adapt, and practice effective study habits, learning becomes an enjoyable and rewarding experience both at home and inside the classroom.

Literacy Strategies and Activities to Promote Study Skills

High-powered teachers also know that students need to be interested and curious about what they are reading, make connections, and also be able to apply study strategies that nurture and enhance their critical-thinking skills. They also know that students need to be aware of and also understand how they cognitively process information. They know that it is vital for students to have the ability to monitor their own learning and engagement as well as evaluate themselves. This process is called **metacognition**. Metacognition is the ability to control one's own cognitive processing. High-powered teachers know for students to be able to think about and control their own learning, they need exposure to a variety of study strategies, monitoring strategies, and also repair strategies before they read, while they are reading, and also after they read. High-powered teachers equip their students with assigned reading material at an instructional level, which means that students will require some form of instructions while they are reading. This enables students to learn how to monitor and control their own learning. The goal is that the teacher does not need to be with students for them to employ their knowledge of and competence with language.

High-powered teachers implement graphic organizers in their daily reading assignments to promote metacognitive thinking, which in turn promotes stronger study skills. They know that the use of a graphic organizer enables students to monitor their own learning through making and recording connections while they are reading, and also after they have read. They know that this strengthens students' metacognitive awareness through applying prior knowledge to new knowledge, which is vital in retaining information.

High-powered teachers implement a **Metacognitive Reading Awareness Inventory** near the beginning of the academic year to help determine which students have established strong-study skills and which students will need further direction (InTASC Standard 7, CCSSO). **Table 10.2** provides an example of a **Metacognitive Reading Awareness Inventory.** Let's practice. Take about 10 minutes and complete the Metacognitive Reading Awareness Inventory to help you gain insight into your own study habits. Reflect on your answers. How can you improve your reading awareness and study skills? Turn and share with a partner.

Table 10.2: Metacognitive Reading Awareness Inventory

1. *What do you do when you encounter a word that you do not know the definition of?*	2. *What do you do if a sentence is unclear to you?*
a. *Read the words or sentence around the word to help determine the meaning.*	**a.** *Reread the sentence.*
b. *Use a resource such as a dictionary.*	**b.** *Ignore it and continue reading.*
c. *Ignore it and read on anyway.*	**c.** *Reread the entire paragraph and the following paragraph to help clarify the sentence.*
d. *Sound the word out to determine the meaning.*	**d.** *Ask a friend.*

Sometimes for (handwritten margin note)

3. Which sentences are most important in a chapter?
   a. Almost all of the sentences are important.
   b. The ones that contain the most words.
   c. Sentences that contain important information and details.
   d. The sentences that are directly related to the main idea.

4. As you read a textbook, which of the following do you do?
   a. Continually make predictions or inferences about what you are reading.
   b. Adjust your pace depending on the difficulty of the text.
   c. Typically read at a constant and steady pace.
   d. Skip over parts that you do not understand.

5. When you read History or Science texts, what do you do to remember important information you've read?
   a. Make connections to or relate it to something you already know.
   b. Question yourself about important information.
   c. Skip sections that you don't understand.
   d. Determine that you should remember certain parts of the information.

6. When you come to section(s) in a text that are confusing, what do you do?
   a. Continue reading until you gain understanding.
   b. Skip those sections completely.
   c. Use context clues to help clarify the confusion.
   d. Ask the teacher.

7. Why should you go back and reread an entire passage a second time?
   a. To underline, highlight, or summarize to study later.
   b. You did not understand the passage.
   c. It seemed like important information to remember.
   d. To clarify a specific or supporting idea.

8. Before you begin reading what kind of plan do you make to help you read better, to understand better, or recall information?
   a. Make sure I can finish reading the entire text in the shortest amount of time possible.
   b. I do not typically have a plan. I just start reading.
   c. Think about what I already know about the topic at hand.
   d. Determine why I am reading the material.

9. While you are reading, what is important to you?
   a. Know that different strategies can be used to help me understand.
   b. Know when I know and when I don't know key ideas.
   c. Know what I already know about the topic that I am reading.
   d. Know that confusing text is not uncommon and that I can usually ignore it.

10. What do you do to help you recall information?
    a. Annotate while I am reading.
    b. Highlight important information.
    c. Reread for a deeper meaning.
    d. All of the above.

KWL Plus Charts

High-powered teachers provide their students with multiple tools to encourage and promote deep thinking and organized thinking. They provide **KWL Plus Charts** prior to assigning reading to help students determine what they already know about the topic or subject. They ask students to complete what I already know about the topic section, and the second section where students record what they want to learn. Once students have completed the K-section and the W-section, they begin reading. After the assigned reading is complete, students will then complete the last section, which is what they have learned from the reading.

After students have completed their **KWL Plus Charts**, high-powered teachers require them to map their findings from the third column. They also require their students to complete a summary of their complete findings. Requiring students to complete the summary encourages them to reflect on what they have read, what they have learned, and also enhances their comprehension and writing skills. High-powered teachers include the KWL Plus Chart in individual assignments and small group activities, which encourages student collaboration, discussion, and also enhances students' comprehension. The addition of the plus column in this graphic organizer takes the ordinary KWL Chart to an entire new level of learning.

SQ3R Strategy

High-powered teachers also know the value of implementing the **SQ3R Strategy** as a study method. This is a study strategy that allows students to independently learn the information they seek. High-powered teachers know that all students do not learn the same or at the same time. They provide assistance where it is needed, but encourage students who are able to work independently to incorporate the SQ3R Strategy often. They teach their students how to include the five basic steps to help them better understand the process. High-powered teachers also require their students to complete the SQ3R Strategy often with various reading assignments, which in turn results in students expecting to complete the SQ3R Strategy. In other words, it becomes second nature for them to automatically apply the questions to their reading. The five steps of the **SQ3R** include as follows

Examine the text
- *Study the visual aids.*
- *Study the organization and presentation of the material.*

Create questions about the selection
- *Convert the chapter title into a question.*
- *Convert subheadings into questions.*

Read, recite, and reread
- *Read the entire selection to answer the questions.*
- *Recite the answers to the questions.*
- *Reread the material to determine if your answers are correct.*

Note-Taking

Taking notes involves several skills. These skills include, knowing how to identify the main idea, understanding what signifies an important part of the text, creating abbreviations, being organized, being able to categorize ideas, being an active-listener, being an accurate speller, good penmanship, and summarization. High-powered teachers know the value of teaching their students how to take notes. They provide their students multiple activities and opportunities to implement the required skills that is necessary for their students to develop a note-taking system that works best for them. First and foremost high-powered teachers teach their students active listening skills. They teach them how to sit up straight in an attentive manner, to listen for details and important information, to ask and answer questions, they also teach them to track the teacher to help them maintain their focus.

High-powered teachers teach students a variety of note-taking methods which include but are not limited to, **double-sided journal entries, two-column notes,** and **three-column notes**. Double-sided journal entries serve several purposes. They require the student to read the text closely, to determine important information, to make personal connections, and also help them to organize their thoughts and notes. When completing **double-sided journal entries**, students record important information on the left and write personal connections on the right. **Two-column notes** require the student to write down main ideas within a passage or text on the left side of the paper and then provide details on the right side. While the **three-column notes** method of note-taking requires students to think deeper about the main ideas. In the three-column method students write main ideas on the left of the paper, record details in the center, and provide examples on the right. High-powered teachers not only teach their students how to take notes, but also how to organize their notes.

High-powered teachers know the importance and benefits of incorporating data-books. They require their students to create and maintain **data-books**. Data-books can be as simple as using a three ring binder for students to collect and be able to retrieve important information. Information may include class syllabi, class schedules, journal entries, class notes, graded worksheets, study-guides, as well as graded written assignments. Data-books can serve as storage, be a method of organizing important material, used as a reflective method of study, while also be used as a general study tool.

Regardless the method of note-taking, high-powered teachers introduce, model, and remodel to ensure that students understand how to take notes effectively. They provide multiple opportunities for students to practice taking notes before requiring them to take notes independently. This can be practiced through incorporating technology and allowing students to listen to recordings and take notes. Note-taking can also be practiced through interaction with a peer. While one student reads, the other may be required to take notes. High-powered teachers also incorporate slides in their instruction with main ideas in red or highlighted to signal students about important information and also to allow students to know what material should be recorded, highlighted, or transferred to their data-book. They may also give them practice articles or text to highlight what they determine to be key ideas, main ideas, or important information. After students have read the material and highlighted their findings, the teacher then allows students to self-assess by providing them with an article that has the important information highlighted, or peer-assess with a partner. The goal is to gradually release responsibility to the students as they become more aware of how to determine what is important and what they should include in their notes. This can be completed through gradually taking away the highlighted text from slide shows and requiring students to determine what is important and what should be recorded in their notes. This method can be incorporated in various grades and modified to fit the needs and learning levels of the students.

Collaborative Peer-Studying

High-powered teachers purposefully partner their students together to read, reflect, discuss, analyze, determine, and apply what they have learned together. This type of activity can be a simple as **think-pair-share** or **read-think-write**. Both of these activities require partners to read text, think about what they have read, and then respond either through oral presentations or written expression. High-powered teachers also incorporate graphic organizers in collaborative studying. An example of collaborative studying is the use of a **Partner-Guided-Reading Map**, which is pictured in **Table 10.3**.

Table 10.3: Partner-Guided-Reading Map

1. *Text walk.*	2. *Skim, read title, subtopics, look at illustrations, captions, graphs, maps, and illustrations if present.*
3. *Make a prediction of what the text is about.*	4. *Record your prediction.*
5. *Read text with a partner.*	6. *Stop and reflect about what you've read.*
7. *Discuss with your partner.*	8. *Summarize what you've learned thus far.*
9. *Reread with a partner.*	10. *What connections can you make? Record your answers.*
11. *Complete assigned reading.*	12. *Discuss with your partner.*
13. *Summarize what you have learned.*	14. *Clarify your predictions.*
15. *Discuss with your partner the main idea, important events, and information.*	16. *Write a brief summary with your partner.*

Language Link

High-powered teachers know that students benefit when using grammar in context of their own writing. They also know that **grammar workshops** are ideal settings for this to happen. Grammar workshops typically occur after explicit instruction of a particular concept. High-powered teachers first implement engaging activities to reteach, reinforce, and enhance students understanding of the concept being taught during grammar workshop. For example, if students are learning how to create and correctly punctuate complex sentences, teachers provide students with text that contains the type of sentences that they have recently been required to include in a writing assignment. Teachers then ask students to identify complex sentences by highlighting them. Students then check their answers through self-assessment using a checklist or completed text.

Second, high-powered teachers provide students with copies of text including complex sentences that are not punctuated correctly. Students are asked to identify the incorrect sentences and rewrite them using correct punctuation. Finally, students should be given a copy of their own writing to identify complex sentences that are not punctuated correctly, or writing that doesn't contain complex sentences, and be asked to create complex sentences within the paper. In other words, high-powered teachers know that grammar workshops are designed to reteach and reinforce students' understanding of grammar through engaging activities and using students' personal writing (InTASC Standard 8, CCSSO).

What Can Parents Do to Help?

High-powered teachers know that parents play a vital role in students' academic success. They also know that the single most important thing that parents can do to help their child study, and also help them to be academically successful, is to make sure that they are informed, aware of, and involved with their children's academic lives. They know that for children to be successful in school, parents need to be actively involved early in the academic year and stay involved throughout the course of the year. High-powered teachers know that if they can get parents involved and interested in their children's education, it typically generates a spark of enthusiasm in both the child and the parent. They continually strive to find new innovative ideas to encourage parents to encourage their children to become readers, and also to apply good study habits. High-powered teachers know that fostering the love of reading within a child is also supplying them with the single most important thing that can help them to succeed in school and in life. They know that reading is key to students' academic success in all content areas, and also to lifelong learning.

High-powered teachers ensure that parents stay well-informed about their children's curriculum. Middle school and secondary teachers make it a yearly goal to supply students and parents with a course outline or syllabus with clear expectations for each assignment. High-powered teachers know the importance of creating a syllabus. They know that it helps them to be better organized, the students to be aware of upcoming assignments, and also helps parents to know what their children are working on, when they are working on particular assignments, as well as future assignments, and also the expectations of the teacher (InTASC Standard 10, CCSSO).

As students advance to middle grades, the homework assignments become tougher, the workload is often heavier, and it becomes more difficult for students to stay ahead or even on top of the workload and the challenges they face. Parents can help their child gain and maintain control of their assignments and studies to help them have a productive and successful academic year simply by helping them get organized. Multitasking homework, tests, and extracurricular activities, parents know that it can be difficult for their child to keep everything organized and all too easy for important assignments and information to slip through the cracks. High-powered teachers require their students to maintain a planner to write down assignments, deadlines, and also to encourage them to maintain a to-do-list. They also encourage them to revisit their planner daily and update as necessary. High-powered teachers make parents aware of their planner policy and encourage them to assist their child in organizing and maintaining their planner.

Parents can also encourage their children to have a designated study area. Study areas should be free of interruptions such as television or high traffic. Cell phones can also become a distracting factor for preteens and teenagers. The teacher can help students to develop a study plan. The plan should include revisiting their planner, creating a study guide, if one is not supplied by the teacher, and breaking study time into segments. Parents can encourage them to study for a particular amount of time over the course of a couple of days up to a week to ensure that students are not

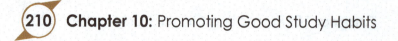
cramming information in the night before an assessment, but rather learning in layers, which can include reading, annotation, quizzing via questioning, or quick recall, flashcards, and also summarizing. Parents can encourage their children to set study goals, setting a designated amount of time to study, and applying study strategies to ensure effective time management tips as well as organizational skills to ensure academic success.

> *"When we teach our students how to study, we have not only given them a study tool, but we have given them a tool that has the power to unlock and open doors of knowledge."*
>
> ~ *Dr. Joyce Bowling*

Author's Tip

Teachers cannot simply assume that their students come to them equipped with the study skills they need to be successful in their classroom or life. I recall walking into various classrooms as a secondary student with a fear of allowing anyone to see my notes that I took during the teachers' lecture. I was afraid for them to see that because I was unsure of my ability to take notes. I had never been taught how to effectively take notes by any of my teachers. I had trouble deciding what was important and what wasn't. I tried to write too much down and in turn lost focus of some of the more valuable information that was being given to the class. As a result of my lack of understanding of how to take notes, I was frustrated with studying as I had to reread the entire content, try to make sense of the notes, and then try to determine what parts of the content I should study. I had to work harder to learn, which in the end didn't affect my grades, but pushed me to find a better way to study.

During my sophomore year of high school I was blessed to have a wise, insightful, and wonderful AP Biology teacher. I recall the excitement that filled the small group of students who awaited details about all of the fun dissection projects that she had in store for us. I envisioned dissecting pigs, bats, and even cats, as I had heard previous students elaborate on their lab experiences. Imagine our surprise when she began the semester with teaching us how to effectively take notes. Yes, that's right, thanks to this wonderful teacher who took time to care about her students, I finally learned several effective methods of note-taking that resulted in studying smarter, not harder.

I promised myself that when I became a teacher, I would teach my students, regardless the grade-level, good study habits and also several strategies to help them study smarter, not harder. I would suggest that you implement the metacognition survey during the first days of school with your new students to help you gain insight into their study habits. Require students to take the study checklist to better determine their areas of strength and also areas for possible improvement. Also, listen to your students, complete running checklists and monitor their progress, and track the data after completed assignments. But, most of all, give your students' academic advantages, give them the tools that are necessary for them to be successful. Teach a wide variety of study strategies and habits to allow them multiple methods of studying. Have clear learning objectives, set goals, teach students to prioritize their assignments and teach them to take responsibility for their learning. Above all, equip them with the knowledge of how to study smarter, not harder. You will be pleasantly surprised how much this will motivate students to learn, and how the motivation will spill over into your classroom atmosphere.

Virtual Study Strategies

One of the most useful lifetime skills that teachers can share with their students is good study habits. Currently, a large majority of high-powered teachers are engaging in some sort of distance learning. Regardless, the setting, high-powered teachers know the importance of teaching, modeling, and equipping students with a variety of study strategies to help students study effectively. They also know the challenges that might arise with virtual students adopting **effective study strategies** due to the amount of independence that's required of them.

High-powered teachers include several key strategies that are flexible and also help promote learning in multiple situations to promote **long-term durable learning**. Many of the strategies have been integrated in classrooms in various ways for many years. High-powered teachers also know their effectiveness in a variety of situations, which include virtual learning. High-powered teachers know that there's not one prescribed method that works for all; therefore, they teach multiple study strategies so that students have multiple strategies to apply when studying. Whether teachers are working with **synchronous**, **virtual/remote**, or **distance learning**, the following strategies can help foster student learning and allow students to choose what works best for them.

High-powered teachers require both in-person and online students to take the **study skills checklist** to allow students to better understand their strengths, areas for improvement, and to help them to devise a study plan that works best for them. They encourage students to pace themselves and also designate **30 minutes** on specific days to review, organize, and rewrite notes, read and reread, and also to prepare for upcoming instruction. They know that creating a schedule and sticking to it is especially important for all students. High-powered teachers encourage students to rewatch recorded videos during their scheduled study time, and also quiz themselves with applications such as **Quizlet**. Virtual students are also encouraged to work as teams in breakout rooms, or as partners to quiz each other.

High-powered teachers also provide students with **concrete examples** as they know that concrete information and examples allow students to make important connections, and also know that concrete examples are easier to recall than abstract information. Thus, concrete examples foster genuine learning. High-powered teachers also involve their students in **probing questions** while working in real time with the online class. They know that asking stimulating questions that involve recalling, analyzing, extending, and applying allows students to make connections, retain the information, and also to retrieve the information when necessary.

Dual coding is a combination of **verbal representation** of information mixed with **visual representations** that might include diagrams or illustrations. High-powered teachers know when students are given both resources and combine them, it allows the students to remember the information as well as retrieve it. High-powered teaches know that when students are studying, they are more likely to recall information when they use multiple representations to show the same idea. High-powered teachers implement dual coding in online video lectures, in real-time lectures, and also through slide shows. They also include pictures and diagrams that students can retrieve to assist them in studying during their designated study time. They also know that all students do not learn the same and dual coding helps to ensure that diverse learners are given resources that will help all students be successful.

High-powered teachers also incorporate and require students to take **low-stakes** or **no-stakes quizzes** in the district approved platform or provided application. They create questions that require deep thinking, thinking beyond the text-book, rather than just extending on the obvious text-based answer. Based on the research, **open-book assessments** can be beneficial for studying.

Therefore, they include questions that allow open-book retrieval opportunities. They also include questions that include a combination of multiple-choice answers, open-ended questions that require students to apply concepts to specific examples, or identify components within an example. For quizzes that are not open-book, high-powered teachers include time limits on completing the quiz to prevent students from retrieving online answers or answers from their textbooks.

Most importantly, high-powered teachers know that when students are aware of, can select, and are exposed to a combination of study materials, and **given choices** of how to study, it is easier for them to understand the information that has been presented. High-powered teachers also pace themselves to prevent information overload, but rather present their students with layers of engaging activities, opportunities to absorb and process the content, and also allow time for them to practice applications. All of the above strategies promote **long-term learning** and learning for both in-person and virtual students. Keep in mind that when implementing either of the above strategies, students are required to take control over more of their own learning. High-powered teachers not only strive for students to learn, but also to retain what they've learned, and later retrieve and apply what they've learned.

Now It's Your Turn

For this assignment you will be required to complete the study skills checklist and reflect on your findings. You will be required to determine what area(s) of improvement you can personally make to enhance your study skills, and also include a plan of action of what you will do to improve your personal study skills. The specific details for this assignment are located on blackboard.

Application

To help guide you through Chapter Ten and upcoming chapters, become familiar with the following key terms for a deeper understanding of Chapter Ten:

- ✦ Study skills checklist
- ✦ Metacognition
- ✦ Metacognitive reading awareness inventory
- ✦ KWL plus
- ✦ SQ3R
- ✦ Double-sided journal entries
- ✦ Two-column notes
- ✦ Three-column notes
- ✦ Data-books
- ✦ Think-pair-share
- ✦ Read-write-think
- ✦ Partner-guided-reading map
- ✦ Grammar workshops

In-Seat Activity

You will be randomly divided into groups. Find your group and collaborate to determine which one of the study strategies your team would like to collaboratively research and present your findings to the class. You will be given in-class time to work collaboratively, research, and prepare for this informal and brief presentation. The object of this assignment is to help you gain a deeper understanding of at least three study strategies that you can use as a student, and also to incorporate in your classroom.

Reflect and Answer the Following Questions

+ *Why are good study habits important in students' learning?*
+ *How can I promote good study habits?*
+ *What is metacognition?*
+ *What literacy strategies promote study skills?*
+ *What activities can I incorporate in my classroom to promote study skills?*
+ *What can parents do to help?*

Student Notes

Annotating is an effective learning strategy. This page is reserved for you to annotate *(take notes)*, record potential questions, and also to refer back to when studying, completing assignments, and to help you gain a better understanding of Chapter Ten.

Student Reflection

High-powered teachers reflect. This page is reserved for you to reflect about information that you found insightful and what you have learned from Chapter Ten.

Chapter References

Council of Chief State School Officers (CCSSO). *Interstate Teacher Assessment and Support Consortium (InTASC) Model Core Teaching Standards*, Apr. 2011, https://www.ccsso.org/sites/default/files/2017-11/InTASC_Model_Core_Teaching_Standards_2011.pdf. Accessed 7 July 2018.

Harris, T., and R. Hodges, editors. *The Literacy Dictionary: The Vocabulary of Reading and Writing*. International Reading Association, 1995.

Chapter 11
Power in Classroom Discussions

Teacher Quote

"When it comes to the education of our children... failure is not an option."
~ President George W. Bush

Chapter Questions

✦ What are classroom discussions and why are they important to learning?
✦ What are the components of a classroom discussion?
✦ How do I conduct a meaningful classroom discussion?
✦ What strategies promote discussion?
✦ How can I use discussions for assessment?

What Are Classroom Discussions and Why Are They Important?

Teachers are being held accountable for students' performances more now than ever before. As a result, developing discussion skills and encouraging discussion often take a backseat to teaching the mandated curriculum, and or preparing students for standardized tests. Some teachers even discourage talking, resulting in students who are *"talk-deprived"* and view classroom discussion as an activity only to be carried on surreptitiously (Alvermann).

215

Through the years as a public school teacher, I found that many teachers fear discussions for a variety of reasons. Some fear that discussion will create a loss of instructional time or decrease test preparation, while others fear that discussions result in loss of classroom management resulting in behavioral problems. This is a tragedy, considering the power that meaningful discussions can bring to the classroom. Many teachers do not understand the impact meaningful discussions can have on instruction, test preparation, classroom management, assessment, and students' learning.

Discussion is a very important tool of learning. Discussions engage students, encourage collaboration, broaden their perspectives, increase classroom rapport, increase deep-thinking, help students make and create necessary connections, enhance comprehension, and also promote high-level thinking and problem-solving. High-powered teachers implement discussions in their classrooms because they know that discussions allow students to explore and gain a better understanding of curriculum. They know that gaining a deeper understanding of the content and concept results in higher level thinking. High-powered teachers also implement and encourage classroom discussions to increase student engagement, which in turn encourages students to take ownership of ideas and increases student participation of all students regardless their literacy level. Meaning is developed, clarified, and altered not only by hearing ideas of others, but also by expressing their own.

Components of a Classroom Discussion

True meaningful discussion is not simply summarizing ideas or searching for the ideal answer, but rather genuinely collaborating in a way that leads to a deeper or a new meaning. Deep meaningful classroom discussion is a process of coproducing meaning that encourages sharing different interpretations based on diverse background knowledge, inferences, and also diverse interests. In other words discussion is an ideal mechanism that promotes thinking and rethinking. High-powered teachers implement discussion to activate prior knowledge, encourage thinking, increase rethinking, encourage reflection, and promote clarifying (InTASC Standard 1, Council of Chief State School Officers [CCSSO]).

Meaning discussions increase and promote **metacognition**. For example, high-powered teachers know that when one student expresses their prior knowledge, the prior knowledge of other students is activated. Thus stimulating further ideas from others and resulting in collaborative construction of meaning for all. In other words, shared prior knowledge about a particular topic or text becomes corporate knowledge as well as students' textual understanding. High-powered teachers know that discussion does not take away from the curriculum. They consider discussion an essential component of the curriculum, just like reading, writing, or any other content area. In this chapter you will learn the importance of meaningful classroom discussions, how to implement classroom discussions, literacy strategies to promote discussions, integrating assessment with discussion, and also inspire students to actively engage in discussions.

Promoting Classroom Discussion

High-powered teachers know that like reading or writing, discussion is not an end in itself and that it is not meant to be isolated. They know that discussions should have a purpose within the content area. Purposeful conversations should lead students toward an established curricular goal, promote new insight, and also guide students in discipline-specific ways of thinking. High-powered teachers promote discussions in all content areas. They know that all content areas have important concepts that are critical for students to learn, which are often related to the established goal(s). Discussions should be purposeful, planned well, and aligned to the objective(s) to help students achieve their academic goal(s), and overall success.

High-powered teachers know that discussion is inclusive and they strive to find and create ways that encourage all students to come to the discussion with access to the ideas and with something to discuss to ensure all students' participation. They know that students' literacy levels are diverse, which can present challenges in reading and preparing for discussions. However, they do not let literacy levels decrease discussions, but work to find creative ways to encourage discussion regardless the literacy level. High-powered teachers partner students to read together prior to discussion or even assign video or audio read-alouds to ensure that all students have a voice in the discussion. All too often students voices are silenced as a result of lack of planning or preparation. High-powered teachers empower all of their students with the tools necessary for deep meaningful discussion through preparation, thus allowing and encouraging all students to join the discussion, express their views, ideas, and learn from each other (InTASC Standard 2, CCSSO).

One of the most important goals of any curriculum is to promote conceptual change. High-powered teachers know that conceptual change occurs when students experience external and also internal conflict within their own thinking. High-powered teachers want their students to gain new insights, expand upon those insights, and also to change perceptions, views, or opinions as a result of exploring the subject of discussion. However, change is not necessarily defined as changing one's point of view. Sometimes a concept or idea is altered dramatically, while other times it might simply be refined, moreover ideas can be strengthened through gaining new insight and understanding of alternative points of view. Regardless, the possibilities of conceptual change are unlimited through meaningful, well-orchestrated discussions.

High-powered teachers implement discussions that are carefully guided by purposeful, well-constructed, and sequenced questions that are established to promote students' development of discipline-specific ways of thinking. They know that this type of choreographed discussion leads their students toward an established concept or a conclusion, which encourages them how to think within the discipline. High-powered teachers also know that they have a meaningful and successful classroom discussion

Literacy Strategies to Encourage Classroom Discussions

"I remember the first class I was enrolled in where discussion was
encouraged, not discouraged. That class, the teacher, the classroom
atmosphere, the engaging conversations, and the level of respect for both
the students and the teacher helped me overcome my fear of sharing
my thoughts aloud in class. That class forever changed the way I that
learn...and the way I teach."

~ *Dr. Joyce Bowling*

Research suggests that grouping is effective and beneficial at all grade-levels. In 1978, L. Vygotsky theorized that a social environment provides learners with the opportunities to observe higher levels of cognitive processing, thereby enabling learners to achieve more because of the assistance of peers in contrast to learning independently. Successful discussions greatly depend on creating a conductive environment. For discussion to flourish and be successful, both the students and the teacher should be prepared and willing to explore new ideas (InTASC Standard 4, CCSSO).

High-powered teachers introduce discussions as a *"we"* journey! In other words, they create and establish a positive atmosphere in their classrooms by allowing students to know that they too are willing to explore new ideas. For example, they might introduce the discussion as, *"Today, we will take an adventure together. We will explore new ideas, theories, and points of view about Shakespeare, and it will be fun."* For discussions to be productive they require the teachers to trust their students as well as the student to trust their teacher. Peers must also feel a sense of trust in each other, as well as trust in themselves. Students need to feel prepared for what they are being asked to do (InTASC Standard 3, CCSSO).

High-powered teachers also know when students are prepared for discussions the discussion results are more profitable. However, not all discussions have to be planned or orchestrated. As we all know some of the most beneficial conversations and discussions are sporadic and inspired. High-powered teachers allow those sporadic and meaningful conversations to lead into grand conversations and discussions at a later date for an additional layer of learning. High-powered teachers recognize worthy discussion opportunities and adjust their instructional plans accordingly (InTASC Standard 7, CCSSO).

Nevertheless, high-powered teachers prep their students for discussion activities. They do not assume that students come to the class prepared for rigorous academic discussions. They prep them for the interactive roles that are necessary for successful discussions. High-powered teachers strive to ensure that all students have a voice, feel comfortable and confident sharing without the fear of being ridiculed (InTASC Standard 3, CCSSO). They also help students develop a level of tolerance for others' opinions, perceptions, and ideas. Through practice students learn how to take a stand and also nurture their belief with confidence.

High-powered teachers are persistent and consistent in cultivating discussion activities and in their expectations that students can participate. High-powered teachers believe that all students should feel confident in their abilities to communicate, both inside and outside the classroom. They know that academic skills as well as life skills are nurtured through discussions. They know that when students are strategically prepared for discussion, the classroom becomes a place where students feel free to share their ideas, thoughts, and feelings, as well as feel emotionally and physically safe. High-powered teachers encourage and promote this type of environment through implementing activities that encourage students to listen, interact, trust, and care about each other (InTASC Standard 3, CCSSO).

Grouping

Two important decisions need to be made about groups and grouping for discussion. The first is whether to group at all. High-powered teachers know that every lesson doesn't require grouping to have a meaningful discussion. They know that small groups are beneficial for some discussion, but not for all. They know that there will be opportunities when whole-group discussions, which involve the entire class, make more sense. Making the decision to group should be based on the purposes of the discussion and on the degree to which the students are ready to work in small groups. Whole-group discussions can be effective and efficient for three main purposes: to provide guidance before students explore a new topic, to follow up after students have explored a new concept or topic, and to model for students as well as give them opportunities to model and practice discussion strategies (InTASC Standard 5, CCSSO).

New teachers often struggle with the decisions whether or not to group their students, and also how to group them. They worry about the number of students per group, the criteria that determines a group, and many other questions. The answer to these questions will vary depending on the number of students per class, academic levels, diversity, students' readiness, as well as physical and emotional needs. However, there are typically three types of grouping, which consist of **informal grouping**, **formal grouping**, and **base groups**. The number of students per group will depend on the activity or level of discussion. Typically, groups can consist of at least two, but usually not more than six students. Your purpose for grouping determines the design and make-up of the group.

+ **Informal Grouping**: Typically involves students working with activities that do not require much time and often occur sporadically. Informal groups have fewer guidelines or established rules. Informal grouping is a grand opportunity for content review. For example, small informal groups of students can turn to their partner or their group and discuss thoughts, ideas, or even summarize completed chapters in a novel, character traits, or make inferences. The possibilities are unlimited, but very rewarding.

+ **Formal Grouping**: Formal grouping involves a group-processing strategy, planning, assigning roles, and more extended classroom activities. Students do not simply turn and work with their partner or a small group, they are assigned roles. For example, jigsaw is a type of formal grouping. For the jigsaw strategy students are assigned topics, disperse into specific groups to discuss a given topic where each person in the group have been given the same topic, character, or story element. Once this group thoroughly discusses their given topic, they return to their home group or base group.

+ **Base Group**: Unlike formal or informal groups that work together only to complete a given task, base groups work together for extended amounts of time. Base groups may work together for the duration of a week, a month, or even a year. Base groups may review work that was completed in both informal and formal groupings that occurred during the day, or even the week. Base groups also set goals, plan, solve problems, work through situations or activities that require extended support, or complete group projects.

Establishing a Group

High-powered teachers know the discussion should be engaging and transformative, and their students must be comfortable and ready to take academic risks. They must be ready to explore the unknown, willing to be optimistic of new perspectives, gain new insights, and also new understandings. Establishing who will be in a group, or how you will establish a group depends on the purpose for the group. Some of the grouping practices include following:

+ **Interest Grouping:** Grouping students who share a common interest to complete projects. Projects can be determined by the group or based on suggestions given by the teacher. This type of grouping and decision-making allows students to voice their opinions, explore new ideas, be flexible and open to other ideas, and also serves as a sense of motivation.

+ **Social Grouping:** Social grouping allows students to work with peers of their choice. This is not an ideal form of grouping to include as a primary method, but is necessary at times to promote social skills.

+ **Random Grouping:** Random grouping involves a random selection made by the teacher. Random selection can be as simplistic as selecting random names from a container, using a

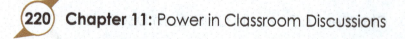

random selector app, or even allowing students to select a name from a container. This type of grouping helps eliminate feelings of the teacher or students being biased.

+ **Ability Grouping:** Ability grouping is grouping students based on their ability to comprehend specified content. This is a wonderful opportunity to use leveled readers or leveled text, which can be created through www.newsela.com. Ability grouping may also consist of students working on projects at different levels. While one group might work on writing a skit based on a chapter in a novel the class is reading, another group might be working on creating a storyboard to retell the important events within the chapter, and yet another group might be writing a poem that retells the chapter. Nevertheless, each group is working toward the same goal to summarize the chapter.

+ **Tutorial Grouping:** Tutorial grouping allows students to learn from each other. Students who have learned the assigned materials are grouped with peers who may be experiencing a little difficulty with the given text. The object is for the students to expand their understanding through questioning and responding.

+ **Needs Grouping:** Needs grouping consists of grouping students according to their strengths and their challenges. Needs grouping is designed to help reduce the amount of time spent reteaching while also providing additional support for students who may require additional help.

Just as whole-group discussion has its purposes, so do small-group discussions. High-powered teachers know that small-group discussions help their students make meaning, assume responsibility for their learning, and also practice effective strategies. They also know that discussion provides opportunities for reflection and revision of meaning, create learning opportunities that are less likely to occur when students work independently. Because students are more likely to speak up in small-group settings than whole-group settings that are teacher-led, small groups are a more comfortable setting for students to gain confidence and also independence (InTASC Standard 4, CCSSO).

Student Roles

Now that you know more about how to group students, and the importance of grouping, let's take a closer look at various roles that students may have within their groups. Student roles can consist of a reader, reporter, illustrator, timekeeper, researcher, and also the encourager. Each role is important and specific to the group. High-powered teachers rotate student's roles to allow all students an opportunity to experience each role, which also reinforces their understanding of how the group should work as a whole. Teachers may also modify the roles or extend them to better fit students' learning styles or their learning levels (InTASC Standard 2, CCSSO).

+ **The Reader:** The reader reads directions, resource material, or the assigned text.
+ **The Reporter:** The reporter reports findings or actions to the other groups.
+ **The Illustrator:** The illustrator illustrates designs for projects.
+ **The Timekeeper:** The timekeeper is in charge of keeping groups aware of time and also working within an assigned amount of time.
+ **The Researcher:** The researcher is responsible for gathering material needed to complete a group project.

✦ **The Encourager:** The encourager keeps notes on the groups' processing, social skills, and also makes sure that all group members have a turn and provides positive feedback to the group to help establish and maintain moral.

Regardless the method or establishment of groups, high-powered teachers ensure that their students know what is expected of them through explicit instructions, modeling, and practice. High-powered teachers allow multiple opportunities for students to work in groups and have established guidelines and expectations that students learn, expect, and follow. They also know that grouping enhances time management, simply because they do not have to reiterate the rules, guidelines, or expectations, because students are well-versed in their knowledge of what to do, the teachers' expectations, as well as their personal goals.

Selecting Questions for Discussion

High-powered teachers know that the quality of discussion is dependent on the quality of the question(s) selected by the teacher. If questions are too hard, students often lack background knowledge, which results in lack of knowledge to bring to the discussion. Thus, the discussion is superficial. Whereas, if the question(s) is too easy, students have little to discuss, simply because there is an obvious answer(s) to the question(s) being asked. Moreover, if the question(s) or the topic is thought of as boring or does not relate to students' lives, they are typically not as willing to put forth the effort to have a meaningful discussion.

High-powered teachers listen to their students, while also considering curricular needs, objectives, current events, and students' interest. The first step in selecting a question for discussion is to identify a curricular goal, objective, or standard that you want to address. The second step is to write a question based on that goal at the application level. Bloom defines *application* as using a concept learned in the classroom in a new situation.

High-powered teachers know that an application question requires their students to synthesize information to solve a real-world problem. They encourage students to make predictions about real-world situations, current events, etc. **Application questions** promote deep thinking, problem-solving, reflecting, and also inferring. Application-level questions are ideal for discussions as they inspire students to get involved. In other words, they engage students because the question(s) often relate to their lives. They have some level of background knowledge, and usually already have a formed opinion about the topic. Application questions are generally not too easy to answer, thus giving students something to discuss.

Once high-powered teachers have identified the curricular goal, they determine the application-level question based on the curricular goal. They prepare students for discussion by giving them a set of warm-up, or prep questions. These questions usually consist of asking simple facts, ensuring that students have read, reviewed, reflected, and gathered the necessary material required to have a meaningful discussion and also an application-level small-group discussion.

High-powered teachers ensure that their students are prepared and have good questions to discuss in small groups. They ensure that students are able to discuss the questions knowledgeably and appropriately. They help students utilize their background knowledge by making them write preparation questions for discussion, and by giving them guidelines for carrying out rich, respectful discussions.

Activating Prior Knowledge

As stated in previous chapters, students come to classrooms year after year with diverse personalities, ethnicities, cultures, socioeconomic status, learning styles, reading levels, home lives, social lives, knowledge, and unique personalities, which can all play a role in students' background knowledge of many topics. However, high-powered teachers know that there are many ways to activate and build students' background knowledge. They help activate, build, and establish students' knowledge through incorporating books, magazines, articles, videos, and other information sources available for students to read, review, and watch. They pair students who have limited prior knowledge with a partner or a small subgroup of student(s) that have established knowledge to read together, discuss, ponder answers to questions, and simply gain enough insight to be able to participate in a grand discussion with a group or in a whole-class discussion. High-powered teachers know when a student gains enough knowledge about the topic to pique their interest, the student will pay more attention to new information and, as a result, gain background knowledge that a less-interested student wouldn't even have noticed. A student who is motivated is typically more eager to learn, pays closer attention to what is being said in the discussion, apply it to what they already know, and as a result will retain and be able to recall more about the topic. Differences in background knowledge can be an asset to discussion when each student has something that they can contribute to the conversation/discussion.

Preparing for Discussion With Writing

High-powered teachers promote rich discussions by giving students sufficient time to prepare for discussion through writing. They know that some students will not properly prepare for discussions on their time. As a result, high-powered teachers create a time for students to prepare for discussions in class time. They know that giving students' time to prepare for an upcoming discussion sends a strong message that preparation is important and key to a productive discussion (InTASC Standard 8, CCSSO).

Incorporating discussion planning sheets require students to reflect on what they already know and separate relevant information from irrelevant information. High-powered teachers know that writing also provides a rehearsal stop to ensure that information is familiar to them and ready to use during discussion. Discussion planning sheets make information readily available for students to refer to when necessary during discussions. In other words, they prepare students and get them ready for discussion by requiring them to identify important facts they want to discuss, separate fact from fiction, and also come to a tentative conclusion based on facts and opinions. They also provide students with a designated space to record thoughts that may arise as a result of what's being said during the discussion. An example of a **discussion planning sheet** is shown in **Table 11.1**.

Journal entries are setup in a similar fashion, but are less structured. Journals serve the same purpose for students as do discussion planners. They serve as a tool for them to record their thoughts, ideas, and also to record new information they may gain through the discussion as well as a reflection tool. Students are required to set their journals up in a similar fashion as the discussion planning sheet. For example, they include the question being asked near the top of the entry, list and organize facts, as well as opinions, and designate a place for conclusions, as well as new thoughts or ideas. High-powered teachers require students to use the discussion planning sheet prior to implementing journal writing as a means of preparing for discussions, simply to ensure that students know what purpose the writing serves, what components are required, and to establish a habit of examining the facts, opinions, and determining what is relevant or irrelevant, as well as coming to a conclusion or answer to the question.

Table 11.1: Discussion Planning Sheet

Discussion Planning Sheet			
Name: _____ Date: _____			
Question(s) or Topic: _____			
Facts	Opinions	Conclusions	My new thoughts after discussion

Discussion Webs

High-powered teachers incorporate **discussion webs** because they know that these encourage students to visualize the key elements of an issue and also quickly recognize and identify opposing points of view on the matter. Discussion webs are an ideal resource for argumentation, debates, and most classroom discussion. Discussion webs are an organizational tool that helps guide discussions at any grade-level. They allow students to determine ideas of contention, to weigh opposing viewpoints, and also critically evaluate the debate, argument, or discussion. Discussion webs can also be a useful tool for readers. This type of organizer helps the reader to determine a clear point or viewpoint. In other words, a discussion web is a visual framework for analyzing texts (InTASC Standard 8, CCSSO).

Discussion Web Steps

1. Distribute reading material to students. Be sure to select an interesting or controversial topic.
2. Ask students to read and then identify the main question of the text. Once a consensus is reached, post the question for quick reference.
3. Divide the class in small groups of four to five students. Provide the groups with copies of the Discussion web graphic organizer (**see Table 11.2**).
4. Ask the groups to write down at least three reasons for answering the question yes and three reasons for answering no.

5. Teacher should then display a simple T-Chart in a visible place recording students' positive and negative responses. Use this list to help promote discussion. Ask students to evaluate each reason as pro or con objectively and fairly.

6. After discussing the individual reasons, encourage each student to decide on a position on the general question. Point out that understanding both sides of an argument or debate does not preclude taking a stand.

7. Finally, have each student write his or her final conclusion on an index card or sticky note. Collect the cards and tally the responses. Share the results with the class and list the most common reason pro and con for these decisions on a shared Discussion Web graphic organizer.

Table 11.2: Discussion Web

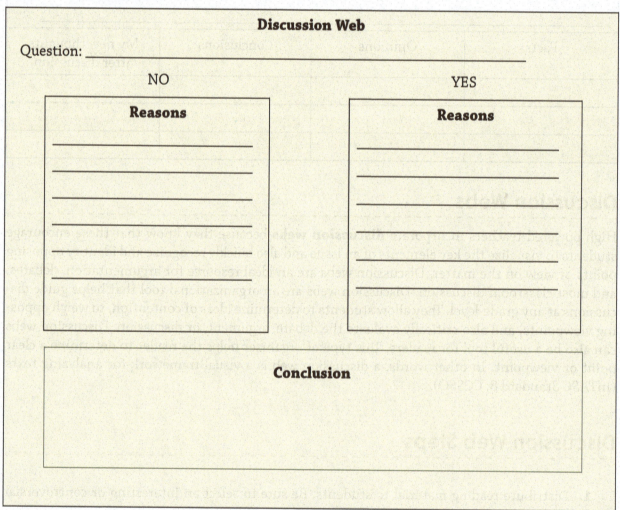

Fishbowl Discussions

Productive classroom discussions involve everyone, not just the social or vocal students who are regular contributors to classroom discussions. High-powered teachers know that the best discussions are those that enrich understanding of disciplinary topics through the exchange of multiple viewpoints and also involve every student. One way to facilitate a discussion that involves everyone in the class is using the fishbowl strategy. The fishbowl strategy involves one group of students looking in on another smaller group of students in a manner similar to watching fish through the clear glass of an aquarium. The smaller group in the inside circle carries on a conversation about the issue or topic while the outside group listens and prepares questions and comments for the participants. These roles are often rotated to ensure that all students play an active part in discussing, listening, and questioning.

High-powered teachers implement the fishbowl strategy during reading because they know that it is particularly well-suited for English Language Learners. They know that students are provided a structured way to listen to a conversation before being expected to participate in discussion. They also know it can be easily adapted in various settings such as smaller groups and online settings. They also implement the fishbowl strategy to increase student engagement, comprehension, and discussion skills (InTASC Standard 8, CCSSO).

Fishbowl Discussion Step-By-Step

1. Identify a question, topic, or focus for discussion. Typically, the more controversial and charged the issue, the greater the level of student engagement.
2. Ask students to turn to their neighbors and talk about his or her ideas or opinions related to the issue or question. Ask students to take notes on their discussion either through the use of a journal or a discussion planning sheet. Allow sufficient time for a reasonable exchange of ideas and viewpoints, which can be determined by moving around the room while you monitor and facilitate.
3. Demonstrate the format and expectations of a fishbowl discussion. This is best accomplished through a practice of the activity. Ask four or five students to volunteer to sit around a table or in a cluster of desks in the middle of the room. Have other students gather in a circle.
4. Get the discussion started by telling the participants sitting in the cluster to begin talking among themselves about the ideas or opinions they raised and recorded during their conversation with their partner.
5. Tell the other students to listen carefully to their classmates while they engage in a small-group discussion. You may also ask them to take notes to share afterward.
6. Allow the students who volunteered to talk for about 5 minutes, getting involved only if the discussion dies down or to ensure everyone is contributing and taking turns.
7. When the small group finishes or has stopped talking, ask the other students to make comments on the discussion they observed or ask questions to the participants. This is an ideal time to model appropriate comments and questions.
8. Create a different small group of volunteer participants and continue the fishbowl processes until all students have had the opportunity to be inside the fishbowl and they are clear about their roles and expectations.

The fishbowl strategy is an ideal method of discussion for literature. For example, a possible question on Shakespeare could be *What if Hamlet had not killed Polonius? Could he have saved himself from a certain life of tragedy? Explain your answers.* While five students begin proposing different possible outcomes of the play and also offering possible rationales, the other students could be asked to watch and listen quietly. After students offer suggested scenarios, the teacher may elicit reactions to the small-group discussion from students watching from the outside of the fishbowl. High-powered teachers know that this approach allows those students looking in on the discussion to critique and assess the ideas of the fishbowl participants and to also formulate their own ideas. The teacher then selects a new group of five students and poses a new question about Hamlet. Thus, students are engaged, recalling information, exercising critical thinking skills, as well as problem-solving skills (InTASC Standard 8, CCSSO).

Discussion and Assessment

Reflective writing can be very beneficial in assessing students' knowledge of a concept that has been at the heart of recent classroom discussions. Reflective writing can be implemented through extended response questions, journal entries, expository writing, essay questions, and also through written summarization. Regardless the type of reflective writing, each type should require the student to recall, describe, and explain why he or she arrived at a conclusion about the topic that was recently discussed. Reflective writing is also an excellent opportunity for students to exercise written expression, grammar, punctuation, and self-expression. High-powered teacher implement reflective writing to enhance and assess students' comprehension, written expression, use of grammar, and also to encourage students to be reflective learners (InTASC Standard 6, CCSSO).

High-powered teachers also implement students' projects as methods of assessment. Students are required to follow a rubric, which details what the final product must contain. Projects can include but are not limited to the following: storyboards, power points, videos, poetry, a speech, skit, comic strips, essays, informational booklet, etc. High-powered teachers require students to choose the type of project that they want to complete. Allowing students to have a voice and a choice in the type of project they want to complete encourages motivation, inspiration, engagement, and to choose a project based on their learning style. High-powered teachers know that students who have a choice, are motivated, and working with a project that fits their learning style and needs, the final product is typically more creative, personal, and a product that students are proud to assume ownership of as well as a deeper understanding of the concept the project is based on (InTASC Standard 8, CCSSO).

Language Link

High-powered teachers cease the moment to integrate discussions with Language Arts. They know that knowledge of the topic is vital to the success of a debate. Before students are asked to select a position of either supporting or opposing the topic of the debate, students should have adequate background knowledge of the topic in an effort to make personal connections necessary to determine their position. High-powered teachers allow students time to research the topic and write a brief summary of their findings with correct citations, thus enhancing written expression of expository text and knowledge of citing sources. They also require their students to include textual evidence found within their articles in their writing (InTASC Standard 8, CCSSO).

Hosting a Virtual Book Club

Recently, high-powered teachers have found that hosting **virtual book clubs** has been a game-changer with student's **motivation** to read. They discovered that by creating an assignment with the title, Book Club, student's interest, participation, and responses increased dramatically. They found that the **"atmosphere"** was more relaxing during the virtual book discussion than in a typical classroom discussion. They also discovered that student's answers were more detailed, honest, and heartfelt. Student questions grew in depth, which extended the classroom discussion beyond the basic answers. The virtual book club discussions engaged students and encouraged them to consider other participant's points of view. The goal of book clubs is to create a **positive** and **affirming** experience that encourages and motivates students to read while also participating in classroom discussions.

High-powered teachers bring a lesson to their online book club chats, just as they would for in-person class. Book clubs can vary in lengths of time depending on the grade-level and also on the novel being discussed. Nevertheless, students are assigned a text to read and all begin reading the same day. **Flexibility is key in virtual book clubs**, as students read on various levels, at diverse speeds, and many will want to read further and deeper in the text than the required page number. Teachers may select to host multiple book clubs for various groups of students based on their reading levels. Book clubs can mimic small group guided reading, but in a more sophisticated and relaxed manner, with the teacher primarily facilitating, guiding, and prompting the discussion rather than guiding instruction.

Teachers may also choose to post **video messages** to the platform that the district is currently using. Video messages can be weekly reminders of pages or chapters to read, prompting questions, and insightful moments to highlight during independent reading. Teachers can also ask students to come to the book club prepared with paper and pencil, as well as the assigned book. Teachers may choose to meet with their book club students twice a week, or even three times a week. Again, high-powered teachers are flexible, and modify the schedule to meet the needs of their students and also to align with the chosen text. Asking students to answer a question during the prerecorded video messages will also help to inspire students to talk, while also equipping them with a starting place for the conversation, and also give them the confidence that they need to voice their opinion during the book conversation.

Many teachers prefer to meet by Zoom, which allows everyone involved in the session to visibly see each other, which provides students with a more collaborative and social experience. High-powered teachers typically begin with an icebreaker to allow students to find their comfort zone. Teachers may choose to open the conversation with a Likert scale rating of the book thus far, or of the entire book when students have completed the book. Likert scales can be visual with students holding up the number of fingers from one to five to rate the book. Once the ice has been broken introduce the conversation with a few probing questions and ask for volunteers to answer. When the conversation is established, most teachers prefer to sit back and observe the students taking the lead. They know that student-to-student conversation is better than student-to-teacher discussion.

Time is important when implementing any type of strategy. Elementary and middle school book club sessions should typically last no longer than 30 minutes. Secondary students can handle longer meetings of up to an hour. Come prepared with prompting questions in case the conversation becomes idle. Ask text-to-self questions that allows students to explore the text, and also self-reflect about their own lives, which leads to self-discovery. Also, high-powered teachers encourage text-to-self connections such as which character they would like to become friends with. Other questions might ask students to consider which character they are more like. Students may be required to complete a Venn Diagram comparing and contrasting themselves to a character in the book. Still other questions can center around the setting allowing students to visualize themselves living in the era of time the book was set, or place where the character lives. This type of questions allows students to make real-life connections, which enhances conversations, motivation, and also learning.

High-powered teachers know that book club settings not only **promote conversation**, but also have the ability to **promote rapport** within their classroom. Because the groups are small with **low stakes**, with **high rewards**, **learning experiences** are very **gratifying**, and also **encourage** students to take **academic risks**, **practice self-reflection**, while also **empowering themselves as learners.** They know that the objective and or overarching goal of virtual book clubs is to promote conversation, enhance comprehension, encourage collaboration, but also to promote a love of literature in a positive and supporting environment that makes learning fun. Even though an online learning experience is different from a classroom experience with the right approach, patience, and creativity, high-powered teachers can use this time to cultivate connections with their students while promoting conversation and the love of reading.

Now It's Your Turn

For this assignment you will research discussion strategies. Select a discussion strategy that you would like to know more about. The strategy cannot be the one described in this chapter. Once you have determined the strategy that you want to research, you will be required to write a five paragraph reflective essay describing the strategy, the steps, and how it should be implemented. Also, include why you chose the strategy of choice. A drop box with more details about the assignment is located on blackboard.

Author's Tip

Preparing your class for discussions can be challenging. Keep in mind that there are many factors to think about when planning discussions. For example, the academic atmosphere of the classroom, the physical size of the classroom as well as the number of students, the composition/layout of the classroom, the nature of the questions being asked, and also the guidelines for appropriate behavior, and finally staying on task. Without careful planning both teachers and students can become discouraged, thus decreasing the quality and end results of the discussion (InTASC Standard 7, CCSSO).

Take time to prepare for small-group discussions, prepare the questions, organize the material, pre-teach, activate prior knowledge, and most all prepare the students. Equip them with the tools that a beneficial and effective discussion requires. Facilitate the discussion to ensure that all members of each group is engaged. Do what it takes to make the discussion productive (InTASC Standard 7, CCSSO).

It is a good idea to create and maintain a running list of topics that lead to spontaneous discussions in your classrooms. Try to identify characteristics of those topics and use the information when selecting topics and questions for more constructive discussions. Above all, do not set students up for failure. What? Model for your students. Model what you expect them to do during discussions. I always found it beneficial to model bad behavior for students to see how teachers perceived students who were not engaged, daydreaming, being argumentative, or being zoned out of the conversation. Practice, practice, practice discussions as a whole group. Discuss the various roles and what each entail, and finally allow students to work in small-group discussions a few times before holding them accountable.

You will find that by establishing a curricular goal, or objective, that the students are well aware of, preparing students and equipping them with material and applicable questions that will stimulate their curiosity, activate prior knowledge, create a desire within them to want to know more, to motivate them to dig deeper, selecting a topic and questions that they can relate to and are interested in, your students will be more engaged in the discussion. Thus, ensuring productive and meaningful discussions.

What Can Parents Do to Help?

The hours in a school day are few and the time a teacher can spend with any one student is limited. For students to be successful in school, parents and families need to be actively involved in their children's learning. Parents should become involved early and remain actively involved throughout the academic school year. In fact, research shows that what the family does is vital and more important to a child's academic success than how much money the family makes or how much education the parents have. In other words, parental involvement is vital to their child's academic success (InTASC Standard 10, CCSSO).

High-powered teachers know that when parents show an interest in their child's education, a spark of enthusiasm is generated, resulting in an increased student motivation and an increase in students' academic achievement, and learning becomes more enjoyable and rewarding. High-powered teachers encourage parents to read selected material about an upcoming discussion with their child to promote a deeper understanding, a sense of motivation, and also to encourage discussion of the topic at hand.

High-powered teachers also invite parents to attend classroom debates as a means of encouraging their child to participate. They might even schedule a parent/student debate over a controversial topic to enhance students' motivation, as well as promote a deeper level of knowledge about the topic at hand. Ideas can range from bring your own device to school policy, school uniforms, school safety, school lunches, dress codes, etc. Parent/student debates can be a departmental project that can implemented to increase students' knowledge of the topic at hand, discussion skills, research skills, oral language, and also increase parental involvement. Regardless the method of parental involvement, high-powered teachers know that an actively involved parent increases the likelihood of student motivation, as well as academic success (InTASC Standard 9, 10, CCSSO).

Applications

+ Metacognition
+ Informal grouping
+ Formal grouping
+ Base groups

+ Interest grouping
+ Social grouping random grouping
+ Ability grouping
+ Needs grouping
+ Tutorial grouping
+ Application questions
+ Prior knowledge
+ Discussion planning sheet
+ Fishbowl discussion

In-Seat Activity

Working with your randomly selected group, select and read one of the articles that is on your table. You may read independently, shared reading, or designate a reader. Once you've read the article, reflect and collaborate to determine what type of discussion strategy would be best suited for the article. The articles have a predetermined grade-level and content area written at the top of the page. Be prepared to present a brief overview of the article and which discussion strategy your team selected for the article. Explain why you chose the strategy and how you anticipate it will enhance students' learning. You will be given an allotted amount of time in class to read, collaborate, and prepare your informal presentation.

Reflect and Answer the Following Questions

+ *What are classroom discussions and why are they important to learning?*
+ *What are the components of a classroom discussion?*
+ *How do I conduct a meaningful classroom discussion?*
+ *What strategies promote discussion?*
+ *How can I use discussions for assessment?*

Student Notes

Annotating is an effective learning strategy. This page is reserved for you to annotate (*take notes*), record potential questions, and also to refer back to when studying, completing assignments, and to help you gain a better understanding of Chapter Eleven.

Student Reflection

High-powered teachers reflect. This page is reserved for you to reflect about information that you found insightful and what you have learned from Chapter Eleven.

Suggested Reading

Become familiar with the work of the following authors as they are representative of those you may be asked to identify on the Praxis. Each author's work brings an element of interest, inspiration, and also rich literature that is excellent to implement with a variety of discussion strategies.

- Louisa May Alcott
- Ray Bradbury
- Emily Dickinson
- Frederick Douglass
- Ralph Waldo Emerson
- F. Scott Fitzgerald
- Anne Frank
- Robert Frost
- S.E. Hinton
- Zora Neale Hurston
- John Keats
- Helen Keller
- Harper Lee
- Madeleine L 'Engle
- C.S. Lewis
- Jack London
- Lois Lowry
- Herman Melville
- George Orwell
- Edgar Allan Poe
- J.D. Salinger
- William Shakespeare

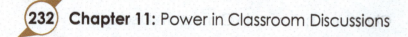

- ✦ Mary Shelley
- ✦ Percy Bysshe Shelley
- ✦ Gary Soto
- ✦ Amy Tan
- ✦ J.R.R. Tolkien
- ✦ Mark Twain
- ✦ Alice Walker
- ✦ H.G. Wells
- ✦ Walt Whitman

Chapter References

Alvermann, D., et al. "Middle and High School Student's Perceptions of How They Experience Text-Based Discussions: A Multi-Case Study." *Reading Research Quarterly*, vol. 31, no. 3, 1996, pp. 244–67.

Bloom, B., editor. *Taxonomy of Educational Objectives*. Longman, 1956.

Council of Chief State School Officers (CCSSO). *Interstate Teacher Assessment and Support Consortium (InTASC) Model Core Teaching Standards*, Apr. 2011, https://www.ccsso.org/sites/default/files/2017-11/InTASC_Model_Core_Teaching_Standards_2011.pdf. Accessed 7 July 2018.

U.S. Department of Education Office of Communications and Outreach *Helping Your Preschool Child*, Washington, D.C., 2005. Accessed 6 Nov. 2019.

Newsela | Instructional Content Platform, 2018, http://newsela.com. Accessed 18 Mar. 2018.

Vygotsky, L. *Mind in Society*. Harvard UP, 1978.

Chapter 12
Increasing Students' Vocabulary

Teacher Quote:

"Vocabulary is a matter of word building. You can't build vocabulary without learning new words. Read daily…the more you read the more words you will know."

~ Dr. Joyce Bowling

Chapter Questions

✦ *What is word-knowledge?*
✦ *How can students increase their word-knowledge?*
✦ *Why is vocabulary vital to students' academic success?*
✦ *What is meant by intentional focus on vocabulary?*
✦ *How does vocabulary affect reading comprehension?*
✦ *What vocabulary strategies enhance students' vocabulary?*

Word-Knowledge

Our oral language and reading vocabularies continue to grow throughout our lifetime. A rapid expansion of language occurs during a child's first 10 years of life. When children enter kindergarten, their vocabulary typically consists of several thousand words, and increases by nearly 3,000 words per year. As students' advance through elementary grades their word knowledge should continue to grow each year. Researchers estimate that every year beginning in fifth grade, students encounter approximately 10,000 unfamiliar words. However, there is a preponderance of evidence that suggests too few middle-school students read at levels needed to learn from required textbooks (American institutes for Research; Heller and Greenleaf; National Center for Education Statistics). The most recent National Assessment of Education Progress (NAEP) results show that only 31% of eighth graders across the nation read proficiently (2017). High-powered teachers know that students need a rich vocabulary to understand what they read. They also know that word knowledge is critical to students' academic success (InTASC Standard 1, Council of Chief State School Officers [CCSSO]). High-powered teachers are lifelong learners who research and implement new innovative vocabulary strategies daily to help engage, inspire, and expand students' vocabulary (InTASC Standards 4, 5, 6, CCSSO).

> *Mark Twain once said, "The difference between the right word and the almost right word is the difference between lightning and a lightning bug."* (Appleton, 1890).

> *~ Mark Twain*

Vocabulary demands of school texts have been cited as a major contributor of students reading problems. Middle-school students need to have a well-developed word-knowledge base in effort to handle reading across content areas in school. High-powered teachers know that reading comprehension is complex and involves the coordination of multiple cognitive processes and knowledge, which is key to deep comprehension and word-knowledge. High-powered teacher know that word-knowledge and reading comprehension are interwoven. They also know that students' reading comprehension increases as their word-knowledge increases (InTASC Standard 4, CCSSO).

Research makes it clear that middle-school students need to study words to better understand the English language. They also need more systematic instruction that helps them to organize their word-knowledge. High-powered teachers' present systematic instruction in an integrated and thought-provoking manner to help their students better understand how words work. They expect their students to have a vast vocabulary and a good understanding of word-knowledge (InTASC Standard 8, CCSSO). In other words, high-powered teachers want their students to know a vast amount of words, but they also want them to know how to use words in written expression and also in oral conversations.

Research suggests that word study at the intermediate level should demonstrate to students how their word-knowledge can be applied to advance their vocabulary, reading comprehension, spelling, and writing. High-powered intermediate and middle-grade teachers apply the following principals to help guide their instruction (InTASC Standard 8, CCSSO).

✦ Actively involve students in the exploration of words to help them develop a positive and curios attitude about words.
✦ Activate students' prior knowledge to engage them through connections that help them learn specialized vocabulary in various content areas.
✦ Encourage students to reflect, consider, and make connections between concepts.
✦ Help students to compare and contrast familiar concepts.
✦ Ensure students have sufficient exposure to words in multiple meaningful settings and contexts.
✦ Teach structural elements such as syllables, affixes, and the effects of affixes on the base words to which they are applied.

High-powered teachers intentionally focus on vocabulary. They know that a deliberate and **explicit approach** can be vital in activating students' prior knowledge about important concepts (InTASC Standard 1, CCSSO). High-powered teachers understand how learners grow and develop. They understand how to connect concepts and use differing perspectives to engage learners in critical thinking and creativity that encourages students to make connections to prior knowledge. High-powered teachers know that prior knowledge is considered as the framework by which students understand new information. Thus, when students retrieve prior knowledge, it becomes easier for them to grasp novel concepts. High-powered teachers implement a variety of instructional strategies to encourage students to develop deep understanding of content. They know by learning or reviewing key vocabulary their students are enabled to think of other associations to the new words, contexts, allowing them to make both academic and personal connections (InTASC Standard 8, CCSSO). High-powered teachers provide support, a support for students with each vocabulary lesson through explicit instruction, innovative strategies, and engaging activities that expand students' word-knowledge, as well as opportunities for students to interact with social concepts (InTASC Standard 3, CCSSO).

It is vital to students' learning to focus on intentional and specific vocabulary strategies daily to help build students word-knowledge, vocabulary, and reading comprehension. High-powered teachers know that competent adults do not refer to a set of rules they have memorized while reading or writing. Instead, adult readers recognize new words by comparing them, or the patterns within them, to words they already know. Therefore, they teach their students to constantly use patterns and strategies when reading, spelling, and writing (InTASC Standard 1, CCSSO).

High-powered teachers realize the difficulty of text(s) and vocabulary that middle grade and secondary curriculum require students to read, comprehend, and apply (InTASC Standard 4, CCSSO). They know students must first understand the academic language that authors use in textbooks to understand the concepts and content in their texts (InTASC Standard 1, CCSSO). High-powered teachers make this challenging language more understandable for all students, including struggling readers, many of whom struggle because of diverse language backgrounds (InTASC Standard 2, CCSSO). High-powered teachers ensure students have every possible advantage such as clarifying content and language objectives before, during, and also after instruction. They teach content vocabulary prior to the reading or writing assignment. High-powered teachers also monitor their students' conversation, collaboration, and written work while they work in small-groups to ensure that they have a full understanding of the text, and also address questions that may arise (InTASC Standard 6, CCSSO). After small-group work, high-powered teachers encourage students to ask questions about words that are still unclear.

High-powered teachers incorporate vocabulary strategies in their daily instruction to introduce students to new words, deepen their understanding of familiar words, while also building their word-knowledge (InTASC Standard 7, CCSSO). They know that students often begin framing concepts in the simplest possible language, which offers them opportunities to use more specific words, as well as new words with which they are gaining familiarity and reinforcing the crucial literacy goal of developing vocabulary. For example, high-powered teachers encourage students to use new words in daily conversation and when questioning and answering questions. An example of asking for a better word may include the following scenario:

Teacher: *Why do you think that Samantha yelled?*
Student: *Samantha yelled because she was scared.*
Teacher: *Can you answer with a synonym for the words, yelled and scared?'*
Student: *Samantha screamed because she was frightened.*

Teacher: *Very good! Now, can you use one of the new vocabulary words to replace either screamed or frightened?*
Student: *Samantha shrieked because she was petrified.*
Teacher: *Very nice job!*

In other words, high-powered teachers are constantly requiring their students to think about words, replace words with richer words, interpret their meanings, make connections, and also asking their students to be prepared to explain their thinking or applying their knowledge of the words in new and diverse ways. They do not simply ask a question, instead they go beyond the obvious *"go to"* questions, which requires students to reflect ordinary words with extraordinary words. They pique students' interest about words, require them to incorporate new words, and also to explore both old and new words on a daily basis (InTASC Standard 8, CCSSO). High-powered teachers want students to not only know a vast amount of words, but also know how to use words correctly in all content areas, written expression, and also in everyday life.

Many teachers simply ask students to use a particular word(s) in a sentence. High-powered teachers will require students to use words in multiple ways. For example, high-powered teachers may not only ask a student to use a word in a complete sentence, but also ask them to rewrite a sentence to have the same meaning, but start with a different word. They may also ask them to change the adjective form of a word, and to use synonyms and antonyms. It's not just what students say that matters, but it's how they communicate it. High-powered teachers realize that for their students to be academically successful, they must take their knowledge and express it in a variety of clear and effective formats to fit the academic demands as well as the demands of society (InTASC Standard 4, CCSSO). It has been said, that the complete sentence is the battering ram that knocks down the door to college (Lemov).

"Students who know more words learn more words."

~ Author unknown

Intentional Focus on Vocabulary

Teaching vocabulary is vitally important for students' academic success. All vocabulary instruction is not equal. High-powered teachers know that beneficial vocabulary instruction begins with a student-friendly definition that is clear and simple. However, the definition is not the final stopping place or the ultimate goal of vocabulary instruction. High-powered teachers begin here, and then take time to allow students to work with the vocabulary words after their initial understanding of the word(s) to increase their knowledge and use of the word(s) through rigorous, engaging, and challenging activities (InTASC Standard 5, CCSSO). In other words, they know that simply recognizing a word does not mean that students know how to effectively use a word. The intentional focus on words, their definitions, and their uses prepares students to effectively use vocabulary functionally while also increasing their reading comprehension.

The skill of inferring vocabulary from context appears frequently on standardized and state assessments. However, teaching vocabulary primarily by context clues is not the most beneficial method and not the only method of inferring and learning new vocabulary. Context can be vague and misleading. When students learn to infer a word correctly, they are still simply making guesses, and often the guess is an erroneous guess. In other words, they still do not have a deep understanding of the word. High-powered teachers know that a more significant, and deep word-knowledge is a better achievement predictor. Strong vocabulary must also be systematically and explicitly taught with rigor, diverse activities, and multiple opportunities to apply the words while reading, writing, and speaking.

Vocabulary Strategies

High-powered reading and language arts teachers challenge their students with vocabulary instruction that challenges them to think deeply about the meanings of words, and also encourage them to explore and understand why and how they are used in sentences. They introduce vocabulary in a fun and challenging way. High-powered teachers engage, challenge, and involve students with words, rather than simply asking for a definition. They involve their students in mini-activities that take ten to fifteen minutes (InTASC Standard 5, CCSSO). For example, high-powered teachers might implement one or more of the following strategies:

+ They ask students to provide the definition and part of speech of new vocabulary words.
+ They ask them for synonyms, ideally one with which they are already familiar with.
+ They also ask them to explain how the vocabulary word is similar but different.
+ They ask students to suggest a time or times when they might use the word, and why?
+ They ask students to use the word in a meaningful sentence and also in a question.
+ They provide students with an illustration or a visual that portrays the vocabulary word and ask them to explain why the picture is a representation of the word.
+ They ask them to write a second sentence using the vocabulary word that reflects the word's meaning in a complete thought.
+ They also ask students to list and discuss variations of the word such as the different parts of speech. For example, how can they make a verb into an adverb simply by changing or adding a suffix?
+ They also play reinforcing vocabulary games that require them to compare, contrast, or combine.

High-powered teachers incorporate a wide-variety of vocabulary strategies into their instruction to help students make connections, gain insight, increase understanding, expand vocabulary, and also increase their knowledge of how to correctly use vocabulary words. Vocabulary activities can be engaging, collaborative, independent activities, and also whole-classroom activities. Each vocabulary strategy and activity is purposeful, planned, and also modeled before students work independently or in collaborative groups to support every student in meeting rigorous learning goals (InTASC Standard 7, CCSSO).

Vocabulary Self-Awareness

High-powered teachers know that teaching and expanding students' vocabulary is vital to their academic success, but they also know that teaching vocabulary can be complicated. Many teachers view learning new vocabulary as a black or white issue; in other words, either a student knows the word or they don't. However, high-powered teachers know that expanding one's vocabulary really exists on a sliding scale. The varied word-knowledge levels of each individual student' in a single classroom is broad and diverse. Each student has a diverse range of word knowledge and word understanding. Students are exposed to a vast amount of words through daily conversations, cultural experiences, family, friends, television, social media, reading, and through academic instruction. High-powered teachers know that students may be familiar with vocabulary words. They may have heard the words, but that they don't actually know the definition of the words. High-powered teachers know that students may recognize rich vocabulary words when other people use them in conversations, but remain unsure of how to implement them in their own oral language. High-powered teachers know that a *"one size fits all"* to teaching vocabulary does not address or meet the needs of all students (InTASC Standards 1, 2, 7, CCSSO).

Vocabulary knowledge impacts students' ability to comprehend what they are reading. Diverse levels of vocabulary results in diverse reading levels. High-powered teacher assess students' vocabulary before assigning reading to better understand their depth of background knowledge, and also to plan meaningful vocabulary instruction that will meet the needs of their students. They have found that pre-assessing students' knowledge is beneficial as it allows students to gain insight into their own understanding of what they know, as what they still need to learn in order to comprehend the assigned reading (InTASC Standards 2, 6, 7, CCSSO).

High-powered teachers incorporate a **Vocabulary Self-Awareness activity**. In this activity, the vocabulary words are introduced at the beginning of the chapter, or at the beginning of a unit. The students then complete a self-assessment of their knowledge of words. An example of a Vocabulary Self-Awareness graph is shown in **Table 12.1**. Step-by-Step instructions include the following steps:

Table 12.1: Vocabulary Self-Awareness Graph

Word	?	☆	✔	Example	Definition

✦ The teacher selects some of the target vocabulary for the lesson. Encourage students to add words to the list as they read. (*This allows them to discover words in context.*)

✦ Students complete the graph prior to reading with symbols. Each vocabulary word should also be rated according to the students understanding, including an example, and a definition. If the word is unfamiliar or unknown to students, they would rate their knowledge with a question mark. If the word is familiar, but they are unsure of the definition, they will give themselves a star. If they know the word and a definition, they give themselves a check.

✦ Over the course of reading the assigned text, students include new information to their chart. The object is for students to replace all of the stars and question marks with check marks. Because students continually revisit their vocabulary charts to review their entries, they are also gaining multiple opportunities to practice and extend their growing understanding of the words.

Word Study

High-powered teachers know that students typically encounter between eight and fifteen new words each day. They also know that some of those words are not necessary for understanding the reading or for communicating their understandings in writing, knowledge of at least one of the words is probably critical to reading that will occur that day.

Table 12.2: Alike Yet Different Graphic Organizer

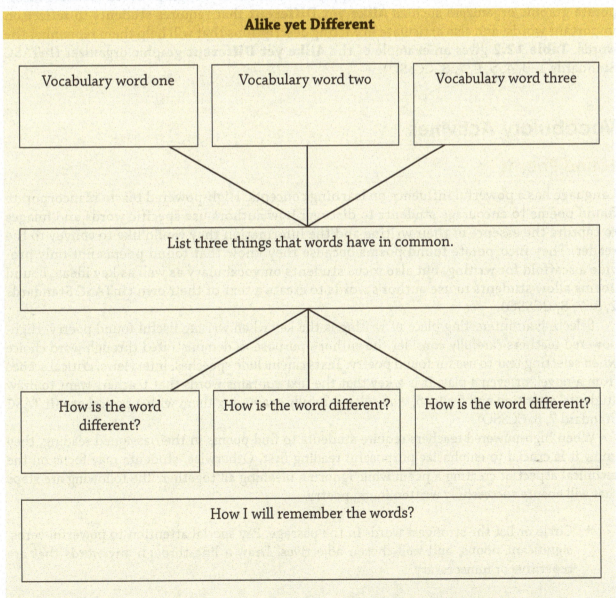

Word study is an intentional examination of specialized words within the context of authentic reading in content classes. High-powered teachers implement a variety of vocabulary strategies to ensure their students are intentionally examining specific words. Strategies include context clues, making connections, structural analysis, comparison/contrast, and also making use of available resources. High-powered teachers plan for and establish multiple ongoing opportunities for students to learn a variety of strategies for gaining word meaning when challenging vocabulary is encountered, thus ensuring improvement in content literacy (InTASC Standards 4, 5, 7, 8, CCSSO).

High-powered teachers know that when students engage in word study on a daily basis their content vocabulary will increase, which also supports reading and writing in content classes. They also know that one of the most difficult and challenging aspects of content reading is understanding the specialized vocabulary used in many textbooks. High-powered teachers challenge their students to explore words that are unknown to increase their reading comprehension. They also design and integrate meaningful activities to establish necessary knowledge that students can recall and apply when necessary. High-powered teachers incorporate graphic organizers such as **Alike yet Different** that requires students to reflect on important words, and also articulate in writing descriptions that will help them remember the words. **Table 12.2** gives an example of the **Alike yet Different** graphic organizer (InTASC Standards 1, 3, 4, 5, 6, 7, 8, CCSSO).

Vocabulary Activities

Found Poems

Language has a powerful influence on learning concepts. High-powered teachers incorporate found poems to encourage students to discover how authors use specific words and images to capture the essence of their writing and the information they would like to convey to the reader. They incorporate found poems because they know that found poems not only provide a scaffold for writing, but also focus students on vocabulary as well as key ideas. Found poems allow students to use author's words to create a text of their own (InTASC Standards 2, 5, 7, 8, CCSSO).

Selecting an interesting piece of writing is the key when writing useful found poetry. High-powered teachers carefully consider the author's purpose as demonstrated through word choice when selecting text to use for found poetry. Texts can include speeches, interviews, critical scenes from a novel, or even a play. It is a key that the text contains words that teachers want to draw students' attention and focus to, while also carefully examining them with a critical eye (InTASC Standard 7, 8, CCSSO).

When high-powered teachers require students to find poems in their assigned reading, they know it is crucial to emphasize purposeful reading first. Otherwise, students may focus on the technical aspect of creating a poem while ignoring meaning all together. The following are steps that will ensure successfully written found poetry.

✦ Circle or list the strongest words in the passage. Pay special attention to powerful verbs, significant nouns, and well-chosen adjectives. Draw a line through any words that are repetitive or unnecessary.

✦ Start the poem with a strong word or even a phrase. Try to honor the authors' original order of words as much as possible. Think about which phrases require emphasis, and consider line breaks accordingly. Strong words and phrases should stand independently/alone.

✦ Edit the poem for verb tense. Added words may have to be incorporated for grammatical purposes, but try to keep them to a minimum.

✦ Title the poem and write a final draft. Don't forget to add citation of the text you used.

Found poem is one of the many vocabulary activities and strategies that high-powered teachers incorporate in their classroom instruction to help students gain a deeper understanding of words, enhance word-knowledge, and enrich their vocabulary (InTASC Standards 7, 8, CCSSO).

Digital Vocabulary Field Trip

High-powered teachers bring excitement to their classrooms through the implementation of digital vocabulary field trips (InTASC Standard 1, 4, CCSSO). They know that digital field trips allow students to travel and explore diverse cultures, outer space, the bottom of the ocean, explore literature, authors, time-travel, and much more. Digital field trips are often referred to as virtual field trips as well. Digital field trips are exciting, informative, engaging, and very beneficial.

Step-by-Step:

1. Select the topic.
2. Create a digital field trip that allows students to click on websites that you have researched. The assigned websites can be pasted in a power point, document, Web Quest, or a free online program called 4Teachers; www.4teachers.org.
3. Post and explain directions that will guide them through the online journey.
4. On the left side of the illustration/picture(s) that represents the topic, list questions on the right, add websites that students will click on to learn more about the concept, topic, and also answer the questions.
5. Students visit websites and make connections. They examine, compare and contrast the information they discovered on the websites. Thus gaining knowledge about words through multiple exposures to different contexts, cultures, and through different media, including reading, viewing, presenting, collaborating, and reflecting.
6. Students will record their newfound information in a graphic organizer, or a summary.

Shades of Meaning

Accomplished writers know that words have the power to create mental images that take the reader outside the text and on a marvelous journey that has no boundaries. Too many times students limit themselves on word use, simply because their vocabulary is limited, or they haven't been taught how to use appropriate resources to incorporate and replace dull and dead words with more eloquent words that takes their writing to the next level.

High-powered teachers know that all students need multiple experiences with terms and words across all content areas. They also know that students need to be encouraged to not only know a wide-variety of words, but also know how to use them correctly when speaking and writing.

High-powered teachers address, InTASC Standard 8, by implementing a fun vocabulary activity titled, Shades of Meaning, to help students understand the relationships that words have with each other and also help them gain insight into incorporating a richer more eloquent vocabulary in their writing and daily language (CCSSO).

Shades of Meaning is fun and engaging activity that can be played with individual players or as a collaborative group. The activity is an inexpensive activity, but a very satisfying one. Teachers can implement Shades of Meaning by using paint chips, which can be found at most department or hardware stores. This is a great resource for a variety of activities and the good news is...they're free! The variation in tint from light to dark serves as a perfect **metaphor** for the "**shades of meaning**" between and among similar words.

Step-by-Step Instructions

1. Pick up paint chips from the local department store or ask a hardware owner to donate them for your classroom to use. (*It's amazing how many donations you will receive for educational purposes.*) Don't be afraid to ask.

2. Distribute paint chips to students as you introduce the concept of shades of meaning.

3. Explain that words and terms are used precisely to describe ideas, concepts, and situations. Tell students that they will experiment with expanding their understanding of the shades of meaning represented by similar terms.

4. Model shades of meaning by using a concrete example of a gradation of meaning. Words can be modified depending on the grade-level. Adjectives are fun to begin with, for example cute, pretty, beautiful, and gorgeous.

5. Initiate the discussion by asking the examples of the ways in which the phenomenon can be described. For instance, words associated with light include dim, glow, dazzle, bright, and glaring. You may even want to use a concrete model, such as a lamp with a dimmer switch to model the concept.

6. After you have garnered a number of responses, ask students to make choices about a continuum of terms. Ask them to write these terms on their paint chips.

7. Attach the paint chips to a piece of notebook paper and ask students to develop sentences using each of the words. Ask students to write the sentences next to each block on the paint chip.

8. Explain that effective writers and speakers understand the subtle differences between related words. Ask students to work with a partner to develop other shades of meaning. Encourage students to use the thesaurus as a source of related terms.

9. The shades of meaning and example sentences can be compiled into a writer's notebook to help support more quality writing.

Vocabulary Resources

According to the International Reading Association literacy educators need to use the tools that the twenty-first-century technologies afford us. High-powered teachers ensure that their students know how and when to use vocabulary resources to enhance their understanding, expand their knowledge, enhance their writing, and also to self-assess. They know that dictionaries, thesauries, and online resources cannot simply be given to a student to use with expectations that they will use the resource proficiently. High-powered teachers instruct and model the use of both a dictionary and thesaurus as well as online resources to ensure that students are using them to their fullest potential. They incorporate a dictionary and a thesaurus in fun engaging vocabulary activities such as a scavenger hunt, digital field trips, daily writing, group activities, independent work, and also encourage students to use vocabulary resources at home as well.

English Language Learners and Differentiation

High-powered teachers know that academic language may resemble the task of learning a third language for English language learners or struggling readers. Thus, special care must be taken to give them every possible advantage in learning academic language, particularly in content areas. For example, research suggests that Spanish-speaking students can be taught to recognize cognates (i.e., *words with similar meanings*) that look and sound alike in two languages, such as operation [*English*] and operacion [*Spanish*] and use cognate information to comprehend English texts.

Reading a wide variety of diverse literature is important for vocabulary development and reading comprehension for all students, regardless their reading level. High-powered teachers know that technology is a major influence on students today. Therefore, they encourage and incorporate technology to scaffold and meet the needs of all students by implementing fun and engaging technological learning opportunities (InTASC Standard 2, CCSSO). They help students increase reading volume, which enhances vocabulary by incorporating listening to digital text with a text-to-speech tool and audio books. Text-to-speech tools can increase struggling readers and ELL students' reading speed, reduce stress, enhance vocabulary, and also improve their comprehension.

Author's Tip

Every week my eighth-grade English teacher would have the class record a list of twenty to twenty-five words from the board. We had to look the words up and copy the words' definitions. She would also ask us to rewrite each word seven times as homework. We took a test every Friday where we were required to spell the word correctly and write the definition. This was definitely a mundane task, or what we now refer to as passive teaching. You may be wondering if this type of assignment worked. Honestly, I can't say that I remember it working.

As a teacher, I vowed to not fall into the pits that some of my teachers dug when I was a student. I wanted more for my students. I wanted to try new and exciting strategies, engaging activities, and meaningful opportunities that were purposeful to help my students establish a vast vocabulary. I researched innovative strategies, different instructional methods, a wide-variety of technology resources and much more to promote and increase students' vocabulary. I discovered a vast amount of research confirming that students need multiple and diverse exposures to a word before they fully understand and can apply the word. I learned that students need to learn words in context, not standalone lists that come and go each week as my teachers drilled us with. Obviously, students can learn words in context or explicitly, by reading, and then by reading some more. I prided myself on my well-stocked and well-organized classroom library. I knew that I would be able to offer my students books from all genres that ranged from classics to newly released novels.

I found that by allowing students to have some say in the vocabulary words was also very beneficial. I often suggested some of the words, and then allowed them to suggest additional words as they read the text. One of the largest mistakes that teachers can make is to determine all of the words and not give students an opportunity to suggest or add words. Selecting vocabulary should be a team effort between the teacher and the students. I found that selecting some of the words prior to reading the text and allowing students to determine more words within the text was most beneficial for sixth grade students. I found that students were reading closer, with a purpose, and with a critical eye when given the opportunity to suggest words. Their attention was more focused and as a result, students' interest in reading expanded, as did their reading comprehension. Allowing students to have a voice also resulted in an even stronger sense of community in our classroom (InTASC Standard 3, CCSSO).

Reflect back to EDUC 332 when you learned about tier one, tier two, and tier three vocabulary. You may turn back to the first section of this book to refresh yourself with these terms. **Tier one** consists of basic words that rarely require instructional focus. These are basic words that students come to school being familiar with. Examples of tier one words include door, table, house, and other common words. **Tier two** words are often referred to as high-frequency words and appear across a variety of domains. Tier two words are crucial when using mature academic language. More instructional focus should be given to tier two words. Examples of tier two words include analysis, coincidental, and reluctant as well as many other words. **Tier three** words are often limited to specific content areas and include words such as isotope, morphemic analysis, and isotope.

Robert Marzano believed that vocabulary instructional strategies are a very beneficial part of teaching in all grade-level vocabulary, but especially beneficial at the middle-school grade-level. His research shows that teachers should stress vocabulary in all content areas and include direct vocabulary instruction in the following six steps (Marzano).

1. The teacher explains a new word, going beyond reciting its definition allows teachers time to tap into students' prior knowledge, and also suggests incorporating imagery.
2. Require students to restate or explain the new word in their own words, which can be verbally or written.
3. Ask student to create a nonlinguistic representation of the word, which can be an illustration, picture, symbol, or representation.
4. Allow students time to engage in activities to deepen their knowledge of the new word. This can include comparing words, classifying terms, writing their own analogies and metaphors.
5. Encourage students to discuss the new words in think-pair-share or elbow talk activities.
6. Students should then be allowed to collaborate and participate in games or activities to review new vocabulary. Games may include, but are not limited to: tossed terms, Jeopardy, and Jenga.

Marzano's six steps were very beneficial to vocabulary learning inside my classroom. It was fun, engaging, students were more vocal, receptive, and also retained understanding, while building a vast and meaningful vocabulary. Don't let time be an enemy to you or your students. You may be thinking there just isn't sufficient time for all of the pre-reading word analysis, direct instruction of vocabulary, or for playing games. You may be more concerned about your content. Keep in mind that a greater understanding of the content can be achieved when students understand what they are reading through knowing the difficult vocabulary included in the content. Remember, vocabulary is the best single predictor of intellectual ability and the best predictor of students' academic success. One final tip; take the time to take your students on a digital vocabulary field trip or engage them in a digital scavenger hunt. Both of these activities can increase students' desire, expand their vocabulary, give insight to new unfamiliar places, or content, and can also provide a fun beneficial learning experience.

What Can Parents Do to Help?

To succeed in school and beyond, children of all ages need to build a robust vocabulary. Children learn a lot from the adults in their lives, including their parents. High-powered teachers know that there are numerous ways parents can help their child learn new words. They ensure that parents are aware and understand what concepts their child is learning in school so they can in turn support them at home. High-powered teachers use the vast amount of technology available today to help keep their parents in the loop, connected, and stay well-informed informed about what their child is learning (InTASC Standard 10, CCSSO).

High-powered teachers use the subtle approach when asking parents to help their children with learning new vocabulary words. A good rule of thumb is to select five unfamiliar words per week to ask parents and family members to incorporate in everyday conversations. They know that the key to a vast vocabulary is exposure to words often in a variety of different ways. They implement those same five words in their daily instruction and classroom conversations as well. Multiple exposure to words can increase students' awareness of the words, how to incorporate the words in daily conversations, and also how to use the newfound words in writing assignments.

Parents can also help their child build their vocabulary by taking them to new places, which exposes them to new and different ideas, thus discovering new vocabulary. Encourage them to read the menu at specialty restaurants, focus attention on dialog in diverse movies, visit museums, and read daily to help expand an ordinary vocabulary to an extraordinary vocabulary. When parents expose their children to a wide-variety of cultural experiences, encourage them to be well read, read with their children, and actually take time to talk to their children and have vocabulary rich conversations, the result is a richer vocabulary and also the knowledge of how to use rich vocabulary in everyday life.

Language Link

Many teachers struggle with incorporating grammar in their daily lessons. They often resort to the multiple choice method of choosing the sentence that isn't punctuated correctly, or spouting a grammatical rule that students are expected to remember and demonstrate in their daily writing. High-powered teachers know that for students to truly understand grammar, the rules of grammar, and how the rules apply to writing, their instruction should be creative and repetitious. Janet Angelillo compares isolating grammar instruction on Friday only as being as successful as dieting on Friday only.

High-powered teachers teach grammar repetitiously and also in daily minilessons. They know for students to use grammar and punctuation correctly, they must teach grammar in a variety of methods on a daily basis. Mini-lessons allow teachers to model for their students and also gives students time to discuss the concept at hand. Mini-lessons also provide students time to apply their newfound or resurrected knowledge in multiple settings.

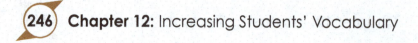

Implementing a **daily correct-all** in a daily five-minute bell ringer, exit slip, or as a five-minute daily oral language review is a great way to revisit and revive previously taught concepts, and also an engaging way to introduce new concepts. Daily consistency is the key to success with implementing a correct-all. Daily correct-all's can be implemented in a variety of methods, but high-powered teachers prefer hand's on mini-activities such as:

+ Taking a sentence from literature that students have or will be expected to read and ask students to discuss the sentence structure, the punctuation, and also interesting words within the sentence.
+ Using the same sentence, teachers may ask students to imitate the sentence by writing one similar to the sentence displayed.
+ Take a relatively difficult sentence and intentionally leave the punctuation out and ask students to punctuate the sentence.
+ Take an anonymous sample sentence from students' writing that contains mistakes and mimic the sentence making the same mistake(s) ask students to identify the mistakes and correct them.
+ Provide students with random words, which can be vocabulary words, and ask them to write a particular type of sentence incorporating the words, and also punctuating it correctly.
+ Finally, ask students to explain during open discussion why they punctuated the sentence as they did.

High-powered teachers strive to create daily fun and engaging mini-grammar lessons to introduce new concepts and also to revisit previously taught concepts. They incorporate activities such as Cloze to help students gain a better understanding as well as use of words, and also to increase their knowledge of grammar, grammar rules, and use of punctuation. For example, the following activity could be given in a five-minute correct-all minilesson to reinforce tense.

Tense Cloze Activity

Walking into science class, I _____ the boy of my dreams sitting in the first desk of the last row. His black hair, swept softly to the left, _____ down on his shoulders. He _____ a bag of chips. Sour cream, my favorite. Could it be more perfect, I _____ to myself. And then he _____ at me. He _____ to speak to me. His eyes, twinkled brown and _____ wide. "What are you looking at?" The sound of my dream deflating _____ in my ear.

see	*saw*
cascades	*cascaded*
eats	*ate*
thinks	*thought*
look	*looked*
is going	*was going*
open	*opening*
hisses	*hissed*

High-powered teachers incorporate both the correct-all and the Cloze activity into their daily instruction. They modify them to match a variety of concepts or content. For example, the Cloze activity can be designed to enhance students' use of transition words, or use of pronouns, or even as a vocabulary activity. Nevertheless, a daily five-minute minilesson or mini-activity is a great way to enhance understanding, practice application, and also a great formative assessment (InTASC Standards 6 & 7, CCSSO).

Virtual Vocabulary Strategies

High-powered teachers know that vocabulary is a foundational component of an effective comprehensive literacy framework. They know that vocabulary influences student's fluency, comprehension, and their overall academic achievement. In addition, vocabulary affects students speaking, listening, reading, and writing skills. With this in mind, effective, strategic, and carefully planned vocabulary instruction is vital for students overall academic success. Vocabulary instruction can be as simple as the **Word of the Day**, or as elaborate as **Digital Field Trips** (see page 241).

Successful vocabulary instruction includes both **direct and indirect word-learning strategies**. With the demand of virtual learning being more prominent than ever before, high-powered teachers provide students with the tools they need to ensure that students are provided with engaging and rigorous instruction, hands-on activities, and the opportunity to incorporate rich-vocabulary in both written and spoken format. In the twenty-first-century classroom, digital tools must coexist alongside more traditional tools. Online tools, compared to traditional methods, provide a more in-depth and diverse array of information about words and word meanings. In addition, digital tools also enable teachers to customize word lists to allow students to visually see the words, hear pronunciations, read words in diverse authentic examples, visually see pictures or illustrations of the word(s), all while reinforcing word learning through playing interactive games. High-powered teachers know that **multiple exposures** to words is key for students to not only recognize, read, and pronounce the words, but also to correctly use the words.

High-powered teachers are successful and strategic planners who integrate vocabulary instruction with strategies such as read alouds, which allow students to hear the word in context. Book clubs are also an effective strategy to allow students to experience words through text, conversation, and rich discussion. This is also a key opportunity for students to collaborate with peers to create their own virtual word walls using various types of software such as a power point. High-powered teachers may also ask students to create a **graffiti word wall**, which allows students to be creative, while having fun, and also enhancing their vocabulary.

Moreover, high-powered teachers introduce students to words, intentionally teach individual words, frontload the words with assigned independent reading, and allow students to experience the words through collaborative and engaging conversations, hear the words in **read alouds**, and have fun learning the words by providing them with the digital tools they need to be successful. The Collocation Dictionary is an online dictionary that can help students effectively study, write, and also speak English. The **freecollocation.com** website can be implemented in both the **in-person** class and also the **virtual** classroom. The Collocation Dictionary website can also be a successful website for English Language Learners. High-powered teachers have also found that, **vocabulary.com** and also **wordsift.org** websites have both been productive and engaging websites that students have enjoyed and that have both been successful in enhancing student's vocabulary.

Now It's Your Turn

For this assignment you will be required to create a vocabulary mini-lesson (activity) using words from the current novel that we are reading in class. Once you have determined the activity and the vocabulary words, you will be required to write a reflection about the vocabulary activity you selected, explaining why you selected the activity, a description of the vocabulary activity, how and when it will be implemented, include how you will scaffold the activity, and also include how you anticipate this activity will increase students' reading comprehension. Include the words that you selected from the novel and a brief explanation of why you chose them. Keep in mind that this type of activity can be included in the lesson plan that you will be required to write and teach this semester. Precise details and a drop box for this assignment can be found on iLearn.

Applications

To help guide you through Chapter Twelve and upcoming chapters, become familiar with the following key terms for a deeper understanding of Chapter Twelve:

+ Word-knowledge
+ Explicit instruction
+ Rigor
+ Mini-lesson
+ Correct-all
+ Cloze activity
+ Vocabulary self-awareness activity
+ Word study
+ Alike yet different
+ Found poems
+ Digital field trips
+ Shades of meaning
+ Metaphor
+ Tense close activity
+ Daily correct all
+ Robert Marzano
+ Tier one vocabulary
+ Tier two vocabulary
+ Tier three vocabulary

In-Seat Activity

Reflect on open and closed word sorts that you learned about last semester in EDUC 332. You may refer to the text if necessary. Then open the envelope of random words on your table. Working collaboratively with the people at your table, using the open word sort strategy, sort and categorize the words into three categories. Once you have sorted the words, decide which tier each group of words belong, and also be prepared to explain how you determined how to categorize the words, and why you selected which tier they belong.

Reflect and Answer the Following Questions

✦ *What is word-knowledge? Why is word-knowledge important to students' academic success?*

✦ *Is word knowledge and vocabulary the same? Why or why not?*

✦ *What is meant by intentional focus on vocabulary?*

✦ *How does word knowledge and vocabulary affect reading comprehension?*

✦ *What vocabulary strategies will you implement in your classroom to enhance students' vocabulary?*

Student Notes

Annotation is an effective learning strategy. Annotating is typically completed along the outer edge of the text within the book. However, sufficient space is not always available. Therefore, this page has been reserved for you to annotate *(take notes)* record potential questions, and also to refer back to when studying, completing assignments and to help you gain a better understanding of Chapter Twelve.

Student Reflection

High-powered teachers reflect. This page is reserved for you to reflect about information that you found insightful and what you have learned from Chapter Twelve.

Suggested Resources

Time For Kids, 2018, https://www.timeforkids.com. Accessed May 18, 2018.

Scholastic Publishes Literacy Resources and Children Books for Kids of All Ages, 2018, https://www.scholastic.com/home/. Accessed May 18, 2018.

National Geographic, 2018, https://www.nationalgeographic.com. Accessed May 18, 2018.

Newsela | Instructional Content Platform, 2018, https://newsela.com. Accessed May 18, 2018.

Dictionary.com | Meanings and Definitions of Words at Dictionary.com, 2018, www.dictionary.com. Accessed May 18, 2018.

Thinkmap Visual Thesaurus, 2018, www.visualthesaurus.com. Accessed May 18, 2018.

Vocabulary Games, English Vocabulary Word Games, 2018, www.vocabulary.co.il. Accessed May 18, 2018.

WordSift, 2018, www.wordsift.org. Accessed May 18, 2018.

Feinberg. J. Wordle--Create, 2014, www.wordle.net/contact. Accessed May 18, 2018.

Reading Rockets | Launching Young Readers, 2018, www.readingrockets.org. Accessed May 18, 2018.

Enchanted Learning, 2018, www.enchantedlearning.com. Accessed May 18, 2018.

Chapter References

American Institutes for Research. *Lessons and Recommendations from the Alabama Reading Initiative: Sustaining Focus on Secondary Reading.* Author, 2006.

Angelillo, J. *A Fresh Approach to Teaching Punctuation.* Holt, 2002.

Council of Chief State School Officers (CCSSO). *Interstate Teacher Assessment and Support Consortium (InTASC) Model Core Teaching Standards*, Apr. 2011, https://www.ccsso.org/sites/default/files/2017-11/InTASC_Model_Core_Teaching_Standards_2011.pdf. Accessed 7 July 2018.

Heller, R., and C. L. Greenleaf. *Literacy Instruction in the Content Areas. Getting to the Core of Middle and High School Improvement.* Alliance for Excellent Education, 2007.

International Reading Association. New Literacies and 21st-Century Technologies (Position Statement), 2009, https://www.literacyworldwide.org/docs/default-source/where-we-stand/new-literacies-21st-century-position-statement.pdf?sfvrsn=ec4ea18e_6. Accessed Apr. 24, 2018.

Lemov, D. *Teach Like a Champion: 49 Techniques That Put Students on the Path to College.* Jossey-Bass, 2010.

Marzano, R. *Teaching Basic and Advanced Vocabulary: A Framework for Direct Instruction.* Heinle, 2009.

National Center for Education Statistics. *The Condition of Education 2014 (NCES 2014-083), Reading Performance,* 2014, http://nces.ed.gov/programs/coe/indicator-cnb.asp. Accessed May 7, 2018.

National Center for Education Statistics. *The Nation's Report Card 2017 (NCES 2017),* 2017, https://nces.ed.gov/nationsreportcard/subject/publications/stt2017/pdf/2018039KY8.pdf. Accessed May 13, 2018.

Twain, M. *The Art of Authorship: Literary Reminiscences, Methods of Work, and Advice to Young Beginners, Personally Contributed by Leading Authors of the Day.* D. Appleton, 1890, pp. 85–8.

Chapter 13

Engaging Students in Comprehension Strategies and Activities

Teacher Quote

"Experience is the catalyst through which comprehension is achieved. For this reason, we must engage students in meaningful collaboration, interaction and active learning in the classroom. An active mind encourages deep and lasting comprehension."

~ Dr. Shannon Deaton
Dean, School of Education
University of the Cumberlands

Chapter Questions

✦ What components makeup reading comprehension?
✦ How do students comprehend?
✦ How should I assess students' reading comprehension?
✦ How should I model reading comprehension for middle-grade students?
✦ How can I engage my students to improve their comprehension?
✦ What strategies are proven to improve students' reading comprehension?

What Is Reading Comprehension?

In recent years, an astounding amount of research has been compiled about the importance of understanding the qualities of good reading instruction in the primary grades. Emphasis on quality reading instruction cannot be overstated. More than half a century of research has proven a very strong correlation between students who learn to read early with ease and academic success in middle and high school. However, according to the U.S. Department of Education, despite progress in recent years, one in four eighth-grade students in the public school system lack basic grade-level reading skills and do not understand grade-appropriate material (Goodman). According to NCES, the nation-wide average reading score for eighth-grade students was lower in 2017, than it was in 2013.

Academic reading (*reading for school purposes*) requires the use of comprehension reading strategies (e.g., Pressley et al.). The purpose of reading is to construct meaning, therefore reading comprehension is the key to long-term reading success. To an average literate person, reading may appear to be a simple task. Looking at letters, which make sounds, which create words that in turn make sentences. However, high-powered teachers know that even an understanding of text depends on numerous invisible thought processes, which work together at lightning speed while the reader is reading.

To fully understand the nature of reading comprehension, we must appreciate the complexity of it. Most educators are fortunate to have had a wide variety of rich literacy experiences including those facilitated by easy access to books, literate parents or caregivers, and also caring and devoted teachers. For those who had a positive learning experience as a result of a combination of the above, the vital thought processes of reading became automatic, creating an automaticity, which ironically tends to hinder the reader from seeing how complex reading comprehension can actually be for the struggling reader, especially in grades 6–12. Reading habits are automatic and unconscious processes that are used in constructing meaning from the text. Comprehension habits are the split-second thoughts that automatically and constantly occur to help proficient readers actively construct meaning. They also make up the majority of the thinking processes we use during reading, even though we seldom notice them (Taylor et al.).

One of the most important processes of reading comprehension is mentally organizing the textual information to match what the author had in mind, which is the ongoing process of seeing and inferring logical connections between chunks of text and using them to create a coherent main idea (Taylor et al.). Organizing is a vital part of comprehension, while other comprehension habits support this process by adding or subtracting key information to and from the evolving main idea.

There are many vital hidden processes that occur in the mind of a reader that constitute the comprehension of a proficient reader including making **connections to prior-knowledge, generating questions, visualizing** and **creating sensory mental images, making inferences, determining importance,** such as the **main idea** of a text, determining the **purpose,** and the **author's purpose,** as well as the **teachers' purpose** for assigning the text. **Synthesizing, monitoring,** and also **applying fix-up strategies** are each an important component of reading comprehension. Other reading comprehension habits include the **reader's purpose, flexibility, categorizing,** and **classifying** (InTASC Standards 1, 5, 8, CCSSO).

While reading the reader constantly tries to make sense of the information being read by connecting the information to two other sources of information, which include concepts found in preceding sentences and the reader's background knowledge. Prior knowledge is the second type of connection that is vital to reading comprehension. Prior knowledge helps the reader visualize text's description and fortify his or her understanding of implicit and explicit ideas in the text. Students' prior knowledge and use of strategies has a tremendous impact on how well they comprehend. Connections to previous concepts found within the text help the reader keep track of elements within the text such as people, objects, events, or ideas.

High-powered teachers teach and model how to ask questions using read-alouds and think-alouds. They know the importance of asking questions while reading occurs, because much of reading comprehension stems from the process of inquiring. They model how proficient readers post questions to themselves as they read. They teach their students that asking questions is the art of carrying on an inner conversation with themselves and with the author. High-powered middle-school teachers also reiterate and reinforce the importance of visualizing through modeling. They teach their students that visualizing and creating mental images is much like bringing life to written text. Proficient readers not only use visual, but also use auditory and other sensory connections to create mental images that help them to envision the plot, characters, and also the author's message (InTASC Standards 4, 5, 8, CCSSO).

However, comprehension involves more than just **reader factors** or **reading habits**. Comprehension also involves three important **text factors**, which include *genres, text structures*, and *text features*. Three broad categories of literature include expository/informational books, nonfiction, and poetry. **Text structures** include how the author organizes texts and also how the author emphasizes the important ideas within the text including sequence, comparison, and cause and effect. Authors use text features to achieve a desired and particular effect in their writing. Literary devices and conventions include symbolism and tone in nonfiction stories. In nonfiction books headings, subheadings, indexes, illustrations, graphs, maps, and captions are important features. While in poetry, the page layout and the use of **figurative language** are both contributing factors to students' reading comprehension.

Much of what is to be understood within the text, must be inferred. Making inferences can be difficult for students. Students may fear being wrong, lack self-confidence, or may have not been previously taught the importance of making inferences, or how to make them. High-powered teachers explain that authors rely on readers to contribute to a text's meaning by linking their background knowledge to information in the text. They also rely on the reader to acknowledge explicit messages or to read between the lines to discern implicit meaning, make predictions, and also to read with a critical eye, which leads to self-questioning and making important inferences about the text (InTASC Standards, 4, 5, 8, CCSSO).

High-powered teachers know that students comprehend and are able to synthesize better when they understand how authors organize and present their ideas (InTASC Standard 4, CCSSO). The knowledge of text factors also serves as a scaffold, which in turn makes comprehension easier. High-powered teachers incorporate **Book-walks** as a strategy to introduce text factors when beginning an unfamiliar genre, or to review a previously taught genre (InTASC Standard 8, CCSSO). Book-walks, require very little time, but prove to be very beneficial. Begin a book walk by introducing the text including the cover, title, blurb, genre, author, and illustrator. Allow students to independently examine the book for 5–10 minutes. Ask students to pay particular attention to pages of the book including text structures and text features. Encourage students to write down any questions, predictions, inspirational ideas, or what I like to refer to as, *"aha moments"* that may spring up during the book-walk. Book-walks ensure that students are aware of and also understand the text factors about the book prior to reading the book. Book-walks also eliminate unnecessary interruptions of reading time, thus ensuring that students' full attention is focused on the content of the book, rather than wondering about confusing the text factors, structure, and features of the book.

Begin With Assessment

High-powered teachers preassess for useful information through authentic assessments that enables them to better know their students, their learning style(s), reading level(s), as well as possible reading difficulties. Preassessments also enable and equip teachers to plan their instruction based on assessment data, which better informs them about what students know, or may not know, what content to teach, and also which strategies to include to enhance and promote students' reading comprehension. High-powered teachers preasses, monitor while students are comprehending, and also assess after they have read (InTASC Standard 6, CCSSO). This enables teachers to see students' strengths and weaknesses in using their comprehension habits to construct meaning.

Assessing reading comprehension is a complex process. To accurately measure the quality, speed, and durability of the numerous connections and processes that occur during reading and interaction with text is an impossible task. It is impossible to see or measure the multitude of immediate inferences that soar through readers' minds as they read. We cannot see what the reader is visualizing. High-powered teachers know that each student brings a diverse and unique set of skills and background knowledge to each text. They also know that ongoing student observations, interactions, and meaningful conversations allow them to sharpen their observation abilities as well as their level of creativity and use of instruments to help them to better know their students as readers.

High-powered teachers monitor students' progress before reading, during reading, and also after reading. Monitoring students allows them to determine students' strengths as well as their weaknesses based on how they construct meaning from the text (InTASC Standard 1, CCSSO). Due to the large number of students, explicit focus on content, and the time constraints of 50–60 minutes classes, middle and secondary teachers are faced with a challenge when monitoring students reading comprehension. However, high-powered teachers modify their instructional activities to also serve as formative assessments.

High-powered teachers also instruct, model, and require students to self-monitor and self-assess their developing reading comprehension, as well as their reading habits. They incorporate reading logs and ongoing running records (you may refer to part one of this book to refresh your knowledge and understanding of both). Students are also required to enter in a journal after reading as a method of self-assessment through reflection. High-powered teachers encourage students to not only monitor their thinking, but also track their thinking to determine their progress. They encourage students to read, reflect, and analyze their own growth, and also encourage them to self-reward themselves for positive growth and obtaining minigoals.

High-powered teachers also provide ongoing applicable and explicit feedback, while also requiring students to reread, rewrite, and rethink to promote a level of deeper thinking, analyzation, and also producing. According to R. J. Marzano et al., teachers must provide ongoing clear feedback to students with regard to their progress. Students want to know their academic strengths and weaknesses. They want to know their scores, how they arrived at the given score, and typically want to know how to increase their score(s).

Proficient readers monitor themselves as they read. They monitor themselves and expect to make necessary adjustments in their strategies. High-powered teachers also require their students to self-monitor and make necessary adjustments because they want to ensure that their students are able to achieve a satisfactory understanding of the text (InTASC Standard 6, CCSSO). Through requiring students to self-assess, self-reflect, self-reward, and also self-correct, students are taking ownership of their reading, reading habits, and ultimately their learning. This ownership combined with a variety of practice activities, coupled with a diverse range of increasingly difficult texts, causes the skills and the strategies to become more of an automatic reaction. In other words, students are reading with a purpose and not just hoping for an understanding of the text at the end of the assigned reading, but rather striving to achieve understanding, while also automatically applying strategies throughout the process of reading the assigned text with the intent to comprehend the text. Students can self-reflect with the comprehension checklist provided in **Table 13.1**.

Table 13.1: Self-Reflection Comprehension Checklist

I Monitored Myself:	Check	While I Read, When I...
I made connections to prior knowledge.		When I...
I ask myself questions.		About...
I was able to visualize.		When I...
I made inferences.		About...
I determined the importance of.		When I...
I made conclusion(s).		About... based on...
I monitored my reading.		When I...
I was able to apply fix-up strategies while I read.		When I...

High-powered teachers know that assessments that allow more student choices, creativity, expression, and also validation of original thought tend to be more motivating and informative, as more explicit feedback can be given, thus enhancing engagement, ownership, and multiple opportunities to improve learning. Whereas a multiple-choice test provides little feedback, resulting in less learning opportunities. According to J. Zwiers, some of the best assessments are the ones that students do not consider to be an assessment.

High-powered teachers use every teaching activity as an opportunity to assess students' reading comprehension (InTASC Standard 6, CCSSO). They predetermine what aspects of comprehension they want to observe/assess and also decide what type of evidence that students can provide to demonstrate and show the quality of comprehension. Evidence can include, but not be limited to, information in a graphic organizer, illustrations, discussions, and written expression. High-powered teachers incorporate checklists that itemize and list what is being observed/assessed and how it is evidenced by the activity.

High-powered teachers familiarize their students with the checklists that they are using, or will use during observations or assessments. (**See Table 13.2 for an example of a middle-school comprehension checklist**.) This is beneficial for informing students about what they are expected to know, what they are expected to do, and also what they are expected to say or even think. Rubrics can also be incorporated as a method of explaining what is expected from students, and also to measure growth. Regardless whether they use a checklist or a rubric, high-powered teachers include a section on the instrument they are using for observations/assessments for notes. They know that making brief annotations during an observation can prove to be very beneficial to them when determining why a student might be having difficulty comprehending, as well as beneficial for planning or modifying instructional strategies that will help meet the needs of their students (InTASC Standards 2, 7, CCSSO).

Finally, high-powered teachers do not withhold their observations from their students, but rather share them with students. Sharing can be on an individual basis with explicit feedback, one-on-one conversations, and also as a whole with the entire class, if the observation was designed for a whole-class observation. Observations can also be completed for small collaborative groups as well. High-powered teachers know that to truly understand a students' learning style, learning level, and learning difficulties that assessments and observations should be completed in all settings. They know that conferencing with students about their learning, learning objectives, and setting goals, improves student–teacher relationships, classroom rapport, and also allows students to take ownership of their learning (InTASC Standards 3, 6, 10, CCSSO).

Educators across the nation know that high-stakes standardized tests are an ever-present influence on what educators do in school. However, high-powered reflective teachers continually strive to motivate, inspire, and take their students to an enriched, meaningful, and higher level of learning than what can be measured through standardized tests (InTASC Standard 5, 6, CCSSO). Students make steady academic progress when they are engaged in authentic learning experiences throughout the academic year. Their ability to reason, infer, judge, interpret, organize, apply, communicate, problem-solve, collaborate, connect, and also comprehend, they are able to readily apply their skills both inside and outside the classroom.

Table 13.2: Middle-School Comprehension Checklist

Making Predictions					Evidence/Notes
Student uses evidence from background knowledge to make prediction.	1	2	3	4	
Student makes logical prediction that relates to the main idea of the text.	1	2	3	4	
Student revises prediction(s) based on new or developing information within the text.	1	2	3	4	

High-powered teachers model what they want their students to learn (InTASC Standard 5, CCSSO). According to L. S. Vygotsky, modeling is a key component of reading comprehension in upper grades. According to research, there is a lack of modeling reading comprehension in grades 6–12, primarily due to lack of teachers' knowledge about how to model comprehension. Many middle and secondary teachers assume that students arrive in their classroom already knowing how to read and comprehend. Teachers' may assume that students just need extra time to figure out the meaning of texts, when in reality many students are not fully prepared to apply the skills and strategies necessary to fully comprehend text.

Lack of knowledge or skills is due to a wide variety of possibilities. Learning gaps can come from students constantly being relocated due to changing schools because of his or her family moving, a student may have gradually drifted below the teachers' radar, and was mistakenly passed on without fully being prepared for the next grade-level, or a student may have been a problematic student who wasn't fully prepared for advancement, but was promoted because of his or her behavior. Moreover, other student(s) may not have encountered the learning experiences, a solid foundation of applying comprehension strategies in previous grades that are necessary for middle-school success.

High-powered teachers know that all students do not come with the same background knowledge or experiences. They know that not all of the students' previous teachers modeled comprehension strategies, or ensured that students were given multiple opportunities to participate in engaging and learning comprehension activities. In other words, all students have not had the opportunity to be an apprentice and are not academically ready to move forward. High-powered teachers get to know their students through daily formative assessments, being a kid-watcher, encouraging collaborative conversations, and carefully planning and providing students with multiple opportunities to engage with them, as well as with their peers (InTASC Standards, 4, 5, 6, 7, 8, CCSSO).

High-powered teachers know that all students need to observe another person modeling academic skills multiple times, even at the middle-grade and secondary level, especially with difficult texts (InTASC Standards 4, 5, CCSSO). High-powered teachers are highly qualified and willing to demonstrate and show students how good readers think. For example, they model their way of thinking with think-alouds when reading difficult or challenging text and while performing tasks such as completing graphic organizers that they may require students to complete independently at a later time. They also model how to draw mental images from text and how to create written responses. They ensure that students are given every available opportunity and necessary tools to become the apprentice that they need to be academically successful in their classroom and beyond (InTASC Standards, 5 & 8, CCSSO).

In the first half of this book, you learned about the academic benefits of read-alouds. High-powered teachers incorporate read-alouds, even at the middle and secondary levels. They know that reading aloud is a powerful form of modeling, while also building conversation, classroom rapport, encouraging collaboration, and also inspiring students to want to read for meaning (InTASC Standards, 4, 5, & 8, CCSSO). Reading aloud is also an effective method of modeling fluency and language. Research shows that many struggling readers did not have this type of positive text-to-language modeling when they were young. It is sad to think of the thousands of pages of exciting stories, rich characters, rich vocabulary, pronunciation, thinking, and discussions of plots, making inferences, predictions, analyzing characters, and much more they did not experience. High-powered middle-school and secondary teachers incorporate think-alouds while reading aloud, as they know this is an effective and beneficial method of modeling how proficient readers think while they are reading.

High-powered teachers know that verbalizing their thoughts while reading can enable students to see the many complex habits that enhance comprehension. Think-alouds also provide a perfect opportunity to model what students should do when they are stuck, confused, or are trying to figure out words or meanings. High-powered teachers use this opportunity to model how to ask questions, make predictions, inferences, use context clues, and also how to reread for a deeper meaning. The possibilities of modeling and learning are unlimited. Each think-aloud and read-aloud can be a unique opportunity to take students' reading comprehension and their desire to read and succeed to the next level (InTASC Standards, 4, 5, 8, CCSSO).

High-powered teachers know that all assessments cannot realistically be fun and engaging. However, they also know that the fun and engaging activities, observations, and multiple formative assessments prepare their students for summative, as well as high-stakes and standardized assessments (InTASC Standard 6, CCSSO). High-powered teachers do not assign reading, ask students to answer the questions at the end of the chapter or unit, assign a grade, and then move forward. Instead, they read with their students, model for their students, engage in purposeful collaborative activities, discuss, formatively asses, then assign independent work, assess, reflect, provide explicit feedback, reteach if necessary, and based on their findings from the summative assessment, they decide whether to move forward or not (InTASC Standards, 3, 5, & 6, CCSSO).

Engaging Students

High-powered teachers plan and design their lessons with explicit instructions, collaborative opportunities, and also with engaging activities that maximize learning and building good academic habits for their students (InTASC Standards, 4, 7, 8, CCSSO). High-powered teachers incorporate a **literacy binder** for quick references while they plan for instruction. Literacy binders serve as a reminder of what activities to incorporate and when to incorporate them. **Table 13.3**, is an example of a literacy binder.

Table 13.3: Literacy Binder

Prereading	During Reading	Postreading
Anticipation guides	Read-aloud/think-aloud	Journaling
K-W-L plus	Jigsaw	Socratic seminar
Think-aloud	Graphic organizers Semantic webbing	Question the author
Shared reading	Reciprocal teaching	Reader's theatre

Applying Reading Strategies?

Reading and writing are complex processes involving both reading strategies and skills. **Strategies** are deliberate, goal-oriented actions. High-powered teachers model reading and writing strategies to engage students, help them think about what they are reading, and help them process text. In other words, high-powered teachers teach students to use strategies to organize, direct, and also problem-solve as they read and write. Strategies include *making connections, asking questions*, *determining importance, inferring, predicting*, *visualizing, and summarizing*. **Skills** are automatic actions that occur without deliberate control or conscious awareness.

Making connections are a vital part of reading comprehension. Text-to-text connections include connections made to text that students have previously read, while text-to-life connections can include movies, conversations, or real-life experiences. High-powered teachers model how to make connections through the use of **read-alouds** and also **think-alouds** during prereading.

High-powered teachers know that there are certain aspects of reading that are observable, while there are also very important dimensions of reading that cannot be seen or heard. When students read silently, they employ a multitude of skills and strategies even the reader themselves may not be aware of. For example, productive readers ask themselves questions, they also monitor their understanding of what they are reading, and then take necessary measures to correct their comprehension when needed. High-powered teachers know for students to be productive readers they need to create visual images of what they are reading, make connections, make inferences, and ask themselves questions.

High-powered teachers model and encourage students to ask themselves what they already know about the topic or concept, to determine if anything similar has ever happened to them, and also to think about how they would feel, if it did happen to them. When high-powered teachers incorporate think-alouds, they model how students should interact with the text and the character(s). They encourage students to think about how or why they relate to a character, and finally encourage students to think about how the story might remind them of something else that has happened in their life. Making and establishing connections promote metacognition, and also help establish background knowledge. High-powered teachers inspire their students to connect themselves to the text, and to go past the obvious (InTASC Standards, 4, 5, 7, & 8 CCSSO).

As stated earlier, high-powered teachers make the reading process more observable to their students through thinking aloud as they read to students. They model how readers check themselves with a question when they encounter text that they don't understand. They encourage students to ask themselves what they don't understand about the text or what they do understand. They teach their students to determine which words they don't understand and also invite them to wonder about the text they are reading. High-powered teachers teach students how to question through explicit instructions and modeling questioning techniques with think-alouds, which is incorporated before independent reading. High-powered teachers incorporate the think-aloud strategy to teach students that productive reading is not passive reading; that the reader can consciously and also deliberately negotiate his or her understanding of the text (InTASC Standards 1, 5, & 8, CCSSO). Think-alouds can be integrated in all content or subject areas to provide students with a glimpse of expert thinking. Below are the step-by-step think-aloud instructions.

Step-by-Step Instructions for Read-Aloud(s) and Think-Aloud(s)

1. Present the strategy in real text, not in workbooks or texts created for skill teaching. In other words use the text or one similar to the text that students are or will be reading.
2. Describe the mental acts readers employ during productive reading as a way of equipping students with the knowledge necessary to take control of their own cognitive thinking and cognitive processing.
3. Provide examples and non-examples that demonstrate the goal of flexible thinking.
4. Combine modeling with opportunities to express their own thinking while they are reading.

Promoting Reading Comprehension

Anticipation guides help to instill interest in the text before reading actually begins. The anticipation guide was developed by M. H. Head and J. E. Readance and draws on the research evidence related to study guides. High-powered teachers know that **determining important information** in a text is vital to students' comprehension. They implement anticipation guides to encourage and also to guide students to make predictions and check for understanding. They also incorporate anticipation guides because they know they are very versatile, and can be crafted as preludes to almost all text. They also know that anticipation guides, when crafted correctly, can prompt students to become active seekers of vital or important information within the text, and also create and establish readers' ideas (InTASC Standards 4, 5, CCSSO). Below are the step-by-step instructions of one method of constructing and implementing anticipation guides. **Table 13.4** is an example of an Anticipation Guide.

Step-by-Step Instructions

1. Begin by reviewing the material to be covered in the upcoming lesson. Identify the most important content. Material or sources may include a textbook, article, lecture notes, a video, websites, virtual or digital field trip, or even a guest speaker.
2. Convert important information and concepts into shorter, more precise statements. Statements should be written in a way that they will pique students' curiosity or grab their attention. All statements do not have to be factually confirmed, as this leaves room for students to make confirmations based on the information they find. A good mix of both factual and nonfactual is recommended.
3. Present the statements to students by writing statements on the board and asking students to copy them, or provide them with copies of the questions. Statements can be reviewed orally as well.

4. Allow students response time and a response option. For example, teachers might require students to respond with either true or false, yes or no, or even agree or disagree.

5. Ask students to look at each statement using the required response option. Keep in mind that this is completed prior to providing students with the source of information (text).

6. After individual students initially respond to the statements, ask them to find a partner or go to their assigned partner and share their responses. This is a vital step to the process as it allows students to express alternative point of views. It also activates students' prior knowledge and increases their anticipation.

7. Gather students' responses and allow volunteers to share whether they agreed or disagreed with the statements. Don't give the answer away at this point. Keep in the mind the more eager students are to find out whether their anticipations are verifiable, the better.

8. Remind students as they read, listen, and also view, they should try to determine whether their initial response about each of the statements are supported by the material, or if they need to make changes. If their answers are supported, then students' after reading and learning response will be the same as their previous (initial) answer. Either way, students should write a brief explanation for their after-reading and learning responses based on relevant information from the content or sources they encounter during the lesson.

9. Present the information source such as the text, article, or website. As material is covered, stop periodically and ask students to discuss with their partners whether they now have relevant information to justify or reject their initial answers.

10. Finally, ask student to volunteer to share both their before answers and their after answers with explanations. This can be completed as partners or independently. Clarify any lingering misconceptions during sharing time.

This is an example of an anticipation guide incorporating chapters from the novel, The Miraculous Journey of Edward Tulane (DiCamillo).

Table 13.4: Format Example of Anticipation Guide

Directions: Before your read the text, read each statement carefully and write T for true and F for false in the space provided in the before blank. After completing the answers, read the assigned text. While you are reading and find information related to each statement, reflect and think about your answers. Decide whether your answer/anticipation should be changed by placing the correct letter in the after blank. Briefly explain your choices.

1. Lolli will do something to remove Edward from her parents' home. Before _____ After _____

   Explain: _____

   _____

2. Bryce will give Edward a new home. Before. _____ After _____

   Explain: _____

   _____

Anticipation guides can be used to entice students to read for content information, important information, make inferences, or predictions, and also to inspire them to read through anticipation of knowing if their previous answers are correct. High-powered teachers incorporate anticipation guides in the entire class, in collaborative groups, and also independently. Anticipation guides can be incorporated with expository text to help students better understand content. For example, high-powered science teachers may include an anticipation guide to help students gain a better understanding of the effects of drugs on their bodies or the dangers of second-hand smoke. Nevertheless, high-powered teachers have found that anticipation guides increase students' engagement with the text, increased reading comprehension, and also encourage students to read closer for important details and information (InTASC Standards, 5, 7, CCSSO).

What Is Close Reading?

Close reading is an instructional practice that has existed for decades (Richards). Even after decades of debate about the effectiveness of the strategy, it is still being used by high-powered teachers based on their belief that it is necessary for the reader to understand the text and what the author is saying before they can have a meaningful interaction with the text. Close reading is a thoughtful, critical analysis of text that focuses on significant details or patterns to help the reader develop a deep, more precise understanding of the text's form, craft, meanings, and is also a key requirement of Common Core State Standards. Many teachers have implemented close reading unknowingly. Close reading is just what it says, it directs the reader's attention to the text itself. Close reading includes using short passages and excerpts that warrant a second read, diving into the text with few prereading activities required, focusing on the text, rereading deliberately with a purpose, annotation, identifying confusing parts of the text, collaboration and discussion, and finally responding to text-dependent questions.

High-powered teachers encourage close reading to enhance students' reading comprehension of complex texts. They also incorporate close reading with texts that require close, careful, critical reading, and are complex enough to warrant a second or even a third reading as well as a thorough investigation of the text. All texts do not demand this level of attention. However, difficult and complex texts warrant close reading. When selecting texts high-powered teachers consider the four components of text-complexity: qualitative measures, quantitative measure, the reader, and the task. Each of these is equally important when considering complexity of the text. High-powered teachers consider the following questions before implementing close reading:

+ Does this text offer ideas or information that further students' understanding of the topic?
+ What background knowledge do my students need to have to be successful with this text?
+ Is the text at an appropriate readability level for my students? How can I scaffold for all learners to ensure students success with this text?
+ How much prior knowledge do my students have about this topic?
+ How interested are they in this text?
+ What difficulties or challenges might students face while reading this text?

High-powered teachers read the text and measure for complexity before requiring students to read. They base the complexity on academic and domain-specific vocabulary, syntax, audience appropriateness, text structure, and also text features. After determining the complexity of the text, they require students to read and reread for different purposes to help them gain insight of the content, which helps when locating text evidence and also to analyze the text's message (InTASC Standard 4, CCSSO). They encourage students to read the initial reading fluently, yet swiftly. They then ask students to reread at a much slower pace while annotating. Students should annotate important words, phrases, key factual information, and also important phrases. High-powered teachers also encourage their students to summarize, analyze, and self-explain to determine the significance of certain ideas and information. Step-by-step instructions are listed below.

Step-by-Step

1. Because close reading can be time-consuming teachers should select short, worthy passages when modeling and practicing close reading.

2. Set the purpose for reading and have students read text independently if possible. The first read can also be done as a read-aloud/think-aloud or paired with a partner for shared reading if necessary.

3. During the first read students are primarily focusing on key ideas and details, main idea, and story elements.

4. Following the first read, students can think-pair-share to assess what they have learned from the text. By listening to students responses, teachers can also determine the focus of the first read.

5. It is important to have repeated readings during close reading. Keep in mind that texts shouldn't reveal the meaning easily. During the second read, teachers can select a portion of the text that they feel is worthy of a close read. Teachers often provide students with text-dependent questions that require them to look for text evidence, examine vocabulary, text structures, or text features.

6. Students are allotted time and encouraged to annotate as they reread.

7. Close reading can even require a third reading, which goes even deeper, and requires students to synthesize and analyze information. Students are encouraged to annotate during the third read or record information in a graphic organizer while they are reading.

8. Students should discuss the text when close reading. This can be whole-class discussion, small-group discussion, or partner discussions. When students interact during close reading, close reading becomes an inquiry process where students, guided by their teacher, investigate the meaning of the text.

9. Finally, high-powered teachers ask text-dependent questions that require the students to revisit the text with each question. Questions can be prewritten or inspired by listening to students' discussion about the text. However, teachers should be prepared to ask a question if the conversation becomes idle or stagnant.

The goal of close reading is for students to read complex texts independently. However, high-powered teachers know that all students will not achieve this immediately. High-powered teachers scaffold instruction and model to support students and gradually release responsibility to the student. High-powered teachers scaffold by incorporating shared reading, interactive read-alouds, prompting and questioning, and also through incorporating think sheets. Regardless the strategy, or the reading level of the student, high-powered teachers offer just the right amount of support to ensure students are successful (InTASC Standards, 1 & 2, CCSSO).

Semantic Webbing

There are many activities that can help students better understand the text they read including semantic webs. Semantic webs and organizers have proven to be a very successful resource in middle-school classrooms. They have long been used effectively and beneficially for hierarchically organizing information. Semantic webs are basically outlines presented in a visual form. They have been referred to as brain mapping, word webbing, and mind mapping. High-powered teachers know that mapping is an effective technique for teaching reading skills and textual patterns of organization, as well as assisting students in organizing their thoughts, and also organizing information.

Many semantic organizers have a central concept, which is also surrounded by key ideas, and key supporting concepts that increase in level of detail as the reader moves away from the central concept or topic. High-powered teachers implement semantic organizers to enhance students' reading comprehension by using the **main idea,** the next spaces shape the headings, and also key supporting concepts, the next spaces would include the subheadings, and finally the last spaces are used for key details.

One of the most useful strategies for reading comprehension is to identify the purpose in reading. High-powered teachers guide students to identify the purpose in reading to get information, to follow instructions to perform a given task, for pleasure, amusement and also enjoyment, and for being curious about a topic. In other words, clear identification of the purpose in reading text is a must for efficient reading. By doing so, the readers know what they are looking for, and are not distracted or overwhelmed by other information within the text. High-powered reading and language arts teachers ensure students know the purpose when they are reading. They incorporate semantic maps by implementing the following steps (InTASC Standards 4, 7, CCSSO):

1. Select a text that lends itself well to semantic webbing. It can include texts that compares, persuades, analyzes, describes, classifies, and interpretive text that all lend themselves well to semantic organizers.

2. For prereading, write a topic or a preview question that relates to the text's key ideas. List some key vocabulary terms under this. Draw a simple semantic organizer on the board visible for all students. Ask students to think about and suggest which terms could be grouped together and which terms might go in the organizers boxes. Discuss with the class as a whole, and fill in the appropriate shape as students give answers. The object is for students to complete the semantic web independently after modeling through incorporating a read-aloud, and emphasizing key words, and details of several terms.

3. After adding the main idea, main headings or categories, students will have a general idea about the text and can summarize what they think the text will cover. (This is also a great opportunity to scaffold to meet the needs of all learners. Students can work collaboratively in think-pair-share conversations to determine what the text will be about and also to summarize what they do know.)

4. During reading, ask students to read silently as they fill out their own semantic organizer. You may differentiate for struggling readers by reading the first part of the text, and requiring students to read the remaining text. You may also differentiate when necessary while reading aloud with the student and placing extra emphasis on key words. Students who may struggle with written expression can also use symbols or illustrations to represent words or key ideas.

5. Ask students to retell the important points of the text to their partners. The listener should remind the student, who is telling, or of any important information that may not have been included. When students put the text into their own words, they are taking ownership of the information, which solidifies it in their minds, which in turn helps the brain build lasting visual-based connections.

6. The semantic organizer also provides a framework for students' text-based writing. The boxes also help provide students with forming paragraphs within the body of the text.

In order to enhance the comprehensibility of reading passages, purposes techniques such as advance organizers, story mapping, story grammars, and semantic mapping as prereading strategies, high-powered teachers allow students to preview new structures and vocabulary to help students make connections between the new and old concepts, which allow them to draw on their background knowledge to aid in comprehension. Semantic webbing has been proven to be a successful instructional technique for English as well as foreign language(s). **Table 13.5** is an example of First Mapping.

Table 13.5: Example of First Mapping

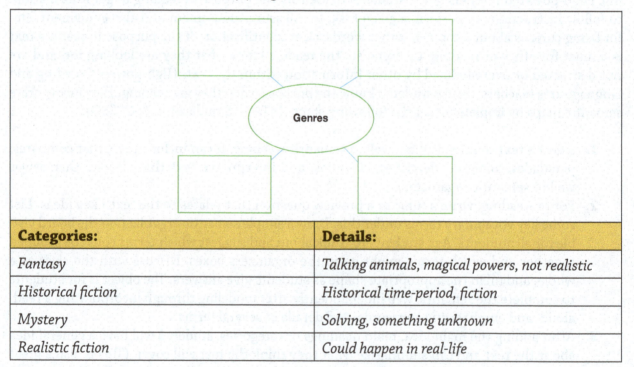

Categories:	Details:
Fantasy	*Talking animals, magical powers, not realistic*
Historical fiction	*Historical time-period, fiction*
Mystery	*Solving, something unknown*
Realistic fiction	*Could happen in real-life*

Reciprocal Teaching

During reading, high-powered teachers implement reciprocal teaching to help move instruction from delivery of their instruction to students' discovery (InTASC Standard 8, CCSSO). Reciprocal teaching is an approach that enables students to directly assist with discovering material and the subsequent construction of meaning, and is ideally suited for classroom teachers' who are intent on placing learning in the hands of their students. Studies suggest that reciprocal teaching increases comprehension, achievement, and also standardized test scores.

High-powered teachers use reciprocal teaching to differentiate and scaffold instruction for struggling readers, and for the multicultural classroom to allow diverse viewpoints, experiences, and information to be considered as part of the discovery of the text. Reciprocal teaching can be used to enhance and improve reading comprehension. With the implementation of reciprocal teaching, students have multiple opportunities to practice cognitive strategies such as predictions, questioning, summarizing, and also clarifying.

High-powered teachers model the process for students individualizing a particular comprehension strategy to ensure that students understand each strategy (InTASC Standard 5, CCSSO). After practicing the strategies and reviewing the process, high-powered teachers reverse the roles of learning from the teachers' instruction to allow students to self-discover for themselves. They provide their students with the tools that they need to help ensure that they are engaged and learning. Tools may include *props, sticky notes, technology, charts*, etc. Teachers may also provide their students with *premade cards* that help guide students through the process. For example, cards may have questions such as *"What is the problem about? What predictions can you make? What information is given? What isn't clear to you? What questions do you have?"* The suggested steps below can be implemented in one lesson or spread out over a series of lessons.

Step-by-Step Instructions

1. Introduce summarizing by sharing several short readings. Readings can be magazine articles, newspaper articles, and very brief stories. Model writing summary statements as a class. As students become more familiar with summarizing, have them work in small collaborative groups of four to read a selected piece of text and work on summarizing specific sections of the text.

2. For predictions ask students to hypothesize about the next event or describe what they think the reading is going to be about. For summarization, ask students to identify and also paraphrase the main ideas in the assigned reading. For clarification, ask students if there is anything that they were confused about that they feel was cleared up through the reading. For questioning, ask students to develop their own questions about the text. Be sure to encourage them to use diverse methods of questioning such as why, when, how, and who. You may also ask students to compare and contrast as they become more proficient with the strategy.

3. Follow this process for each remaining comprehension process that comprise reciprocal teaching such as predicting, questioning, and clarifying. It will vary, but this will typically take a few days or a week for students to understand each of the tasks and the types of conversations they should have with their group using these processes.

4. Once students are confident and understand each of the four components of reciprocal teaching, identify a reading passage or passages. Identify specific places in the text where you want students to focus. Collaborative groups of four should then stop and have their reciprocal teaching conversation. Students should take turns supplying their group with information. This can be divided into discussion points.

5. Once teachers have modeled several times and students have practiced several times, distribute the student copies of the assigned text. Keep in mind that this can be diverse reading material about the same topic, which allows the teacher to scaffold the reading as necessary for their students.

6. Invite students to take the lead in identifying, and locating places to stop and have their reciprocal conversations. Follow, by asking them to share their thinking about how they arrived at their decisions.

Question the Author

After students complete reading, high-powered teachers incorporate **Question the Author** (QTA), strategy. They know that implementing **QTA** encourages readers to interact with the text and the information within the text, which helps build meaning from the text by analyzing the author's purpose in writing. The questions that students create are then used for classroom or collaborative group discussions or prompts. The QTA strategy also allows teachers to scaffold for diverse learners by providing diverse reading levels of text and also multicultural text. The questions as well as the discussion help students to develop their own ideas and not simply restate information that they pull from the text.

High-powered teachers incorporate QTA to encourage students to take responsibility for their thinking and also for constructing meaning (InTASC Standards 5, 8, CCSSO). I. L. Beck and M. G. McKeown state that over time, students realize that the author is challenging them to build their own ideas and concepts as they interact with the ideas and concepts of the author. The goals of the QTA typically remain the same: to construct meaning of the text, to help the students to dig deep and go beyond what is stated in print, to think figuratively, and to use prior-knowledge to make connections. High-powered teachers act as a facilitator and allow students to work the text independently or collaboratively. The following steps will guide you when implementing the QTA strategy:

1. Locate reading material that will generate a good conversation. I find poetry to be very engaging and always strikes up a good conversation.
2. Instruct and encourage students to ask questions of the author. Model questioning for students and also provide them with questioning prompt cards, or posters until they become comfortable with the strategy.
3. Allow students to work collaboratively, as a team or as a class to discuss their opinions or their difference of opinions.
4. **QTA Example:** I have found it fun, engaging, and a very good learning experience to read a particular book, article, or poem written by a local author. Poetry or short stories often work best and are more accessible. We discuss as a class or in collaborative groups or teams and formulate questions that students have. I then require students to read a second piece of the authors' work, and formulate their own questions. I invite the author to our classroom, so that students can actually pose their questions to the author, and compare the authors' answers to their established assumptions about the text. This can also be completed online if the author cannot attend, which integrates the use of technology with the lesson.

Differentiation, Cultural Diversity, and Comprehension

Reading comprehension can be challenging for a struggling reader. Comprehension can also be challenging for linguistically or culturally diverse students who reside in a home where English language is not a primary language. Culturally diverse students arrive in classrooms across the United States with varying degrees of literacy in their native language at a steadily growing rate. In many incidents, little thought or preparation is given to their level of proficiency or readiness for classes in English language arts, or other content classes. Unfortunately, many educators are not prepared or knowledgeable of thinking patterns that differ from their own, primarily due to lack of experience, or lack of thinking outside their own cultural linguistic boxes. However, there are multiple strategies that have proven to be helpful.

High-powered teachers strive to know their students and the factors that shape their learning. There are many factors that shape patterns, habits, and attitudes of culturally diverse students. Some factors may include war, loss of family members, cultural shock, poverty, racism, linguistic prejudice, differing religious views, family literacy, frequent movements, and more. Other factors that many students from all cultures experience include drugs, divorce, lack of family interaction, isolation, violence, physical and sexual abuse, and more. The number of factors that affect the way children learn is unlimited. Moreover, these factors may be compounded by obvious and radical diverse educational experiences that students have had in previous schools, both inside the United States and in their home countries.

High-powered teachers strive to see classroom learning through the eyes of all of their students and provide texts, instructions, and attitudes that correlate to their diverse background and interests and the necessary explicit instructions and support to develop grade-level comprehension abilities in all learners. High-powered teachers provide this support with additional modeling, multiple opportunities to practice, immediate applicable feedback, and also scaffolding instruction and assignments (InTASC Standards 1 & 2, CCSSO). They also collaborate with colleagues who have more experience and success with working with English Language Learners (ELL) students. They invite them to observe in their classroom and discuss possible strategies that can be implemented to increase students' as well as teachers' understanding. High-powered teachers also communicate directly with ELL students' families to ensure that they are pronouncing students' names correctly, gain a better understanding of their home-life, as well as gain other important information that will help them be better prepared to teach ELL students (InTASC Standard 10, CCSSO). Finally, high-powered teachers reassure students that their first language is important and also acceptable.

High-powered teachers scaffold instruction and assignment to ensure students are successful, and also that they are given equal opportunities as their peers. They emphasize key words for ELL students, incorporate visuals, objects, maps, illustrations, and videos to build background knowledge, and also increase comprehension. They also incorporate explicit instruction, direct definitions, simplifications, and include analogies that help students comprehend better. High-powered teachers also incorporate auditory reinforcement by allowing ELL students to listen to text in their native language, and then listen a second time in English. They summarize for students to gain and maintain focus on key concepts and important information. Finally, high-powered teachers make bilingual dictionaries readily available for ELL students, and also encourage them to use them as needed. Overall, high-powered teachers do not isolate ELL students with specific strategies but plan, scaffold, and ensure that they have the tools and the support necessary to be successful using strategies that other students are using, participate in activities that other students are participating in, and completing assignments and projects that other students are required to complete. They know that all learners do not develop the same or learn the same. By getting to know their students academically, their strengths, and their areas of struggle, high-powered teachers plan accordingly with each student in mind to ensure they are learning and prepared to move forward academically, socially, and in real-life (InTASC Standards, 1, 2, 3, 4, 5, 6, 7, 8, CCSSO).

Language Link

To help students discover grammar, high-powered teachers emphasize and demonstrate to their students that they can discover grammar wherever they find language. They incorporate grammar through daily oral language, worksheets, and also textbooks. However, they do not solely rely on textbooks and worksheets to dominate or dictate how they teach grammar. Worksheets and textbooks are meant to reinforce students' understanding of the concept at hand, not establish understanding. High-powered teachers teach grammar from a wide-variety of authentic texts to help their students better understand the use of grammar in different settings or genres (InTASC Standards 1, 6, CCSSO).

High-powered teachers incorporate newspapers, graphic novels, comic strips, short stories, novels, speeches, and many other types of text to demonstrate or teach diverse grammar lessons. Incorporating a wide variety of texts also allows teachers to differentiate and scaffold, while also providing students with diverse reading material, while enhancing students' grammar and writing skills. For example, high-powered teachers may ask students to compare and contrast in their grammar instruction by incorporating two texts about the same subject. The teacher then asks the students to compare the grammatical differences between the two texts. For example, students may read a short narrative about a specific person of interest, and also read an expository article about the same person. Students can compare and contrast the use of grammar in both texts. Poetry also provides multiple opportunities for teachers to teach grammar. The possibilities are endless. High-powered teachers know that by incorporating grammar with authentic texts their students are increasing reading skills, analyzing skills, and also increasing their grammar skills (InTASC Standards 4, 5, CCSSO).

Virtual Literature Circles

Distance learning doesn't mean that students have to settle for less engaging and rigorous reading instruction. **Literature circles** is a preferred reading strategy both inside the classroom and online by many teachers. Literature circles provide teachers with an easy way to incorporate rich literature, diverse genres, **expand vocabulary**, promote peer collaboration, motivate students, and also promote **reading comprehension** through exploration of engaging literature with peers.

Teachers may choose how to group their circles. Many teachers find that circles are successful when they're based on student's reading levels. While other teachers choose to create more diverse circles with various levels of learners within each circle. High-powered teachers know the importance of **student choice**. They provide their students with at least four choices of books for each placement level within the literature circles. Each book is filled with diverse characters, themes, and cultures. Each circle will then vote to select their group's choice of books. Much like read alouds, literature circles are rooted in making predictions, asking questions, and making inferences. High-powered teachers use breakout rooms for their circles. Online literature circles look much like they do in the physical classroom. Literature circles are conducted during **asynchronous instruction**. Each student is given a role, and students hold each other accountable/responsible in terms of preparation.

Roles may consist of the following:

+ **Discussion Master:** The discussion master is responsible for guiding the literature circle through the discussion of the selected chapter(s). The discussion master is also responsible for keeping the members of their group on task and to ensure that all members are participating. They may also redirect the discussion if necessary.

+ **Passage Master:** The passage master is responsible for finding and documenting key passages found throughout the reading selection. The passage master also documents the passages that group members find memorable. This allows the passage master to focus on literary merits of the selection, "aha" moments, emotions, and personal revelations that members may have.

+ **Word Wizard:** The word wizard is responsible for finding and documenting unfamiliar vocabulary words, while also documenting unfamiliar words that other circles may find within the text. The word wizard is responsible for citing key words that the author uses to describe, enhance, or create curiosity within the reader.

+ **Summarizer:** After reading the assigned selection, the summarizer is required to take careful notes from the text that he/she will share with the circle during their discussion. The role of the summarizer is to briefly discuss their notes with the group and then document critical discussion points, conclusions, predictions that the group derives from the actual discussion itself. The summarizer also presents their summary during the grand conversation when the circles reconvene as a whole group.

+ **Connector:** The role of a connector in literature circles is to make connections between the elements in the reading selection to student's lives, the lives of others, or between characters in the book. They may also make valid connections between the character in the selected text and characters in other texts.

Literature circles have been a successful tool both inside the classroom and online by promoting natural conversation from within the circles, as well as engagement and collaboration, and most of all creating and ensuring authentic learning is taking place. High-powered teachers know that through literature circles, students are given the opportunity to internalize concepts such as empathy and courage while digging deeper into the lives of the characters, the plot, and the theme, and also promoting reading comprehension and inspiring their students to read.

Now It's Your Turn

You will be required to work in collaborative teams for this assignment. Teams will be randomly selected by the professor. Teams will consist of a team leader, a researcher, an interviewer, a technology person, and a planner. Teams will be provided with a list of four–five reading comprehension strategies or activities to research. After the initial team meeting, each team should have selected a team leader and come to a consensus about the strategy that their team will research. The team leader will then email the professor to identify themselves as the team leader with the team's preferred strategy (InTASC Standard 8, CCSSO).

The team will collaboratively decide on the role and job duty that each member will be responsible for. For example, one person may be the researcher who will be responsible for locating two scholarly articles about the strategy. While another team member may be responsible for interviewing two teachers who have implemented the chosen strategy. Another team member would then be required to find two lesson plans that integrate the chosen strategy. While another person can be the one who puts it all together into a power point, prezi, etc. (InTASC Standards, 7, 8, CCSSO). Each team member will email the technology person their information to construct the presentation. How your team organizes and divides the work will be a team decision and may vary from other teams. The team leader will be the contact person and will also submit the final presentation in drop box.

Teams will also be required to present their strategy to the class on the specified date. Each team member will also be required to write a reflection about their collaborative experience completing the project and also presenting the presentation. Each member will also self-assess their team with the provided rubric (InTASC Standard 6, CCSSO). Each member of the team will submit their completed reflections after their presentation.

This assignment is designed to enhance your collaborative skills, increase your knowledge about a reading strategy, enhance leadership skills, written reflection, self-assessment, and also speaking and listening skills. Each person in the class will also complete a TAG rubric after listening to their peers present to provide them with constructive feedback of what they thought, whether the team did well, and also suggested areas of growth (InTASC 1, 2, 3, 4, 5, 6, 7, 8, CCSSO). Specific details about this assignment are located on the content page in the Collaborative Group Project folder. Teams and strategies are also located in this folder.

Author's Tip

I cannot express how much having grand conversations enhances student engagement, as well as reading comprehension. Grand conversations also provide multiple opportunities for you to formatively assess your students. I enjoyed incorporating grand conversations in the classroom in every grade-level that I taught. I learned a lot about my students, as they also learned from each other. Grand conversations can be planned or they can be inspired through collaborative discussions about an assigned reading, student responses, debatable issues occurring within the school, or current events. Nevertheless, grand conversations are a great way to get students to think, analyze, respond, and present their own ideas. When students feel that they have a voice in the classroom, they feel a stronger sense of community, safer to take academic risks, while also creating and enhancing the rapport in the classroom.

I found that incorporating most reading comprehension strategies with grand conversations was a double-win for students' reading comprehension. These conversations created an interest among the students, a desire to dig a little deeper, read a little closer, to search for textual evidence to back up their claim, their statements, and their beliefs. Grand conversations are a great source of motivation, collaboration, and also content enrichment. I would suggest establishing rules for grand conversations early in the year. Rules can include, but not be limited to, only one person can speak at a time, mutual respect must be given, negativity is not allowed, and everyone must contribute something to the conversation. I also required sixth-grade students to complete a journal entry after grand conversations. I incorporated an online method of journaling through a district-approved website where students recorded their brief summary of the conversation, their top three takeaways, and what they would like to know more about. This can also be completed through the use of an exit slip. Grand conversations provide unlimited opportunities for educators as well as students.

Don't be afraid of conversations in your classroom, the benefits will surpass the fear of letting go and allowing students to discuss debatable topics, share points of view, and discuss rich literature. Benefits include but are not limited to enhanced comprehension, social skills, speaking and listening skills, formative assessment opportunities, community, increased knowledge of diverse topics, writing skills, and many more. Above all, do more than encourage your students to read... inspire them to read!

> *"The more time students spend reading each day, the more it becomes a daily habit."*
>
> ~ *Donna Miller*

What Parents Can Do to Help?

A Southwest Educational Laboratory synthesis of research on parent involvement over the past decade reported that students with parents who are involved in their education benefit in a number of ways:

- ✦ They earn higher grades and achieve higher test scores.
- ✦ They pass classes, are promoted, and earn credits at a higher rate than most of their peers.
- ✦ Their attendance is higher and more consistent.
- ✦ They possess better social skills, improved behavior, and also adapt easily with change in school.
- ✦ Their graduation rate is higher and the rate of postsecondary enrollment is higher.

This research also indicates that schools and teachers play an important role in determining the level of parental involvement. It is up to you, the teacher, to find methods of communication and collaboration, as well as involvement in their child's education, and in the school. The strongest and most consistent predictors of parent involvement at home and in the school are the existence of specific school programs and teacher practices that both encourage parental involvement at school and also guide parents in how to help their children with school work at home (Williams and Chavkin).

Parental involvement, or lack there of, is reflective in student's academic success, regardless their age. It is up to you the teacher, to locate and implement innovative ideas and resources that will assist and also encourage parents to want to know what their child is working on in school, and encourage as well as guide them with what they can do to help. Below are suggestions that you can implement to get to know your students' parents better, gain insight into their busy schedules, and also encourage parents to be involved in their child's education.

1. Create a video introducing yourself to parents. The video should be posted on your classroom webpage. You could actually invite the principal to join you in the video as well, as he or she is a very important part of children's education. This method provides a time for

parents to get to know you, and the principal, at their convenience, and also an opportunity for you to discuss your expectations for their child, as well as for them.

2. You can also email the parents a survey, or use survey monkey for their convenience. There is much to be discovered about parents through surveys such as their interests, schedules, expertise, and etc.

3. You may also create a how-to video for parents to watch about how to help their child. This can be reading together, discussing difficult literature together, encouraging them to offer positive feedback, explaining how to ask thought-provoking questions, as well as high-order questions. It can also be a video explaining how to encourage their child to be goal-oriented and create and maintain a daily calendar.

4. Also be the consistent teacher who communicates the class schedule, assignments, updated, important dates, and sends reminders to parents via your classroom website, classroom dojo, remind 101, or various other methods of technology. Remember, what you send home with students in the form of paper does not always arrive at home, or may often go unnoticed on the kitchen table, entry table, or even tossed in the garbage before it's opened.

Above all encourage parents to engage in collaborative conversations about the text that their child is currently reading. Provide them with questions that they can use to initiate the conversation. Don't expect the parents to do all the work, be their support as well. You will be amazed how many parents want to be more involved, but are unsure of how to help their child, due to their own insecurities of the content. I found that providing parents with a few weekly thought-provoking questions truly enhanced the quality of time that parents actually spent with their child.

I am an advocate of implementing classroom websites. The dissertation that I completed for my doctoral degree was titled, *Teachers' Perceptions of Classroom Websites and Their Effect on Parental Involvement*. As a researcher, I examined teachers' perceptions of interactive classroom websites and their effects on parental involvement. Data showed that teachers agreed for parents to check classroom websites on a regular basis. Data also showed a significant difference indicating that teachers with a website perceive that technology increases communication between parents and teachers more than teachers who did not have a website (Bowling).

Of course you will have some students whose parents simply will not help. Teachers' typically discover this early in the year. I found it beneficial to have mini-discussion groups for those students. I paired a couple of students who were effective communicators and well-read, and also who enjoyed peer-tutoring with the students who lacked parental help to discuss the questions that were meant for parents. What I discovered was that both the well-read students and the students who lacked parental involvement benefited. I implemented the same strategy for students whose parents may have been absent for the weekend due to work, medical emergencies, and etc., in an effort to prevent them from falling behind and also to ensure that they experienced the collaborative conversation.

High-powered teachers are effective teachers who go above and beyond the ordinary and strive to be extraordinary. They work tirelessly to get to know their students, even if they have 170 middle-school students, as well as their parents. High-powered teachers involve both the parents and the community to ensure that their students are receiving every possible benefit of a top-quality education.

Applications

To help guide you through Chapter Thirteen and upcoming chapters, become familiar with the following key terms for a deeper understanding of Chapter Thirteen:

- ✦ Reading comprehension
- ✦ Reader connections
- ✦ Visualizing
- ✦ Inferences
- ✦ Authors' purpose
- ✦ Main idea
- ✦ Synthesize
- ✦ Fix-up strategies
- ✦ Reader factors/reading habits
- ✦ Text factors
- ✦ Genre
- ✦ Text structures
- ✦ Figurative language
- ✦ Book walks
- ✦ Self-reflection comprehension checklist
- ✦ Comprehension checklist
- ✦ Literacy folder
- ✦ Anticipation guides
- ✦ Close reading
- ✦ Semantic webbing
- ✦ Question the author
- ✦ Cultural diversity
- ✦ Grand conversation

In-Seat Activity

Work in teams of four and search the Internet to learn more about one of the following strategies to better enhance your understanding and equip you with a wide variety of reading comprehension strategies. Be prepared to summarize your findings with the class.

- ✦ *Three-level guide*
- ✦ *QAR—question–answer relationships*
- ✦ *Directed reading-thinking activity*
- ✦ *Critical thinking map*
- ✦ *Framed outline*
- ✦ *Multipass*

Reflect and Answer the Following Questions

✦ *What components makeup reading comprehension?*
✦ *How do students comprehend?*
✦ *How should I assess students' reading comprehension?*
✦ *How should I model reading comprehension for middle-grade students?*
✦ *How can I engage my students to improve their comprehension?*
✦ *What strategies are proven to improve students' reading comprehension?*

Student Notes

Annotation is an effective learning strategy. Annotating is typically completed along the outer edge of the text within the book. However, sufficient space is not always available. Therefore, this page has been reserved for you to annotate *(take notes)*, record potential questions, and also to refer back to when studying, completing assignments, and to help you gain a better understanding of Chapter Thirteen.

Student Reflection

High-powered teachers reflect. This page is reserved for you to reflect about information that you found insightful and what you have learned from Chapter Thirteen.

Suggested Readings and Resources

https://static1.squarespace.com/static/59887cb1ebbd1aa4144128da/t/599497f6c534a5408 38f3e41/1502910460714/Flipgrid_language_arts.pdf

https://www.readworks.org/

http://wac.colostate.edu/books/grammar/alive.pdf

Chapter References

Beck, I. L., and M. G. McKeown. "Questioning the Author: Making Sense of Social Studies." *Educational Leadership*, vol. 60, no. 3, 2002, pp. 44–7.

Bowling, J. *Teachers' Perceptions of Interactive Classroom Websites and Their Effects on Parental Involvement*. University of the Cumberlands, 2013.

Council of Chief State School Officers (CCSSO). *Interstate Teacher Assessment and Support Consortium (InTASC) Model Core Teaching Standards*, Apr. 2011, https://www.ccsso.org/sites/ default/files/2017-11/InTASC_Model_Core_Teaching_Standards_2011.pdf. Accessed 7 July 2018.

DiCamillo, K. *The Miraculous Journey of Edward Tulane*. Candlewick Press, 2006.

Goodman, A. "Voices from the Middle: The Middle School High Five: Strategies Can Triumph." *Voices from the Middle*, vol. 13, no. 2, 2005, pp. 12–9. http://www.ncte.org/library/NCTEFiles/ Resources/Journals/VM/0132-dec05/VM0132Middle.pdf. Accessed 14 May 2018.

Head, M. H., and J. E. Readance. "Anticipation Guides: Meaning through Prediction." *Reading in the Content Areas*, edited by F. K. Dishner, et al. Kendall/Hunt, 1986, pp. 229–34.

Marzano, R. J., et al. *Classroom Instruction That Words: Research-Based Strategies for Increasing Student Achievement*. Association for Supervision and Curriculum Development, 2001.

Miller, D. *The Book Whisperer: Awakening the Inner Reader in Every Child*. Scholastic, 2011.

National Center for Education Statistics. *Digest of Education Statistics: 2016*. NCES 2017-094, Feb. 2018, https://nces.ed.gov/programs/digest/d16/. Accessed 15 May 2018.

Pressley, M., et al. *Cognitive Strategy Instruction*. Brookline, 1990.

Richards, I. A. *Practical Criticism*. Cambridge UP, 1929.

Taylor, B. M., et al. *Reading for Meaning: Fostering Comprehension in the Middle Grades*. Teachers College Press, International Reading Association, 2000.

Vygotsky, L. S. *Mind in Society: The Development of Higher Psychological Processes*. Translated and edited by M. Cole, et al. Harvard UP, 1978. (Original work published 1934).

Williams, D., and N. Chavkin. "Essential Elements of Strong Parent Involvement Programs." *Educational Leadership*, vol. 47, 1989, pp. 18–20.

Zwiers, J. *Building Reading Comprehension Habits in Grades 6–e12: A Toolkit of Classroom Activities*. International Reading Association Inc., 2010.

Chapter 14
Teaching Students to Write Effectively

Teacher Quote

"A sentence should be alive…Sentences need good energy to make the meaning jump off the page and into the reader's head. As a writer you must embed energy in the sentence—coil the spring, set the trap."

~ Peter Elbow

Chapter Questions

✦ *What is the writing process?*
✦ *How can I inspire my students to write?*
✦ *What writing strategies should I incorporate to enhance students' writing?*
✦ *What genres of writing should I teach?*
✦ *How does vocabulary enhance writing?*
✦ *How can I integrate writing mechanics and grammar in writing?*
✦ *How should I assess students' writing?*

According to National Assessment of Educational Progress, three-quarters of both 12th and 8th graders lack proficiency in writing. According to the data, it also revealed that 40% of those who took the ACT writing exam in the high school class of 2016 lacked the reading and writing skills necessary to successfully complete a college-level English composition class (NCES).

There is a shortage of good quality research on the teaching of writing, but the available studies point toward a couple of concrete strategies that help improve the quality of student writing, and also help them to perform better on writing tests. Research shows that students need to learn how to transcribe their thoughts by hand as well as typing on the computer. According to research, teachers report that many of their students who can produce a multitude of text on their cellphones are still unable to work effectively using a laptop, or even on paper.

Many educators agree that children have become so anchored and accustomed to the small mobile screen that larger formats intimidate and seem to overwhelm them. They further explain that through the use of quick communication and texting on mobile devices, the rules of grammar and punctuation have become nearly obsolete to them, both of which are vital to academic writing. However, high-powered teachers at every grade-level strive to motivate their students and also to provide them with explicit instructions, model good quality writing, provide them ongoing explicit and applicable feedback, and also give them multiple daily opportunities to experience a wide variety of writing styles through collaborative writing, independent writing, and multimodal writing. They also provide students with opportunities to experience writing in all content areas (InTASC Standard 8, Council of Chief State School Officers [CCSSO]).

High-powered primary teachers require primary students to practice writing good sentences, that also vary in length, on a daily basis. Primary students also begin writing quality paragraphs to prepare for intermediate grades, where on-demand writing is a large part of state-mandated testing. High-powered teachers believe that when teachers work consistently across all grade-levels to ensure students are mastering the writing standards at each grade-level before advancing to the next grade, they are ensuring that students are prepared for on-demand writing, state-mandated and standardized tests, content writing, and also preparing them to be college- and career-ready (InTASC Standard 4, CCSSO). High-powered teachers believe that students with higher confidence in their writing ability perform better in the classroom, on tests, and in life.

"Every great story you've ever read, started with a single sentence."

~ *Dr. Joyce Bowling*

Author Reflection

I've always enjoyed writing. Even when I was learning to hold a pencil correctly, I had a strong desire to put words on paper. I inherited the gift of storytelling from my grandparents, who could spin a tale that was vivid, alive, and full of excitement, danger, suspense, and many other emotions. At the very young age of eight, I began writing and telling stories for my third-grade teacher. Each Friday she would randomly select a specific number of students to share an object, a story, or even a song with the class. My name was finally drawn from the big fishbowl of names. This was a grand opportunity, the chance that I had been waiting on. I would share one of my stories that I had written with the entire class.

Excitement consumed me as Friday drew closer and closer. I couldn't wait to share my story about the giant who lived just over the hill with the class. I thought my heart would pound out of my chest as I approached the front of the class to face my peers. My mother's words rang out loud and clear in my mind. She would always encourage me to participate in school and church plays. She would simply say, *"Don't be afraid, find three objects on the back wall, just above the audience's head and focus on them. Don't look directly at anyone, until you're ready to."* She taught me to train my eyes to maintain my focus on those objects, at least until I felt more confident about looking directly at my audience. I took a deep breath, and focused on the bulletin board behind my classmates and began my fable. It worked! I overcame my nerves, told the story, focused on the three objects on the back wall, and eventually was comfortable enough to look at my audience, smile at them, speak fluently with emphasis on certain words, and even use animated voices. My audience was hooked and captivated from the first two lines of the story, so was my teacher.

You may be wondering what that story has to do with teaching students to write effectively. Let me just say, my mother and my third-grade teacher were two of the biggest influences on my writing, career choice, and my desire to succeed in all aspects of life. My mom always listened and provided feedback and support. My third-grade teacher instilled the love of reading and writing within me. She gave me encouragement, guidance, support, feedback, constructive criticism, and also many opportunities to write and share many stories that were burning inside of me. My third-grade teacher, Mrs. Penny Robinson, encouraged me throughout my school years, and also into my adult years. She was a teacher who taught with creativity, passion, fire, and encouraged her students, regardless their socioeconomic status, learning level, or their behavior. She believed in her students and she inspired her students! She motivated them and challenged them to challenge themselves (InTASC Standard 3, CCSSO).

I'll never forget the words she spoke to me on the last day of third grade. She left me with words that helped mold me, helped me believe in myself, and also caused me to challenge myself. She stated, *"You will one day be a teacher who cares about your students and teaches with compassion. You will be a storyteller, and I know that one day, you will be a published author. Keep inspiring, telling, teaching, and don't ever stop writing."* I have recalled those words often. Mrs. Robinson cared about me, my future, and above all, she believed in me. My advice to you as you embark on this incredible journey of teaching is inspire your students. Challenge them to challenge themselves. Encourage students to write daily. Increase a desire in them to never stop learning, motivate them, and above all, believe in your students, just as Mrs. Robinson believed in me. Be a high-powered teacher that makes a difference in the lives of your students.

Reading and Writing Are Reciprocal

You learned in the first half of this textbook, reading and writing are **reciprocal**. Reading and writing should not be taught in isolation, instead should be integrated and taught together. High-powered teachers know that better readers make better writers and better writers make better readers. Both reading and writing involve a five-step process. Writing is a mental, physical, and focusing process that consists of arranging ideas to form an impression that leads to writing a clear message in the form of text.

The Writing Process

You also learned about the writing process in the first half of this textbook. Regardless the grade-level, **the writing process** remains the same. However, the depth and level of writing becomes more rigorous and diverse at the middle-school level. When we think of the writing process, we think of the steps that writers go through as they develop a piece of writing. The writing process steps include *prewriting, drafting, revising, proofreading, editing,* and *publishing*.

Prewriting

Prewriting can consists of **unfocused** and **focused prewriting**. Unfocused prewriting can be implemented when students do not have an idea for their topic. Whereas, focused prewriting is used when students have an established writing topic in mind. Prewriting can involve several components. High-powered teachers begin writing assignments with reading. The type of reading will mostly depend on the type of writing students will be required to do. For example, if the writing assignment is to write a poem, high-powered teachers would begin the lesson with reading poetry to the class, allowing students to read aloud and read together. They would take this opportunity to explore different authors, their techniques, and also review the guidelines for writing the specified style of poetry. In other words, when high-powered teachers are expecting students to complete a specific style of writing, they teach, model, and allow them opportunities to experience the genre and style of writing, before independent writing is assigned.

High-powered teachers model, read, and provide their students with the necessary tools to be successful writers, and then allow their students' time to reflect and think about what they want to write about. They encourage them to brainstorm, plan, incorporate semantic mapping, and have a graphic organizer during the prewriting stage. If the writing assignment consists of an argumentative speech, high-powered teachers may allow students to watch a video where someone is giving a speech, or read a speech aloud to the class. They would also discuss the components that make-up an argument as well as what is expected within a speech. High-powered teachers prepare their students to write by ensuring they have appropriate background knowledge, providing them with explicit instructions, time to practice, and instilling within them the confidence necessary to meet the demands of the writing assignment (InTASC Standards 4, 5, 7, CCSSO).

Tools for Prewriting

High-powered teachers provide and teach their students how to use tools that will enhance their writing. They integrate teaching and learning tools such as *graphic organizers, dictionaries, thesauri, acronyms*, *visual images*, *examples*, *rubrics, checklists*, and also provide them with *explicit instructions*. Graphic organizers are visual representations that provide students with successful methods of organizing, interpreting, analyzing, and applying. High-powered teachers know that graphic organizers are an invaluable teaching as well as learning tool. They know that graphic organizers help their students develop thinking skills, while also helping them organize their thoughts on paper. Graphic organizer are also a great resource to help students plan their writing (InTASC Standards, 4, 5, 7, 8, CCSSO).

Unfocused Prewriting

The primary purpose of **unfocused prewriting** is to encourage students to think about and explore topics or focus on the topic before they begin writing the initial draft. High-powered teachers encourage free, unfocused prewriting because they feel that it is valuable to provide students with an opportunity to write without restrictions or rules. According to Elbow, *"the goal of freewriting is the thinking process, not the product."* During unfocused prewriting, high-powered teachers ask their students to write continually for a specified amount of time asking students to not focus on the mechanics of their writing, but rather their ideas. Unfocused prewriting has also been referred to as freewriting and **brainstorming**. Nevertheless, the end product should be the same, which is unfocused ideas recorded on paper. Once students' time is exhausted and they have their thoughts on paper, high-powered teachers ask students to read what they have written to identify the main idea. They then record their main idea in their graphic organizer. Once students have established a topic, they may begin to identify key ideas, determine which ideas to include in their writing, and what information they want to exclude. Students then complete the remaining sections of their graphic organizer (InTASC Standards, 5, 8, CCSSO).

Focused Prewriting

As stated earlier, **focused prewriting** is a type of freewriting that is best suited for students who have a topic in mind and are ready to complete a graphic organizer. By integrating a graphic organizer in focused prewriting, students are able to either narrow or broaden their scope of the topic. Focused prewriting allows students to formulate their ideas, organize them, and allows them time to think about different ways to approach their writing topic (InTASC Standard 5, CCSSO).

"Focused freewriting is the heart and soul of a story."

~ Dr. Joyce Bowling

Graphic Organizer

Graphic organizers are beneficial for students writing, regardless the style of writing. High-powered teachers implement Graphic organizers in both reading and writing. They know that graphic organizers are powerful tools that can help students identify and determine cause and effect, to teach sequencing, activate background knowledge, to compare and contrast information, characters, plots, topics and more. Graphic organizers come in all shapes and sizes including, *mapping*, *webs*, *diagrams*, *grids*, and *charts*. High-powered teachers implement graphic organizers with writing in multiple ways such as organizing ideas, reasons, categorizing importance, and creating characters for narratives. They incorporate graphic organizer to help students identify the main idea, build a story, organize vocabulary, etc. High-powered teachers know that graphic organizers also motivate the visual learner, and the struggling writer (InTASC Standard 2, CCSSO).

Example 14.1 is an example of a simplistic graphic organizer to encourage students to identify the problem of a story, characters, setting, and the solution, while building the backbone of their story from the ground up, just as you would build a house.

High-powered teachers know that graphic organizers take on all shapes, sizes, and forms. Their primary focus is not on the shape or style of the organizer, but on what students are recording within the organizer. The graphic organizer that I found to be most successful with sixth-and seventh-grade students was very simple, producible by the student, and could be implemented with all writing genres. I asked students to outline the shape of their right hand on a separate sheet of paper. When completing a persuasive or argumentative writing, students were required to record the working title on the palm of the hand, the thumb was for writing the opening statement, rhetorical question, or the hook in the opening paragraph. The forefinger was designated for information for the first body paragraph, their primary reason for

Example 14.1: Building a Story

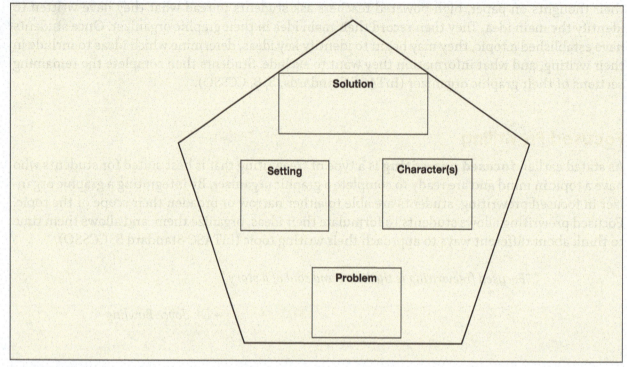

Source: Joyce Bowling

persuasion, first problem, or their strongest reason for supporting, opposing, or reason for asking, etc. The middle and third fingers were to record their remaining reasons, arguments, conflicts in order of their importance. Each finger also suggested where students should change paragraphs. The fifth and final finger, was to write the concluding statement in the final paragraph that should drive their point home, conclude the story, leave a lasting impression, and remind their reader of previous statements, etc. This organizer worked well when students were taking state-mandated tests, as it allowed them to create their own graphic organizer in their answer booklet, organize their thoughts quickly, and plan and prewrite in a time-efficient manner (InTASC Standards 1, 3, 4, 5, 7, 8, CCSSO). An example of the hand graphic organizer is shown in **Example 14.2.**

The focused prewriting stage is also a time for planning. During the focused prewriting stage, students should determine their purpose, who their audience is, and also identify the task that has been given to them. High-powered teachers teach students how to use different acronyms to help organize their thoughts and narrow their focus during the planning stage.

You learned about PAT in the first half of the book. This is a great method of organization for all grade-levels. I found that incorporating the simple acronym, **PAT**, into the graphic organizer helped students to determine why they were writing and who their audience was. High-powered teachers ask students to record the acronym on the side of their graphic organizer in the style of an acrostic poem. The letter P represents the **purpose** for the writing. The letter A represents **audience**, who will read the final product. And finally, the letter T represents the **task** required. For example, students may be asked to write a letter, a speech, an email, an article, etc. An example of **PAT** is shown in **Example 14.3.**

Example 14.2: Hand Graphic Organizer

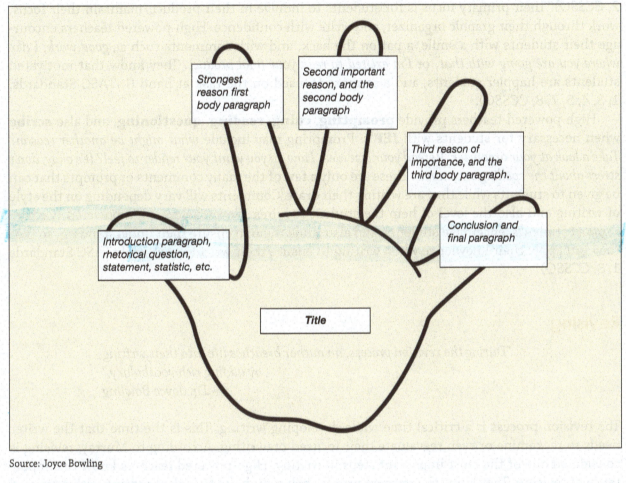

Source: Joyce Bowling

Example 14.3: PAT

P = *persuade the governor*
A = *the governor*
T = *write a letter*

Drafting

Drafting is the stage of writing when students refer to their graphic organizer and begin writing the first draft of their paper. High-powered teachers know the importance of this stage and encourage students to write their drafts legibly, and label the top of their paper as DRAFT. They teach students to skip one or two lines in-between as they are writing, which allows room for revisions and annotations that may occur during the revision process. Drafting should be writing that is not pressured, but more focused than prewriting. High-powered teachers ask students to incorporate basic punctuation as they write, but not to stress over attention to fine details as they will focus more on details of mechanics during the editing stage of writing (InTASC Standards 4, 5, 8, CCSSO).

During the drafting stage of writing, high-powered teachers monitor their students' writing to help keep them on task, but they do not hover over students or critique their work. However, they

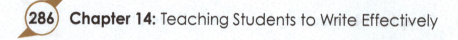

make themselves available for questions, and also to assist struggling writers (InTASC Standard 2, CCSSO). Their primary focus is for students to indulge in their product, maintain their focus, work through their graphic organizer, and write with confidence. High-powered teachers encourage their students with a smile, a pat on the back, and with comments such as *good work, I like where you are going with that*, or *I'm excited to read your final product*. They know that motivated students are happier students, and also more focused on the task at hand (InTASC Standards, 1, 3, 4, 5, 7, 8, CCSSO).

High-powered teachers provide **prompting**, **cuing**, **reading**, **questioning**, and also **scribe** when necessary for students with **IEP's**. Prompting may include *what might be another reason? Take a look at your organizer. Reread your last idea. How do you want your reader to feel? It's okay, don't stress about the spelling or commas*. These are only a few of the many comments or prompts that can be given to students while they are writing their draft. Comments will vary depending on the style of writing and also the level of help the student requires. Nevertheless, high-powered teachers support students, encourage students, and also guide them to ensure their understanding, so that they can apply their knowledge when writing to ensure their writing success (InTASC Standards 1, 3, CCSSO).

Revising

> *"During the revision process, an author breathes life into their writing*
> *by adding rich vocabulary."*
> *~ Dr. Joyce Bowling*

The revision process is a critical time while developing writing. This is the time that the writer needs to reexamine or even reevaluate their focused prewriting. According to Murray, revising is considered one of the most important steps in writing. High-powered teachers know the importance of revising. They know the revision process helps students to look at writing with a focused and critical eye, and as a writer and a reader. They also know that it promotes reading with a critical eye, thinking metacognitively, and encourages grammatical growth (InTASC Standard 1, 4, 8, CCSSO).

Revision can be a very difficult part of the writing process for students. High-powered teachers believe that revision can be difficult for students simply because it is often difficult to change perspectives, such as from the writer's perspective to the readers' perspective. They further explain that it is difficult for young writers to identify where change is required within their own writing. There are also cognitive and language reasons why revising can be difficult for young writers. Revising requires rethinking, refining, possibly reorganizing, and also rewriting their first draft. Until students become confident that their writing focuses on content and organization of that content as well as the words used by the writer, with a focus on the purpose of the writing and their audience, they will continue to struggle with revision. **PAT** helps students gain focus, purpose, and think about who the audience is, thus alleviating some of their insecurities about revising their writing (InTASC Standards 1, 4, 5, 8, CCSSO).

High-powered teachers encourage their students to use a checklist as they are rereading their drafts. (**See Table 14.1**, *for an example of a **Revising Checklist** for informational writing*.) They encourage students to read with a purposeful eye to see if they have incorporated the correct words, such as strong verbs, descriptive adjectives, transition words, transitional phrases, structure of their writing, and much more. High-powered teachers require their students to make two

Table 14.1: Revision Checklist for Informative Writing

Did I Do the Following?	1st Revision	Revision With a Partner
I checked required elements against the rubric.		
I have a strong, clear, and precise introduction.		
I established a clear purpose.		
I provided factual information.		
I varied the length of sentences.		
My Paragraphs are the appropriate length.		
I incorporated transition words, or transitional phrases throughout the paper.		
I used correct words: strong verbs, descriptive adjectives, and rich vocabulary.		
My paragraphs include an introduction, at least three body paragraphs, and a strong conclusion.		
I wrote with the audience in mind.		

revisions before moving to the next stage of writing. They ask them to reread their draft while using the checklist or rubric to ensure that they have included each required component. They ask them to revise their draft accordingly, and then work with a peer to revise it a second time. Students should read their revised draft aloud to their partners, which encourages them to hear and recognize possible mistakes, confusing words, and other possible errors. The partner is used primarily as a means of support, not to do the actual revision. High-powered teachers teach their students how to work collaboratively. They teach them how they should prompt their partner to look deeper, read more critically, think analytically, and offer suggestions without directly revealing the answer(s) to their partner (InTASC Standards 1, 2, 3, 4, 5, 6, 7, 8, CCSSO).

In other words, revising allows young writers to go backward and forward to see what they had in mind and actually what their writing reveals. Revision is also the link in the writing process between the intention, the purpose, and the audience of the writer, and the final outcome of their writing, which is the content and audiences' response. High-powered teachers know that revising is a very difficult stage of the writing process for young writers. Therefore, they teach their students and even provide and post the following guidelines on their wall or create a bookmark to serve as a reminder (InTASC Standards 7, 8, CCSSO).

+ *All writing does not require revision.*
+ *All writing should be reviewed, discussed, and also evaluated.*
+ *Revising should include a checklist and a rubric.*
+ *Revision focuses on the quality and organization of ideas, not on mechanics, or spelling.*
+ *Revision requires purposeful thinking of the audience and the main idea of the writing.*
+ *Revision comments should encourage students to rethink and rewrite with confidence.*

+ *Revision comments should be applicable comments.*
+ *Revision refines great ideas.*
+ *Revision is meant to be encouraging, not discouraging.*

High-powered teachers provide, review, and explain rubrics that students' writing will be scored by. They also provide them a different checklist for each style of assigned writing. Providing students with checklists allows students to become familiar and gradually gain confidence as well as academic knowledge of the required elements of each style of writing. High-powered teachers know when they provide their students with the tools they need to be successful throughout the year, their students write with the required knowledge and confidence necessary to write with proficiency on standardized tests (InTASC 1, 4, 6, CCSSO).

Revising Techniques and Strategies

High-powered teachers include a variety of revision techniques and strategies throughout the year, which helps increase students' comfort level, deepen their understanding of the content, the writing process, and also helps them differentiate and scaffold to meet the needs of all learners (InTASC Standards 3, 4, 8, CCSSO). They ensure that revising is purposeful and focused on specific revision skills. They know that other revising sessions can be more generalized. High-powered teachers know that the closer the revising goals in a writing assignment are to purpose, audience, and content of the assignment, the more productive the revising efforts will be. Strategies can include but are not limited to the following strategies.

Author Conferences

Author conferences are informal conferences that focus on the students as authors. They focus on the needs or the concerns that students may have about a writing assignment that is in progress, the writing process in general, or students' abilities as a developing writer. High-powered teachers' conference with their students one-on-one, and also allow students to conference with a peer (InTASC Standard 8, CCSSO).

Nevertheless, author's conferences are meant to be encouraging and inspiring, as well as developmental. High-powered teachers know that the key to success with author's conferences is for students to receive feedback that encourages the student/author to want to write again. The following questions can be incorporated during an author's conference. Note that author's conferences can happen at any time during the writing process, and also the following questions can be modified to fit any of the writing stage.

+ *What is your topic?*
+ *What is the purpose for this writing?*
+ *What is your assigned task?*
+ *What do you need to find out?*
+ *Who are you writing this for?*
+ *Who will read your writing?*
+ *Do you think you have enough information?*

✦ *Do you think you'll need all of this information?*
✦ *How do you feel about your progress?*
✦ *Have you used your checklist?*
✦ *What might be another way to write this?*
✦ *Do you have enough details for your audience?*
✦ *Did you use enough transition words or phrases?*
✦ *What would be a stronger word to describe this?*
✦ *What do you want the reader to learn from reading your writing?*
✦ *What have you learned while writing this?*

Writing Groups

High-powered teachers' classrooms are collaborative and engaging, even during the revision stage of the writing process. Collaborative learning allows students to peer assess, learn from each other, while also helping the teacher differentiate and scaffold for all learners. High-powered teachers incorporate writing groups during the revision process to help shift the responsibility of revising from the teacher to the students. They know that when writing groups are used effectively, they can provide a supportive audience for young writers with revision needs, regardless of when their needs arise. They also know that writing groups promote a sense of community, peer-to-peer collaboration, and a collaborative and cooperative rapport in the classroom (InTASC Standard 3, 8, CCSSO).

Writers' groups also allow time and offer support for young writers to help them manage new writing formats, narrow their focus, or define a writing topic. High-powered teachers also know that writer's groups can help students to organize their thoughts and response to a writing assignment. This is also a time for supportive, conductive, and applicable feedback. When students work collaboratively, they create a shared responsibility for each member's writing efforts (InTASC Standard 8, CCSSO). High-powered teachers provide explicit instruction for writing groups, model, and provide them with a posted list of requirements. This list may include the following:

✦ *All members of a writing group should be* **good listeners** *and listen carefully to what is being read.*
✦ *All members should* **think about** *what the writing says to them about the topic, the ideas being expressed, and the purpose.*
✦ *All members should* **react** *to specific features in the writing. Features such as content, vocabulary, organization, transition words, phrases, or visual images.*
✦ *All members should* **remember** *what makes them uneasy about writing and revising.*
✦ *All members should* **provide** *productive feedback.*
✦ *All members should* **respond** *in encouraging ways that will make the writer want to write again.*

Revision Centers

High-powered teachers also incorporate **revision centers** with a wide variety of objectives. They create a revision center in their classroom that offers a quiet and private setting where students can focus on their writing, read aloud to themselves, or where they can record themselves reading their written work. High-powered teachers know that when students record themselves reading, they not only hear their own voice reading, but they can also analyze what they are hearing. They have the ability to stop and rewind to listen again to allow them to determine what they need to do to make their writing flow smoother, deepen the meaning of their writing, or what words should be replaced to make their writing more meaningful. Listening to one's self-read also allows students to hear grammatical errors. High-powered teachers provide students with a rubric, and also a checklist in the writing center, which allows the student to self-assess, reflect, analyze, and also self-correct (InTASC Standards, 2, 3, 4, 6, 8, CCSSO).

High-powered teachers implement and encourage revision centers to help students analyze and evaluate their own writing. Clear objectives are posted in the revision center that remind students of the purpose of the center. Objectives may include *reflection, understanding, analyzing, evaluating, modifying, creating*, and *applying objectives*. Revision centers encourage students to reflect on their own learning, analyze, and also apply what they know and what they need to do to correct and make necessary changes, which may include applying correct grammar, rich vocabulary, transition words and more elements that ensure their writing is strong, precise, and purposeful. Thus, creating a finished product that they can be proud of (InTASC Standard 8, CCSSO).

A high-powered teacher creates a revision center that is also suitable for peer-revision to ensure that all learners' needs are met. Their revision centers are designed to allow English Language Learner (ELL) students, struggling writers, culturally diverse students, and students who need a little guidance to work with a peer or the teacher to revise their writing. Revision centers include resource tools that will enhance students' writing such as checklists, thesauri, dictionaries, bilingual dictionaries, lists of power verbs, lists of transition words and transitional phrases, reference handbooks, and also an encyclopedia of quotes (InTASC Standard 2, 8, CCSSO). Students are encouraged to use the reference tools to strengthen their knowledge of what constitutes quality writing, encourage repetitive use of resource tools, and also to ensure that students are creating a final product that meets the objectives, rubrics, expectations, standards, that they can take ownership of and be proud of.

> *"If you want students to be successful...give them the tools they need to build their success."*
>
> ~ Dr. Joyce Bowling

Proofreading and Editing

Proofreading and **editing** are the final stages of writing. Teachers often confuse the two, or sometimes eliminate one of the stages. However, high-powered teachers teach their students that each step is necessary and each stage of the writing process has a purpose and is equally important (InTASC Standards 4, 8, CCSSO). When students proofread, they are proofing for grammatical, mechanical, and spelling errors. High-powered teachers model how students should read with a purposeful and critical eye. They teach them to focus on the use and the overuse of commas, to ensure that sentences are complete and are also punctuated correctly. Proofreading is vital to the final product. If commas are omitted or the body of the text contains run-on sentences, or misspelled words, the reader becomes distracted as their focus is on the grammar, and not on the purpose of the paper.

The revision stage encourages students to reflect on and address the purpose, content, and their audience, while proofreading draws their attention to grammar, spelling, and punctuation. Proofreading is at the very heart of the editing stage. While students are editing they are required to make final revision to the mistakes that they found while proofreading. They are also focusing on the visual appearance of the final product. For example, high-powered teachers require students to proofread and edit their final format to ensure that their writing contains all of the required elements for the assigned format. For example, if students are asked to write a business letter, they assess their writing with the provided rubric/checklist to ensure that their letter contains the following: *a heading that contains the address of the sender and who the letter is being sent to, the greeting, the body, the closing, and the signature.* High-powered teachers provide students with checklists and rubrics that allow them to self-assess during proofreading and editing stages (InTASC Standards 4, 5, 6, 8, CCSSO). An example of an **editing checklist** is shown in **Example 14.4**.

Example 14.4: Editing Checklist

Did I use correct spelling?	
Did I indent paragraphs?	
Do my verbs agree with my nouns?	
Did I use correct capitalization?	
Did I use correct verb tense?	
Did I use correct punctuation?	
Did I use the correct format and include all elements?	

High-powered teachers know that through *explicit instructions, modeling, available resource tools,* and *multiple opportunities* that allow and encourage *student engagement* and *self-assessment,* they are preparing students to be successful writers in all content areas, on **standardized tests** and **state-mandated assessments**, to write **on-demand**, and to have the knowledge and skills that are necessary to be competent successful writers in daily life in the real world (InTASC Standards 1, 2, 3, 4, 5, 6, 7, 8, CCSSO).

Publishing

Publishing is the final phase in the process of writing and is one of the most important reasons for writing. The final phase is what causes writers to ponder, toil, make revisions, and often times the purpose for all of the other stages of writing. Publishing can also be a very emotional stage for students as well as professional writers. Methods of publishing consist of submitting a completed paper to the teacher, sending a letter to the principal, submitting writing for competitions, answering extended responses, writing a book review, a social media post, submitting an article to the school newspaper, writing a blog, sending an email, reading a final product orally to the class, replying to an on-demand scenario, as well as many more stages of publications.

Publishing, regardless the method, is a very public and personal experience. Students and professional writers find themselves with many questions including *Will the reader like my work? Did I include all of the required components? What if the reader doesn't like my writing?* However, high-powered teachers also know that the publishing stage can be an exhilarating feeling of accomplishment, a feeling of ownership, and a reason for students to feel proud of their final product (InTASC Standards 5, 8, CCSSO).

Standard-Based Writing

Good quality **standard-based writing** assignments are an important element in public classrooms. High-powered teachers prepare their students to produce quality standard-based writing through explicit instructions, differentiation, modeling, engaging, and also provide them with multiple ongoing opportunities to practice, create, and apply their writing. Teaching students what the expectations for standard-based writing are and also allowing students to practice it as well, helps prepare students for standardized and state-mandated writing tests in public schools, and also for college. Thus, ensuring that students are college-and career-ready (InTASC Standards 5, 7, 8, CCSSO). Guidelines for standard-based writing assignments may include the following:

1. *To encourage students to write because they care about the assignment and their writing.*
2. *To challenge students to acquire and provide information during the course of completing the assignments.*
3. *For students to use the most appropriate writing style(s) to convey their message to their readers.*
4. *To provide students with multiple opportunities to explore and create.*
5. *To ensure that students know and apply all stages of the writing process.*
6. *To encourage and promote critical and analytical thinking, problem-solving, and also to develop new insights.*
7. *To involve the reader as a writer.*
8. *To promote and encourage self-assessment and peer-assessment.*
9. *To allow students multiple opportunities to gain insight and experience multiple methods of feedback.*
10. *To help students prepare for state-mandated, standards-based writing assessments, and also how to apply standards to all writing assignments.*

Engaging Writing Strategies

High-powered teachers know the value and benefits of incorporating **story maps** in their instruction to help enhance students' writing (InTASC Standard 8, CCSSO). They incorporate story maps to help students generate ideas for stories. They also help draw their attention to key or important elements found in most stories including, characters, plot, resolution, or even conflict. High-powered teachers know that the use of story maps helps their students when creating and writing their own stories. They encourage students to use a variety of story maps to help them think about and prepare for story writing. Story maps are very beneficial for narrative writing. Story maps help students formulate the beginning, middle, and ending of their story. Typically, mapping is used as a graphic organizer that students complete during the prewriting stage of writing. However, story mapping can be implemented with felt boards or illustrations for struggling writers, tactile learners, or ELL students. Mapping can be differentiated to fit the needs of all learners and learning levels (InTASC Standard 2, CCSSO).

Cubing is another strategy that high-powered teachers integrate during unfocused prewriting, or even as a strategy to help build students understanding of story structure, and also enhance their writing skills. Cubing in a sense is a form of a graphic organizer as it encourages students to explore writing topics from a number of perspectives. The term cubing refers to the fact that students think of a topic as being a cube, which has six sides. Each side of the cube represents one perspective on the topic or one way of exploring the topic. Cubing can be completed in a variety of ways. One way to complete cubing is to ask students to complete six steps that include, describe it, compare it, analyze it, apply it, and argue it, either opposing or supporting it. High-powered teachers enjoy this method of cubing as it is comparable to **Bloom's six levels of comprehension**. Each of the above steps is recorded on one side of the cube, and regardless the side of the cube that the student rolls, they are required to think. This is a hands-on type of learning that most students enjoy as it is engaging and fun (InTASC Standards 3, 4, 5, 8, CCSSO).

Cubing can also be used to strengthen sequencing events and skills of telling a story. High-powered teachers implement cubing in this manner by using a different picture on each of the six sides of the cube or even using multiple cubes for students to roll. Either way, the student is required to roll the die or dice and then begin the story based on the picture that is facing upward. Teachers require students to have a logical sequence of events, incorporate transition words, and transitional phrases, and also have a beginning, middle, and ending based on the pictures on the dice. This can also be modified by replacing illustrations/pictures with carefully chosen words. Words can include the eight parts of speech to reinforce use of adjectives, adverbs, verbs, and etc. High-powered teachers know that the academic uses for cubing are limitless, and each one is very beneficial. Cubing is beneficial as a method of prompting for ELL students, struggling readers and writers. Reusable dry-erase cubes can be purchased, premade story cubes can also be purchased, or cubes can actually be made by the teacher or the student from paper (InTASC Standard 2, 8, CCSSO).

Vocabulary Enhances Writing

Words are a writer's most valuable tool. High-powered teachers know that rich vocabulary enhances students' reading experience and also their writing, which is why high-powered teachers teach vocabulary and give their students the tools needed for successful writing. They know that rich vocabulary has the ability to take ordinary writing to extraordinary writing (InTASC Standards 4, 7, 8, CCSSO).

High-powered teachers model an enthusiasm for and also a curiosity about new words through their own attitude, teaching, and their writing to inspire students to dig deeper for more meaningful vocabulary words to incorporate in their writing. They look for those teachable moments throughout the day as they occur while reading, teaching, or through conversations. They encourage students to explore new words in alternative methods of expressing concepts, and also when expressing colorful and descriptive ways of speaking and also writing (InTASC Standard 8, CCSSO).

High-powered teachers deliver explicit writing vocabulary instruction, model how rich vocabulary has the ability to paint mental images for the reader that allows them to visualize the setting, the characters or the plot (InTASC 4, 7, 8, CCSSO). Incorporating rich vocabulary also helps pique and even maintain the readers' focus on the content of the text. High-powered teachers use creative strategies to enhance students' writing vocabulary (InTASC Strategy 8, CCSSO). They also know that practice and repetition are also important methods by which students become familiar and gain understanding of how to incorporate words correctly. High-powered teachers use explicit instruction, discussions, and also engage their students in rich vocabulary activities and strategies that enhance their speaking, listening, and reading skills, and also their writing skills. Strategies may include but are not limited to the following: Shades of Meaning, Tossed Terms, Vocabulary Cards, Thesauri Scavenger Hunt, vocabulary graffiti, and also story pyramids (InTASC Standards 4, 8, CCSSO).

Story Pyramids

High-powered teachers incorporate **story pyramids** during creative writing. They know that story pyramids helps students develop vocabulary and develop ideas for writing. A story map can act as an outline for the beginning of a narrative. An example of a story map is shown below.

+ *The first line is one word that names the character.*
+ *The second line describes the character using two words.*
+ *The third line describes the setting, or can be a descriptive line using three words.*
+ *The fourth line describes the main even, or can describe the setting using four words.*
+ *The fifth line states a problem using five words.*
+ *The sixth line describes a second event using six letters.*
+ *The seventh and eighth line describe the third event, and the solution using seven and eight words.*

High-powered teachers know that this type of organization enhances creativity, engages the student with critical thinking, enhances vocabulary, while also creating visual images of a newly formed story in a fun graphic organizer (InTASC Standards, 4, 7, 5, 8, CCSSO).

Word Banks

Word banks are a great source of inspiration for writers who struggle with ideas. High-powered teachers incorporate word banks for multiple styles of writing such as narratives, fables, fairytales, and even tall tales. Word banks can be as simple as a designated area on the white board where lists of random words are posted that students may choose to incorporate in their writing. Word banks can also be totally random. For example, teachers can use a bag, box, or some type of storage container and fill it with small slips of paper with a menagerie of random and fun words that includes nouns, proper nouns, pronouns, adjectives, verbs and more. Students are asked to reach in and randomly select a specific number of words. The object of this type of word bank is that students must incorporate all of their selected words within their writing. Students gain inspiration from the words and begin to formulate a story, plot, and add characters based on the words they selected (InTASC Standards 2, 8, CCSSO).

Example 14.5: Story Pyramid

> Sam
> Likes fishing
> Sam fishes daily
> He likes ocean fishing
> Sam's boat sprang a leak
> He doesn't have a bailing bucket
> Sam doesn't even have a rowing oar
> Instead of panicking, he quickly radios for help

Source: Joyce Bowling

Voice

Author's Voice is the individual writing style of an author. **Author's Voice** is also a combination of usage of tone, style, syntax, diction, use of punctuation, character development, and the use of dialogue within the body of text. I like to think of voice as an author's own unique style. An author's voice can also take on different meanings according to the genre or the purpose. Don't confuse author's voice with voice. For example, in a narrative, there is no place for **author's/writers' voice**. Yes, that's correct. The voice that emerges in a narrative must belong to the character, not the author. However, if the writer is writing expository text, then most definitely there's a place for the author's voice. Since the author is writing to inform the reader, there should be a relationship between the author and the reader (InTASC Standard 5, CCSSO).

High-powered teachers know that developing voice in expository writing is not as difficult for students as developing voice in narrative writing. For expository writing, students want their personality and ideas to shine through. When writing a narrative, they must think like the character and write like the character would speak in an effort for the reader to make connections and form a relationship with the character. For example, when a reader is reading a novel, they are not hearing the voice of the author inside their head, they are hearing and visualizing the voice of the character.

High-powered teachers also allow their students to create **character analysis maps** during the prewriting stage of writing to allow them to create their character, and also bring life to their character by giving them both internal and external characteristics and qualities. They encourage students to give their characters hair color, eye color, freckles, etc. To help them visualize the character and also give them voice. Narrative writing can be fun, engaging, and a building process that is worthy of time, repetition, and engaging in creative and collaborative activities. Narratives are a great source of motivating students to write, and also a reading motivation as well (InTASC Standards 1, 3, 4, 5, 7, 8, CCSSO).

Assessment

High-powered teachers know that assessment is a teaching requirement, but also a learning requirement. They also know that assessment is an opportunity to provide their students with constructive and applicable feedback (InTASC Standard 6, CCSSO). They teach their students to not fear assessment and also to share the responsibility with them (InTASC Standard 3, CCSSO). High-powered teachers follow the listed **assessment guidelines**:

1. **Assessment of students' writing should be ongoing and continuous:** *Students should see assessment as a method of providing them with helpful feedback.*

2. **Assessment isn't synonymous with grading:** *High-powered teachers use formative assessment more than summative assessment for instructional strategies.*

3. **Students are involved with their writing assessments:** *This allows students to take more responsibility and authorship for their writing.*

4. **High-powered teachers look for common writing problems when assessing students' writing to enhance future instruction:** *Typically students' writing will cluster. When high-powered teachers look for commonalities in students' writing, it allows them to plan for collaborative instruction, collaborative experiences, as well as whole-group and small-group discussions.*

5. **High-powered teachers build assessment criteria into writing assignments:** *This encourages students to keep in mind how their writing will be evaluated as they complete writing assignments.*

6. **Uses assessment criteria consistently:** *This prevents students' confusion about how they will be assessed and also alleviates frustration while writing.*

7. **Not all writing must be graded:** *Allowing students to select from several pieces of writing to submit encourages students to analyze and critique their own writing gives them a choice and a voice, and also helps them to take ownership and authorship for their written work.*

Writing Assessment Strategies

Authentic writing assessment means taking a closer look at students' writing. Graphic organizers are a performance based-model of assessment and are ideal for including in student portfolios, since they require students to demonstrate both their grasp of the concept(s) and also their reasoning. Writing folders/portfolios are a great method of both monitoring and assessing students writing. High-powered teachers teach students to organize their writing folders, update them with revisions, allow students to self-assess their work as they progress, and also review folders to measure student growth, provide students with applicable feedback, conference with students, and make consistent modifications to their entries throughout the year. As students revise their drafts and prepare for their final submissions, they are also able to visually see and monitor their own growth. High-powered teachers provide students with rubrics for each style of required writing, checklists, and encourage them to maintain a neat and orderly portfolio with dated entries (InTASC Standard 6, CCSSO).

Direct observations are also a method of assessment. As stated earlier, be a kid-watcher. In other words, observe your students daily while they are reading and also while students are writing. Be observant when students are finding or determining a topic, what prewriting strategies are they using, who works well with a peer, which students require help with resources, creating a graphic organizer, which students need to incorporate transition words, or rich vocabulary, etc. High-powered teachers know that by observing their students in daily classroom writing, they are giving them an opportunity to practice writing without the feeling of pressure that often comes with timed or standardized assessment. They know that they are also allowing students valuable opportunities to practice a wide variety of writing formats, while also gaining insight about students' strong areas in writing, as well as the areas they are still struggling in (InTASC Standards 2, 6, CCSSO).

New teachers may struggle with time spent assessing students' writing. Note that all written work does not have to be formally graded. Grade one in every three to four papers and allow students to select the paper they would like for you to score. Self-assessment also alleviates some of the pressures of grading students' writing. Model peer-assessment with your students, provide them with the necessary resources- and allow them to peer-assess at least once a week.

As a fifth- and sixth-grade language arts and on-demand writing teacher, I found myself overwhelmed with the amount of writing papers that my students were turning in as a daily practice. After much thought, deliberation, as well as trial and error, I discovered a method of assessment that worked well for me and my 157 students. For example, if my students were working on writing a persuasive article we followed the calendar below:

- ✦ Monday was a day of explicit instruction about the style of writing students were going to be asked to write, daily oral language, and modeling.
- ✦ Tuesday was a brief summary of Monday, daily oral language, and a collaborative activity.
- ✦ Wednesday, daily oral language, and students began planning and brainstorming.
- ✦ Thursday, daily oral language, students worked on their drafts.
- ✦ Friday, daily oral language, and students worked on revising their draft.
- ✦ Monday, daily oral language, a summary, and review of the week before students began proofreading.
- ✦ Tuesday, daily oral language, students' edited their paper.
- ✦ Wednesday and Thursday daily oral language, and students worked on their final product.
- ✦ Friday, daily oral language, writing time to complete assignment, and students submitted their papers.

You may be wondering what I was doing while they were working. I was observing, assisting scribing when necessary, and monitoring students' productivity. The results of the above suggested calendar was, a final paper was submitted on Friday. Rather than accumulating 750 papers by Friday when I was requiring students to submit a paper each day. Of course this plan was not always repetitious as there were weeks that we worked on multimedia writing, researching for expository assignments, novels, and experienced whole-class activities, such as jigsaw, reader's theater, and held classroom debates (InTASC Standard 8, CCSSO). Each of the activities were designed with a purpose to enhance students' writing, for them to experience peer collaboration, increase their understanding, apply their knowledge and skills, create projects, analyze information and more, but each enhanced both their reading and writing skills as well as classroom rapport (InTASC Standard 3, CCSSO). Remember, reading and writing are reciprocal. The more the students read the better writers they will be. The more students write the better readers they will be. The more you inspire and engage your students, the better teacher you will be.

Language Link

- -

High-powered teachers use literature to teach students about sentence structure and word use, as well as punctuation and capitalization. Students can also focus on the use of stronger nouns, verbs, adjectives, and adverbs by depicting them visually. **Concrete poems** are a great tool to help students visualize and strengthen their use of the English language. High-powered teachers teach students about concrete poetry, and also modeling the process of writing concrete poetry.

Students participate in collaborative settings to create concrete poems, and also as a whole class (InTASC Standards, 7, 8, CCSSO).

High-powered teachers know that through engaging students in writing a concrete poem they are encouraging students to think critically, creatively, and also emphasizing the importance and incorporating the use of stronger words, thus enriching their language and writing skills (InTASC Standard 4, CCSSO). The process of writing concrete poems may vary depending on the grade-level. Concrete poetry can be integrated into multiple disciplines as well. A suggested guide for writing concrete poems is listed as follows:

1. *Students to determine a place/location, person, a thing/object, or activity that they like or enjoy.*
2. *Students to draw an outline of the shape of their topic. For example, if a student chooses to write about a house, or a home, they would draw the outline of a house. If a student decided to write about a flower, they would draw the outline of a flower, etc.*
3. *Students brainstorm two to five strong nouns, verbs, adjectives, and adverbs that describe their idea. (The number of words will vary with grade-levels.)*
4. *Once students have an idea for their topic, their chosen words, students begin to fill the shape with lines of poetry that contains words from their lists.*
5. *Idealistically, the lines of the poem should fit and fill the shape of the poem outline.*

High-powered teachers integrate grammar, punctuation, and mechanics with literature to make the learning experience more meaningful, applicable, and also to emphasize the importance of using correct grammar, punctuation, spelling, and mechanics when writing. They also know that integrating reading, writing, and language arts makes lessons more memorable, and their knowledge of these three is more applicable when creating final projects. High-powered teachers emphasize sentence structure, subject–verb agreement, and more through various styles of writing including fables, fairytales, speeches, biopoems, free-writing, conversational poetry, imagery. They know that engaging students in the written process of poetry in a fun way, increases writing skills, reading skills, creativity, while also decreasing, alleviating, or eliminating fear, doubts, misconceptions, or intimidating thoughts that students may have about poetry (InTASC Standards 4, 5, 7, 8, CCSSO).

Virtual Creative Response Writing

High-powered teachers know that **writing is thinking**. They also know that writing is the most disciplined form of thinking and that it allows each student the opportunity to uniquely express themselves. Writing also allows students to reflect, express, and evaluate themselves as well as the topic at hand and the world around them, while also making valuable connections. High-powered teachers know the importance and the challenges of both inspiring students to write creatively, while also teaching them the conventions of writing both inside the classroom and inside the virtual classroom. They have found that incorporating the **quill.org** website to be beneficial in engaging students with creative grammatical scenarios that both challenges and enhances their writing skills.

Many writing assignments are viewed as ways of measuring what students have learned, but high-powered teachers know that writing is an important component in the process of learning. They know that writing can **create experiences** that allows students to **self-explore**, **increase comprehension**, and also **self-reflect**. Response writing is a research-based strategy that allows students to **reflect**, **explore**, and **respond**, while also **enhance** their **writing skills**.

With the demands of online teaching and learning, high-powered teachers have risen to meet those demands by strategically implementing **Creative Response Writing** within their class-room and also with online students. They know that **student choice** is crucial when inspiring middle-school students to write. Research has proven that when students follow their interests and their own innate curiosity, they are more likely to respond with honest and compelling writing. However, high-powered teachers know that if total choice is left to the students, they sometimes write about topics that don't promote higher-order thinking, create **comprehensive thinking**, or allow room for **meaningful connections**. Thus, teachers have found that while reading a novel with their students and creating diverse writing prompts that allow student choice, student responses and motivation increased. For example, teachers may ask students to create and introduce a new character within the story, or include themselves as the newly created character. They may also ask students to change an event, or the ending of a specified chapter. High-powered teachers are creative, flexible, and willing to modify writing prompts as they become inspired by the novel, or to align with the current novel being read. Teachers may also encourage students to create and submit ideas for prompts while reading the text.

High-powered teachers know that meaningful writing helps students think beyond the actual experience to which they are responding and explore through making connections, linking information, expanding upon the new information, and then applying what they have learned in written format. In other words, students should be encouraged to expand, apply, and or evaluate their own creative writing, rather than simply regurgitating information. Creating fun and engaging writing prompts are beneficial to engage students in their writing, inspiring them, and also motivating them to step outside their comfort zone. High-powered teachers know the key to productive **Creative Response Writing** is the understanding that there is no one correct answer. Answers will vary among writers. However, high-powered teachers craft their writing prompts so that they scaffold student's thinking rather than evaluate it. They have found the following to be beneficial with both in-person and online students.

+ Provide students with a rubric or checklist to allow them to know what you are looking for in their writing, which should include length, format, and grammatical expectations.
+ Encourage students to brainstorm prior to writing.
+ Provide students with rich vocabulary word walls or word banks to help inspire their use of vocabulary.
+ Encourage students to put themselves in the position of the character in the novel, to think about and evaluate the circumstance(s) that the character is experiencing, or what they might be thinking.
+ Ask students to complete a graphic organizer to help organize their thoughts on paper prior to writing.
+ Encourage students to write creatively from the heart, with a focus on the literary elements.

High-powered teachers have discovered that writing in response to any learning opportunity whether it is in response to lecture, conversation, or to literature, allows students to **expand** their **thinking** about the concept or topic at hand while also providing them with the opportunity to consider new information on their own. A written response differs from an oral response or a discussion because students have the choice to think without interruption, to add to their thinking, or change their thinking upon further reflection. Creative Writing Responses are also beneficial in strengthening students reading skills, use of grammar, and promoting effective and creative writing skills.

Now It's Your Turn

For this assignment you will assume the role of a first year teacher. You will be required to write a friendly opening-day letter to the parents/guardians of your students (InTASC Standard 10, CCSSO). Your letter must include the following: *heading*, *greeting*, *introduction paragraph*, at least *three body paragraphs*, a *conclusion*, and a *signature*. A drop box, specific details, and other requirements for this assignment, as well as an example of a friendly letter, are located on the content page of blackboard. This assignment is designed to help you think like a teacher and also to prepare you for a realistic expectation of a teacher.

Author's Tip

Being a living example of what you teach is one of the most inspiring things a teacher can do to motivate their students. If you are teaching your students to be a reader, you should also be a reader. If you are teaching them to be a writer, then be a writer. Inspire your students through your own written expression, through the use of technology, academic competition, showcasing their writing, and giving them a purpose to write. Be the high-powered teacher who is also a **life-long learner**. Attend professional developments about writing, explore websites, read articles published by professional writers, study authors' work, interview successful authors, and above all strive to increase your knowledge of writing, engaging students, creative lesson plans, and methods of inspiring students to be the best writers that they can be. Offer multiple ongoing opportunities that allow students to experience writing in various different settings, genres, and to publish in more ways than turning-in a paper (InTASC Standards 9, 10, CCSSO).

Allow students to write persuasive speeches, and also give those speeches in front of the class. Encourage students to explore fun and interesting topics to promote research skills. Allow students to write persuasive commercials that they also must perform collaboratively before an audience. Create writing prompts that require them to think like a historian and write from a historical perspective. Provide them with interesting and inspiring visual images to pique their curiosity and motivate them to write poetry using **imagery**. Bring in fragrances that stir their senses and trigger memories as well as background knowledge. Invite guest speakers who are published authors to inspire your students to write. Create a class newsletter that allows them to explore **expository** writing (InTASC Standards 7, 8, CCSSO).

Be a high-powered teacher that allows ongoing opportunities for students to practice timed on-demand style of writing to prepare them for timed state-mandated tests. Host poetry slams for students to showcase their poetry. Teach, instruct, and allow students opportunities to learn about writing a **narrative**, through exciting action-packed stories, teach them how to write an **argumentative** paper with a supporting or opposing view. Teach them the secrets to writing a successful **persuasive** letter or speech. Be the high-powered writing teacher who explores all genres of writing with a spirit of enthusiasm, inspiration, motivation, and creativity. This list could continue for pages, but overall, be a high-powered teacher that thinks outside the box.

Be the teacher that demonstrates confidence, boldness, and that teaches writing with passion. Give your students the tools required for successful writing, the opportunities to practice writing in various formats, the encouragement that they need to be confident, and the keys that they need to master and unlock their own writing success.

What Can Parents Do to Help?

One of the greatest assets to students learning is to have supportive and encouraging parents. Parental involvement and support increase students' desire to accept academic challenges, to be successful. It also offers students an additional source that can be accessed most anytime (InTASC Standard 10, CCSSO). Parents serve as a source of inspiration, motivation, encouragement, to listen to students as they read their writing, as a reader, someone to bounce ideas off of, and also a means of moral support. High-powered teachers strive to keep parents "in the educational loop" making them aware of the standard students are striving to master, content they are covering, and providing them with samples of their child's completed and graded work.

In reality, high-powered teachers know that not all parents are truly involved in their child's academic life, and sometimes not in their lives at all. However, they make every effort to keep them informed regardless of their personal situation at home. They also provide them with academic support through peers, and also teacher support. High-powered teachers know that some students need to rise up and face the challenge of writing, while other students need a support system and someone to listen to them and believe in them. High-powered teachers inform, invite, and encourage parents/guardians to attend parent–teacher conferences. They also encourage parents to request parent–teacher meetings if they feel the need (InTASC Standard 10, CCSSO).

Applications

To help guide you through Chapter Fourteen and upcoming chapters, become familiar with the following key terms for a deeper understanding of Chapter Fourteen:

+ The writing process
+ Prewriting
+ Unfocused prewriting
+ Focused prewriting
+ Drafting
+ Graphic organizers
+ Revising
+ Revision checklists
+ Revision center
+ Proofreading
+ Editing
+ Publishing
+ Editing checklist
+ Standard-based writing
+ Cubing
+ Story maps
+ Word banks
+ Argumentative
+ Narrative
+ On-demand
+ Expository
+ Persuasive

- Author's voice
- Voice
- Character analysis map
- State-mandated assessments
- Standardized assessments
- Writing resources
- Bloom's taxonomy
- Imagery
- Life-long learner
- Author's voice
- Writer's conferences
- Concrete poems

Reflect and Answer the Following Questions

- *What is the writing process?*
- *How can I inspire my students to write?*
- *What writing strategies should I incorporate to enhance students' writing?*
- *What genres of writing should I teach?*
- *How does vocabulary enhance writing?*
- *How can I integrate writing mechanics and grammar in writing?*
- *How should I assess students' writing?*

In-Seat Activity

Bloom's Taxonomy is used by high-powered teachers as a basis for creating and writing objectives. Using the Bloom's Taxonomy example below, work with a partner to create writing objectives that align with each level of Blooms. Be prepared to share.

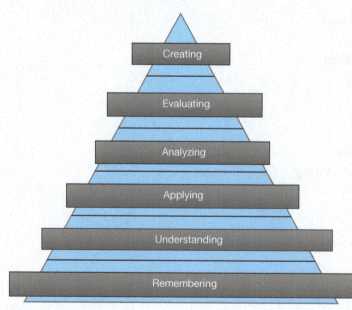

Source: Joyce Bowling

Student Notes

Annotation is an effective learning strategy. Annotating is typically completed along the outer edge of the text within the book. However, sufficient space is not always available. Therefore, this page has been reserved for you to annotate *(take notes)*, record potential questions, and also to refer back to when studying, completing assignments, and to help you gain a better understanding of Chapter Fourteen.

Student Reflection

High-powered teachers reflect. This page is reserved for you to reflect about information that you found insightful and what you have learned from Chapter Fourteen.

Chapter References

Council of Chief State School Officers (CCSSO). *Interstate Teacher Assessment and Support Consortium (InTASC) Model Core Teaching Standards.* Apr. 2011. https://www.ccsso.org/sites/default/files/2017-11/InTASC_Model_Core_Teaching_Standards_2011.pdf. Accessed 7 July 2018.

Elbow, P. *Writing with Power: Techniques for Mastering the Writing Process.* Oxford U Press, 1983.

Murray, D. *A Writer Teaches Writing.* 2nd ed., Heinle, 2004.

National Center for Education Statistics. *Digest of Education Statistics: 2016.* NCES 2017–094. https://nces.ed.gov/nationsreportcard/. Accessed May 21, 2018.

Chapter 15
Literature and Strategies

Teacher Quote

"Learners need time and opportunities to use and practice new learning in realistic ways."

~ Brian Cambourne

Chapter Questions

✦ *Why is it important to teach all genres of literature?*
✦ *What is quality literature?*
✦ *What is narrative text?*
✦ *What are the literary elements of literature?*
✦ *What is expository text?*
✦ *How are narrative texts and expository texts different?*
✦ *What creative strategies can I implement to teach poetry?*
✦ *How can figurative language be taught?*
✦ *What strategies enhance literature?*

Author Reflection

Over the years, while teaching literature, I have been asked numerous times, why do we have to learn about this? I have even encountered parents who were curious about the importance of literature, while also suggesting that our time be more wisely spent teaching factual information and current events instead of learning about things or events that aren't even real. Of course

I responded with a logical explanation, while on the inside, I couldn't help but feel that the question of why teach literature was ludicrous. Why wouldn't you teach literature to expand students' knowledge, creativity, enhance comprehension, teach culture, reading skills, problem-solving, critical thinking, analytical thinking, entertainment, to foster the love of reading, and so many other beneficial reasons.

I reminded my students, and assured their parents, that literature is important. I explain the diverse ways that literature really does contribute to a student's education, explaining to them that through requiring them to read rich literature, I am encouraging them to use and foster their critical thinking skills, strengthen their reading and writing skills, and also encouraging them to gain a better understanding of the real-world. For example, diverse cultures are built on stories. Stories are in forms of myths, legends, fables, religions, and etc. By learning about culture through engaging rich literature, students are enhancing their critical thinking skills, vocabulary, cultural experiences, finding a great source of entertainment, preparing for standardized and state mandated tests, while also learning to appreciate, understand, and also learning to live in their own culture through gaining insight and knowledge of the multitude of cultures within society today.

Consider the following statement: *school should be a place where students read what they would not normally read on their own*. Let's face it, in the *"microwave society"* of instant gratification, reading is not always on the top of students' priority list. Requiring students to read and discuss diverse rich literature in school, ensures that students are at least being exposed to, and have some experience with literature. Secondly, when students are discussing literature in collaborative groups or engaging in whole-class discussions, they are able to hear other students' perspectives about the story, character(s), or plot, which may also lead to the refining of their own understanding of the topic at hand, while gaining valuable collaboration skills and learning from their peers.

While teaching sixth grade language arts, I always encouraged students to read deep and wide in order to experience different cultures, diverse societies, and explore the unknown. One particular young man springs into my mind when I think about the importance of literature. This young man was a student who performed at an average level, but had the talent and intellect to be far more than average. He was a bit on the lazy side, he didn't willingly participate during class conversations, appeared disinterested in the content, and always appeared sleepy. He was also a former first-grade student in my class several years prior and displayed many of the same qualities that he displayed during his sixth-grade year then too. It was a constant battle then to motivate him, and a continued daily struggle to find something that interested him, engaged him, or motivated him. However, I found that once he was motivated, interested, or simply wanted to apply himself, he was an above average student. I saw a great potential in this student, even if he didn't see it within himself.

During his sixth grade year we were reading and exploring a wide variety of genres when I noticed that he had taken a particular liking to Greek mythology in a short story which we were reading. As educators say, the light-bulb came on, not for him, but for me. I began to scour the library shelves for books containing **Greek mythology**, seek the advice of secondary English teachers, and pull a few favorites from my own personal library. I gave a considerable amount of thought to how I would approach the student with my idea. I finally decided that I would make the books available, as a ***genre bulletin board*** with exciting and captivating blurbs, pictures, and reviews. I also displayed books from each genre on a shelf beneath the bulletin board, making them available to students through a classroom checkout app on their smartphones, which also intrigued and enticed them, and added another layer of technology in our class.

I had high hopes that this would encourage all students to read and explore diverse genres. I explained that I would not require a written report about the books, but would really like for them to post a review of the books they read on our classroom website. The books vanished off the shelf at a fast rate. While some students returned books unread or half-finished, other students kept books for weeks and returned them completely finished with enthusiastic smiles and positive comments. One day I noticed the young man who had inspired the genre bulletin board taking an interest in a book about Greek mythology. My heart felt like it took a leap as I waited and hoped he wouldn't return the book to the shelf. I was beyond pleased when he left my classroom with a book tucked carefully under his arm.

One week later, he returned the book and quietly picked up a second book. Anxiously, I checked the classroom website for book reviews. Slowly they began to trickle in, and after about four weeks of anticipation, the young man's book review had been posted. *He was hooked!* This same young man devoured every book about Greek Mythology he could find, explored fantasy science-fiction that contained mythical creatures, and even explored and read some historical fiction as well. This once unmotivated student, flourished through middle school, and high-school, he performed in theater in high-school and went on to attend college, where he also participated in theater.

I admit, I lost track of him after a number of years after he graduated from public school, but I must say that over the course of his years as a student, both inside my class and beyond, we had many wonderful and meaningful conversations about literature, Greek mythology, and about life in general. I am, and will always be, eternally grateful that I did not give up, or give in to this student just being an average student who didn't have a desire to read, write, or perform. I knew deep down inside of him, he was an above average student with much talent to explore, and tremendous talent to offer the world.

Reading literature with students is a grand opportunity for teachers to implement reading strategies, thought-processing strategies, writing strategies, practice fluency, increase comprehension, enhance critical thinking, foster the love of reading, encourage peer collaboration, allow students to view literature from diverse perspectives, create projects that are representative of the literature they are reading, enhance test-taking skills, increase standardized test scores, and so much more (InTASC Standard 7, CCSSO). Literature is not simply about a character, or time-period, or even the genre. We, as high-powered teachers, must teach the child and integrate skills, strategies, content, and most of all engage our students with power thinking, recalling, processing, applying, and creating through rich literature and inspiring literature content and literature strategies to ensure that our students are well-rounded, well-educated, and also **college, career, and life-ready**.

What Constitutes Quality Literature?

It has been said that for a book to be *"high-quality"* it must have literary merit and appeal to the reader(s). However, it can be difficult to classify and also make the claim that a piece of literature has literary merit. However, high-powered middle school teachers look for **quality literary features** when selecting texts that they warrant as being, *high-quality*, to assign for reading in their classrooms (InTASC Standard 4, CCSSO). Some of those features include the following:

+ *The **protagonist** is typically the age, or near the age of the target audience.*
+ *The **literary elements** consist of a believable **plot**, engaging writing style, and compelling themes.*
+ *The **theme** is age-appropriate and interesting to students and also allows them to make **real-world connections**.*

✦ *The text broadens understanding and perspective of the world and opens up new possibilities as well as the capacity for* **empathy***.*
✦ ***Characters*** *whom students can make connections with, visualize, relate to, and form relationships.*
✦ *Engaging and appropriate* ***dialogue****.*
✦ ***Descriptive writing*** *that compels the reader to want to read more.*

However, keep in mind that what an adult constitutes as being high-quality may not be the book that students would have selected. High-powered teachers know that in reality the high qualities are not what students base the criteria of their book choice on. Instead, students usually base books on referrals from friends, the cover, a familiar author, an interesting blurb on the back of the cover, and if the book has been, or planned to be, in movies.

Narrative Text

Narrative texts consist of stories that are fiction and also nonfiction. Narrative texts contain a *character(s)*, *setting*, *plot*, *point of view*, *style*, and *theme*. When high-powered teachers select a narrative text to implement in the classroom, they consider the reading skills required to understand the selection, and also the topic. They also consider the quality of the text to determine if it is appropriate for the intended skill(s) they plan to integrate with the text. For example, does the text promote critical thinking, could it be used to teach **cause and effect**? Would it enhance understanding of plot or theme? In other words, high-powered teachers seek out literature that they can integrate that interests their students, and also enhances the skill(s) they are currently or will be teaching. They seek out literature that helps their students master required standard-based skills, as well as life-skills (InTASC Standard 1, 4, 5, 7, & 8, CCSSO).

For example, high-powered teachers may integrate a text where the character is encountering a problem that students are encountering, could encounter, or one that their peers have encountered. Problems such as bullying, illness, overcoming a social issue, or the character may be facing the same problem that students have read about that is occurring in the real-world. In other words, they select texts that students may have some background knowledge about, an interest in the topic, or one they want students to create an interest in the topic to build background knowledge for future connections (InTASC Standard 5, CCSSO).

Literary Elements of Narrative Texts

High-powered teachers are readers and planners; they are reflective, and also diverse. High-powered teachers are not just readers, they are well read, and continually seek out new literature to incorporate in their content area. They are life-long learners who plan and design instruction, activities, and assignments around a wide-variety of literature (InTASC Standards 7, 8, & 9, CCSSO). High-powered teachers know that when the elements of literature are skillfully woven within a text, they consider the book to have literary merit. They carefully select texts to implement in their curriculum to encourage student's reading, writing, further their knowledge of literature, enhance their vocabulary, while also meeting the needs of all learners, learning styles, and learning levels (InTASC Standards 2, 4, 5, & 7, CCSSO).

Style

Style refers to how the author conveys their message, in other words, the author's personal and distinctive way of writing. High-powered teachers know that style is reflective in the author's choice of words, how they arrange the words, and how the sentence is constructed. An author's unique writing style is also evident in how their story comes together, in what makes the character(s) come alive, in the setting, and what makes the plot convincing, compelling, and what draws the reader to the inside of the story. An author's writing style creates and sets the mood, or the atmosphere, the story, the tone, and also the pace of the story.

High-powered teachers explore the use of style in literature to help their students understand how language conveys images, mood, and also meaning, while enhancing their own writing skills as well. Examining the author's style of writing enables students to dig deeper into the text, and look closely at particular literary elements to consider and think about how the author crafted the story. High-powered teachers select literature that purposefully requires students to explore the use of words, phrases, and clauses in particular literary passages (InTASC Standard 7, CCSSO).

High-powered teachers also guide their students through the process of developing their own unique style of writing through everyday opportunities to explore reading rich narratives. They seek out texts that contain characters that have the ability to draw the reader inside the plot, a timeline of interesting events that encourages the reader to delve deeper, read closer, make connections, want to know more, and also question the author. They implement texts that have compelling plots, rich characters, and texts that have identifiable traits that signify the author's unique writing style (InTASC Standards 4, 5, & 7, CCSSO).

Point of View

High-powered teachers also implement compelling activities, engaging experiencing, and interesting text to teach students about point of view (InTASC Standard 7, CCSSO). They know that **point of view** is also a very important component of style. Point of view is the position the narrator assumes in telling the story. Most stories are written from **first person point of view**, which is told with the word, I. First person is used when the main character is telling the story. The reader can only experience the story through this person's eyes, which allows the reader to know about the characters/people or the events that this character, *I*, has personally experienced.

Third person point of view is used when the narrator is not a character in the story. Third person also uses the words, *he* or *she* and sometimes, the word *it*. There are **three main types of third person point of view**. **Third person limited** means that the point of view is limited to only one character. **Third person multiple point of view** is still in the *he*, *she*, or *it* category, but the narrator can now follow multiple characters within the story. This can be a challenge for the reader, as the reader must be able to determine when the point of view is changing from one character to another character. **Third person omniscient is the point of view** that still uses *he*, *she*, or *it* in narration, but now the narrator knows it all. The narrator isn't limited by what an individual character knows, and also knows what other characters may not know. High-powered teachers know that students enjoy writing from third person omniscient, simply because it flows more naturally, but they teach and encourage students to write in all three types of third person point of view (InTASC Standards 4 & 5, CCSSO).

Setting

Setting is *where and when the story takes place*. The story can be set in the ***present, past***, or in the ***future***. High-powered teachers know that the setting directly affects the plot, characters, and the theme of the story. Setting helps initiate the main backdrop and mood for the story. Setting elements allow the reader to time-travel, embark on, and experience *cultural adventures*, *historical adventures*, and also *futuristic adventures*. High-powered teachers integrate literature that encourages students to explore and interact with the text and to learn about topics such as diverse regions, neighborhoods, weather, historical events, the future, and also diverse cultures that students otherwise may not have the opportunities to explore or even experience. They know that literature can enrich and enhance students' understanding of the world around them today, gain insight into history that helped shape the world, while also providing them with opportunities to explore the future (InTASC Standard 4, CCSSO).

Character

High-powered teachers know that the **character(s)** in a story must be *well-developed, believable*, and one that the reader can make *connections* with. In other words, authors must create characters that the reader can become involved with and also care about, or characters they dislike. High-powered teachers select literature that contains rich characters students will either love or love to hate (InTASC Standard 4 & 7, CCSSO). Characters can compel the reader or discourage the reader. When a character drives the reader and inspires them to return to the pages, or continue reading a series, the author has created a well-developed character.

High-powered teachers not only know the importance of **characters** in literature, they teach their students about the various types of characters a story may include (InTASC Standard 4 & 7, CCSSO). Character can be defined as *any person*, *animal*, or even a *figure represented in literature*. There are many types of characters that exist in literature, each possessing their own development and also their own function. Characters serve particular roles in literature. For example, the **protagonist** is the character responsible for handling the *main problem*, and also the one in *most need of change*, while the **antagonist** is typically the *bad guy* in the story. The antagonist is the character that *opposes the protagonist* outright on all counts, physically, and also emotionally. Other character roles include the ***mentor, tempter, sidekick, skeptic***, and the ***emotional*** and ***logical character***.

The role of the **mentor** is often carefully woven into the story as being the ***protagonists' conscience***. The mentor voices or represents the lesson that must be learned by the protagonist, in order to change for the betterment, or to achieve the goal. The character role of the **tempter** is often the *right-hand* to the antagonist. The tempter doesn't need to know the antagonist, but they both stand for and represent the same thing, which is usually stopping the protagonist from achieving the protagonist's goal. The tempter often tries to manipulate and convince the protagonist to join the *"other side*, or the *dark side."* However, in the end, the tempter can also change his or her, or its mind to realize that the benefits of joining the good guys prevail.

The character role of the **sidekick** is that of the protagonist's unconditionally loving friend. The character of the sidekick can become frustrated with the protagonist, and even have doubts, but will always stand by the side of the protagonist in the end. Often, the sidekick embodies the theme without even realizing it. The **skeptic**, however, is the *lone objector*. The skeptic does not believe in theme or the importance of the protagonist achieving his or her goal. The skeptic is on their own path alone, without loyalties to the protagonist. Keep in the mind that the skeptic may not even like the protagonist or want the protagonist to succeed, they may display jealousy, envy, or voice their opinion at the cost of their own goal. However, the skeptic can have a change of heart as well.

The role of the **emotional** character acts according to their instincts and allows their motions and emotions to fuel decisions. They are *impulsive* and *reactive* and sometimes the emotional character is right and succeeds in ways that a thinking person would never have tried, but the emotional character may also experience trouble or reap the repercussions of leaping before thinking. The role of the **logical character** is the *rational thinker*. The character who *plans* things out, seeks out *logical solutions*, and also gives *reasonable, matter of fact answers to questions*. However, the logical character can sometimes deepen the understanding within the reader that the head needs to also listen to the heart to work at its best.

Plot

High-powered teachers know that **plot** also drives a story (InTASC Standard 4, CCSSO). *Plot is the action of the story* and usually consists of a *beginning, rising action/middle, climax, and falling action or resolution*. For a plot to be complete it must have a conflict of some kind. The resolution of that conflict should carry through the conclusion. Plots also have pacing, which refers to the how quickly the action moves, it can be steady throughout the story, or move at a faster or slower pace. Plot also contains *suspense* and *tension*. These create a *level of interest* in the plot, thus enticing the reader to continue reading. Good authors create a plot that is natural and not contrived of coincidental incidents, which in turn makes the plot more believable.

Theme

High-powered teachers know that students often have difficulty determining the **theme of literature**. *Theme is basically the central idea of the entire story*. The idea that lies beneath the surface of the story. High-powered teachers select literature with themes that students can connect with and have identifiable traits, to teach theme. They incorporate literature with themes such as overcoming fear, themes of friendship, or acceptance. However, the theme should not overpower or dictate the plot or characters (InTASC Standards 1, 5, & 7, CCSSO).

High-powered teachers find creative ways to teach the elements of literature to help students gain a vivid understanding of each element, while also exposing them to cultural opportunities, rich characters, and compelling plots (InTASC Standards 1, 2, 4, 7, & 8, CCSSO). High-powered teachers incorporate interactive engaging semantic maps that allow students to dissect, analyze, and determine the elements of literature through mapping. Semantic maps serve as an aid for the visual leaner, as well as an engaging activity that can be completed in collaborative groups, peer-to-peer, independently, or as a whole-group activity. Nevertheless, high-powered teachers involve, engage, and activate students thinking in multiple daily opportunities to expand their knowledge, instill confidence, and help them to better understand literature as well as apply what they know to create literature-based as well as standard-based projects such as slideshows, written essays, student performances, art, and much more (InTASC Standards 5, 7, & 8, CCSSO).

Expository Text

High-powered teachers not only know that most elementary students are exposed to, and have read, a fair amount of **expository text**, but also know that they have read more narrative text. However, they also know that it isn't until middle-school or even high-school that students are expected and required to read more expository text than narrative text, and often are required to compare and contrast the two (InTASC Standard 4, CCSSO). Students know to expect characters, plots, and other literary elements in a narrative text. Whereas, with expository text, the reader is involved with text that can sometimes be quite challenging for young readers. The structure of the text is different, the concepts are often difficult, and the vocabulary becomes specialized, as well as the presentation of the material is not always predictable, which often causes students to lose interest, focus, and become disengaged.

Expository text *informs the reader through explanations, compare/contrast, problem/solution, and also through definition/example*. High-powered teachers guide and instruct students how to recognize the patterns listed above. Expository, unlike narrative text, has very few cues to prompt the reader. High-powered teachers strive to meet students' academic needs dealing with expository text. Needs such as *study skills, organizational skills,* and *referencing skills* are vital to guide students through expository text. Expository text does not always appeal to students as it does not have a compelling plot with rich characters. However, there are some students that enjoy reading expository text and have little to no difficulty reading, exploring, analyzing, or referencing the text. But for those student who do not read and process expository text with such ease, high-powered teachers incorporate tools and activities that guide and help students to better be able to understand expository text (InTASC Standards 4, 7, & 8, CCSSO).

They know that difficult text should be graphically organized with *outlines* or *semantic maps*. They also encourage students to *annotate* while reading, make *double-sided journal entries, split-notes*, which can also double as study guides. High-powered teachers know that the use of study guides will help students sort, categorize, and process the most important information within the text (InTASC Standard 4, CCSSO). High-powered teachers incorporate articles from accredited websites, newspapers, scholarly magazines, and other supplementary sources that provide an overview of content that delves deep within the vein of ideas and events that teachers and student both like, but that also encourages *critical thinking, problem-solving, connects* to real-life situations, and also promotes reading, factual information, *information processing skills,* and **written expression** while meeting the cultural needs of students as well as the needs of all learning style, or reading levels (InTASC Standard 2, CCSSO).

Genres

High-powered middle-school teachers know the importance of teaching students about the various **genres** of literature (InTASC Standard 1, CCSSO). The main categories that actually separate the diverse genres of literature include **poetry**, **drama, prose**, **fiction**, and **nonfiction**. A genre is a broad term that translates from the French to mean "kind" or "type." Each genre varies in *style, structure, subject matter,* and also in the use of *figurative language*. Genres also raise certain expectations in what the reader anticipates will happen within the text. It is important to know which category/genre a piece of literature is classified as, simply because the reader will already have a certain amount of expectations based on the criteria of the genre, before he or she even begins to read the selection.

High-powered teachers know the importance of teaching the different roles of genres (InTASC Standard 4, CCSSO). They may select *drama* and *fiction* genres to enhance students reading and writing skills, as well as their communication skills. Whereas, teachers might incorporate poetry to enhance students' *imagination, figurative language,* and their ability to read and make *inferences*, rather than rely on literal information. For example, students read and allow their imagination, connections, and their emotions to guide them, rather than the facts within a text. Reading poetry can help students learn to read between the lines to gain insight into what the author is implying. Whereas, nonfictional texts and essays help students/readers to develop *analytical* and *persuasive capabilities*. Keep in the mind that the primary purpose and function of each genre is not only to inform the reader, as well as entertain the reader, but also to establish connections, a form of behavior, and to create and establish a relationship between the author and the reader (InTASC Standard 1, CCSSO).

Poetry is also a main genre in literature. All poetry shares specific characterizations. For example, poetry is written in lines, and stanzas, instead of structured sentences and paragraphs. High-powered teachers guide students to help alleviate possible fear(s) they may have about poetry, and also to help them gain a better understanding about the rules and characteristics of poetry (InTASC Standard 1, 2, 4, 5, 6, & 7, CCSSO). For example, all poetry doesn't follow a strict set of rules about the number and length of lines or stanzas, and flow more freely. Whereas, other styles of poetry require a certain number of lines, a specified number of words per line, and certain ending words to rhyme, and are more structured. High-powered teachers often begin teaching poetry with less intimidating rules to help students gain confidence and feel more comfortable while learning about the genre of poetry (InTASC Standard 5, CCSSO).

Most poetry contains an abundance of **figurative language**. For example, poetry may contain ***similes, metaphors, hyperboles, personification, imagery, symbolism, onomatopoeias, alliteration, rhyme***, as well as other types of figurative language. Poetry requires thought, imagination, emotions, and heartfelt ideas. Often the reader has to *read figuratively*, while also making *inferences* and *interpretations*. High-powered teachers teach students that every reader may not have the same interpretation of a poem, as each reader may read the poem with their own unique and personal connections (InTASC Standard 2, CCSSO).

Poetry is usually shorter than the other genres. However, some poems may be classified as **epic poetry**, which is a long-narrative style poem chronicling heroic deeds, or serious subject matter. While other poems may contain less information and be complete in four to five lines. Poetry is expressive and can be written about any object, event, person, or animal. High-powered teachers review poetry, the elements, characteristics, types of poetry, and also read poetry with their students to help them gain insight, understanding, and prepare them for poetry that may be required of them in high-school, and also on standardized tests. They prepare them for a wide-variety of styles of poetry which may include but not be limited to *sonnets, ballads, elegies, haikus, melodramas, acrostic*, and also *free-verse/free-form*. High-powered middle-school teachers also enjoy poetry with their students, and allow them to use imagery to prompt them, write collaboratively, incorporate strategies that help them to grow in understanding and also give them multiple opportunities to analyze poetry, respond to poetry, and also create poetry (InTASC Standards, 1, 2, 3, 4, 5, 7, & 8, CCSSO).

Drama is a form of text that is performed in front of an audience. It is also referred to as a play. The written text contains dialogue, and also stage directions. Drama can be categorized in individual categories such as *comedy, tragedy*, or *tragicomedy*. High-powered teachers create lessons that allow students to explore various types of drama through the use of videos, written text, hands-on experiences, engaging in collaborative activities such as Readers' Theater, and also creating and performing their own drama. High-powered teachers know that student performance also allows them to assess students' speaking and listening skills, as well as critique their written and social skills (InTASC Standard 6, CCSSO). They also know that allowing students to be creative and expressive enhances students' collaborative skills as well as classroom rapport, while also preparing them for in-depth drama that they will be required to read (InTASC 3, 4, & 5, CCSSO). Dramas could include *Taming of the Shrew*, *Romeo & Juliet*, *Hamlet*, or *Oedipus*.

Poetry and drama are not the only genres that incorporates figurative language. Fiction often incorporates the use of figurative language, which can be elaborated, simply because fiction isn't real and authors' can be as creative as they need to, or want to be while writing. **Fiction** is more structured than poetry, and can be defined as narrative literary works whose content is produced by imagination. Fiction is not necessarily based on fact. Fictional stories can consist of *imaginary* or *invented characters* and *plots*. In other words, fiction stories are usually made up stories, but can also be based on factual information. Fiction can be characterized into three broad categories that include *realistic*, *nonrealistic*, and *semi-fiction*. A fictional work may incorporate *fantastical* or *imaginary ideas* from everyday life, but nevertheless, each work of fiction includes a *plot*, *characters*, *setting*, *exposition*, *foreshadowing*, *rising action*, *climax*, *falling action*, and some type of *resolution*.

Traditional fiction also includes *folk tales*, *fairy tales*, *myths*, and *legends* as well as *tall tales*, and *fables*. Other subcategories of fiction include the ever-popular, genre of fantasy. **Fantasy fiction** is highly imaginative which contains highly imaginative worlds where anything is possible. Fantasy science fiction is also popular among middle-school students. High-powered teachers encourage students to read in all genres, including fantasy, as they know that students have to think in a nonliteral manner, figuratively, and also use their imaginations, and think futuristic. They also know how difficult fantasy literature can be, as it requires imagination, thinking beyond the obvious, and also often follows a rigorous multidimensional plot with rich characters (InTASC Standard 4, CCSSO).

Whereas **realistic fiction** often involve plots, characters, and events that are similar to and within the realm of possibility of reality. High-powered teachers know that middle-school students enjoy realistic fiction, as they usually can make real-life connections with the characters, or the plot. **Historical fiction** is another subcategory of fiction that high-powered teachers incorporate and encourage students to read. Historical fiction can be incorporated as supplemental reading in social studies or history class as it is based on historical figures, eras of time, as well as historical events, regardless the genre, or the category. High-powered teachers are well-read, and explore diverse genres and texts to integrate in their classrooms to further students' knowledge, and also prepare them for their academic future, while also fostering the love of reading within them (InTASC Standards 4, 7, 8, & 9 CCSSO).

High-powered teacher know that **nonfiction** is a vast category that also has *subgenres* such as *personal essays*, *biographies*, *memoirs*, *journals*, *articles*, *informational books*, *speeches*, *diaries*, *autobiographies*, and more. They teach their students to recognize and know the characteristics of nonfiction includes *deals with real-events*, and *real people*, *characters* and *settings* and *events come from what is true*, the story *is not manipulated by the author's imagination*, in other words, the author *states the facts*, and tells it as it is, with the events being true rather than imagined. High-powered middle-school teachers strive to find interesting nonfiction text that students can relate to and are interested in to teach the elements of nonfiction, as well as promote reading skills, thinking skills, and enhance content knowledge (InTASC Standards, 1, 4, 5, 7, & 8, CCSSO).

Prose is also a genre of literature and encompasses any literary text which is not arranged in a poetic form. In other words, prose is the opposite of poetry. Prose contains sentences, paragraphs, and also includes forms of writing such as novels, short stories, journals, letters, and can also be classified in both fiction and nonfiction, depending on the content. High-powered teachers incorporate prose in their classrooms in various formats, to meet various academic standards. For example, high-powered teachers may require students to reflect in journals after completing projects, or assignments. They may also ask them to write short stories when working on characterization or plot. They know that the academic learning possibilities from incorporating prose in any content area are unlimited (InTASC Standards 4 & 7, CCSSO).

> *"When teachers involve their students in the learning process...they empower them with knowledge and skills that they will carry with them for the rest of their lives."*
>
> *~ Dr. Joyce Bowling*

Promoting Literature Through Literacy Strategies

High-powered teachers incorporate a wide-variety of literacy strategies in their classrooms to promote literature, enhance reading skills, enhance content, expand vocabulary and also increase reading comprehension, as well as insight to the diverse genres of literature, and more (InTASC Standard 7 & 8, CCSSO). They incorporate literacy strategies before reading, during reading, and after reading, depending on the reason for the strategy or activity.

High-powered middle-school teachers implement literacy strategies *before reading* to help prepare the students for the type of literature they are going to read, and also to prepare them for what they will be required to do once they've read the text. Strategies that are incorporated *during reading* are planned to encourage students to *think deeply*, *read closely*, *answer questions*, *analyze* the text, *look beneath the surface of the text itself*, and to *read between the lines* to gain insight into what the author is trying to convey. While strategies that are implemented *after reading* the text allow the teacher to determine if students understood *what they read*, *can apply* what they have learned, and also *create* projects, *complete assignments*, and use the knowledge that they gained from the text correctly. In other words, every strategy or activity is planned with an academic purpose in mind. They also promote *student engagement*, *classroom rapport*, *prepare students for standardized* or state *mandated assessments*, while also preparing them for the next grade-level (InTASC Standards 1.2,3, 4, 5, 6, 7, & 8, CCSSO). Strategies include but are not limited to the following.

Student Questions for Purposeful Learning

High-powered middle and secondary teachers strive to develop students' abilities to read, listen, and also learn with a purpose (InTASC Standard 7, CCSSO). They know that purposeful learning is associated and also connected to higher levels of engagement, which leads to higher levels of achievement. Purposeful learning guides students and helps them gain and maintain focus. High-powered teachers integrate purposeful learning strategies to make learning more engaging, help students to make connections, and also to enhance students' sustained attention span, and attention stamina (InTASC Standard 7 & 8, CCSSO). They incorporate **Student Questions for Purposeful Learning (SQPL)** as an approach designed to gain and hold students' interest in the material or topic that questions will be based on, and also required reading material. The theory behind SQPL is that students become more motivated as they pay more attention to the information source for answers to their questions.

SQPL begins with a teacher prompt to encourage, motivate, and also stimulate an interest, as well as inspire student questions, the process can become internalized, which leads students to

start questioning and also answering questions about the content independently. SQPL also provides a source of legitimate student-based questions that are valuable to students' learning. High-powered teachers know that students who participate in the SPQL strategy become the questioner, instead of being questioned. They encourage SPQL to be *implemented before reading*, as it reinforces students' desire to explore the text for the information that they want to know, and also explore ideas with a purpose and with focused attention. High-powered middle-school teachers follow the step-by-step guide, listed below, to incorporate the SPQL strategy:

1. Teachers review the material to be read and covered in the day's planned lesson. Then the teacher thinks of a statement related to the text that would pique students' curiosity, to cause them to wonder, that also challenge them and make them question the text. *Keep in mind that the statement doesn't have to be factual information, as long as it piques curiosity and is motivating.*

2. Present the statement to students or display it on the whiteboard, or have it copied on their handout, if one is being used.

3. Pair students with their partner and, based on the statement, generate up to three questions that the students would like to have answered. The questions must be related to the teacher statement.

4. When partners have thought of their questions, ask the partners to share their questions with the class.

5. Once students ask their questions orally, record the answers on the board. You, the teacher, will know when questions become repetitious. At this point, flag those questions with a star, or underline the number.

6. Once all of the students' questions has been shared and recorded, you may decide if further questions should be added. Additional questions may be necessary if students did not ask questions that are vital to the purpose of the text, or the information that you want them to learn. You may simply state that you also have a few questions, or keep the motivation high, by stating that their questions has created a few question of your own. (Students like to feel that they inspire the teacher.)

7. At this point ask students to review the questions silently to themselves, if they are working independently, if they are working with a peer one can read quietly to the other. Students will be ready for the information source (text) so they can seek out and search for the answers to their questions. Explain to them as they read to pay close attention to information that helps answer a question that is written on the board. They should also be especially specifically focused on material that pertains to the questions that you flagged, as these questions could be considered class consensus questions.

8. Require students to periodically stop and discuss the text with their partners. If students are working independently, they should stop and reflect on the text periodically. Partners can also discuss the answers to their questions, and also volunteer to share with the class.

9. High-powered teachers also ask students to maintain a copy of their questions and answers to use as a study guide before taking an assessment.

High-powered teachers incorporate the SQPL strategy with multiple genres, but find it to be very beneficial with nonfiction text. They know the diverse value and the effectiveness of this strategy, as it is a great source for differentiating for multiple reading levels, diverse learning styles, and also a great way to scaffold instruction to help meet the needs of all students

(InTASC Standard 2, CCSSO). SQPL is also a very good strategy to enhance students' vocabulary, comprehension, questioning techniques, as well as their critical thinking. Student questions for purposeful learning can be implemented in all content areas, which also promotes closer content reading in all content areas.

Opinionnaire

High-powered teachers incorporate **opinionnaires** as a strategy and also a tool that elicits attitudes about a specified topic. High-powered middle-school teachers typically incorporate an opinionnaire as a *pre-reading strategy/activity* to promote and encourage students to consider and also evaluate the authors' use of important themes and ideas by helping them to connect literature to life.

High-powered teachers know that opinionnaires have been used by teachers for many years and has been modified to fit the needs of the content, students, and also grade-level (InTASC Standard 4, 7, & 8, CCSSO). Nevertheless, incorporating opinionnaires is a method of seeking students' opinions about a specific topic. High-powered teachers' alter the format to fit their instructional purpose. However, most opinionnaires' consist of a series of statements that are meant to be enticing or even controversial. Nevertheless, the statements or questions should promote a curiosity within the reader. They also do not allow for a neutral response, but rather requires a statement of agree or disagree. Other responses can include strongly agree, agree, disagree, or strongly disagree. It is optional to leave a space for students to leave a reason for their answer.

Finally, high-powered teachers incorporate opinionnaires for various reasons and implement them in several different ways. They may use the instrument as a pre-and post-reading activity, where students can express a change of opinion based on new information. High-powered teachers also find them beneficial to use to ask for thoughts about a character(s) in a novel. Nevertheless, high-powered teachers in all content areas know that an opinionnaire is a tool that helps them gain insight into students' thoughts about a topic, character, text, and etc. while also encouraging students to think analytical, reflect, and make connections to the text and to life. They also know that opinionnaires offer student opportunities to voice their opinions. Step-by-step instructions are listed as follows:

1. Teachers will create an opinionnaire of typically 10 statements. This allows students time to think carefully about their opinions rather than rushing too quickly through a long list. The statements should be stated in a bold manner that is worthy of a debate or deep discussion.
2. Decide how you want students to respond. Will you allow them to respond through agree or disagree only or will you include strongly agree, agree, disagree, or strongly disagree? This can be modified by the teacher to fit the purpose of the opinionnaire.
3. Consider whether you want students to explain their answers. Keep in mind that insight into their reasons for their answers can be valuable for you to better understand their reasons, and to design upcoming lessons. Reasons also promote the desire to debate, and can cause others to rethink their answers, or even defend their point of view.
4. Teachers may also want to make the opinionnaire anonymous so that you can elicit more authentic answers. Keep in mind that some students will provide more honest answers, depending on the topic, if they are not required to provide their name.

5. Opinionnaires generally lead to great discussion naturally when given adequate time. Be sure to review the rules for classroom discussions or debates. Remind them that everyone's opinions are valued, and also that there isn't a right wrong opinion.

6. Select a reading to follow the opinionnaire. The opinionnaire is meant to inspire and encourage their interpretive reasoning and also help them reflect on and also gain background knowledge. The text should be interesting and thought-provoking about the statements in the opinionnaires as well as provide new information that they can consider.

7. Once students have read the assigned material, follow up with further discussion about the assigned topic. Encourage all students to use evidence from text to support their reasons, or their arguments. The follow up discussion will differ from the first discussion, as students should now have textual evidence to support their opinion.

8. Finally, give students the opportunity to rethink or revisit their opinions. You may administer a new opinionnaire, or simply provide an opinion before and after reading opinion on the first opinionnaire. Students should revisit their first response and determine any changes in their beliefs, opinions, and also their reasons listed.

9. Ask students to write a brief reflection of their experience explaining their original opinions and as well as what they have learned, confirmed, or changes that may have occurred through reading the text, and why. (This step is optional, but reinforces written expression, reflective thinking, and also allows students to measure their growth.)

High-powered teachers implement opinionnaires typically when working with expository or nonfiction text. They use it as *pre-reading activity*, and follow up by administering the opinionnaire a second time as *post-reading activity* (InTASC Standard 6, CCSSO). High-powered teachers also know that opinionnaires can be scaffold to fit the needs of all learners and also promote critical thinking, enhance reading comprehension, as well as vocabulary. Opinionnaires can also be incorporated in all content areas and be modified to fit the needs of all students, regardless the learning style, learning level, or grade-level (InTASC Standard 2, CCSSO).

Annotations

High-powered teachers teach their students to annotate while they are reading. **Annotation** is a form of notetaking. Students annotate while they read and write notes directly on the text. Annotation has been referred to as reading with a pen, or pencil. High-powered teachers encourage their students to annotate as they know that annotating helps students to *recall important information*, *key details*, *deepen their understanding* of the text, and also make and establish *connections*. They know that annotations promote reading comprehension, while also enhancing students' writing (InTASC Standard 4, 7 & 8, CCSSO). High-powered teachers teach students how to annotate by doing the following:

+ *Underlining* major or key points.
+ Placing *parenthesis or a bracket* around longer statements that are too long to underline.
+ Placing an *asterisk* in the margin to emphasize the top ten most important statements.
+ Placing *numbers* in the margin to signify a sequence of major points made by the author in the development of an argument.

✦ *Circling* important phrases or keywords that serves much like underlining, but can allow the reader to distinguish the difference between major points and keywords.

✦ Writing *questions* that may spring to mind while reading in the top or bottom margin.

1. High-powered teachers give explicit instruction about each of the above types of annotations to help students become familiar with them, and know when to incorporate them.

2. High-powered teachers make copies of the text available for every student to practice annotation, and also when annotation is required while they read.

3. High-powered teachers circulate around the room to provide assistance where needed when students are learning to annotate.

4. High-powered teachers collect students' annotation to determine if they are annotating correctly. They also take this opportunity to formatively assess their students, as well as plan their future instruction and determine if they should reteach a part of annotation.

Again, high-powered teachers teach and model the process of annotation, and also provide students with multiple opportunities to practice annotating. They know that annotating encourages students to read close, think deep, make connections, pick out keywords, important information, while also enhancing their reading comprehension as well as their vocabulary. High-powered teachers know that annotating engages the students with the text and is a beneficial skill that they will use throughout school, and also in the real-world. High-powered teachers also know that annotation can be beneficial for students understanding in all genres, but find it very beneficial with nonfiction text.

Character Analysis Maps

Character analysis maps take on many different shapes, sizes, and forms, but nevertheless, the purpose remains the same, to gain a better understanding of a character(s). High-powered teachers incorporate character analysis maps both *during and after reading a text* (InTASC 4, 6, & 8, CCSSO). While students are reading a story they can complete a character map as they determine important information about the character. Character maps can also be completed after reading, which requires the student to reflect, recall, and then complete the map. Character maps can include external characteristics of a character as well as their internal characteristics, which requires students to make inferences about the characters personality based on what they know from the text. High-powered teachers require more than just a word, they also ask students to add textual evidence as to why they have documented on the character map that a character has a temper. Or a student may state that a character has an empathetic heart, or a love for children. With each character trait that a student lists, they must give an explanation of their reason for adding the trait, and also add textual evidence.

Character analysis maps may appear as webbing, a diagram, or a graph. Nevertheless, character maps encourage students to read close with a purpose, make inferences, and engage with the text. High-powered teachers encourage character maps in narratives, fiction, and also an occasional nonfiction text such as a biography. They also encourage students to go beyond the map and ask them to reflect on the story, their map, and write a brief reflection entry in their journal describing the character in written form incorporating rich adjectives as they describe their character(s).

Take 6

High-powered middle-school and high-school teachers know the value and benefits of engaging their students with a wide variety of strategies and activities that enhance their understanding of a topic, increase their reading, writing, and speaking skills, and also promote problem-solving, analytical thinking, critical thinking and much more (InTASC Standards 7 & 8, CCSSO). However, they also know that instruction time is valuable as well as limited with the large number of students that they teach daily. High-powered teachers incorporate a strategy referred to as, **Take 6**, *after reading* to increase students reading comprehension, expand their vocabulary, and also enhance peer-collaboration after reading an assigned text. They implement **Take 6** by completing the following simple steps:

1. High-powered teachers provide students with a few minutes to review the assigned task, and the reading material. This can be modified to fit the need of any genre. For example, a teacher may require students to read a fictional short story that involves two characters or read a chapter of a novel that includes two characters. They may ask students to describe the two characters in short statements for Take 6.
2. High-powered teachers ask students to partner with their assigned classmate, and then give each team a pair of dice.
3. They ask both team mates to roll a dice, with the student who rolls the largest number begins the written review of the character, or specified assignment. The first student continues writing while the second student continues to rolls the dice.
4. When the student rolling the dice lands on six, the partners then change roles, allowing the second student to write, while the first student rolls the dice.
5. Students change roles each time the dice lands on six. The option is for both students to record as many key points about the text, the character, or the assigned task, as they can write in the predetermined amount of time that is set before students begin. Most teachers display the time on the smartboard and typically allow 6 minutes for this brief but beneficial activity.

Language Link

High-powered teachers require students to read in all genres and also create in all genres. They provide students with multiple hands-on activities that include collaborative activities where students engage with peers to explore and create in diverse genres, while also providing them multiple opportunities to compete independent daily work and independent assignments/projects. Nevertheless, each opportunity is created with a purpose. Integrating daily opportunities to help strengthen students' knowledge and understanding of language arts is at the top of high-powered middle-school teachers' list of priorities (InTASC Standards 1, 4, 5, 6, 7, & 8, CCSSO).

For example, high-powered language art teachers require their students to write in their journal daily, complete daily journal entries, which enhances their writing skills, as well as their use of mechanics. They guide, instruct, and model diverse genres of writing. For example, if the daily lesson is based on poetry, high-powered teachers require students to create a specified style of poetry that will also serve as their daily reflection/journal entry. Students may be required to describe the lesson through an acrostic poem, if that was the style of poetry they learned about that day. If the daily lesson was about narrative poetry, then high-powered teachers would require their students to write a narrative style poem reflecting on what they had learned in the daily lesson(s), and etc.

In other words, high-powered teachers base the daily writing on the genre that students are currently learning about. This ensures that students are experiencing the genre through lecture, modeling, hands-on activities/strategies, and also through written expressions. Thus, deepening their understanding of the genre, enhancing their writing skills, and also giving them daily opportunities to explore and create their own written work, while applying the characteristics of the genre they are learning about, as well as correct spelling, and appropriate mechanics. Daily journal writing can include fiction, nonfiction, and all of the subcategories of each. When students are given the opportunity to express themselves they are also making necessary connections to previously learned material, while exploring new possibilities. High-powered teachers know that journal entries are a *win–win situation* students are creating daily, which also provide them with samples of work that they can formatively assess to gain insight into upcoming instructions, as well as gain insight into how well students are progressing (InTASC Standard 6, CCSSO).

What Can Parents Do to Help?

Middle-school reading content can be challenging for some students, even the student who is "the reader" who reads freely without being told to. Middle-school is a time during students' academic career when they are required to read more sophisticated literature, and also use sophisticated reading skills such as analyzing literature. Reading becomes a powerful resource for students to locate information that helps make sense of complex material in all content areas. Therefore, high-powered middle-school teachers focus on refining and strengthening their students' existing reading skills. They also encourage and invite parental involvement with their child's academic journey (InTASC Standard 10, CCSSO).

First and foremost, high-powered teachers keep parents well-informed about their child's academic goals, the teachers' expectations, grades, progress, curriculum, both current and upcoming assignments, current reading material, and also about any and all assessments that their child will be required to take. They maintain a classroom website, create a newsletter, blog, or some method of contact to ensure that parents know about important dates, standards that their child is working to master, as well as current and upcoming assignments (InTASC Standard 10, CCSSO).

High-powered teachers welcome parents' feedback and offer suggestions to parents through their chosen method of contact with ideas of how to help or encourage their children to strategically read with a purpose when they're reading at home. They provide weekly reading skills and strategies to help strengthen their child's reading. For example, a high-powered teacher wouldn't only post that her or his class would be working on analyzing characters next week. They would explain the purpose of analyzing characters, the importance of this topic, what a character analysis map is, provide an example, and offer suggestions of how parents could help their child with analyzing characters. Research shows that many middle-school parents want to help their child, but are not sure how to help them. High-powered middle-school teachers ensure that parents are informed and have the information and tools necessary to help their child accomplish tasks, meet goals, and to be academically successful.

You may be thinking that the above example is quite a bit of work. You might even be wondering when you would have time to maintain a classroom website or blog. High-powered teachers

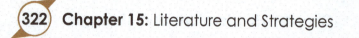

make time to ensure that they are doing everything possible to ensure that their students not only succeed, but also go above and beyond and exceed their expectations to master the required skills necessary for academic progress, prepare them to be college-and career-ready, as well as prepare them for the real-world. Be the high-powered middle-school teacher that parents will thank for keeping them informed, equipped, and also accountable for helping their child be prepared for what awaits them both inside the classroom and in the world.

> *"I have a love for reading, whether it's a book, article, a complete work of fiction, informational, or even a simple essay. Regardless the content I read, when finished, I have gained knowledge, and that excites me."*
>
> ~ *Mr. Tom Hurt*

Author's Tip(s)

One of the greatest gifts that a child can receive is to have a caring and nurturing teacher as well as loving involved parent(s) or guardians that support and motivate them both at home and inside the classroom. However, in the real-world we know that every student does not have a nurturing, loving, or even a supportive home life. Research shows that the majority of students whose parents were involved in their education performed better in the classroom and also on assessments. So, what do we, as teachers, do to supplement for those students who are lacking in support and involvement from home? I found that partnering students with a peer or with a mentoring teacher was very beneficial. I interviewed colleagues and ask them if they would be willing to be a mentor for a student or two students in the aspect of being available for questions, offering advice, periodically checking on their assigned student(s), and being there to listen. I was overwhelmed with the number of teachers who were willing to take a little time out of their busy week to ensure the students who were not receiving help at home, or from a relative, received what they needed from them. This act of kindness proved to be very beneficial on students grades, attitudes, and also beneficial for the teacher. Several teachers adopted this same policy and soon were asking other teachers to be a mentor for students. As a whole, our school was also able to see a visible difference. A little time, caring, consideration, guidance, and just being available to listen goes a long way.

Additionally, I wanted to suggest a style of poetry that I used to introduce my sixth-grade students to the genre of with. They found it fun, less intimidating than diving right into analyzing poetry, or writing poetry that had strict rules or characteristics. I read, *Where I'm From*, written by George Ella Lyon (Kentucky Arts Council). The students' response was overwhelming and also unanimous. They loved the poem! I then asked students to brainstorm and create and complete an organizer that was filled with facts that described them, much like Lyon's poem described him. They followed the writing process and in the end produced their own unique poem that described them. I asked students to read their poem with the class and also peer-assess each other as they read aloud. This simple poetry lesson opened up doors to many deep discussions about poetry, projects, more poetry being written, and soon the fear and intimidation of poetry had subsided in the majority of the students.

With each new style of poetry that we discussed, read, analyzed, and wrote...the love of poetry grew within the students. I felt confident as we approached testing time where I knew that it was highly possible that students would be faced with reading a poem and comparing it to a narrative on their state-mandated test. I felt confident they would master the skills necessary to advance to the next grade-level equipped with the necessary knowledge to be successful there as well. I also had hopes that they would carry with them the desire to continue reading and writing poetry throughout their educational career and as an adult.

I would like to leave you with a final tip about annotation. I realize how difficult time management is in modern classrooms. Time is probably the resource that teachers lack the most. I found that it was even difficult to find time to make copies, or that I had exceeded the number of copies that I was allotted for the month, to make copies of the text that I wanted my students to have to practice annotation. I soon discovered that students of all ages loved using self-stick notes. They were even a bit more excited about applying the annotations to the sticky notes than directly on the text. This was not a perfect solution, but it helped students to read closer with purpose, and then gradually gravitate to annotating directly within the text and in the margins of the text. I kept sticky notes as it was one of my required items on my supply list, and many students enjoyed bringing their own notes. This was a great time saver that proved to be very beneficial to students' annotating skills. It also alleviated the pressure and concerns of making mistakes when writing directly on the text, as they were disposable and also flexible to be moved from location to location.

Be the high-powered teacher that thinks outside the box, continues learning, researching, mentoring, and reading with their students, as well as writing with their students. Attain and maintain contact with parents, collaborate with your colleagues, and get involved in the bigger picture within your school. Strive to make each academic year better than the year before. Grow with your students as you learn with them. Be motivating, inspiring, dedicated, build classroom rapport, and most of all respect and love what you do, and why you do it. Be the best high-powered teacher that you can be, the teacher that your students deserve.

Virtual Socratic Seminars

High-powered teachers are readers and also planners. They are reflective, and also diverse. High-powered teachers are not just readers, they are well-read, and strive to motivate and foster the love of reading within their students through research proven strategies that can be implemented both inside the classroom and online. They have found that **Socratic Seminars** have been successful for both in-person and virtual students.

The Socratic seminar is basically an **extended discussion** that is centered on a **complex text**. It is an inquiry-based approach that is meant to prompt critical thinking. Socratic seminar is a challenging but rewarding routine that teachers have found to be successful with the entire class or in small groups, who may be observed by a larger group. For online sessions, teachers have found one large group to be successful. Sessions typically range from 30 to 60 minutes, depending on the grade and age level of the students. The teacher's role in a Socratic seminar is primarily to facilitate the conversation by posing questions that are not readily answered and do not have a single correct response to **encourage conversation, diverse points of view**, as well as **promoting deep thought** and **analytical thinking**.

High-powered teachers are planners. They plan and prepare questions to ensure the Socratic seminar is successful. Opening questions may be presented to the group to help initiate and **inspire conversation** and discussion. The opening question(s) should be thought-provoking and based on the text itself. Also, throughout the discussion, the teacher takes notes on behalf of the class, asks follow-up questions, and also ensures that all students are involved and engaged in the discussion. Although, the teacher is part of the circle or group of students, the goal is to encourage students to speak to each other, rather than answer the teacher. The facilitator typically ensures that students keep answers as neutral as possible at this point of the seminar and allow closing questions to invite students to **summarize** the **interpretations** discussed during the seminar. High-powered teachers keep in mind that although the discussion eventually comes to an end, the critical thinking does not. They create postseminar activities that may include **self-reflection, self-evaluation, exploration**, and **extended written responses** in the form of **analyzing** the text.

Steps for a Socratic Seminar include the Following:

+ Selecting a text that is **complex** and subject to more than one interpretation.
+ Be **specific** with length of required reading.
+ Prepare and plan for students to have sufficient time to read and understand the text in days leading up to the seminar. Teachers may choose to read the text with students or allow for independent reading. The seminar is the **capstone** for the text.
+ **Provide** online students with information for logging into the platform where the seminar will take place.
+ Post an initial question to **encourage rich discussion**. The question shouldn't be a question that can be answered quickly and can also serve as a place to return to if the conversation or discussion begins to slow.
+ Teachers should be **mindful** of students who may be dominating the discussion, or those who are not participating.
+ Encourage students to provide **text-evidence** when referring to text. Provide listeners with page numbers, and paragraph.
+ Pose closing questions that **encourage** students to make **meaningful connections** to the text. Connections may be from character to character, from self to character, or from previous time to current era of time.
+ Teachers should **take notes** during the discussion, while also encouraging students to take notes to refer to when working on postassignments.
+ After the seminar, **invite** students to **reflect** and **self-assess** on their contribution to the discussion. Ask them to identify their strengths and also their areas for growth for future seminars.

High-powered teachers incorporate **Socratic seminars** in their in-person classrooms and their online classrooms to allow students to experience a strategy that encourages deeper thinking, and also a deeper understanding about the ideas and values within the assigned text. They also know that this type of seminar promotes **classroom rapport, addresses diversity, encourages active listening, participation**, and also **peer collaboration** and **text-to-self** experiences that enrich the lives of each of their students, all while promoting and **fostering the love of rich literature** within their students.

Now It's Your Turn

For this assignment you will be required to explore the following website and also read George Ella Lyon's poem, *Where I'm From*, http://www.georgeellalyon.com/where.html. Create and complete a graphic organizer that will help you organize your thoughts and data about yourself. Write a similar poem describing you, and where you are from. What makes you, you? This is meant to be a cultural look at yourself, your youth, your life, and what helped mold you and define you. A drop box will be provided with more explicit details and directions for the poem, and the written reflection. The object of this assignment is to help you begin thinking about how you will teach poetry, give you a better understanding of cultural poetry, provide you with a resource that you can implement in your classroom, and help you gain insight into what truly makes you, you. This assignment also promotes culture, individuality, self-reflection, and writing skills.

Applications

To help guide you through Chapter Fifteen and upcoming chapters, become familiar with the following key terms for a deeper understanding of Chapter Fifteen:

- ✦ Quality literature
- ✦ Narrative texts
- ✦ Characters
- ✦ Plot, setting, point of view, and theme
- ✦ Style
- ✦ First person point of view, third person point of view, and third person multiple point of view
- ✦ Third person omniscient point of view
- ✦ Protagonist, antagonist
- ✦ Mentor, tempter, sidekick, skeptic, and emotional character
- ✦ Expository text
- ✦ Genres
- ✦ Poetry, drama, prose
- ✦ Fiction
- ✦ Nonfiction
- ✦ Figurative language, similes, metaphors, hyperboles, personification, and imagery
- ✦ Symbolism, onomatopoeia, and alliteration
- ✦ Rhyme, sonnets, ballads, elegy, haiku, melodrama, acrostic, and free-verse
- ✦ Traditional fiction, fantasy fiction, realistic fiction, historical fiction, and science fiction
- ✦ SQPL, opinionnaire, annotation, character analysis map, and take 6

Work with your group or with a partner research the following activities/strategies in your group and be prepared to share your findings with the class. Include a brief description of the strategy, if it should be implemented before, during, or after reading.

✦ *Text structures*
✦ *Pop-corn review*
✦ *Venn diagram*
✦ *Writing frames*

In-Seat Activity

Working with your team, review the roles of characters. Briefly define each role, and also collaborate to determine a text that is grade-level and content appropriate for middle-school students that also contains character(s) that fit one or more of the character roles that you've defined. Cite the book that you select for each character, and also give an explanation of why you selected the text, and how you determined the character role for the characters that you chose. Be prepared to share your findings with the class. You may create and complete a character analysis map/web for each character to help organize your thoughts.

Reflect and Answer the Following Questions

✦ *Why is it important to teach all genres of literature?*
✦ *What is quality literature?*
✦ *What is narrative text?*
✦ *What are the literary elements of literature?*
✦ *What is expository text?*
✦ *How are narrative texts and expository texts different?*
✦ *What creative strategies can I implement to teach poetry?*
✦ *How can figurative language be taught?*
✦ *What strategies enhance literature?*

Student Notes

Annotation is an effective learning strategy. Annotating is typically completed along the outer edge of the text within the book. However, sufficient space is not always available. Therefore, this page has been reserved for you to annotate *(take notes)* record potential questions, and also to refer back to when studying, completing assignments, and to help you gain a better understanding of Chapter Fifteen.

Student Reflection

High-powered teachers reflect. This page is reserved for you to reflect about information that you found insightful and what you have learned from Chapter Fifteen.

Suggested Readings and Resources

Lyon, George Ella. *"Where I'm From,"* http://artscouncil.ky.gov/KAC/Vibrant/WhereFromAbout. htm. Accessed July 12, 2018.

Chapter References

Cambourne, B. *The Whole Story: Natural Learning and the Acquisition of Literacy in the Classroom.* Scholastic, 1993.

Council of Chief State School Officers (CCSSO). *Interstate Teacher Assessment and Support Consortium (InTASC) Model Core Teaching Standards,* Apr. 2011, https://www.ccsso.org/sites/default/files/2017-11/InTASC_Model_Core_Teaching_Standards_2011.pdf. Accessed July, 7 2018.

Lyon, George Ella., http://www.georgeellalyon.com/where.html. Accessed May 28, 2018.

Kentucky Arts Council, http://artscouncil.ky.gov/KAC/Vibrant/WhereFromAbout.htm. Accessed May 31, 2018.

Chapter 16
Inspiring the Joys of Reading and Writing

Teacher Quote

"Looking back, I can visibly see how reading lead to many significant and life-changing opportunities for me. Reading has helped me to become the person that I am today...well-read and happy."

~ Dr. Joyce Bowling

Chapter Questions

✦ *What is a well-read teacher?*
✦ *How can I motivate the unmotivated reader?*
✦ *What are the benefits of reading and writing with my students?*
✦ *How can I increase student engagement with reading and writing?*
✦ *How can I incorporate technology to increase students' interest in reading?*

Research shows that the number of children who are daily readers drops markedly from childhood to *tween* and *teenage years*. One study, (Scholastic) documents a drop from 48% of 6- to 8-year olds down to 24% of 15- to 17-year olds who are daily readers. Another (NCES) shows a drop from 53% of 9-year olds to 19% of 17-year olds. What does this all mean? According to studies, since 1984 the number of tweens and teens who read for pleasure once a week or more has dropped from 81% to 76% and is steadily declining.

High-powered teachers are continually looking for ways to learn how to motivate their students to love reading and writing. They know the rewards of reading are immense, as well as its impact on communication skills. They also know that reading is well known for reducing stress, increases knowledge, and much more. Nevertheless, high-powered middle-school teachers as well as secondary and elementary teachers are fighting a constant battle to inspire and motivate students to read as more and more students cringe at the thought of reading a book.

Research suggests that motivation, or lack thereof, is the direct result of an individual's self-efficacy related to the task. Bandura further defines self-efficacy as the beliefs we have about ourselves that cause us to make choices, put forth effort, and persist in the face of difficulty. High-powered teachers know that one of the most powerful sources of self-efficacy is mastery experience. They know that there are a number of factors that are important to reading motivation including self-concept and value of reading, choice, and also time spent talking about literature as well as reading, which include the availability of diverse texts, and collaboration and engagement. Take a few minutes to read the next section and then do a little reflection to determine your self-efficacy, motivation, and your desire to inspire and motivate your students to love reading.

Quote

- -

"In school there is no greater motivation for a student than the knowledge that at least one adult knows them well and cares about what happens to them."

~J. Mathews, Washington Post Education Columnist

I recall my days of youth while growing up deep in the southeastern Appalachian Mountains of Kentucky. I thought that I was the luckiest girl alive. I thought I was lucky to live in, and explore the vast beauty of the Appalachian Mountains. I enjoyed exploring the mountains, observing wildlife, collecting wild flowers, watching the amazing life of the creatures that lived beneath the clear flowing streams, and also the joys of allowing my imagination to run wild with my surroundings. My imagination soared with the comforting sounds of the tree frogs, the nightly chirping of the crickets, the serine cooing of the beautiful gray doves, and the late evening lonesome call of the whipper will. Inspiration engulfed me, even at the tender age of seven and eight, I imagined characters, stories, and dramatic plots. The inspiration I gained from nature, the mountains, my culture, and my family continued throughout my life. I had many stories to tell, to write, and share with the world.

Today, as an adult, I still consider it a blessing to live in the same mountains that I explored as a child, listening to the tree frogs sing in the late evenings of spring, watching the colors of the leaves change with each season, and I will forever love the lonesome call of the whipper will, and the beautiful cooing of the doves that fill the afternoon with a sense of peace, a bit of sadness, and also a sense of hope and encouragement within me. I admit that I am not a long-distant traveler. I have traveled outside the country, enjoyed some of the magnificent wonders of the world, enjoyed the salty ocean water, and experienced life in the big city of New York. However, my happy place lies within the mountains of Kentucky. I find joy in the serenity of the mountains, the traditions of my culture, the history of my Cherokee heritage, my family, and the tranquility of the beautiful nature around me. Yes, I am inspired by each of those things.

The mountains are not my only source of inspiration. I also discovered as a young child growing up in the hills of Appalachia, that I could find adventure beyond the mountains that I called home. I discovered the joys of reading. I learned that I didn't have to leave the peaceful comfort of my clubhouse, back porch, or my favorite thinking spot, which was the banks of the creek that flowed carelessly and freely beside our house. I discovered that I could find adventure, meet new and exciting people, travel to other countries, time-travel, and explore the unknown, all while reading a book. My love and passion for reading grew as I grew. My choice of summertime activities changed and evolved into interests other than climbing trees or catching frogs, just as my love for reading became more diverse. I discovered that anything was possible in fiction. I learned that there was more to know about historical figures than what the history book at school divulged. I found that characters in a book could be anything or anyone that the author wanted them to be. So came the desire to tell the countless number of stories that had been held captive in my own imagination. It was time to share my characters, my plots, my poetry, my mysteries, hopes, dreams, and my heart with others. I confess, I've always been a bit of a story teller who could embellish to fit the needs and desires of my audience, but I hadn't really put my stories down on paper. So it began, I found myself once again, sitting by the creek on the soft green moss, and began writing daily and freely about my surroundings, the mountains, traditions, my culture, and all of the things that inspired me. I couldn't wait to return every day. I would write for hours on end, dreaming, imagining, reflecting, and indulging in the rewards of creating my own stories.

Today, I am still inspired to write while listening to the creek water flow from the Appalachian Mountains. I find peace and tranquility in hearing the waters flowing over the time-worn stones of yesteryears. Exploring the past and dreaming of tomorrow. **Example 16.1** is an example of my poetry that was inspired while sitting on the banks of the creek listening to the water flow only weeks ago.

Example 16.1: Appalachian Mornings

> *"Appalachian Mornings"*
> *Rising early was nothing new.*
> *For folks in the mountains, it was what we did, and some still do.*
> *As the rooster crowed his good morning announcement, the day had arrived*
> *Thick fog blanketed the garden we had planted and nurtured with love.*
> *The harvest was needed for our family's survival.*
> *The aroma of buttermilk biscuits baking filled the house.*
> *It was a distinct smell like no other, but a pleasant aroma of days gone by.*
> *The dough had been carefully rolled to perfection...*
> *cut to just the right size by the floured rim of a drinking glass.*
> *Coffee brewing in the kitchen...teased and enticed my nose.*
> *The glowing cinders were stoked, to kindle the fire to warm our small feet and tiny toes.*
> *Water was heated in a big tea-kettle on top of the cook stove...*
> *Just the right temperature to wash away leftover sleep from our eyes and faces.*
> *The crowded little kitchen was filled with life...*
> *While outside the gentle black cattle moved softly on the mountainside,*
> *Mamaw's change would soon rattle from her big cookie tin*
> *as she unlocked her little country store that provided for us all.*
> *Mommy, was always humming while she sewed in the early morning light*
> *another garment was now sewn and completed just before daylight.*
> *Each morning, our brother complained about going to school.*
> *While my sister and I would hurry for the bus...knowing the driver wouldn't wait.*
> *Arriving anxiously and waiting by the road...*
> *The smell of the damp morning mountain soil filled the air.*

(Continued)

Example 16.1: Appalachian Mornings (*Continued*)

> *I loved that morning smell...I breathed it deeply into my being.*
> *I would cherish it, remember it, and allow it to consume me.*
> *Watching from the small foggy window of the yellow bus...*
> *I cleared a tiny spot so I could see mommy standing on the porch waving good-bye.*
> *A sadness stung my heart...*
> *as the bus chugged down the winding country road.*
> *I never really knew why.*
> *As the bus rounded the next curve...*
> *and our home and mommy slowly faded out of sight.*
>
> ~ *Dr. Joyce Bowling, 2018*

Are you inspired yet? Maybe not. I learned a long time ago, and know that research also supports, that what inspires a teacher, does not necessarily inspire their students. However, I also know that when I was inspired, even by a different topic, different book, a movie, a new source of technology, poetry or whatever it may be, inspiration became contagious. My inspiration spilled over to my students. I discovered that when I got excited about a new book, and enthusiasm filled my face as I described the rich new character, or the strange and unusual setting...my students suddenly wanted to read and explore new books. When I talked with enthusiasm about writing, they wanted to create new adventurous stories. I discovered that inspiration truly was contagious, just as negativity can be contagious (InTASC Standard 3, CCSSO).

Be the teacher who inspires their students to do all of the great things that they were created to do. Don't be a doom and gloom teacher, just because you may have had a bad day, or be having what you consider a bad day. Maybe your students are not performing the way you would like for them to perform, or behaving the way you expect them to behave. Don't be a gloomy teacher because your neighbor/colleague has a gloomy outlook on life today. Each day is a new opportunity to start over, to be inspired, to wipe the slate clean, and a new opportunity to breathe hope, inspiration, and motivation into you and your students. Remove yourself from negative people's company when possible. Wake up each morning with a zeal for life, a zeal for your students to be happy, to learn, to be successful. Keep in mind that you may be the only bright spot in a child's life. They are expecting you to come in and teach with joy, inspire them, motivate them, teach them to go beyond the normal, to reach for the stars, and to be creative. Don't lose sight of the joy and inspiration to teach that you felt as you walked across the stage with your diploma, new adventures ahead of you, and a repertoire full of ideas, material, and dreams (InTASC Standard 3, CCSSO).

> *"The only person you are destined to become is the person that you decide to be."*
>
> ~ *Ralph Waldo Emerson*

Are You a Reader?

In 2004, S. Krashen's research revealed that independent reading over the past 40+ years, revealed that no single literacy activity had more positive effect on *students' comprehension, vocabulary knowledge, spelling, writing ability,* and *overall academic achievement* than **free-reading**. Are you a reader? Will you promote free-reading in your classroom? First, let's define free-reading. Free-reading can be defined as students reading independently in their free time, while they are not involved in, or participating in traditional classroom lectures, instructions, activities, assessments, discussions, or collaborations. S. Krashen also states that students are more likely to read a book at home if they've started reading the book at school.

High-powered teachers are readers. They provide students with ongoing opportunities to read independently in their classrooms (InTASC Standard 1, CCSSO). They have found that their students overall achievement has increased as well as their inspiration to read after ensuring that they have free-reading time. Free-reading time can be the final 10 minutes of class, or the first 10 minutes of class. Students can enjoy free-reading time after completing daily assignments, and also can be cleverly woven into/integrated into instructional lessons.

Throughout this text, I have stated the importance of teachers being a reader. Do a **little self-reflection**, and answer the following questions:

In-Seat Activity

1. *Do you enjoy reading?*
2. *Do you enjoy going to the library?*
3. *What do you like to read?*
4. *Do you have reading goals?*
5. *Is reading important to you?*
6. *Is reading important to your growth as an educator?*
7. *Do you require your students to read?*
8. *Why do you encourage your students to read?*
9. *Do you think reading expands one's knowledge?*
10. *How does reading apply to real-life?*

After answering the questions above, review your answers and reflect on why you answered the questions as you did. What did you learn about yourself? For the second half of this activity complete the following statements:

1. *I will motivate myself to read more by...*
2. *I will explore the genre of ...next week.*
3. *I will read from either a digital device, or from a book.*
4. *I will go to the library...*
5. *My reading goal each month will be...*
6. *Reading is important because...*
7. *I need to read to improve my teaching because...*
8. *I will read with my students because...*
9. *One thing I want to learn more about is...*
10. *Reading applies to my life because...*

When you have completed both sections of the questionnaire think about a reading goal that you want to set for yourself. Be realistic, but make it somewhat of a challenge. Write your goal down. Keep in mind your goal may be to explore and read novels that you want your students to read, novels that will enhance your instruction as well as students' comprehension. You may want to read new *how to or informational* books for teachers each year to expand your knowledge of teaching, gain new innovative ideas, or you may simply decide to read a new novel each month in your spare time. You may also be inspired and motivated to read from each of the above.

After you have written your goal(s), you will be required to write a brief letter to yourself explaining what you have learned about yourself as a reader, and what your reading goal(s) are, as well as what you aspire to accomplish from your goals. Sign and date your letter and place it where you can go back and revisit it often to remind yourself of your goals, the importance of them, and to also help you to remain focused. Set mini-goals to help you achieve your ultimate goals. I encourage you to revisit your goals on good days and bad days. Draw inspiration from within and push forward to be the reader that has the ability to encourage, inspire, and motivate your students.

A Well-Read High-Powered Teacher

> *"I always loved books. I don't remember learning to read, it was just something I always did. I was hungry for knowledge, I guess, and information; I was a curious kid. I still am." (AZ Quotes, 2018).*
>
> ~ Dolly Parton

What is a **well-read high-powered teacher**? A well-read teacher is a high-powered teacher that is also a lifelong learner (InTASC Standard 9, CCSSO). A well-read high-powered teacher reads for enjoyment, they read for improvement, they read for information, they read to advance their career, and they read to inspire their students. Well-read high-powered teachers read for entertainment and also read from all genres. They read to be prepared for questions that may arise in their classroom, to offer reading suggestions, to meet new and interesting characters, to learn about places they've never physically gone before, and to explore the unknown. A well-read high-powered teacher is a teacher who inspires, motivates, encourages, and a teacher that fosters a genuine love of reading in their students. They see potential in all students. They do not give up on their students, and will work tirelessly to help struggling readers be successful readers (InTASC Standards 1, 2, 3, & 4, CCSSO).

Being a well-read high-powered teacher means reading classics, science fiction, poetry, and also stepping outside of your comfort zone, and reading genres you've never read before. High-powered teachers are also willing to sacrifice a little time away from electronics or whatever distracts you or discourages you from picking up a book to read. Research indicates that reading for pleasure is on the decline all across the nation for various reasons. Parents are not reading to their children as much as they once were. Instead, children are often given an electronic device before they are toilet trained or placed in front of a colorful television for entertainment, and as a result of various factors, the joy of reading is dissipating at a ridiculous rate. Well-read teachers take time to read daily, to promote reading as well as the use of technology, and ensure that their students have multiple daily opportunities to read inside their classroom. They know that otherwise their students may not be reading at all.

A well-read teacher implements reading from all genres in their classroom to enhance their instruction, ensure that students are reading from all genres, meet state standards, ensure that students are experiencing reading from diverse points of view, helping themselves as well as their students to understand diverse cultures, and also providing reading opportunities that meet all of their students' needs, both academic needs and cultural needs. Well-read high-powered teachers read from and incorporate all diverse genres in their classrooms to offer students' choices to read based on interest, topic, or genre. They also incorporate a wide-variety of texts to encourage questioning, promote student interaction, and maximize student engagement by using diverse learning experiences (InTASC Standards 1, 2, 3, 4, 5, 7, 8, CCSSO).

Motivation

High-powered teachers know that motivation is an important key to students' success. They know that motivation can be viewed from two perspectives: whether the motivation comes from within the student or from another source, such as the teacher, family, or peers. **Internal motivation** is also known as **intrinsic** motivation. Motivation from other sources is a form of **external motivation**, also known as **extrinsic motivation**.

Intrinsic motivation is something that teachers desire all students to possess. Intrinsic motivation is that drive that causes us to do something because we know that it brings us a source of pleasure, happiness, or a sense of accomplishment, and even recognition. Intrinsic motivation also causes students to challenge themselves to do better, to learn more, to go above and beyond the expected and also to think outside the box, whereas extrinsic motivation comes from the outside source. The outside source can be a teacher, peer, or a family member, or even a motivational speaker, sports figure, or a friend. Nevertheless, regardless of where or who the source of motivation is, or comes from, the desire and intent are the same, to promote and encourage, as well as inspire and motivate another person. Elementary high-powered teachers often offer a reward system to help motivate students. Rewards can be as simple as a sticker or as elaborate as 10 free-reading minutes in the library, or add five points to their lowest grade.

However, high-powered teachers encourage *all students* and provide all students with positive feedback, pats on the back, high-fives, and words of praise regardless if they are intrinsically motivated or extrinsically motivated. They also offer incentives of praise, explicit feedback, words of advice, take time to talk to them and also are willing to listen to all students. They present a positive disposition for all students regardless of how they learn, their level of motivation, learning level, ethnicity, social status, race, gender, or behavior (InTASC Standards 2, 3, CCSSO). High-powered teacher present themselves as a form of motivation through their love and passion for reading and writing with a high-energy, equality, creativity, and also as being a real-person who cares about their students. They read, research, plan, and create exciting opportunities to engage and support all learners, to stimulate their interest, motivate them to be motivated, and challenge them to be the best both inside and outside the classroom.

Motivation and Differentiation

> *"When I am inspired, I give one-hundred and ten percent of myself."*
> ~ *Dr. Joyce Bowling*

Well-read high-powered teachers differentiate their instruction by changing their teaching pace, teaching style, and level of instruction based on student differences, and student need. Student differences may include readiness levels, interests, learning styles, and also learning preferences. Well-read high-powered teachers read and search out new strategies to implement in their classes to ensure that they are responding to the needs of all students, including English Language Learners, challenging gifted and talented learners, and accommodating students with disabilities, and students who learn different at different rates. Well-read teachers continually strive to improve their instruction and knowledge to ensure that they are differentiating in their content, their process, the product, and to ensure the learning environment is a comfortable and accepting environment where all students can learn and be productive (InTASC Standards 3, 7, 8, CCSSO).

High-powered well-read teachers are not afraid of change. They accept reading suggestions and challenges from their students, and also offer students reading challenges and suggestions. A well-read teacher knows something about every genre, and is also familiar with both old and new authors. They also plan for and utilize anchor activities rather than busy work for early finishers. A well-read high-powered middle-school teacher has books available from all genres for students to read. They also have resources available that reflect a variety of reading levels to ensure that all students have something to read. Finally, a high-powered well-read teacher ensures multiple ongoing opportunities for students to read orally, silently, collaboratively, and also read independently (InTASC Standards 2, 3, 7, 8, CCSSO). They want their students to become immersed in what they are reading. As D. Miller states in *The Book Whisperer* "I want my students to lose and find themselves in books."

Modeling for Inspiration

"If your actions create a legacy that inspires others to dream more, learn more, do more and become more, then, you are an excellent leader."
(Goodreads, 2018).

~ Dolly Parton

Research shows that modeling is one of the most beneficial ways to engage, and also to inspire students. Research also confirms that student motivation is a key factor in successful reading (Gambrell and Marinak). High-powered teachers model reading with excitement. They select rich literature that piques students' interest, creates a sense of wonder within them, has rich diverse characters, and makes reading exciting through engagement. High-powered teachers model their love of reading as well as their curiosity when reading through read-alouds and think-alouds (InTASC Standard 7, 8, CCSSO). They read aloud from diverse genres to demonstrate how to read poetry, how to read with anticipation, read with a *detectives' eye*, how to read like researcher, how to read with a sense of humor, and also how to read with a *critical eye* and an open mind. High-powered teachers model the kind of reader, they want their students to be. They model with excitement, enthusiasm, and with a flare that ignites a spark within their students that creates a desire within them to be a reader (InTASC Standard 5, CCSSO).

High-powered teachers also know the value of modeling their love of reading, even when they are not teaching. They model their love of reading through having a wide-variety of books available inside the class, displaying reading quotes on the classroom walls, offering book suggestions to students and to other teachers, and also through conversations about books with students, parents, and colleagues. They set an example for students by visibly reading while eating lunch, while the students are reading, before school begins, and after the bell rings. In other words, high-powered teachers are known by their students as a reader, the teacher who loves to read, even when they don't have to. Be the reader and the writer that you want and expect your students to be (InTASC Standards 3, 4, 5, 10, CCSSO).

Engaging Students With Fun Activities

According to R. Allington, he states that above all, students need time to engage in reading in order to get better at reading. High-powered teachers support and agree that *students need time to read, access to books they find fascinating, and they need exert instruction*. High-powered well-read teachers understand and strive to make reading interesting, diverse, and also exciting and engaging by using a variety of instructional strategies to encourage learners to develop deep understanding of content areas and connection, and also to build skills to apply knowledge in meaningful ways. They are always on the look-out for new innovative ways to engage students through activities not only that motivate their students to read, but also that they can integrate into their instruction, enhance students' comprehension, as well as increase their reading skills (InTASC Standards 7, 8, CCSSO).

High-powered well-read teachers open the doors to opportunities by inviting local authors to be **guest speakers** in their classrooms, or in their school. They also invite local poets, and storytellers to come and share their work, their passion, and motivating words of wisdom with their students to help bring reading and writing alive inside the school (InTASC Standards 7, 8, 9, 10, CCSSO). They also encourage students to read about the guest speaker before they arrive so that they have background knowledge and can make connections both prior to the guest speaker(s) speaking and also to be better prepared for asking and also answering questions. Guest speakers have the ability to allow students to view both reading and writing from diverse perspectives, cultures, and style. Poetry in music is rewarding, as well as culture in storytelling. High-powered teachers know that the possibilities of engaging students with fun activities are vast, but well worth the time, effort, and hard-work. The rewards are as vast as the multitudes of activities awaiting the high-powered teacher and their students.

Book Clubs

High-powered teachers create and invite students to participate in **book clubs**. Book clubs can be a very inspiring opportunity for students to socialize, discuss literature, become motivated, and also explore a wide variety of literature that maybe otherwise they wouldn't have read (InTASC Standards 3, 5, 7, & 8 CCSSO). Book clubs can be established during school, if schedules and time permits. However, they can also be established after school. With parent permission, after school book clubs can be beneficial for the parents, students, and the teacher.

When I taught sixth grade, I surveyed students to determine how many students would be interested in attending book clubs. I was overwhelmed at the positive responses that I received. I met with the principal and we decided that early morning when students arrived at school would be a perfect time to offer book club. This allowed students a structured place to be before the school officially began, increased their desire to read, it provided them a place to discuss their books, silent read, and also a sense of belonging, of being a part of something in the school. I was already at school anyway and usually read at my desk, graded papers, planned or worked on bulletin boards. Nevertheless, I was available as were many of the students who were either hanging out in the lunchroom, stairwells, or in the hallways (InTASC Standard 3, CCSSO).

I made the announcement, included the information on my classroom website, and sent home notes about book club. I was so excited that I could hardly sleep the night before the first official meeting. I decided that I would not hold students' accountable for reading the same novel, but offer them a choice of reading their own books. I had read and researched about how student choice influenced students reading and also motivated them. Studies showed that when students selected their own books, it did indeed boost their reading ability, and desire to read. According to V. Strauss, 91% of students' ages 6 to 17 agreed that their favorite books were books that they selected for themselves. This was enough proof and information for me.

The morning of the first book club meeting had arrived and students slowly began to filter in my classroom at 7:05 A.M. with curious faces, and most with a book in hand. I explained that we would begin by using this time as free-reading time, and that they could read a book of choice. I showed them the classroom library, and encouraged them to browse the titles. Within minutes, most students were either looking through the class library, sitting on cushioned top crates that sufficed as seating for students, while others sat at desks. I quickly did a head-count and was excited to discover that twelve students had made the commitment to arrive early, and sacrifice their own time to read. The club continued and advanced into a writing club as well. The students wrote, edited, and published monthly newsletters, read novels, socialized, learned, and also flourished until I retired from teaching in the public school.

I was pleasantly pleased and also a bit surprised when the students who were regular book club members asked if we could continue having book club, even after I retired. Tears filled my eyes with emotions as I realized that I had accomplished what I sat out to do a couple of years prior, to motivate students, and foster a love of reading and writing within them. To see them be intrinsically motivated, by extrinsically motivating them with what started out to be a simple book club. Our book club continued at the local coffee shop a couple of times a month for a number of years. The book club grew and young tweens and teens from around the county attended as well as many of their parents. We read a wide-variety of diverse literature including classics, fantasy science fiction, non-fiction, and many more (InTASC Standard 9 & 10, CCSSO). I discovered new series of books, new authors, formed new relationships, and watched students whom I had known since they were students in my first-grade classroom graduate and move on to college, careers, and also well-read adults.

Book Commercials

High-powered teachers inspire their students to think creatively, write creatively, and also write persuasively. They incorporate **book commercials** in their classrooms to help students get involved in reading, reading close for meaning, thinking critically, as well as problem-solving, enhancing their ability to persuade an audience, increase their use of persuasive vocabulary, enhance writing skills, while also having fun with reading and creating and performing book commercials. Book commercials are basically advertisements that are short, impromptu testimonials from students about the books that they have read and most of all that they have enjoyed. High-powered teachers integrate book commercials to provide students with a forum for sharing the books that students love, and also as an opportunity to recommend those books to others (InTASC Standards 3, 4, 5, 7, & 8, CCSSO).

Book commercials can be as simple as you want them to be, or as elaborate as you would like for them to be. They can be informal presentations, or formal presentations, which include a grading rubric, and specified requirements. Nevertheless, both informal and formal commercials are meant to be persuasive. High-powered teachers typically begin book commercials with informal presentations, which lead up to a formal presentation. Formal book commercials may include a written paper or a power point as a final project as well as a formal presentation. High-powered teachers know that book commercials provide opportunities to assess students' speaking, listening, writing, and also their creativity skills (InTASC Standard 5, 6, 7, & 8, CCSSO).

Students are asked to annotate for key ideas, quotes, or for ideas in the text that would help them to persuade their peers, and possibly the teacher to read their book while they are reading. High-powered teacher encourage students to create an outline that will help guide them as well as remind them of key points during the commercial. Once a week, typically on Fridays at the end of class time, teachers ask students for one to two volunteers to share their books through a persuasive informal book commercial. High-powered teachers know that book commercials create an excitement among the students, increase classroom rapport, and inspire students to read (InTASC Standard 3, CCSSO). Book commercials also provide students with an opportunity to share new and exciting plots, characters, while also providing an opportunity to motivate the unmotivated student to read. High-powered teachers post a tracking system, which can be as simple as a graph, to monitor who's presented an informal book commercial, whereas a grade is taken for formal commercials. **Step-by-step directions** are listed below (*keep in mind steps can be modified to fit the needs of individuals' classrooms*):

1. Provide students with **descriptions** and **procedures** for both **informal** and **formal** book commercials.
2. Students may present informal commercials beside their desks with a time limit of 3 to 5 minutes. Students share the **title**, **author genre**, and a **hook**, which is meant to entice and inspire the other students, as well as three reasons they want others to read their book. The hook should be the **BIG WHY** of why they want someone else to read their book.
3. Both informal and formal commercials **shouldn't divulge the complete summary** of the book. Keep in mind that anticipation leads to persuasion, which leads to inspiration.
4. **Formal** commercials can be presented **independently**, with a **partner**, or in a **small group** and require planning, whereas an informal book commercial can be sporadic.
5. Students should be given a **rubric for formal book commercials**.
6. Formal book commercials should also reveal the **title, author**, and a **brief summary, a hook and** with at least **three reasons** why they want others to read their book.
7. Formal book commercials should **be timed** and also presented at the front of the class.
8. Formal book commercials can involve **technology** as a visual.
9. Formal book commercials should be a **creative summary** of a book, whereas an informal book commercial should be more of a brief summary of a book.
10. Each book commercial should be followed with a brief amount of time for **questions** from the audience. Teachers may limit the number of questions allowed per book commercial.

Book Talks

Book talks are similar to book commercials, except they do not have to be persuasive, and are more informative. High-powered teachers integrate book talks to allow students to express themselves, recommend a book, and to inform others about the book and the author. Book talks are presented as a summary of their book similar to a book report. High-powered teachers encourage students to participate in book talks to help increase their comprehension, ability to make important connections, and enhances their speaking and listening skills, as well as their social skills. Book talks also promotes classroom rapport, allows everyone the opportunity to be heard, voice opinions and also encourages and inspires students to read (InTASC Standards 2, 3, 4, 5, 6, 7, & 8, CCSSO). High-powered teachers may incorporate book talks on specific days, or incorporate them in the last 5 minutes of class on specified days. Rules for book talks are also clearly posted as well as the objective(s) for book talks. Book talks also allow teachers to assess students speaking and listening skills (InTASC Standard 6, CCSSO). High-powered teachers may require students to present at least two book talks during a semester, or only one, depending on the number of students. They track students who have given book talks either with a checklist or a graph that can be displayed inside the classroom.

Reading With Students

Allow your students to visibly see you as a reader. If you are going to inspire and encourage your students to read, then you need to ensure that you are leading by example. Instead of grading papers when students are silent reading, read a book while your students are reading. Discuss the book that you are reading with your students, and also how you can't wait to read before you go to bed. Allow them to see a genuine enthusiasm for reading in you. Students will know if you are a phony, especially at the middle-school grade-level, so don't try to bluff them into thinking that you are a reader, if you're not.

As stated previously, students enjoy having a choice in what they read. However, realistically, we know that there is some literature that students are expected to be familiar with, know passages from, recognize characters, and also recall the authors. Quite often those novels are assigned to students to read independently on their own, and required to be responsible and to be prepared for discussions, and also be ready to answer questions about their assigned reading. Many students become disengaged with this traditional approach to reading. When surveyed, an overwhelming number of middle-school students admitted that they never read all of the text, but instead, read cliff notes and summaries, thus leading to less than satisfying grades, and never truly giving the text a chance. To prevent this type of stagnant learning, and unbeneficial reading, high-powered well-read middle-school teachers read with their students (InTASC Standards 4, 5, & 8, CCSSO).

They also create ways to make the reading engaging, by involving the students in a challenging or difficult plot by implementing *Readers' Theater*, *literacy circles*, *grand-discussions*, making *predictions*, conducting a *debate*, *role-play*, and many more rewarding and satisfying as well as engaging activities that help bring the characters to life, create an interest in the plot, and that also allows students to make inferences and connections (InTASC Standards 4, 5, 7, & 8, CCSSO). High-powered teachers allow their students to see their level of involvement with the plot, characters, and also with the class as they embark on literary journeys together.

Writing With Students

High-powered teachers read as well as write with their students. When they ask their students to write poetry, they too write poetry. If they require their students to write a personal narrative, they also write a personal narrative. They also use their own writing to inspire their students. High-powered teachers use their writing as examples while teaching. For example, if they are teaching students about writing an argumentative paper, they provide students with a sample of their writing, such as an argumentative letter that they wrote to the governor about an important issue, or an article they submitted to the local newspaper.

Keep in mind that all teachers' writing samples do not always have to be legitimate samples of writing that was actually mailed to the governor, or the mayor, or submitted to a newspaper, but can be just that an example. However, if you have legitimate artifacts that you've written, by all means, if they meet the criteria and expectations that you have for students, use them to inspire your students. High-powered teachers understand how to connect concepts and use different perspectives to engage learners in critical thinking, creativity, and problem solving related to authentic local and even global issues. They know that when students see them and visualize them as authentic writers and readers, it inspires them to read and write. Teach by example for students to self-discover and become intrinsically motivated (InTASC Standard 5, CCSSO).

"Inspiration is contagious! Inspire your students to do great things!"

~ Dr. Joyce Bowling

Promoting Reading and Writing

High-powered teachers promote reading and writing. They promote reading and writing by being an advocate for reading. They seek ways to expand their own reading repertoire by challenging themselves to read novels in diverse genres, reading outside their comfort zone, attending reading and writing conferences, attending reading and writing professional developments, furthering their education, researching innovative reading and writing strategies to enhance students' interest, their reading and writing skills, and also seek opportunities to promote reading and writing throughout their school or district (InTASC Standards 5, 7, 9, & 10, CCSSO). A well-read high-powered teacher also seeks opportunities to engage the entire school, families, and even the community in both reading and writing. They host read-athons, poetry slams, reading challenges, host book clubs; encourage students to compete in reading and writing competitions; and also take every available opportunity to promote the love of reading and writing to students, colleagues, and also to parents (InTASC Standard 9 & 10, CCSSO).

In other words, high-powered teachers become role models for student interest. They deliver their instruction and their presentation of ideas about books with energy and enthusiasm. When high-powered teachers display motivation, their passion motivates their students. They make reading personal and allow their students to know why they choose the literature that they read. They find, create, and take opportunities to talk about what they are reading, and also opportunities to make real-life connections to what they are reading. In other words, they use examples freely to show why a concept or technique is useful and how it ties to reading, writing, and to real-life.

High-powered teachers also promote their love of reading by incorporating a wide variety of fun engaging reading and writing activities that allow students to be expressive, creative, and collaborative (InTASC Standard 8, CCSSO). They teach by discovery, allowing students to find reasoning through problem solving and discovering the underlying principle on their own. They encourage cooperative and collaborative learning activities that are particularly effective as they also provide positive social interaction and social skills (InTASC Standard 3, CCSSO). High-powered teachers present realistic and achievable goals to help ensure that students can achieve a level of mastery while discovering, and also being inspired to read and write.

High-powered teachers are free with praise and constructive criticism. Any negative comments that they have strictly relates to the performance, not the performer/student. They provide non-judgmental feedback on students' work, they also provide opportunities for students to improve and look for ways to promote and stimulate their advancement, while avoiding a division in the classroom. They promote unity, classroom respect, and also treat all students equal. High-powered motivated teachers know that when students feel a sense of belonging, regardless their reading level, writing level, or learning level. They work harder, have more confidence, and feel better about themselves and their work (InTASC Standards, 1, 2, 3, 4, 5, 7, & 8, CCSSO).

High-powered teachers have high expectations. However, they do not place their primary emphasis on testing, but place an appropriate emphasis on formative assessment, grading, and applicable feedback throughout the year. They understand and use multiple methods of assessment to engage students in their own academic growth, and also to monitor students' academic progress. High-powered teachers know that summative assessment is used to show what students have mastered, not what they have not. Therefore, they do not set their students up for failure by withholding the information that they will need to be successful on assessments, but rather provide them with information, opportunities, and also answer any questions or concerns that students may have prior to assessing. They also provide ample opportunities for students to be formatively assessed, to reflect on their learning experiences, formatively assess again, to prepare themselves academically, and also to guide the teachers' and the students' decision making before summative assessments are given (InTASC Standard 6, CCSSO).

High-powered teachers teach. They teach, they listen, they participate, they create, they inspire, they provide, and they prepare. What does that all mean? It means that high-powered teachers teach and encourage throughout the weeks, months, and semesters to prepare students for year-end assessments through explicit instruction, engaging activities, experiences, and through purposeful assignments to be prepared to take year-end assessments without pointing out that they are preparing for assessment, which leads to learning in a more in-depth manner, thus retaining and being able to apply what they have learned without the stress of the word test (InTASC Standard 6, CCSSO).

Author's Tip

"Write it on your heart that every day is the best day of the year."
~ Ralph Waldo Emmerson

As a primary teacher I discovered that promoting reading and writing wasn't a very difficult task, as primary students were typically eager to please their teacher. The majority of the students were still excited about discovering the joys of reading, and also writing creatively. However, when I advanced to intermediate and middle grades, I soon discovered that many of my previous primary students that once loved reading and writing had lost that zeal for reading and especially writing, and they no longer wanted to write those intriguing and fascinating stories with rich and vibrant characters. What had happened?

I determined that my students had discovered the joys of having a social life, the wonders and instant gratification of social media, and also, they had become tweens. The excitement that I had as I entered this new and unknown territory of intermediate learners was suddenly challenged by worries of how I would encourage, promote, inspire, and promote reading and writing with excitement as I had for all those years in the primary grades. I reflected on methods that I had implemented, my students, reviewed scores, browsed their permanent folders, administered reading surveys, self-interest surveys, and researched ideas to help inspire me, so I could inspire and motivate my students (InTASC Standard 9, CCSSO).

I attended reading and writing conferences, sought the help of experienced colleagues, and did some deep soul searching and reminiscing of my own days spent inside the classroom at this very emotional and difficult stage of life. I also reflected on what had been successful for many of my now 154 students when they were students in my first-grade classroom, only 4 and 5 short years ago. I was the same teacher, my love and passion for both reading and writing hadn't changed, other than to grow even stronger. Again, I reviewed the students' reading-interest surveys, their interest surveys, and thought deeply about how I could bring genres and topics that they were interested in into the classroom, while also motivating them to read deeply, write with heart, and once again discover the joys of reading and writing (InTASC Standard 7, 8, 9, & 10, CCSSO).

I was determined that by allowing students to have a choice, a voice in what we read, what we wrote about, as well as inside the classroom would spark an interest and classroom rapport for all 154 students (InTASC Standard 3, CCSSO). An interest that I hoped would ignite a flame of contagious motivation. I began to incorporate more technology with reading and writing, allowing students to read from their devices, answer questions through the use of interactive software, locating definitions, synonyms, antonyms, and more. The students responded very well and seemed to be enjoying the ability to incorporate their electronic devices in the classroom (InTASC Standards 4, 5, 6, 7, & 8, CCSSO).

I continued to research new innovative methods of engaging students with reading. My nights were spent browsing the Internet, researching, and simply just searching (InTASC Standard 9, CCSSO). When I received a notification one evening on my cellphone about watching a movie trailer for an upcoming movie, inspiration engulfed me. Carefully, filled with excitement, I began to formulate a plan. I could hardly sleep that night as excitement filled me. This would work! This would inspire the uninspired reader (InTASC Standard 7, CCSSO). The next day, I began instruction with a movie trailer. Students were engulfed in the short clip of the upcoming movie. They were excited to talk about their thoughts, make predictions, and also display their motivation to watch the movie. That's when I announced that our next reading and writing project would include a **book-trailer**. I awaited their responses with a bit of anticipation, only to discover the majority of the students were nodding their heads, giving inquisitive looks of curiosity, smiling and a few disconnected and apprehensive students. I explained that a book-trailer worked much like a movie trailer. It divulged only enough about the book to interest the audience, and create an excitement and anticipation within them to want to read the book, much like a movie trailer creates a buzz about watching a movie. Then excitement filled the classroom as they better understood what book-trailer actually was.

I worked and collaborated closely with the librarian, the computer lab teacher, and with the students in small groups (InTASC Standard 10, CCSSO). Students selected their own novel, read in their free-reading time, wrote five paragraph book reports about their books, and began working on their book-trailers. The excitement grew as students snapped pictures with their phones to include in their trailers, and began to add music. When the trailers were complete the librarian was so impressed that she volunteered to display the students' book-trailers as a slideshow on the big screen television in the school atrium.

An excitement for reading was generated and began to spread through the school...an excitement about reading. The excitement about wanting to read the novels that were depicted so beautifully on the screen in the atrium created a positive rapport that spread throughout the school. Students were excited to see their work on the screen, teachers were proud of their students, parents enjoyed and marveled at their child's work as they entered the school, and the principal was very pleased with the overall outcome. The librarian was thrilled with the new excitement for reading as well.

Teachers were reading more, students were reading again, and the love for reading had been reignited. I loved working with the librarian, she was not only a colleague, and tremendous resource, but was also a good friend of mine. She asked if my students would be interested in writing blurbs for the library books that they read. The blurbs would be posted on the library website for other students to read and help them determine if they wanted to read a book or not. I thanked her and gladly jumped at the opportunity for my students to write about reading. The blurbs were successful, and also very helpful. *"Instead of blaming technology for students' decreased desire to read and write, I used and embraced the unlimited possibilities of technology to reignite the love for reading and writing."*

What Can Parents Do to Help?

Throughout this text, you have read how parents influence can impact students' desire to succeed, impact their grades, impact their attitude, and their overall academic performance. It cannot be reiterated often enough to be the educator who establishes and maintains good open communication with their students' parents (InTASC Standard 9 & 10, CCSSO). Parents can encourage reading by keeping books in the home, reading themselves, and setting aside time every day for their children to read as well as read with their children.

There is a strong correlation that exists between these parental activities and the frequency with which children read. For example, among children who are frequent readers, scholastic research (2013) shows that 57% of their parents set aside time each day for their child to read, compared to 16% of parents of children who are infrequent readers. Stay focused, remain positive, continually encourage, maintain open communication, be consistent and send reminders. Remember, parents are often very busy, and sometimes, they simply forget. Encourage free-reading, allowing student to begin books at school and encourage them to continue reading at home. Encourage parents to read with their child. Reiterate how reading children's novels keeps reading fresh, young, and also opens up new perspectives about reading, while also involves the parents in the literature that their child is currently reading.

Motivating In-Person and Online Students

High-powered teachers are passionate about their career, their students, their content, their school, and also their community. High-powered teachers are also **motivators**. They motivate the unmotivated. They are always working to inspire their students and their colleagues. High-powered teachers are **flexible** and willing to make changes. High-powered teachers are also **academic risk-takers** who step outside of their comfort zone and who are willing to delve deep into new strategies, content, or curriculum. They are also **strategic planners** who plan new and innovative strategies. They plan and create **collaborative opportunities** that involves their students in **grand-discussion**, as well as strategies to ensure students are engaged, inspired, motivated, and also experiencing rich and diverse literature. High-powered teachers are also **researchers**. High-powered teachers strive to ensure that all students learn and are academically challenged, and academically successful and prepared for their next level of education. High-powered teachers **care** about their student's well-being and their **academic performance**. High-powered teachers are **life-time learners** who are consistently striving to gain a deeper understanding of their **content, methods, strategies, concepts**, and also use and implementation of student and teacher **technology**. They teach from the heart, regardless of the classroom setting. They research new and innovate methods of connecting with their students both **in-person** and **online**. High-powered teachers provide **opportunities** for all students to grow both **academically** and **socially** to help prepare them for the **challenges** and **opportunities** of life. *Will you be that high-powered teacher?*

Now It's Your Turn

As the semester comes to a close and student teaching is within your grasp, begin thinking and planning ways to inspire students to read while in your placement, and your future students. Think about the books that you will read to become that well-read high-powered teacher. For your final assignment create an annotated bibliography power point that you can use as a resource in your future classroom, or even in your student teaching placement. Your power point should contain an introduction slide that contains an inspiring quote, a brief bio of your love for reading, and introduction of your power point. The power point should contain one or two books per slide with no less than eighteen books, and no more than twenty books. You should have included a book from every genre. Each book should contain a small blurb, citation, and a picture of the cover. Think outside the box, explore the Internet, browse the library, and go beyond the obvious go-to books. If you have a favorite, by all means include it, but try to incorporate and explore new titles that you would like to read and incorporate in your class. Make your power point interesting, be tech savvy, and add all the "bells and whistles" that power point has to offer. Make this a autobiography that will inspire your students to want to read the books that you have listed.

Applications

To help guide you through Chapter Sixteen, become familiar with the following key terms for a deeper understanding of Chapter Sixteen:

- ✦ Self-reflection
- ✦ Free-reading
- ✦ Well-read high-powered teacher
- ✦ Book talks
- ✦ Book clubs
- ✦ Book commercials
- ✦ Unmotivated reader
- ✦ Intrinsic motivation
- ✦ Extrinsic motivation
- ✦ Speaking and listening skills
- ✦ Book-trailers
- ✦ Guest speakers
- ✦ Prezi

In-Seat Activity

Working with your partner, you will have a number of days to collaborate and create a book-trailer with Prezi. You may access the software at www.prezi.com. Create an exciting book-trailer about a book of your choice. Your trailer may also be about, *The Miraculous Journey of Edward Tulane* (DeCamillo).

Your trailer should be no less than 3 minutes in length and no longer than five. You should include pictures of the novel, and also music. Your trailer should be compelling, motivating, and exciting. Make your audience want to read your book. You will present your book-trailer the last week in class to the class. You will also be required to write a five paragraph reflection about your experience creating the book-trailer, including your areas of strength, what you gained, how you grew, and your struggles. Include what you might do differently if given this opportunity again. More details for this in-seat assignment are posted on blackboard. You will be given time each week to work on this assignment, but may also work in your own time. Be inspired, be motivating, and be creative.

Reflect and Answer the Following Questions

- ✦ *What is a well-read teacher?*
- ✦ *How can I motivate the unmotivated reader?*
- ✦ *What are the benefits of reading and writing with my students?*
- ✦ *How can I increase student engagement with reading and writing?*
- ✦ *How can I incorporate technology to increase students' interest in reading?*

Student Notes

Annotation is an effective learning strategy. Annotating is typically completed along the outer edge of the text within the book. However, sufficient space is not always available. Therefore, this page has been reserved for you to annotate (*take notes*) record potential questions, and also to refer back to when studying, completing assignments and to help you gain a better understanding of Chapter Sixteen.

Student Reflections

High-powered teachers reflect. This page is reserved for you to reflect about information that you found insightful and what you have learned from Chapter Sixteen.

Suggested Readings and Research

Miller, D. *The Book Whisperer*. Scholastic, 2009.
Miller, D. *Reading in the Wild*. Scholastic, 2014.
Sheldrick, W. *Motivating Your Students: A Simple, Six Step Action Plan to Increase Student Motivation in Your Class*. ICT Publishing, 2013.

Chapter References

Allington, R. *What Really Matters for Middle School Readers: From Research to Practice*. Mass. Pearson, 2015.

Council of Chief State School Officers (CCSSO). *Interstate Teacher Assessment and Support Consortium (InTASC) Model Core Teaching Standards*, Apr. 2011, https://www.ccsso.org/sites/default/files/2017-11/InTASC_Model_Core_Teaching_Standards_2011.pdf. Accessed July 7, 2018.

DeCamillo, K. *The Miraculous Journey of Edward Tulane*. Candlewick Press, 2006.

Dolly Parton. AZQuotes.com, n.d., http://www.azquotes.com/quote/1154293. Accessed June 1, 2018.

Emmerson, W. AZQuotes.com, n.d., http://www.azquotes.com/author/4490-Ralph_Waldo_Emerson. Accessed May 28, 2018.

Gambrell, L., and B. Marinak. *Reading Motivation: What the Research Says*, 2009, http://www.readingrockets.org. Accessed May 23, 2018.

Goodreads. Parton, D. 21, 2018, https://www.goodreads.com/author/quotes/144067.Dolly_Parton. Accessed May 2018.

Krashen, S. *The Power of Reading: Insights from the Research*. Heinemann, 2004.

Miller, D. *The Book Whisperer*. Scholastic, 2009.

National Center for Education Statistics. *Digest of Education Statistics: 2016*. NCES 2017-094. https://nces.ed.gov/nationsreportcard/. Accessed May 23, 2018.

Scholastic. *Kids and Family Reading Report*, 4th ed., 2013, http://mediaroom.scholastic.com/kfrr. Accessed May 21, 2018.

Strauss, V. *How to Get Kids to Read Independently: The Washington Post*, 2015, https://www.washingtonpost.com/news/answer-sheet/wp/2015/03/09/how-to-get-kids-to-read-independently/?noredirect=on&utm_term=.cc1e19e5c61b. Accessed May 4, 2018.